Globalization's Muse

Globalization's Muse:
Universities and Higher Education Systems in a Changing World

John Aubrey Douglass, C. Judson King, and Irwin Feller, editors

2009
Berkeley Public Policy Press
Institute of Governmental Studies
University of California, Berkeley

Library of Congress Cataloging-in-Publication Data

Globalization's muse : universities and higher education systems in a changing
world / John Aubrey Douglass, C. Judson King, Irwin Feller (editors).
    p. cm.
    Includes bibliographical references.
    ISBN 978-0-87772-432-2
    1. Universities and colleges—Cross-cultural studies. 2. Educational change—
Cross-cultural studies. 3. Globalization. I. Douglass, John Aubrey. II. King, C.
Judson (Cary Judson), 1934– III. Feller, Irwin. IV. University of California,
Berkeley. Center for Studies in Higher Education. V. University of California,
Berkeley. Institute of Governmental Studies.
    LB2322.2.G57 2009
    378—dc22

                                                            2009015750

Acknowledgements

Our thanks to the authors for their contributions and participation in the Center for Studies in Higher Education's series of events held on the University of California's Berkeley campus that focused on higher education reforms throughout the world. James Lee and Emily Hilligoss were critical in helping to compile and edit the manuscript, and their hard work is much appreciated. Joyce Bee provided the design for the cover and the book's related website. Our special thanks to the Carnegie Corporation and the Spencer Foundation for their support for two conferences, *The Crisis of the Publics*, and *A Reflection and Prospectus on Globalization and Higher Education,* which drew experts on higher education from throughout the world and generated many first drafts. The first of these events was organized in association with the Berkeley Roundtable on the International Economy, and with advice and guidance by Professor John Zysman. And finally, we wish to express our appreciation to Ethan Rarick and Maria Wolf at the Institute of Governmental Studies' Public Policy Press for their contribution to the final editing and publication of the book that follows.

Contents

A Room with a View: Globalization, Universities, and the Imperative of a Broader U.S. Perspective

John Aubrey Douglass
C. Judson King
Irwin Feller[1]

Universities and higher education systems, for both real and romanticized reasons, have become globalization's muse: in essence, a widely recognized and worshipped route for full participation in the knowledge society. Research universities, in particular, are viewed as an unparalleled source of new thinking and artful innovation, the generator and continuing source of modern science, an unequaled generator of talent, a nearly required path for socio-economic mobility in the postmodern world, and an essential ingredient for participating in the global economy. Hence it is not surprising that building, shaping, nurturing, and sustaining globally competitive research universities, and higher education systems more generally, is now a major focus of national, regional, and local policymaking throughout much of the world.

This book describes and analyzes the changing global landscape in higher education, with special attention to the themes of convergence, competition, and congruity of policies and practices. Written largely before the worldwide financial

---

[1] Center for Studies in Higher Education—UC Berkeley.

1

meltdown, the contributions here offer a long view, discussing trends, past and future. The narrative draws upon the varied perspectives and experiences of leading international scholars and practitioners in higher education, many of whom provide broad analysis of the changing landscape of higher education internationally, and others of whom focus on specific national and institutional reforms and their progress and problems. A thesis knitting the chapters together is that both developed economies, such as OECD member nations, and developing economies, such as China and India, are engaged in significant higher education reforms with some commonality in approach, informed by a growing international conversation, and with tangible and often spectacular results.

The chapters that follow offer a focused view down into the agora, where the market for students is rapidly changing, where higher education leaders and institutions are trading ideas and seeking collaborations, where universal high bandwidth communications is transforming academic activity, and where national governments and new supranational entities, including the European Commission but also international trade agreements, are rapidly changing the structure of higher education systems. It is a complex and quickly evolving story rooted in a new paradigm of significant policy transfer.

In part, the intention of the book is to help inform American lawmakers and the higher education community, students, scholars, and practitioners alike, of these profound changes in the world's higher education landscape, and to suggest that the United States should begin to take stock of the new competition and learn from international reform efforts. At the same time, the book offers a comparative perspective about the strengths and weakness of the U.S.'s famed higher education systems and institutions that will be informative and useful to an international audience. Many foreign observers have a romanticized view about the relative strength of the U.S. higher education system, and that of its vast network of colleges and universities. The following chapters offer a refreshing dose of comparative reality, including the emergence of similar approaches to access, funding, accountability, and promoting institutional quality; the global sense of competition driving policymaking; and thoughts on lessons learned by the chapter contributors. Arguably, we are at the edge of a dramatic shift in flow and supply of talent, and witness to the emergence of new centers for promoting science, technology, and innovation that mark a stark contrast to the past.

1. Globalization Then and Now

Why has the U.S. been such a focal point for international envy regarding its universities and colleges? One major reason is America's spectacular past success. Since at least the beginning of the twentieth century, the United States has been a leader in the development of mass higher education. Since at least the end of World War II, it has occupied a dominant position in academic research and graduate education. In combination, these two characteristics have produced distinctive comparative benefits. American colleges and universities emerged as significant sources of highly skilled labor, proved vital routes for upward socio-economic mobility, and became major producers of new knowledge and technical and scientific innovation. International observers have noted two hallmarks of America's higher education: the achievement of broad access and the general high quality and coherence of its vast array of private and public colleges and universities. Effectively balancing the achievement of both mass and elite goals has been a major triumph. Over the past century, for example, the U.S. led the world in the number of young people going to college and graduating. At the same time, the quality of its major research universities has been the envy of the world.

In looking out into the world, we are essentially turning the tables. For years, the international community has peered over oceans and continents toward the U.S., looking for models such as California's celebrated public higher education system and the building blocks for its network of highly productive research universities. Now, we suggest, the U.S. needs to look outward, and not just for clues to innovative domestic policies related to higher education. Our isolationist impulse in this regard, and our reliance on being the lonely superpower who cannot be informed by the progress of other nations, is a dangerous and, ultimately, failed policy approach.

Yet the centrality of higher education as the means for creating a modern and progressive society, either as an ideal or an accomplishment, is no longer unique to the United States. Universities and higher education systems, for both real and romanticized reasons, have become globalization's muse: in essence, a widely recognized and worshipped route for full participation in the knowledge society, an unparalleled source of knowledge and artful innovation, a foundation for modern science, an unequaled generator of talent, and a nearly required path for socio-economic mobility in the postmodern world.

A greater understanding of this powerful movement among other nations is critical for the U.S. There are a number of signs that America no longer retains its higher education advantage in the global marketplace. Over time, and particularly recently, many nations have adopted elements of the U.S. model on their own political and social terms. They are making great progress (although still too slowly for many critics). New and productive centers of research are emerging in both developed and developing economies; international collaborations among universities are growing; and many OECD countries now exceed the United States in higher education participation and degree attainment rates for young adults. This is all new.

To a degree only recently realized, universities have become the anointed agents of social and economic transformation in the 21st century. There has been a trend in the United States, and throughout the world, to emphasize individual benefits to a greater extent than public benefits—one rationale for the growing role of fees and tuition in which students and their families are asked to contribute increasingly more to the cost of their university education. But the public benefits from higher education, arguably, will be even more important in the future for creating economic and social progress. Good public policy related to higher education, we argue, will tend to emphasize the public over the private good of a university education—a macro view that seeks to understand and shape the collective impact of higher education.

But another important driver of higher education reforms, and the elevated role of universities, is just as important: an acute sense of competition among developed and developing economies, informed by a relatively new premise that goes something like this: Those nation-states that have the highest tertiary access and graduation rates, who are the most effective at attracting talent, and who develop the most vibrant research centers, will likely be the economic winners of the future. It is a hypothesis that is influenced by the past economic performance of developed nations, but that is not fully proven. Perhaps just as important, it is a hypothesis that has gained tremendous political consensus among political and higher education leaders who drive policymaking and have fully embraced the idea and rhetoric of the knowledge economy.

Among the many by-products of globalization and ready and rapid communication is an expanded and increasingly powerful process of policy transfer. National political leaders, and in some cases supranational entities such as the European Commission, seek policy reforms and innovation in their higher education systems and among their colleges and universities always informed, to some degree, by the advances or policy efforts of other nations. There is a growing sense of common challenges, common language on goals and solutions, and a remarkable increase in the interest and knowledge of how other nations and regions are approaching the development of their higher education sectors.

To some degree, the process of policy transfer has always existed in higher education, in part influenced by colonialism. This process is very different in the modern era in the extent of its influence, its sources, and correlating with the increased sense of importance of the higher education sector in national competitiveness and prosperity. How might we decipher the characteristics of past, present, and possibly future changes in higher education with an international comparative and global view?

Phase 1—Higher Education as an Extension of National Culture

Approximately 50 years ago, many nations in Europe and in other parts of the world embarked on a path for building their mass higher education systems. They often looked to the United States to help guide their efforts, but their respective systems remained largely as manifestations of their earlier network of colleges and universities—an extension of their national culture. For example, Germany, France, and the U.K. had distinctly different system approaches and degree standards, and higher education systems in most developing nations were influenced largely by their colonial heritages.

The policy-transfer process was limited, constrained by each nation's own political and cultural roots and focused on national and regional markets for students. With the exception of the U.S., and to a lesser extent the colonial networks of

Table 1. Phase 1: Major Forces Influencing Higher Education 50 Years Ago

- Initial era for building mass higher education systems
- Higher education seen as largely a public good
- Limited adoption of international higher education models and practices—higher education as an extension of national culture
- National and regional markets for undergraduate students and institutional prestige
- Marginal international market for faculty and research talent
- High institutional autonomy—limited accountability measures
- Government as partner with the higher education community
- National accreditation and quality review
- Traditional pedagogy—limited technological adoption
- Substantial government subsidization
- Small for-profit sector—mostly in U.S.
- Beginnings of a burgeoning scientific community
- Limits on cross-national knowledge sharing and communications

---

former, largely European nations, most nations engaged in hiring faculty almost exclusively from within their own national university systems. International collaborations between institutions and between their faculty members were rather limited. These collaborations were perhaps most pronounced among a growing community of scientists and engineers.

In promoting mass higher education, governments tended to be partners with existing higher education institutions and were nearly the sole source of funding. Higher education was emerging as a public good, a decided break from its past in that often elite institutions had linked with existing social and political caste systems. Again, with the exception of the U.S. and later Japan, most nations had small to nonexistent private-sector colleges and universities.

At the same time, America's unique position as the pioneer in mass higher education reinforced its largely isolationist impulse, with few academic leaders and policymakers looking abroad at higher education reform efforts. In this first era of globalization, the lack of a comparative international view in the U.S. had no significant adverse effects; indeed, it may have been a benefit, as America built on its unique strengths, which included a highly diverse higher education system and willingness to accept talent from around the world.

Phase 2—The New Globalization

Since that post–World War II era, much has changed. Globalization is a phenomenon often described as a process of opening and expanding markets for educational services. Beyond market forces, there are also the influences of technological advances in broadband communications and other areas and the broad influences of a globalizing economy that have shaped the need for skill and professional labor. Higher education institutions are also undergoing organizational and behavioral changes as they seek new financial resources, face new competition, and seek greater prestige domestically and internationally. A variety of trends demonstrate the significant influence of the globalization process on higher education. Most tug and pull at the traditional notion of national boundaries as the critical political and economic environment for higher education.

One result is that the command economy approaches for creating and regulating mass higher education in many parts of the world are withering. As is discussed in one of the following chapters, what is emerging is a "structured opportunity market" in higher education—essentially, a convergence, in some form of the effort of nation-states to create a more lightly regulated and more flexible network of public higher education institutions. For example, efforts are being made internationally to converge and standardize undergraduate and graduate degree programs, most notably under the Bologna Agreement. International collaborations with other academic institutions and businesses are now commonplace. Universities seek new avenues to fund and promote the commoditization of their knowledge-production capabilities.

When compared to 50 years ago, the global network and marketplace for academic researchers has grown significantly. Many higher education institutions are also recruiting relatively new pools of students outside national borders. In this quest, most are seeking to apply new instructional technologies to expand enrollment and to enhance the viability and profitability of international ventures. Facilitated by these technologies, there is the specter of a competitive environment between existing and new providers, including the rise of new nontraditional and for-profit competitors. With this more competitive global framework has come talk of a need for international accreditation processes and new efforts at quality review.

We are in a relatively new era marked by a consensus that the educational attainment of a population and increasingly the growth in access to postsecondary education are factors that, more than ever, will determine the fate of nations in the modern world. This widely understood fact is causing a worldwide effort to reform and reshape higher education systems focused on making national higher education systems not just widely accessible, but of higher quality and more accountable.

Table 2. Phase 2: The New Globalization

- Maturing era for mass higher education systems in most developed nations
- Higher education increasingly viewed as a private good
- Growing international adoption and convergence of higher education practices and models—higher education as an extension of globalization
- Growing international and supranational market for undergraduate students and institutional prestige
- Growing international market for faculty and research talent
- Eroding institutional autonomy—growing accountability measures
- Government as adversary with the higher education community
- Possible international accreditation and quality review
- Changing pedagogy—growing technological adoption
- Declining government subsidization—rising student fees, growing diversity of funding sources/privatization
- Growing for-profit sector
- Established scientific community
  Global knowledge sharing and communications

Thinking of Phase 3—Post-Globalization Dreaming

What will the future hold for national higher education systems? Many scholars of globalization argue that the process of globalization is a force more powerful than industrialization, urbanization, and secularization combined. Globalization, notes one observer, is the "inexorable integration of markets, nation-states, and technologies to a degree never witnessed before—in a way that is enabling individuals, corporations, and nation-states to reach around the world farther, faster, deeper, and cheaper than ever before."[2] In contrast, some scholars and activists view globalization not as an inexorable process but rather as a deliberate ideological project of economic liberalization that subjects states, institutions, and individuals to more intense market forces.

Whatever the sources of globalization, most globalist scholars predict an acute and sweeping effect on higher education. There are two main and interconnected reasons for this prediction. First, the opening of what were previously largely closed national markets dominated by state-subsidized providers will enable a reconfiguration of the higher education sector, thus opening opportunities for new providers. Second, new providers will have a competitive advantage, in large part because of their ability to adopt more efficient instructional technologies

---

[2] Thomas L. Friedman, *The Lexus and the Olive Tree* (New York: Anchor Books, May 2000).

quickly. This futurist vision, focused largely on the delivery of educational teaching services, predicted that a ubiquitous mode of delivery (online courses) would replace another (the classroom). Successful, less labor-intensive, and cheaper modes of delivery will push out the older modes. This will also have dire implications for many if not most research universities, which are built around the idea of a community of scholars (not simply providers of teaching services), and also rely on various forms of revenue sharing to support the entire enterprise. The most radical of futurists thought the brick and mortar world of colleges and universities would soon collapse with the research enterprise drifting into more specialized institutional forms.

Many of these predictions came early in the development of online courses and study of globalization and the networked society. It seems clear now that the market, the needs of society, and the ability of existing institutions to adapt are resulting in a far more complex process of reform and transformation. Many sophisticated observers of higher education are dubious about whether the ongoing and predicted market shifts will foster homogeneity and convergence to the degree still anticipated by some. Might these forces of change foster a greater diversity of institutional types and culturally related institutions? Have the complexities of policymaking and markets been fully appreciated? This is one among a number of widely debated topics discussed by the various authors in the chapters that follow.

Whatever the view, it is clear that there are similar emerging approaches to key policy areas that stretch from the national to the institutional level. Some have called this the "Americanization" of higher education, in part because of the iconic and, we dare say, somewhat romanticized advantages of the U.S. model. But we argue that that characterization is a misnomer, in large part because some of the most dramatic higher education reforms are occurring in other parts of the world, providing the new models in key areas such as access and financing. What is emerging is a much more dynamic and global policy-transfer environment. That does not mean that national political culture and the great variety of other factors that distinguish one nation from another will become irrelevant. China's emerging higher education system will not look like India's, or the United States'. But there are goals and national and institutional practices that have emerged, informed by the relatively new *higher education policy transfer network* in higher education.

This network has different operative venues. It includes national leaders who meet and reinforce their macrosystem consensus views of higher education access and research productivity as the driver for participation in the evolving and highly competitive knowledge economy. It includes university and industry leaders who think the same and share ideas and experiences and seek models for collaboration and for increased productivity and quality. It increasingly includes middle managers in higher education institutions looking for policies and practices to help meet evolving national and institutional goals. It also includes the relatively new supranational agreements and associations (most particularly in Europe), the emergence of international rankings that hold the attention of lawmakers and institutions alike, new alliances of often similar universities attempting to share information collectively and influence national and supranational policymaking, and a caste of new journals and other publications reflective of the now pervasive interest in, nay infatuation with, globalization and higher education. All of this portends an acceleration in the scope and influence of the higher education policy transfer network in which national and higher education leaders, faculty, staff, and consumers, are now working and making choices within what was once a largely national, and even regional, knowledge base.

2. A Time of Competition

One present reality of this new and evolving and competitive environment is that national systems of public higher education are in a state of flux. Throughout the world, a shift is occurring in the support and perception of the purpose of public research universities. Many national governments are attempting to bend their higher education systems to meet their perceived long-term socio-economic needs. At the same time, there are relatively new supranational influences on higher education markets and practices that will grow in influence over time, including the Bologna Agreement, the European Commission, the pending General Agreement on Trade and Services, and globalization associated with broadband communication and internationalization of corporations.

England has embarked on a large range of higher education reforms intended to expand access, bolster accountability measures, and revise funding, including the inclusion of postgraduation fees and a new infusion of monies from the national government. Australia has experimented also with income-contingent postgraduation repayment of loaned fees and has adjusted to lower levels of government funding by embarking upon a major mission of expanding revenue through accommodation of students from Asian countries.

The Bologna Agreement has led to structural reforms in Europe, particularly in Germany and Italy, and the development of matriculation agreements, a rising transnational flow of students, and a proposal for an MIT-like European Institute of Technology. Japan is accomplishing major systematic change in the organization and funding of its public universities. China has announced an ambitious plan for the creation of 20 world-class research universities on par with the best U.S. universities.

In the United States, reforms are focused largely on ways to cope with declining rates of public investment in public higher education, rising operating costs, and maintaining access despite fee increases. There is also interest in incorporating new accountability schemes.

As visible as these changes are, little systematic analysis exists about how the sources of change and the reforms adopted or advanced in one country derive from or affect other countries, let alone how they might inform U.S. higher education. American higher education and American political culture have tended to be insular in their approaches to policymaking and ideas on reform. Changes in other countries have followed careful observation of what has made the United States successful, but the United States has not examined closely what has been done overseas in the context of the situations of individual countries.

While recognizing that there are many reform efforts that relate to the peculiar political cultures and needs of individual nations, it is our assertion that there is significant commonality in the challenges facing public universities internationally, including:

- The need to expand or maintain access and improve graduation rates.
- Increasing expectations by governments and the public to serve the broad social needs of society.
- Disinvestment by state governments and the need for new financial models.
- Avenues for increasing efficiencies in teaching and university management.
- Increased reliance on research universities as drivers of economic development.
- Growing emphasis on professionalism and scientific and technological prowess.
- Relatively new global markets for academics and research excellence.
- The rise of relatively new and for-profit competitors in much of the world.
- Increased global collaborations with other universities and businesses in research and teaching programs.

There is much that can be learned from a systematic and comparative analysis of how nations/states and research universities are approaching this new policy environment. Indeed, for the benefit of the United States, there may be some common or transferable approaches to issues such as mission, funding, and access; there are also national or regional political, cultural, and economic-specific examples that must be considered for public universities to adapt and change successfully. Defining commonalities and differences is vital for investigating the viabilities of a broad range of policy options.

3. The Organization of this Book

The following chapters are written by a group of scholars and practitioners, all of whom in one way another have a deep knowledge of higher education in the United States and others with specific knowledge and experience in the recent reforms in pertinent foreign countries. We asked them to structure their contributions around one or more of four major policy areas that we feel capture the sweep of policy challenges facing higher education globally. They include:

- Fees and Finance Models
- Access, Quality, and Accountability
- Science, Technology, and Regional Economies
- Organization and Governance

We also asked our non-U.S. contributors to think about how their experiences, combined with their knowledge of global higher education reforms, might inform and influence U.S. policymaking. The hope was not to create actual policy proposals, as the cross-cultural and institutional differences between nations are too great and complex for easy analysis. That would be an unrealistic ambition. Instead, we view the chapters as structures to learn from one another, and as part of a path to envision how the U.S. might adapt to meet the challenges it faces in falling behind in higher education access and graduation rates. To this end, we struggled somewhat with how to capture the broad range of national higher education reform efforts. Our choice was primarily to attempt a focus on economies within the OECD, as well as on Asia and the United States.

In the course of our effort, we convened a workshop followed by a symposium on the Berkeley campus, with most of the authors of this book present at both events. At the workshop and symposium, participants shared comparative information and analysis, discussed major issues facing national and supranational systems of higher education and the role of research universities, and identified the most promising avenues for further investigation. Within these chapters is a snapshot that is limited by the geographic and cultural biases of its authors, yet, we think, an interesting opening dialogue—particularly for the U.S.

The Carnegie Corporation of New York and the Spencer Foundation generously provided funding for these two conferences organized by CSHE and, for one of them, in association with BRIE.

I. A Look at the Global Higher Education
    Landscape

Chapter 1

An OECD Scan of Public and Private Higher Education

Stéphan Vincent-Lancrin[1]

There is growing concern in the United States that public higher education institutions, and particularly public research universities, are losing ground compared to private research universities: This is the so-called "crisis of the publics." In other OECD countries,[2] there is also a feeling of a "crisis" of public higher education, relating to the perception of an underfunding of public tertiary

---

[1] The author is a senior education analyst at the OECD Centre for Educational Research and Innovation (CERI) (OECD, Directorate for Education). He gratefully acknowledges Kiira Kärkkäinen for her statistical assistance and an analysis of private and public funding she carried out in 2006 for the OECD project on the future of higher education. This chapter was written during a Fulbright-supported research visit at Teachers College, Columbia University. The views expressed are the author's and are not necessarily those of the OECD and its member countries. Contact: Stephan.Vincent-Lancrin@oecd.org.

[2] The OECD has 30 member countries: Australia, Austria, Belgium, Canada, Czech Republic, Denmark, Finland, France, Germany, Greece, Hungary, Iceland, Ireland, Italy, Japan, Korea, Luxembourg, Mexico, The Netherlands, New Zealand, Norway, Poland, Portugal, Slovak Republic, Spain, Sweden, Switzerland, Turkey, the United Kingdom, the United States of America.

education, especially when compared to U.S. tertiary education, and some concerns about the rise of competition, trade, private providers, and market mechanisms. Many observers see the traditional public model governing tertiary education changing, for better or for worse. Something is changing in tertiary education, and tertiary education currently ranks higher in policy debates than it used to: Anecdotal evidence is that OECD education ministers decided to devote their 2006 meeting to higher education. Several projects discussing the possible future of higher education, such as the Spelling Commission on the Future of Higher Education in the United States[3] and the OECD international project on the future of higher education,[4] also point to this widespread perceived urge to engage in a dialogue about recent trends and possible and desirable changes in higher education in the coming decades.

Is public tertiary education really in a crisis, and, if yes, what is the crisis about? This chapter gives an answer to this question by analyzing international aggregated data and examining to what extent there has been a crisis of public tertiary education in the OECD area in the past decade, with an emphasis on research universities when the data enable it. The first section focuses on relative enrollments in the public and the private sector and shows that enrollments in the public sector have not significantly declined and only marginally benefited the private for-profit sector. The second section analyzes changes in the funding of tertiary education from the perspectives of tertiary education institutions, students, and governments and shows that it is mainly students who faced a recent crisis of funding and of public funding of tertiary education. The third section concludes by pointing to other possible reasons for the perceived crisis. Throughout the chapter, the differences in the structure of public/private enrollments and funding in the United States and other OECD countries are emphasized, and help to better understand the differences in tertiary education policy debates in the United States and most other OECD countries.

A Crisis of Enrollments in the Public Sector?

Is the crisis of public tertiary education about enrollments in the public sector? Along the discussion on the inclusion of education services in the General Agreement on Trade in Services (GATS) under the World Trade Organization (WTO) and on the "commodification" of higher education (OECD 2004), there has been a lot of public concern about the emergence of new types of providers, in particular for-profit providers (Cunningham et al. 2000; Knight 2004). There is a perception of an expansion and increasing competition from the private for-profit sector in a sector that has traditionally been public or not-for-profit. This perception is pervasive in all segments of the tertiary education sector, from research universities to community colleges (Bailey 2006).

---

[3] See <http://www.ed.gov/about/bdscomm/list/hiedfuture/about.html>.

[4] See <http://www.oecd.org/edu/universityfutures>.

To what extent is tertiary education still a public enterprise? Is the private sector becoming more attractive to students? One way to answer these questions and see whether public tertiary education is in crisis is to look at the relative importance of enrollments in private and public tertiary education institutions in OECD countries and how this has changed over time. Given the way international statistics are collected (and that the concept of a "research university" does not exist in all OECD countries), enrollments in advanced research programs (ISCED)[5] will be the closest indicator of what happens in research universities.

Public and private, and for-profit and not-for-profit, institutions refer to different animals across OECD countries, with different conditions of operation and relationships to public authorities and their stakeholders. In international statistics (OECD 2006), the definitions of public and private are the following:

- a *public* institution is "controlled and managed directly by a public education authority or agency or; is controlled and managed either by a government agency directly or by a governing body (council, committee etc.), most of whose members are appointed by a public authority or elected by public franchise";

- a *private* institution is "controlled and managed by a nongovernmental organisation (e.g., a church, trade union or business enterprise), or its Governing Board consists mostly of members not selected by a public agency."

An additional dimension to the definition of a private institution is the source of funding. Otherwise, the difference between public and private could be purely formal or legal. There is thus an additional distinction between private institutions: Depending on their funding, some are *government-dependent* while others are *independent* private institutions. Government-dependent private institutions receive (by definition) more than 50 percent of their core funding from government agencies, and independent private institutions, less than 50 percent. Hence, independent private institutions are the institutions generally referred to as private (or the closest to the common understanding).

Public and government-dependent private institutions are not necessarily very different, at least in public perception. For example, in the United Kingdom, higher education institutions are generally considered public, although they are technically government-dependent private. Australia has a system very close to the British system, but almost all institutions are actually public, although their funding comes to a larger extent from private sources than in the United Kingdom.

In 2004, a new law incurring some changes in the composition of governing boards of Dutch universities including more members from nongovernmental organizations has changed the formerly "public" higher education institutions into government-dependent private institutions, although most observers would not describe this particular aspect of the reform as a radical change in the Dutch university system. In statistical terms, it implies that the public sector has become a "not applicable" category (see Table 1.1). The recent "incorporation" of Japanese public universities will lead to the same outcome in future international statistics

---

[5] ISCED stands for International Standard Classification of Education.

Table 1.1. Change in the Distribution of Students Enrolled in Tertiary Education and Advanced Research Programs, 1998–2004 (%)

	Tertiary Education			Advanced Research Programs		
	Public Inst.	Gov't Dependent Private	Independent Private	Public Inst.	Gov't Dependent Private	Independent Private
Netherlands	-32.2	32.2	0.0	m	m	m
Poland	-9.0	0.0	9.0	-0.3	0.0	0.3
Iceland	-8.9	8.9	0.0	0.0	0.0	0.0
Mexico	-6.4	0.0	6.4	m	m	m
Austria	-6.1	6.1	0.0	0.0	0.0	0.0
N. Zealand	-5.5	7.1	-1.6	0.0	0.0	0.0
Switzerland	-3.9	2.5	1.4	0.0	0.0	0.0
Hungary	-3.7	3.7	0.0	-2.2	2.2	0.0
Norway	-3.6	0.0	0.0	-0.8	0.0	0.0
France	-3.4	-0.2	3.6	-0.3	0.0	0.3
Czech Rep.	-3.3	-1.0	4.3	0.0	0.0	0.0
Spain	-2.7	1.9	0.9	-0.3	0.0	0.3
Turkey	-2.4	-1.5	3.9	-2.7	0.0	2.7
Ireland	-1.7	0.0	1.7	-3.5	0.0	3.5
Sweden	-1.6	1.6	0.0	-1.5	1.5	0.0
Denmark	-1.0	1.0	0.0	0.0	0.0	0.0
South Korea	-0.6	0.0	0.6	-0.2	0.0	0.2
Australia	-0.2	-0.1	0.3	-0.2	0.0	0.2
Greece	0.0	0.0	0.0	0.0	0.0	0.0
UK	0.0	0.0	0.0	0.0	0.0	0.0
Germany	0.1	0.0	0.0	m	m	m
Finland	0.5	-0.5	0.0	0.0	0.0	0.0
Canada	0.9	-0.9	0.0	0.0	0.0	0.0
Japan	1.8	0.0	-1.8	0.2	0.0	-0.2
U.S.	2.3	0.0	-2.3	0.3	0.0	-0.3
Italy	6.4	0.0	-6.4	0.4	0.0	-0.3
Portugal	7.5	0.0	-7.5	-0.4	0.0	0.4
Mean	-2.8	2.3	0.5	-0.5	0.2	0.3

Note: m: missing
Source: OECD education database

about Japan. And the recent law (July 2007) giving full autonomy to public universities in France might lead to the same outcome.

First of all, higher education is (still) structurally a public enterprise in almost all OECD countries (Figure 1.1). Independent private institutions are a small segment of the system in most OECD countries, even when growing. The (independ-

Figure 1.1. Distribution of Tertiary Education Enrollment by Control of Institution, 2004

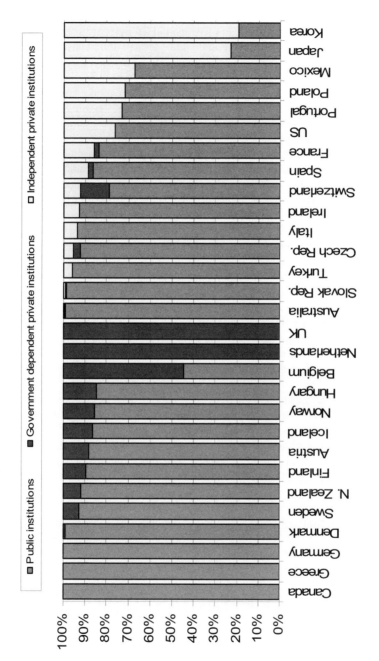

Source: OECD

ent) private sector represents slightly more than 10 percent of total tertiary education enrollments in Spain and France, around 25 percent in the United States and Portugal, about 30 percent in Poland and Mexico, and over three-quarters of enrollments in Japan and Korea. While it is more important in other economically advanced non-OECD countries, especially in Asia and South America, it is only in Japan and Korea that private enrollments overtake the public sector within the OECD area. The share of enrollments in the private sector is consistently and significantly lower for advanced research programs, except in the United States where the share of enrollments increases to 34 percent (Figure 1.2). In many countries, independent private institutions are on average smaller and less prestigious (and thus, one would be tempted to add, less research-intensive) than public institutions. Japan and Korea are good counter-examples, though, as they have a good public/private balance at the top of their national institutional hierarchy— and some other countries have their counter-examples, too, but they are more scattered.

While most students are enrolled in public or government-dependent private tertiary education institutions, a rapid change in the distribution of enrollments in favor of independent private higher education institutions would certainly be a sign of an OECD-wide crisis of the public tertiary education sector. Table 1.1 shows recent changes in the distribution of enrollments: The share of total enrollments in public institutions has dropped by 2.8 percent on average between 1998 and 2004 (and by 1.7 percent when the large shift in the Netherlands is excluded). However, the independent private sector benefited from only 0.5 percent of this average shift. Most of the enrollment shift went to government-dependent private institutions.

Poland, Mexico, the Czech Republic, Turkey, and France are the countries where private institutions have expanded their share the most against both public and government-dependent private institutions. In Portugal and Italy, the public sector has regained ground after the recent growth of the private sector. However, the structure of enrollments in advanced research programs (ISCED 6), that is, those that are typically the most relevant for research universities, has virtually not changed.

While data have the advantage of being comparable over this seven-year period as they were all collected according to the latest ISCED classification, maybe the time series is too short to show the erosion of the public sector in terms of enrollments. At this aggregated level, one can also look further back without too many comparability problems, but for a smaller number of countries. One should be cautious with the data, though. It is only in 1992 that the distinction between government-dependent and independent private was introduced. However, data were already collected between public and private institutions in 1985 and are available for 1985 and 2004 in 18 OECD countries. Over this 20-year period, the drop in the share of tertiary education enrollments in public institutions is more marked, at about five percent, but it is still modest (see Table 1.2)—and even more so if the Netherlands is excluded (the means become -3 percent and -1 percent for the two periods). What the data indicate too is a slowdown of the decreasing share

Figure 1.2. Distribution of Enrollment in Advanced Research Programs by Control of Institution, 2004

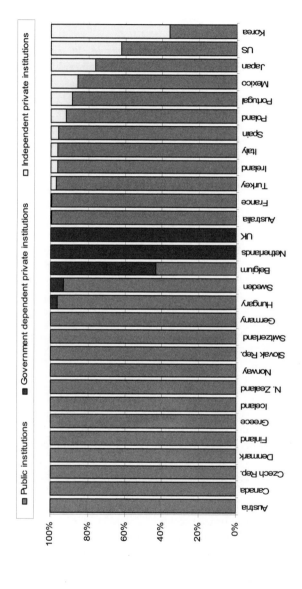

Source: OECD

Stéphan Vincent-Lancrin

Table 1.2. Change in the Share of Tertiary Education Students Enrolled in Public Institutions (Full-Time and Part-Time) (%)

	1985–2004	1998–2004
Netherlands	-42	-32
Portugal	-14	7
Austria	-9	-6
New Zealand	-8	-6
Finland	-8	1
France	-5	-3
Ireland	-5	-2
Switzerland	-5	-4
Spain	-5	-3
Turkey	-4	-2
United States	-1	2
Denmark	-1	-1
Australia	-1	0
Italy	0	6
Czech Republic	-2	-3
Norway	3	-4
Japan	4	2
Canada	10	1
Country mean	-5	-3

of public institutions in most countries: the Czech Republic and Norway are the sole countries where the relative decrease has accelerated in the most recent period. In the United States, the relative share of public institutions has slightly decreased over this longer period, although the contrary is true in recent years.

It is noteworthy that a loss in the relative share of public institutions in total tertiary education enrollments does not imply an absolute decrease in enrollments. In almost all countries, enrollments in public institutions have increased in the same period, sometimes significantly. Again, it does not imply either that students hemorrhaged to the independent private sector.

These enrollment patterns may be interpreted as a crisis of the public higher education sector, but arguably not a critical one, and one that has only modestly benefited the independent private sector. Moreover, the change is almost negligible for advanced research programs, so that there is less evidence of a crisis of public research institutions (by this indicator). In the United States, the structure of enrollments has not changed for advanced research students, and public institutions have actually increased their enrollment share of tertiary students by 2.3 percent between 1998 and 2004, in spite of a small relative decline of one percent since 1985.

Although the Republic of Korea relies more heavily than any other OECD country on independent private institutions for its research training, the United States ranks second and is the only country where the private sector seems to have a strong presence and competitive advantage in advanced research programs compared to other types of institutions. The United States is the only OECD country where the share of enrolments of independent private institutions is bigger for advanced research programs than for all tertiary enrolments (see Figures 1.1 and 1.2). One reason why the crisis of public "research universities" is (generally) not perceived in relation to private education outside the United States may come from this difference: There are few countries where public research universities have strong private competitors, only because the (independent) private sector is generally much less important. This does not mean that public research universities do not feel ill-equipped to compete with U.S. private research universities, as U.S. public universities sometimes do, but this is rather perceived as a loss of *global* competitiveness and a crisis of their domestic public higher education in a changing global environment.

Three conclusions follow from this section:

1. The (independent) private sector has grown, sometimes significantly in some countries, but it is relatively small in most OECD countries and even more so for advanced research programs.

2. The growth of the government-dependent private sector is likely a sign of a change in public governance and management of higher education rather than an evidence of a rapid growth of the private sector. Public institutions are increasingly changing status to become more autonomous and at arm's length from public authorities, without becoming "independent private." This shift is not pervasive, though, and the traditional public sector remains the norm in most OECD countries.

3. Except in the United States, public research universities have little domestic competition for their enrollments in advanced research programs. This might explain why the "crisis of the publics" is not debated in terms of a public-private competition in most OECD countries, but rather in terms of a crisis or transformation of the public governance in higher education and of a loss of global competitiveness.

A Crisis of Public Funding?

More than a crisis of enrollments and attractiveness to students, the crisis of the publics may be a crisis of funding of public tertiary education or a crisis of public funding of higher education. Clearly, private research universities topping U.S. and international rankings are more affluent than their public counterparts. Yale University, one of the top private U.S. universities, had an operating budget of USD 1.67 billion in 2005, for 13,000 students and 1,430 faculty, and an endowment of USD 18 billion. By comparison, the University of California, Berkeley, one of the top public U.S. research universities, had an operating budget of USD 1.54 billion in 2005, for 33,000 students and 2,000 hired and international faculty. The University of Vienna, one of the top Austrian research universities, had an operating budget of USD 451 million (EUR 391.6 million, transformed in PPPs) for about 66,000 students and 5,000 hired faculty in 2005.[6]

In other words, Yale had thrice as much financial resources per student as Berkeley, and 19 times as much as the University of Vienna, and, per faculty, 1.5 times as much as Berkeley and 13 times as much as Vienna. But U.S. public universities tend to be more affluent than other public universities in the OECD: Berkeley had seven times as much resources per student as Vienna and nine times as much per faculty. In Austria, a system relying almost exclusively on public funds and reasonably well-resourced by OECD standards, the operating budget for all tertiary education institutions equated USD 3.2 billion (in power purchasing parities) in 2004, for 238,500 students and about 29,000 faculty—that is, twice as much as Yale University to serve almost 18 times more students and 20 times more faculty. The figures speak for themselves.

There is a wide consensus in some OECD countries that the expansion of higher education systems has led to their underfunding, especially where they rely on a traditional public governance model. However, it should be remembered that there is no objective benchmark in this respect. While more money certainly means better resources, it does not necessarily imply better quality or cost-effectiveness; some less well-funded systems might compare favorably to better-resourced ones. Nobody knows what the optimal level of tertiary education funding ought to be.

The funding issue has many facets and varies according to the standpoints. Typically, governments, students (and their families), higher education institutions, and their staff will have different perspectives on and interests in this. In other words, a crisis of public funding does not necessarily imply a crisis of funding generally and several conflicting perceptions may be accurate (depending on one's perspective). This section explores how the funding of tertiary education has changed at the macro level. Here, international statistics do not allow one to see what happened in "research universities": the only thing that can be looked at is what happened in the funding of academic research (Vincent-Lancrin 2006).

The Institutional Perspective

From tertiary education institutions' perspectives, a crisis of public funding could take different forms: an absolute and/or relative decline in public funding, and, in countries where there is a significant private sector, a relative impoverish-

---

[6] The figures come from activity reports posted on the respective institutional websites (and from the common dataset for faculty figures for Yale and Berkeley). For University of Vienna: *Tätigkeitbericht* 2005.

ment of public higher education institutions compared to their independent private counterparts. This can have an effect for education funding and research funding, but also for education and research facilities.

The funding of tertiary education institutions has increased in all OECD countries between 1995 and 2003, both as a percentage of GDP and in real terms. On average, countries spent 46 percent more for tertiary education institutions in 2003 than in 1995 (see Figure 1.3). While slower than the OECD average, there has also been a 33 percent growth in the United States. Research expenditures in the academic sector have not suffered either: overall, research universities and academic centers have increased their share of research and development compared to other sectors between 1981 and 2003, and their funding accounted for 0.39 percent of GDP in 2003, against 0.28 percent in 1981. In real terms (constant prices), research expenditures have tripled during that time (Vincent-Lancrin 2006).

However, the budget growth has been more modest when the expansion of enrollments is taken into account, and has even decreased in five countries. The budget per student of tertiary education institutions has increased by six percent on average. This time the growth has been slightly above the OECD average in the United States, at 10 percent. See Figure 1.4.

While the resources of tertiary education institutions have actually increased in recent years, the share of their public resources has on average diminished by nine percent (Table 1.3). However, in most OECD countries, their resources remain overwhelmingly public (Figure 1.5). Only in four countries, including the United States, do public resources represent less than 50 percent on average of an institution's budget, whereas they represent more than 70 percent in 21 countries. Table 1.3 shows that there were marked differences in changes across countries: The decrease in the share of public funding has been significant (over 30 percent) in some countries (Australia, Canada, New Zealand, United Kingdom), but more modest or very small in most countries. In the United States, the share of public funding in institutions' budgets has dropped by seven percent on average between 1992 and 2003.

A relative decrease in public funding does not necessarily imply an absolute decrease in public funding: It can also result from the quicker growth of other sources of funding. Between 1992 and 2003, there was an absolute decrease in direct public funding to tertiary education institutions in three countries (among those for which information was available for both years): Australia, Canada, and Italy. Over the same period, the public funding *per student* has decreased in absolute terms in seven countries (with only one overlap with the former indicator): Czech Republic, Finland, Hungary, Italy, the Netherlands, New Zealand, and the United Kingdom. If one looks at a shorter period of time, between 1998 and 2003, the picture changes somewhat: In Australia, Austria, and Iceland, there is a decrease in public funding *and* in public funding per student, while institutions have experienced a decrease in public funding per student in Greece, the Netherlands, New Zealand, Norway, Poland, and Sweden.

Research performed by the higher education sector is largely government-funded in the OECD area. In 2003, the government sector funded directly or indi-

Figure 1.3. Change in Expenditure on Educational Institutions in 2003 Constant Prices, 1995–2003 (1995 = 100)

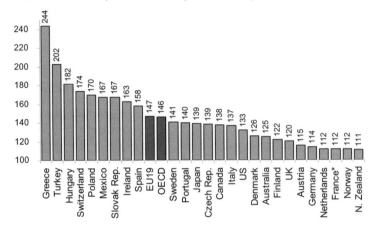

Note: * 2002 instead of 2003
Source: OECD (2006)

Figure 1.4. Change in Expenditure on Educational Institutions for All Services Per Student for Tertiary Education (1995, 2003)

Index of change between 1995 and 2003 (GDP deflator 1995=100, 2003 constant prices)

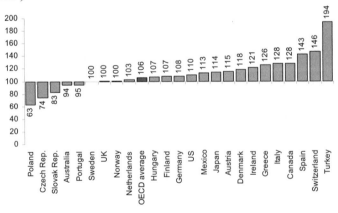

Source: OECD (2006)

Table 1.3. Change in the Distribution of Funding to Higher Education Institutions by Stakeholder between 1992 and 2003 and Change in Public Funding and Public Funding per Student (1998–2003)

	2003			Shift 1992–2003			% change in public funding (PPPs) between 1998-2003	% change in public funding per student (PPPs) 1998-2003
	Government	House-holds	Other private entities (firms, etc.)	Govern-ment share	House-holds share	Other private entities (firms, etc.) share		
Australia	48%	35%	17%	-33%	16%	17%	-3	-16
Austria	93%	6%	1%	-6%	5%	1%	-18	-12
Belgium	85%	9%	4%	-30%	18%	12%	44	m
Canada	59%	23%	18%	m	m	m	51	m
Czech Rep.	83%	7%	9%	-1%	3%	-2%	45	9
Denmark	97%	3%	0%	-1%	m	m	23	11
Finland	96%	4%	m	-3%	0%	m	19	2
France	80%	12%	7%	-3%	m	3%	31	25
Germany	86%	m	14%	m	m	m	12	4
Greece	93%	0%	2%	m	m	m	37	-9
Hungary	78%	5%	16%	6%	m	m	67	9
Iceland	89%	11%	0%	-4%	4%	0%	m	m
Ireland	82%	14%	1%	8%	-9%	-1%	42	12
Italy	72%	19%	9%	-14%	9%	5%	15	12

	2003			Shift 1992–2003			% change in public funding (PPPs) between 1998–2003	% change in public funding per student (PPPs) 1998–2003
	Government	Households	Other private entities (firms, etc.)	Government share	Households share	Other private entities (firms, etc.) share		
Japan	40%	60%	0%	0%	1%	-1%	23	23
Korea, Rep. of	23%	57%	20%	5%	-23%	19%	112	74
Mexico	69%	30%	0%	-12%	11%	0%	33	2
Netherlands	79%	11%	10%	-8%	-2%	10%	9	-4
New Zealand	61%	39%	0%	-39%	39%	0%	11	-9
Norway	97%	3%	0%	-3%	3%	0%	16	0
Poland	69%	31%	0%	0%	-1%	0%	10	-34
Portugal	91%	8%	0%				18	4
Slovak Republic	85%	6%	8%	m	m	m	m	m
Spain	77%	19%	4%	-5%	4%	2%	42	35
Sweden	90%	0%	10%	-9%	0%	9%	27	-14
Switzerland	100%	0%	0%	0%	0%	0%	60	31
Turkey	95%	5%	0%	-3%	3%	0%	44	5
United Kingdom	70%	19%	11%	-30%	19%	11%	33	13
United States	43%	37%	20%	-7%	0%	7%	29	4
Country mean	77%	17%	7%	-9%	5%	4%	31	7

Note: The sum of the changes does not always equate zero because of rounding. Missing data for 1992 were replaced by a close year (1991 or 1993) if available. (e) notes estimates. Source: OECD.

Figure 1.5. Distribution of Funding for Higher Education Institutions, 2003

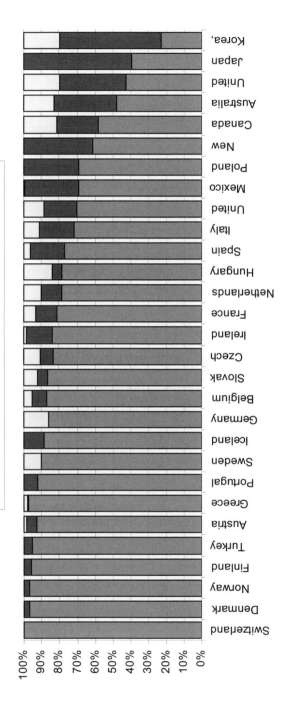

rectly 72 percent on average of academic research; that year, government funding amounted to more than 80 percent of academic research in 16 out of the 28 OECD countries for which information is available. Between 1981 and 2003, the share of government funding has dropped from nine percent, most of the decrease having occurred before 1992 where this share was at 74 percent. In the United States, 68 percent of the funding for academic research came from public sources in 2003, against 67 percent in 1992 and 74 percent in 1981 (Vincent-Lancrin 2006).

U.S. tertiary education institutions have not experienced an absolute decline in public funding or in public funding per student during these periods (in real terms). Figure 1.6 shows that they are the second best-resourced institutions after Switzerland in the OECD area with a unique, relatively balanced tripartite origin of income. In absolute terms, U.S. tertiary education institutions are the ones that get the most money from households and from private sources other than households, and they rank seventh in terms of public resources they receive (for countries for which information is available).

The crisis can also come from a change in the structure of institutions' expenditures. International data on institutional cost structures are available, but they are difficult to interpret in this light without being supplemented by institutional case studies. Between 1998 and 2003, the share of capital expenditures in institutional budgets has decreased on average by three percent (and represented 10 percent on average of an OECD country's institutional budget). On one hand, a decrease in the share of capital expenditure can correspond to an underinvestment in capital (and can thus be interpreted as evidence of budget pressures), but it can also mean there is more available income for current teaching and research activities (budget relief). Conversely, a significant increase in the share of capital expenditures could correspond to an upgrade of facilities, having a positive impact on work conditions for teaching and research.

Between 1998 and 2003, the share of current expenditures other than staff compensation has increased by five percent in institutions' budgets (to 34.5 percent of their budget on average). Where it has actually fallen, for example in France (-10 percent), this could indicate that available income for teaching and research has diminished: such a decrease could be due to the aging of staff (whose compensation grows more quickly than the total budget). But more compensation for staff could also be due to the expansion of staff and represent less rather than more pressure on institutional budgets and conditions of work. No conclusions about budget pressure or crisis can thus be drawn from these data alone.

The main conclusion is a trend toward a smaller share of public resources in institutional budgets, generally because of a quicker growth of other sources of income: This has happened in 19 countries (in different magnitudes). Tertiary education institutions have experienced an increase in their budgets (or expenditures) in all OECD countries over the past decade, but their funding per student has decreased in six countries. Overall, their public funding has increased (save in three countries) as well as their public funding per student (save in seven countries). Three countries stand out and may indeed be experiencing a funding crisis: in

Figure 1.6. Annual Expenditure Per Student on Core Services, Ancillary Services and R&D by Source of Funding (2003) (in equivalent U.S. dollars Converted Using PPPs for GDP, Based on Full-Time Equivalents [FTE])

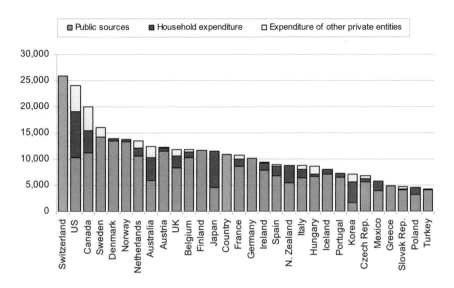

Notes: In Switzerland, the distribution between sources is missing; Canada: 2002 instead of 2003; Canada, Hungary, Italy, Poland, Portugal, Turkey: public institutions only; Mexico: R&D expenditures (and thus total) underestimated.

Source: OECD.

Australia, there was a decrease in funding per student, in public funding, and in the share of public funding (although the decrease was small and there was no decrease in public funding per student); in Italy, there was a decrease in the share of public funding, but also in public funding and in public funding per student; finally, the Czech institutions experienced a drop in funding per student as well as in public funding per student. Like the tertiary education institutions of nine other OECD countries, U.S. institutions only experienced a decrease in their share of public funding between 1992 and 2003: while this may be the consequence of insufficient public funding, it is not strong evidence of a major public funding crisis.

A caveat to this discussion is that averages can hide big variations within countries and the average stories can vary greatly from the individual ones. The distribution of public funding within countries may have become more concentrated and left a majority of institutions less well off than they used to be (even if the average story is different). Conversely, the distribution of public funding may have become less concentrated and some top research universities may feel they have been inadequately funded compared to other national institutions or their foreign counterparts.

The Student (Household) Perspective

From a student perspective, there has been a small crisis of (public) funding in recent years in the sense that, overall, students (and their families) have made a greater contribution to the cost of their higher education than in the past, both in absolute and relative terms. In most OECD countries, though, their tertiary education is still subsidized to a great extent.

In international statistics, the best estimate of the cost of tertiary education for students is the households' contribution to the expenditures (or budget) of tertiary education institutions. This contribution typically consists of tuition fees, but it can include other components like boarding fees and all other payments made to institutions (e.g., for meals, textbooks, and other instructional material, etc.). Given the differences of habits regarding boarding and provision of services other than teaching by the institutions themselves, the data are only imperfectly comparable: an institution offering catering or boarding to students will, for example, get more student contribution than one where catering and housing are left to external providers, although the cost of tertiary education to the student would in all cases include living costs. However, in most countries nonfee revenues are small enough to make it a fairly good proxy.

While institutions' resources have increased, the share coming from households has increased by five percent on average between 1992 and 2003. Figure 1.7 shows that there have been marked differences across countries: in most countries, this share has been fairly stable, as was the case in the United States. Changes toward more household contribution have occurred in New Zealand, the United Kingdom, Canada, and Australia—while changes in Korea have taken the opposite direction.

The relative stability of students' shares of the expenditures of tertiary education institutions in most countries (except in four Anglo-Saxon countries and in Korea) does not mean that there was no change in the cost to students and their families. Indeed, as shown in the previous section, the expenditures of tertiary education institutions have risen. In absolute terms, the level of the household contribution in constant prices has increased in almost all countries for which information was available for both years—with the exception of Ireland (-33 percent) and the Netherlands (-12 percent). In the United States, student expenditures on institutions have increased by 52 percent in real terms (constant prices) between 1992 and 2003, with a slowdown of this increase in recent years (+10 percent between 1998 and 2003).

It is noteworthy that tuition fees were first introduced in several countries during that period: before 1998, tertiary education students did not for example

Figure 1.7. Change in the Share of Resources Coming from Households in Tertiary Education Institutions' Expenditures, 1992–2003

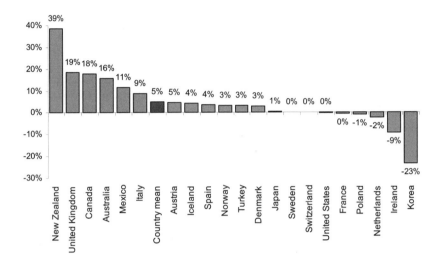

Source: OECD.

pay fees in the United Kingdom, while student payments represented 19 percent of British institutions' budgets in 2003. Given that the distribution of enrollments in the private and public sector has remained more or less stable over that period, the increase has occurred across the board rather than as a mechanical impact of the growth of the private sector.

In power purchasing parities, the average contribution of students to tertiary education institutions' expenditures amounted to USD 2,011 in 2003, while the median was at USD 1,372. Figure 1.8 shows that household contribution varies significantly across countries. These average costs can also hide a large variance within countries. The cost of tertiary education to students is significantly higher in the United States and in Japan than in other countries. U.S. households contribute the most to tertiary education institutions, with an average contribution per student of USD 8,900. While boarding costs probably weigh in more than in many other countries, this figure is mainly due to higher tuition fees. In 2003 tuition fees represented 58 percent of U.S. undergraduate students' contribution to public four-year institutions, and 27 percent for private four-year institutions (while there is typically no boarding at two-year institutions that enroll about 40 percent of U.S. students) (College Board 2003).

In the United States, the cost of tertiary education to families (including tuition fees) varies significantly for public two-year colleges, public four-year institutions, and private four-year institutions. In 2003, costs to *undergraduate* students

Figure 1.8. Contribution of Households to the Expenditures of Tertiary Education Institutions, 2003 (USD and PPPs, based on FTE)

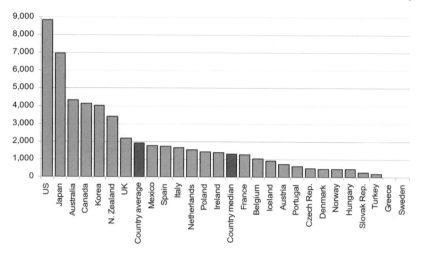

Notes: Same as Figure 6.
Source: OECD.

averaged USD 1,735 at public two-year institutions, USD 9,663 (including 4,081 in tuition and fees) at public four-year institutions, USD 16,206 (including USD 9,890 in tuition fees) at private two-year institutions, and USD 25,052 (including USD 18,273 in tuition fees) at private four-year institutions.[7]

The cost of tertiary education to students (and their families) can be alleviated by student aid, but student aid does not have a big impact on the cost per student on average (although it has a big positive impact on those receiving it, according to many studies [e.g., Dynarski 2003, 2004]). Only 0.4 percent of the private funding of tertiary education institutions was actually an indirect public subsidy in 2003 in OECD countries (OECD 2006). In many countries, student aid is supposed to support living costs rather than tuition fees (especially as they are often low and publicly subsidized in the OECD area). Moreover, part of it can take the form of loans that will be repaid (and are thus a temporary aid). While the contribution of students to tertiary education institutions increased, public student aid also increased per student by 93 percent on average between 1992 and 2003 (but

---

[7] The price has continued to rise since 2003. Total charges to families amounted to US $2,272 at public two-year institutions, US $12,796 at private two-year institutions (including US $5,836 of tuition and fees), and USD 30,367 at private four-year institutions (including USD 22,218 of tuition and fees). After student aid (grants and tax benefits), the prices for full time students fall to US $72, US $9,696 and US $21,367, respectively (College Board, 2007).

with strong variations: the median increase is 25 percent). It amounted to an average USD 1,629 in 2003 (with a median at USD 1,057).

However, in spite of their increasing contributions to the expenditures of tertiary education institutions, students and their families still benefit from generally high levels of public subsidization. Student payments represent on average 17 percent of tertiary education institutions' expenditures in OECD countries. See Figure 1.9. There are only seven countries where students (and their households) contribute more than 30 percent on average of tertiary institutions' budgets, including the United States (37 percent), with only two countries (Japan and Korea) where these contributions are the main income source in institutions' budgets. While this means that students are still publicly subsidized in most if not all OECD countries, it is noteworthy that unsubsidized students would generally contribute less than 100 percent of institutions' revenues: Tertiary education institutions provide nonteaching services like research and services to the community (participation in boards, peer reviewing, work with private companies, etc.) that would not necessarily be paid for by (all) students and their families in a marketplace.

In conclusion, students and their households have faced a small crisis of public funding in OECD countries, actually mainly concentrated in a few countries. However, in most OECD countries students are still very far from paying unsubsidized market prices for their tertiary education. It is likely that tuition fees will be raised in the coming years in public systems where they are very low or nonexistent (although this may take some time in some countries for political reasons): with higher tuition fees paid after graduation through a public (income-contingent) loan scheme, the financing models of Australia, New Zealand, and now England have become the most appealing to many tertiary education experts and economists (OECD 2008a; Johnstone 2005).

The debate takes the opposite direction in the United States or in Japan: The affordability of tertiary education to students has become a big concern and the question is more about cost containment or, in the case of Japan, a possible increase in public funding. While tertiary education can be expensive to students in the United States, notably if they study in private selective universities, it remains largely subsidized for the bulk of tertiary education students: In 2003, about 70 percent of U.S. undergraduate students attended tertiary education institutions charging less than USD 7,000 for tuition fees (College Board 2003). Given the coming demographic pressure on U.S. tertiary education, whose enrollments are projected to increase significantly in the coming decades, costs to students and their families is likely to remain a big issue in the coming decades (OECD 2008b).

The Government Perspective

From a government perspective, a decline in public spending is less likely to be regarded as a crisis than a rapid increase (although a decrease could also be a

Figure 1.9. Percentage of Direct Expenditures to Tertiary Education Institutions Coming from Households, 2003

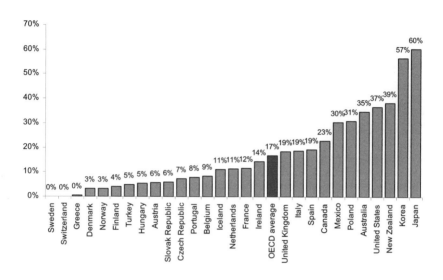

Source: OECD.

sign of underfunding). Overall, government spending on higher education and on academic research has increased in the past decades, but not in a critical way. The share of public expenditures on tertiary education (including all transfers to students, other private entities, and tertiary education institutions) has increased by about 0.4 percent on average since 1993, to reach 3.1 percent in 2003. Canada, the Czech Republic, and the United Kingdom are the only three countries (for which information is available on both years) where the public spending on higher education has declined as a share of total public spending. These public expenditures represented on average 1.3 percent of an OECD country's GDP in 2003, as they did in 1998. And as real GDP has grown in all countries over that period (constant prices), this is also the case of real public expenditures on tertiary education. In 2003, the United States was the ninth top public spender on tertiary education relative to GDP in the OECD area, at 1.5 percent of its GDP (against 1.3 percent in 1998). See Table 1.4.

Between 1992 and 2003, there has been little change in the pattern of public funding for higher education. On average, 83.2 percent of a country's public budget for tertiary education still directly funds tertiary education institutions in the OECD area. This share has slightly decreased (-2 percent on average) between 1992 and 2003 (Table 1.5). Governments and other public authorities have spent a

Table 1.4. Total Public Expenditure on Tertiary Education as a Percentage of Public Expenditure and as a Percentage of GDP

	Public expenditure on education as a percentage of total public expenditure		Public expenditure on tertiary education as a percentage of GDP	
OECD countries	**2003**	**1993**	**1994**	**2003**
Australia	m	3.8	1.36	1.1
Austria	2.5	2.1	0.9	1.3
Belgium	2.6	1.7	1	1.3
Canada	4.3	4.7	2.27	1.7
Czech Republic	1.8	2.1	0.8	0.9
Denmark	4.5	3.4	1.4	2.5
Finland	4.1	3.6	1.5	2.1
France	2.2	1.8	0.9	1.2
Germany	2.5	2.1	0.91	1.2
Greece	2.5	2.3	0.7	1.5
Hungary	m	3	0.9	1.2
Iceland	2.9	2.9	0.7	1.4
Ireland	m	2.9	1.12	1.1
Italy	1.6	1.5	0.72	0.8
Japan	1.8	1.1	0.5	0.6
Korea	2.0	1.3	0.3	0.6
Luxembourg	m	m	m	m
Mexico	4.0	m	0.9	1.0
Netherlands	m	2.9	1.33	1.3
New Zealand	5.5	4.4	1.1	1.6
Norway	4.8	3.9	1.4	2.3
Poland	m	m	m	1.1
Portugal	2.2	m	0.8	1.1
Slovak Republic	2.2	m	m	0.9
Spain	m	2.1	0.8	1.0
Sweden	3.7	2.9	1.5	2.2
Switzerland	3.5	3.3	1.11	1.6
Turkey	m	m	1.25	1.2
United Kingdom	2.4	2.6	0.97	1.1

United States	4.0	3.6	1.12	1.5
OECD average	3.1	2.8		1.3
EU19 average	2.7	2.5		1.3

Source: OECD.

higher proportion of their budget for financial aid for students (part of which is only a temporary disbursement when it takes the form of a student loan that will typically be repaid and later represent a source of public income). In some countries (Australia, Austria, Canada, Italy, Japan, New Zealand, Turkey, and the United States), this shift toward student financial aid (and less direct funding to institutions as a share of their budget) has been above eight percent. The opposite trend could be observed in a smaller number of countries (Belgium, Iceland, Slovak Republic, and Sweden). The structure of spending did not change much in other countries.

Between 1998 and 2003, the share of the public budget for tertiary education going directly to institutions has virtually not changed: it increased by 0.4 percent on average. The share of public expenditures for financial aid to students also remained stable at 17 percent of public expenditures for tertiary education—and 0.27 percent of countries' GDP. The only noticeable change is that the relative importance of funding for grants and scholarships has decreased by two percent and benefited student loans, with 10 percent of public funding being devoted to grants and seven percent to student loans in 2003. That being said, publicly subsidized (and/or administered) student loans are still unavailable or of a negligible amount in 11 of the 28 OECD countries for which information was available in 2003. Apart from a few exceptions, notably the United Kingdom, there has been little change in the structure of public expenditures on tertiary education between 1998 and 2003.

In most countries for which information is available, only a small part of financial aid to students ultimately seems to go to educational institutions: It can thus generally not be seen as a new way of indirectly financing tertiary education institutions through more competitive market mechanisms or vouchers. In the case of research, there is more evidence of a shift toward a different allocation of public funding: Between 1981 and 2003, the percentage of public research funding allocated through general university funds has dropped from 78 percent to 65 percent in the 16 OECD countries for which information is available for both years. While general university funds still funded over 70 percent of academic research in 2003 in eight OECD countries, they have decreased by more than 13 percent in New Zealand, Ireland, the United Kingdom, Australia, Finland, Denmark, Greece, Spain, and Turkey (Vincent-Lancrin 2006). Moreover, the allocation of these general university funds has been increasingly (partially) performance-related in many

Table 1.5. Subsidies for Education to Private Entities (2003)

OECD Country	Direct Expenditure for Institutions	Financial Aid: Household Grants	Financial Aid: Student Loans	Financial Aid Total	Household Grants Attributable for Institutions	Payment to other Private Entities	Total	
Australia	65.0	13.5	21.5	35.0	1.2	n	35.0	-13.0
Austria	82.0	16.6	a	16.6	m	1.4	18.0	-13.8
Belgium	84.2	15.8	n	15.8	4.6	n	15.8	12.2
Canada	78.0	16.8	3.9	20.7	m	1.3	22.0	-8.9
Czech Rep.	93.8	6.2	a	6.2	m	n	6.2	-3.2
Denmark	67.8	26.8	5.5	32.2	m	n	32.2	4.9
Finland	82.1	17.4	n	17.4	n	0.5	17.9	-1.7
France	91.8	8.2	a	8.2	2.6	a	8.2	-0.1
Germany	82.8	13.5	3.7	17.2	n	n	17.2	-6.0
Greece	94.0	6.0	m	6.0	m	a	6.0	2.2
Hungary	85.3	14.7	a	14.7	n	n	14.7	-1.7
Iceland	75.9	n	21.4	21.4	n	2.7	24.1	8.4
Ireland	86.2	13.8	n	13.8	4.3	n	13.8	6.1
Italy	83.0	17.0	n	17.0	5.2	n	17.0	-13.7

OECD Country	Direct Expenditure for Institutions	Financial Aid: Household Grants	Financial Aid: Student Loans	Financial Aid Total	Household Grants Attributable for Institutions	Payment to Other Private Entities	Total	
Korea	95.4	3.3	1.2	4.6	2.9	0.1	4.6	1.1
Luxembourg	m	m	m	m	m	m	m	m
Mexico	94.1	3.5	2.4	5.9	1.1	n	5.9	-2.7
Netherlands	74.1	12.1	13.7	25.9	1.4	m	25.9	3.6
New Zealand	56.6	13.7	29.8	43.4	m	a	43.4	-13.5
Norway	63.3	14.9	21.8	36.7	m	n	36.7	-1.2
Poland	97.7	0.4	a	0.4	m	2.0	2.3	1.9
Portugal	97.4	2.2	a	2.2	m	0.5	2.6	6.3
Slovak Republic	91.5	6.8	1.8	8.5	m	a	8.5	9.0
Spain	92.1	7.9	n	7.9	2.4	n	7.9	-0.5
Sweden	71.6	10.4	18.0	28.4	a	a	28.4	8.2
Switzerland	98.0	1.2	0.1	1.3	m	0.6	2.0	4.5
Turkey	86.8	3.2	10.0	13.2	n	m	13.2	-7.4
United Kingdom	75.3	1.6	23.2	24.7	0.7	n	24.7	-2.4
United States	82.2	13.9	3.9	17.8	m	a	17.8	-8.8
OECD average	83.1	9.8	7.1	16.6	1.6	0.3	16.9	-1.7

Notes: Canada: 2002 instead of 2003; m: missing, n: negligible, a: not applicable. Source: OECD.

countries, generally based on university research evaluation that was introduced in several countries in the late 1980s and 1990s (Geuna and Martin 2003).

In conclusion, in the past decade the structure of public expenditures for higher education has remained fairly stable on average in most OECD countries. In some countries, including the United States, there was a notable decrease of the share of direct public expenditures for tertiary education institutions at the beginning of the 1990s. In recent years, while the share of public expenditures devoted to student financial aid has remained stable, there has been a tendency toward less expenditures for grants and more for student loan programs in relative terms. However, Table 1.5 shows that the structure of public expenditures for tertiary education varies considerably across countries.

Concluding Remarks

The present analysis shows that there was no general crisis of enrollments, of funding, or of public funding in public tertiary education in OECD countries. At the macro level, on the contrary, there was overall a remarkable stability in the distribution of enrollments and in the funding patterns of tertiary education in the past decade. Except for Japan and Korea, tertiary education is still predominantly a public enterprise in the OECD area; the private for-profit sector is still marginal in a large majority of countries, and even more so for advanced research programs. However, the small shift toward enrollments in private government-dependent institutions corresponds to recent shifts in policy thinking and policy reforms making tertiary education institutions more autonomous from public authorities and more remote from traditional administrative models of public governance.

As for funding, tertiary education institutions have not faced a major crisis either: Their budgets have increased over the past years, in most cases per student, and their public funding per student has also increased in most countries. The share of public funding in their budget has decreased on average, but this is mainly due to the quicker growth of (additional) private funding. Students (and their households) have arguably faced the most serious crisis as they contribute more to the expenditures of tertiary education institutions than they used to; however, in most countries their tertiary education is still significantly publicly subsidized. In brief, the crisis, if any, is limited—and actually limited to a few countries. In the United States, there is no evidence of a crisis of enrollments in the public sector, nor of funding or public funding per student; tertiary education is overwhelmingly public. While students' contributions to tertiary education institutions have remained stable, the cost of tertiary education to students and their families has increased in real terms while tertiary education institutions' expenditures increased.

Does this mean that there is no crisis of public tertiary education (or "crisis of the publics")? Not necessarily. Country averages can hide large variations within countries and case studies or less aggregated data could help better understand this widespread perception of a crisis. In the case of academic research, there is for example a well-established trend toward allocating public research funding through competitive bids, as has long been the case in the United States, whereas a large share of public research funding used to go directly to tertiary education institutions (Vincent-Lancrin 2006; Geuna and Martin 2003). As a result, public funding may become more concentrated in a few institutions, leaving a large number of public universities with fewer resources and research facilities (even if the public funding increases); most institutions could thus legitimately feel they are in crisis, a few being better off.

Another important reason could be that the crisis rests in factors other than enrollments or funding levels. A mental revolution is underway in tertiary education with the qualitative transformation of the public governance and economics of tertiary education, the frontrunners being Australia, New Zealand, and the United Kingdom—the United States is following a different trend because of a different tradition and a different history of its higher education. This can be seen in several changes in the way institutions, governments, and experts think about tertiary education, regardless of the implementation of these changes. These changes can take the following forms:

- Changes in the legal and funding relationships of (public) tertiary education institutions and public authorities, which are encouraged to raise more private funds and act in a more entrepreneurial way; this results in a cost sharing that is less favorable to students compared to what it used to be, in more endeavors to raise (or use) private funds for academic research, and in new ways of publicly funding tertiary education;

- Changes in the employment system and job content of academics: While faculty are still civil servants or tenured professionals in a number of OECD countries, tertiary education institutions use more temporary or adjunct professors than in the past, and the academic profession is changing to become closer to a business-like employer-employee relationship (Enders and Musselin 2008; Schuster and Finkelstein 2006);

- changes in the perception of the sector, which is increasingly seen as a regular economic sector: While the sector can hardly be described as a regular marketplace, some ways of thinking about it would have been difficult decades ago: the inclusion of tertiary education in the GATS, the competition for foreign (and sometimes domestic) fee-paying students and for funding is indeed transforming the perception (and to a large extent self-perception) of tertiary education from a public service into a service industry, even in countries that are not directly affected by these changes.

In most countries, these changes are driven (or at least viewed as driven) by globalization, either directly or indirectly, as a response to or preparation for it, with demography being another important factor. Public governance practices have got closer, though not converged, as information and "best practices" circulate more quickly internationally. Globalization has also brought innovation and human capital development to the fore of public policies. As a result, tertiary education is now perceived as playing a major role in maintaining the economic standards of economically advanced nations—and governments now try to make their public education competitive globally. International rankings have recently been prominent in policy reform discussions and explain why some countries try to build up "world-class" universities (although a few world-class departments located in different universities may actually be enough if excellence were the only objective). While international competition and competitiveness become more important in public tertiary education, perhaps is it not so surprising to see public tertiary education transforming itself. Given that relatively affluent U.S. universities top international rankings, giving the rest of the world a benchmark of what world-class universities are, most OECD countries try to help their institutions to raise as many resources and to be able to compete with the U.S. universities by attracting (or retaining) their best faculty; this will probably remain a major driver of change in public tertiary education in the coming decade outside of the United States.

Because of the prominence of U.S. research universities worldwide, the pressure of globalization and competitiveness is not perceived in the same way in the United States as it is in most other OECD countries. While U.S. public research universities find it more difficult to compete financially with U.S. private research universities, some U.S. public research universities belong to these "world-class" universities and are much more affluent than the most affluent public universities in other countries. Many of the changes underway in other OECD countries have long been features of U.S. tertiary education. Research funding is becoming more concentrated in many countries, as has long been the case in the United States; countries are starting to openly differentiate their public tertiary education hierarchically, a hierarchy that has long been in place in the United States; private funding is becoming more important in the economy of tertiary education institutions, whereas this has long been a part of public tertiary education in the United States; and many countries are considering having students cover a more significant share of the cost of their tertiary education in order to increase their institutions' resources, as has long been the case in the United States.

In the United States, the major challenge related to globalization lies in the qualification or tertiary educational attainment of its workforce: In spite of high access to tertiary education, tertiary educational attainment has stagnated while it has continued to increase in most other OECD countries. The cost (or "affordability") of tertiary education to students is part of the equation: while many OECD countries are in the process of increasing the contribution of households to their public tertiary education, the policy agenda in the United States is about maintaining or reducing it. While the research excellence of U.S. research universities makes the United States a benchmark for other countries, one question about the U.S. model is whether quality in teaching and excellence in research can be achieved at a lower cost to students and taxpayers. The search for the answer will probably lead to a further transformation of public tertiary education, both in the United States and in other OECD countries.

References

Bailey, T. 2006. "Increasing competition and Growth of the For-Profits." In *Defending the Community College Equity Agenda*, ed. Thomas Bailey and Vanessa Smith Morest. Baltimore: Johns Hopkins.

College Board. 2003. *Trends in College Pricing*. Washington, D.C.

———. 2006. *Trends in College Pricing*. Washington, D.C.

Cunningham, S., Y. Ryan, L. Stedman, S. Tapsall, S. Bagdon, T. Flew, and P. Coaldrake. 2000. *The Business of Borderless Education*. Australian Department of Education, Training and Youth Affairs. Canberra.

Dynarski, S. 2003. "Does Aid Matter? Measuring the Effect of Student Aid on College Attendance and Completion." *American Economic Review* 93(1): 279–88.

———. 2004. "The New Merit Aid." In *College Choices: The Economics of Where to Go, When to Ggo, and How to Pay for It*, ed. Caroline Hoxby. Chicago and London: The University of Chicago Press.

Enders, J., and C. Musselin. 2008. "Back to the Future? The Academic Profession in the 21st Century." In OECD, *Higher Education 2030: Volume 1: Demography*, OECD editions, Paris.

Geuna, A., and B. R. Martin. 2003. "University Rresearch Evaluation and Funding: An International Comparison." *Minerva* 41: 277–304.

Johnstone, B. 2005. "Higher Education Accessibility and Financial Viability: The Role of Student Loans." In *Higher Education in the World 2006: The Financing of Universities*. GUNI series. Basingstoke: Palgrave McMillan.

Kärkkäinen, K. 2006. "Emergence of Private Higher Education Funding in the OECD Area." Mimeo, <http://www.oecd.org/dataoecd/19/20/38621229.pdf>.

Knight, J. 2004. "Internationalization Remodeled: Definition, Approaches, and Rationales." *Journal of Studies in International Education* 8(1): 5–31.

OECD. 2004. *Internationalisation and Trade in Higher Education*. OECD editions, Paris.

———. 2006. *Education at a Glance*. OECD editions, Paris.

———. 2008a. *Tertiary Education for the Knowledge Society*. OECD editions, Paris.

———. 2008b. *Higher Education 2030. vol. 1: Demography*. OECD editions, Paris.

Salmi, J., and A. Saroyan. 2006. "League Tables as Policy Instruments: Uses and Misuses." Mimeo.

Schuster, J., and M. Finkelstein. 2006. *The American Faculty: The Restructuring of Academic Work and Careers*. Baltimore: Johns Hopkins.

Vincent-Lancrin, S. 2006. "What is Changing in Academic Research? Trends and future Scenarios." *European Journal of Education* 41(2): 169–202.

Chapter 2

The Race for Human Capital

John Aubrey Douglass[1]

In the United States, developing human capital for both economic and social benefits is an idea as old as the nation itself and led to the world's first mass higher education system. Now most other nations are deliberately racing to expand access to universities and colleges and to expand their role in society. Higher education is growing markedly in its importance for promoting human capital, for expanding social economic mobility, for creating what might be termed a "culture of aspiration," and for, ultimately, determining national economic competitiveness. Among the OECD's 30-member nations alone, for example, the average growth rate in enrollment exceeds 20 percent over the last decade.[2] Enrollments in China have grown by an astounding 20 million students over that same period, and India recently announced plans to open some 90 new universities and technical institutes by 2013. Higher education is truly one of the biggest growth sectors in the world.

This chapter briefly discusses the vital role of human capital for national economies, past and future. It also examines the public and private benefits of higher education, the effort of nation-states and regions to build tertiary systems,

---

[1] Center for Studies in Higher Education, UC Berkeley.
[2] OECD, Education at a Glance 2008, September 2008.

and outlines a convergence in government-led efforts toward building what I call a *structured opportunity market* in higher education—including diversified and mission-differentiated providers, new finance structures, and expanding enrollment and program capacity.

Increasingly, institutions and developed and developing nations, and, in some cases, supranational entities such as the European Union, will move to most if not all of the components of this structured opportunity market (SOM), in part influenced by a global process of policy transfer. Those that don't will be compelled to offer in both domestic and international forums a rational reason why they are not adopting some aspects of the model. One important result of this debate within and among nations is the emergence, in some form, of more comprehensive and perhaps eventually more coherent visions of the structure and respective roles of higher education within their societies.

Human Capital and the Fate of Nations

Developing human capital has long been the objective of building national systems of higher education, but it was not until the 1960s that economists began to offer significant analysis of its key role in economic development. Gary Becker and T. W. Schultz famously offered evidence that more than 30 percent of the increased per capita income between the 1930s and the 1960s was attributable to increased schooling, and that investment in a college-educated workforce provided a greater rate of return than any other single investment, such as machinery. They also predicted that for an individual, the private rate of return of attending and graduating from college would grow substantially when compared to those who attained only a high school diploma.[3]

The work of Becker and Schultz, and others, spawned a significant body of economic research on human capital formation and the role of education in the U.S. economy, with increasing interest in the link of investment in higher education with technological innovation. A 1999 study by Claudia Goldin and Lawrence F. Katz estimated that during the last century about a quarter of U.S. growth in income per worker was due to the rise in educational attainment.[4]

Similarly, David Mitch found that investment in secondary and postsecondary education in Europe over the last century had a large impact on general economic growth, although not as large as in the U.S.[5] "Education plays an impor-

---

[3] Gary Becker, *Investment in Human Capital* (New York: Columbia University Press, 1964); T. W. Schultz, Investment in *Human Capital* (New York: The Free Press, 1971).

[4] For a synthesis of these and other studies see Elhanan Helpman, *The Mystery of Economic Growth* (Cambridge, Mass.: Belknap Press, 2004), 42.

[5] David Mitch, "The Rise of Mass Education and Its Contribution to Economic Growth in Europe, 1800–2000," Forth European Historical Economics Society Conference, Merton College, Oxford, 2001.

tant role in accounting for the time pattern of economic growth and the cross-country variation in income per capita," explains economist Elhanan Helpman.[6] And that assertion holds not just for those who attend college; there is evidence that in U.S. cities with large concentrations of college graduates, wages are higher for other workers. "This implies," noted Helpman, "that the social rate of return on higher education is higher than the private rates of return."[7]

Other recent studies continue to demonstrate the importance of college participation rates and how they produce both private and public benefits vital to nations, particularly those with postmodern economies. The private benefit afforded individuals who participate in higher education, and particularly those who graduate with a degree, has continued to grow.[8]

While salaries for all Americans have generally been stagnant over the past five years, the gap between the lifetime income of college graduates and that of high school graduates continues to grow and is the highest among OECD countries; the income gap is also, not surprisingly, growing dramatically between college graduates and the nation's growing pool of high school dropouts.[9] In 2004, the workforce population over age 25 with a bachelor's degree had an average personal income of $48,400; those with only a high school diploma earned on average only $23,000.[10]

Those who attend college have, in addition, much higher rates of employment and much greater opportunities for both social and economic mobility and status. They also have longer life spans and vote at higher rates than other portions of the population. And their children are more likely to attend and graduate from college—essentially receiving from the previous generation the cultural capital that spawns a general desire for education and self-improvement.[11]

Arguably, the public benefit of high participation rates is even more important. Society has a vested interest in generally encouraging a significant proportion of the population to go to college and gain a degree because college education creates a more flexible, talented, and productive workforce, encourages both social and economic equity, and reduces unemployment rates and welfare rolls. It places a downward pressure on crime rates, increases social tolerance, and correlates with high voter participation and rates of charitable giving.

---

[6] *Ibid.*

[7] *Ibid.*

[8] Claudia Golden and Lawrence F. Katz, "The Returns to Skill in the United State across the Twentieth Century," National Bureau of Economic Research, Working Paper No. 7126, May 1999.

[9] OECD Education at a Glance 2005, "OECD Briefing Notes for the United States," Organisation for Economic Cooperation and Development, September 2005.

[10] *The Investment Payoff: A 50-State Analysis of the Public and Private Benefits of Higher Education* (Washington, D.C.: Institute for Higher Education Policy, 2005).

[11] Sandy Baum and Kathleen Payea, *Education Pays 2004: The Benefits of Higher Education for Individuals and Society*, College Entrance Examination Board, revised edition, 2005.

These are all general benefits that are now widely recognized by national governments and higher-education leaders and advocates. Table 2.1 offers a matrix that outlines these and other private and public attributes of high participation rates.[12]

The Character of Mass Higher Education Systems

Nation-states are aggressively racing to increase the educational attainment of their populations, expanding or building mass higher education systems to help in that cause for the first time. How might we assess nascent and mature mass systems of higher education? What commonalities do they have?

One paradigm offered for simply categorizing the status of mass higher education systems was offered in the early 1970s, using a simple definition based on the percentage of the "college aged" population (18- to 21-year-olds) participating in tertiary education. At that time, the idea of mass higher education remained fixated on this traditional college-age cohort. If less than 15 percent participated, then it was elite; if some 15 to 40 percent participated, then it was a true mass education system; and if participation of the assigned cohort was over 40 percent, then it was universal in its character—virtually open to anyone.[13] Numerous studies in the 1970s predicted a steady progress from elite, to mass, to universal access, with participation rates of possibly 80 percent among the traditional college-aged cohort.

Under the simple percentage paradigm, most of the United States developed mass higher education systems by 1940, and most state systems emerged as universal access systems before 1970. A state like California, which aggressively attempted to expand access to higher education, created a mass system as early as 1935, and a universal system by 1960. The U.K. and most other E.U. countries, in contrast, entered the realm of mass systems only in the 1970s. As late as 1965, E.U. countries had only about 10 percent of the 18-to-21 age cohort in tertiary education (all forms).[14]

There are some problems with such figures and comparisons. Americans have always taken an expansive view of what constitutes higher education. Much of the enrollment in the U.S. has been in postsecondary programs that

---

[12] John Aubrey Douglass, *The Conditions for Admission: Access, Equity and the Social Contract of Public Universities* (Stanford, Calif.: Stanford University Press, 2007).

[13] M. Trow, "Problems in the Transition from Elite to Mass Higher Education," in *Policies for Higher Education, from the General Report on the Conference on Future Structures of Post-Secondary Education* (Paris: OECD, 1974); M. Trow, "Comparative Perspectives on Access" in O. Fulton (ed), *Access to Higher Education* (Guildford, England: Society for Research into Higher Education, 1981), 89–121.

[14] According to DFEE data, the participation rate of students under 21 years of age in higher education in Great Britain rose from approximately 12 percent to 15 percent from 1980 to 1989, and then increased rapidly to 35 percent by 2001 with the inclusion of the polytechnics in the higher education system and rapid expansion.

Table 2.1. Private and Public Benefits of Higher Education Participation

	Private Benefits	Public Benefits
Economic	Greater economic mobility Higher lifetime income Higher employment rates Higher levels of personal saving	Greater economic equity Lower unemployment rates Greater productivity More flexible workforce Lower welfare rates
Social	Greater social mobility Improved health/lifespan Improved economic/health chances for offspring Improved consumers	Greater social equity Greater social tolerance Greater civic involvement Increased charitable giving Lower crime rates Higher education persistence rates among next generation

Source: John Aubrey Douglass, *The Conditions for Admission: Access, Equity, and the Social Contract of Public Universities* (Stanford, Calif.: Stanford University Press, 2007).

many European countries consider more appropriate to secondary education, or that they believe should be defined as vocational training. Yet clearly, America has been bold in its attempt to foster both a great variety of educational institutions and to encourage participation in higher education.

A further and more nuanced exploration of the character of mass systems might include other variables related to the perceived demand for higher education and its supply. On the demand side, one could weigh three general variables:

- Social and political expectations of the population;
- Perceived labor needs and other products of higher education (e.g., knowledge production and societal and economic benefits of science and technology);
- Broader ideas on the role of higher education in developing civic and cultural values, and in promoting self-enlightenment, opportunity, and equity.

The supply-side variables are rather simple, including the organizational structure that might meet demand; institutional infrastructure; system governance and mission differentiation; funding capabilities; and, I would argue, significant institutional autonomy to manage the academic enterprise and sources of funding.

In the case of the United Kingdom, for example, the intent to create a mass system arguably began officially in 1963 with the Robbins Report that presented the case for a significant expansion of the prevailing university system. Yet this institutional infrastructure took some three decades to build. In 1963, there were only 24 universities in the U.K., with six "new" universities being planned. Approximately three-quarters of Britain's contemporary universities and a relatively new nonuniversity sector have emerged over the four decades since the Robbins Report.[15]

In a rudimentary manner, the three variables noted offer a framework for analyzing the character of mass higher education systems and the match between demand and supply. To some extent, the U.S. has been progressive *both* in developing demand and creating the appropriate infrastructure to meet this demand. Indeed, the extent to which supply drives demand creates an interesting dynamic.

Among the supply-side characteristics of the U.S. system: a diversity of institutional types, relatively low fees (although this is rapidly changing),[16] financial aid programs, local or regional access to colleges and universities, as well as a curricular system that enables students to accumulate course credits and allows them to matriculate between institutions in their path to a degree. One analysis indicates, for instance, that some 33 percent of students who eventually gain a bachelor's degree in the U.S. attend more than one institution—a rate unmatched in any other part of the world, thus far.

Another important aspect of the American system is the relatively high level of mission differentiation. This has had a huge effect not only on providing different paths for students of different abilities to enter some form of postsecondary education. It has also provided, in association with the ability to matriculate from one institution to another, a rationale for the development of so-called elite public institutions —public universities that are highly selective and focused on a broad range of purposes, including research and public service.

In states like California, the pioneering development of the community college in the early part of the 20th century proved vital both for expanding access to higher education and for solidifying the role of the University of California as the most selective part of the emerging mass higher education system. This gave the university the major responsibility of creating and promoting professional and doctoral degree programs as the state's primary research institution. Regional colleges later emerged—what is now the California State University—as an additional and important provider of higher education, but with a heavy emphasis on teaching. These other vital components in California's mass higher education system were linked by the ability of a student to transfer (or matriculate) between, for example, a community college and the University of California. The logic of this system allowed the University of California to pursue the emerging American model of the public research university, with teaching, research, and public service

---

[15] P. Scott, *The Meanings of Mass Higher Education* (London: Open University Press, 1995).

[16] For an analysis of rising fees in public universities, see David Ward and John Aubrey Douglass, "Higher Education and the Specter of Variable Fees: Public Policy and Institutional Responses in the United States and United Kingdom," *Higher Education Management and Policy* (OECD), vol. 18, no. 1 (2006): 1–28.

functions—including interaction with and support of local and regional economic players and communities. (See Figure 2.1 for the functions of the American public research university model.)

Supply and some combination of the demand-side variables noted (the quality of the secondary and lower schools, expectations of the population, labor needs, and the political saliency of higher education for promoting civically engaged citizens, and perceived and real opportunity) are essential prerequisites for mass systems.

Considering the Array of Human Intelligence

Another prerequisite, I would argue, is an understanding that human intelligence and creativity comes in many forms and is decidedly not uniform. Further, depending on socio-economic circumstance, political culture, and many other factors, humans develop their cognitive abilities at decidedly different rates over time.

Understanding, in some form, these differences is one reason nation-states need to develop an array of different postsecondary institutions that match the needs of both the student and the future labor market, and more importantly society in general. The following outlines different types of human capital, each of which influence the path from the school to a postsecondary education, and one hopes a degree, and then to the world of work and society. Each is important for the economic development of nations, and for creating robust systems that promote socio-economic mobility.[17]

- *Cultural Capital*, defined as family traits and cultural backgrounds that influence individuals, including perceived ethnic and racial ties, language, neighborhoods, and community. An increasing number of studies indicate that what happens in early childhood, including socio-economic and family influences, often determines chances later in life and is perhaps more influential than a student's school experiences.

- *Economic and Educational Capital*, the high correlation of family economic background and educational attainment with life chances, remains significant in society. While many young people from lower-income families, often with relatively low levels of educational attainment, do manage to excel in society (as political/community leaders, as professionals or in business, or as academics) the odds are much lower than for those from upper-income groups, or with relatively high levels of educational attainment among family members.

- *Social Capital*, essentially behavioral knowledge on how to best use opportunities, to understand the workings and manners of society and its institutions, and perhaps most importantly, the ability to navigate through the treacherous waters of growing bureaucracies.

---

[17] Adapted from Douglass, *The Conditions for Admission*, 279–81.

Figure 2.1. The American Public Research University Model

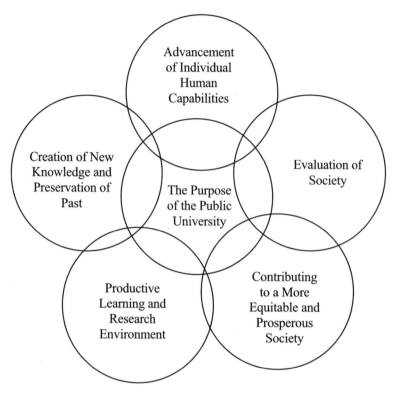

- *Cognitive Capital*, the notion that there are different kinds of intelligence. Their distribution is not even, or localized in one particular social, racial, or economic group.
- *Aspiration Capital*, the recognition that social capital and cognitive capital are influenced by ambition. Ambition plays an important role, in part influenced by environmental factors (e.g., real opportunities) and by personal traits. The combination of social and cognitive abilities with ambition helps explain why a significant number of successful CEOs in the United States were not particularly stellar students or did not come from elite universities and colleges.

In a reiterative process, these different forms of human capital, all essential to developed and developing postmodern economies, affect the individual's path to higher education and are bolstered by effective mass higher education systems.

National Higher Education Goals

National systems of higher education need sufficiently stable organizational structures and levels of funding to support and sustain high-quality academic programs. It is a decidedly accumulative process of building institutions and perceptions and expectations in all sectors of society that a higher education is in reach of the "common man."

Yet it is important to note that these evolving systems of higher education must have organizational flexibility to meet new and expanding societal demands, and on occasion to anticipate them. One might argue that the contemporary proliferation of higher education reforms by nation-states seeks this equilibrium, conditioned by their historical mix of tertiary institutions, their contemporary political culture, and, increasingly, the influence of seemingly successful models in other nations. This is creating a sort of convergence in higher education policymaking among nations, and in the organization and activities of universities and institution building.

For example, at the macro level of national policymaking, and reflecting the political salience of higher education as a primary means for national economic competitiveness, many nations are setting goals for their emerging mass higher education systems. The Labour Party's 1997 manifesto stated a goal of having 50 percent of all younger students participating in higher education (in some form).

Similar goals exist in many other E.U. countries (there is no stated goal in the United States at the federal level or by state governments, yet). In France, the goal is that some 80 percent of the secondary school population should enter the baccalaureate level; Germany has a more modest 40 percent target, and Sweden 50 percent.[18] Informal goals are discussed by ministers and proponents of higher education in other countries, such as in Brazil where the goal is eventually meeting the OECD average of around 30 percent.

Such targets are in part framed by the structure of the nations' postsecondary systems; none are based on a careful analysis of the supply and demand related to labor needs. Critics of government-induced plans to expand access to higher education accurately note that the plots of ministries favor access over quality. Further, the drive for bolstering access to tertiary institutions ignores both the capacity of a nation's population to actually benefit from a postsecondary education, which is most often linked to the balance of graduates with immediate job opportunities.

Reflecting similar debates in the U.S. during the 1970s, some observers in the U.K., for example, have argued that perhaps too many students are entering universities and are, in a sense, overeducated, representing a misplacement of resources and unnecessary strains on an overexpanded network of higher education institutions.

---

[18] Alison Wolf, "Education and Economic Performance: Simplistic Theories and Their Consequences," *Oxford Review of Economic Policy*, vol. 20, no. 2 (2004): 315–33.

Certainly, there is a need for national systems, and in turn individual institutions, to correlate their degree production to, in some form, match existing and perceived labor needs in a country, particularly in professional fields—ignoring for the moment global labor markets. But it is also clear that anticipating market needs is a precarious and complex endeavor. Who should decide: governments or institutions? Is an undersupply better then an oversupply?

In a number of European countries with traditional ties to command economies (where the national government has had a heavy hand in regulating its economy) and where public higher education is dominant, national ministries of education (and not institutions themselves) once set quotas and targets for how many students should enter a particular field—sometimes by limiting admissions to specific universities and colleges or by restricting funds for student positions.

But this has often led to a suppression of demand. In fields such as the humanities, social sciences, and even in science and engineering, matching supply and demand is difficult to assess. Particularly at the undergraduate level, students gain knowledge and skills with wide and often serendipitous uses over their working careers—a trend that will become more dynamic in the coming years. National governments tend to see the advantages of an oversupply and, I would argue, they are correct. As we have discussed, there are many benefits to higher levels of educational attainment that largely outweigh problems with, for example, temporary mismatches between graduates in specific fields and immediate job opportunities.

Cultural differences abound in the socio-economic aspirations of the population in different nations. The United States offers one case example. In part because of the relatively low social consciousness of class differences, the historically robust nature of its economy, demographic trends (including succeeding surges of immigrants), and arguably, because of its particular mass higher education system, one sees incredibly high rates of socio-economic aspirations among Americans. Indeed, their aspirations exceed the ability of the contemporary economy to actually fulfill their expectations.

Data from the OECD indicate that the occupational expectations of 15-year-olds in the United States are that, by age thirty, 80 percent anticipate high-skilled jobs that require postsecondary education. Table 2.2 provides a barometer of aspiration among a population, reflecting the perceived opportunities in the job market, and the perceived accessibility of higher education for those anticipating a high-skilled job. Only eight percent believe they will have white-collar low-skilled jobs; a meager six percent expect to be in low-skilled service and manual labor jobs. In contrast, 57 percent of those in the United Kingdom expect to have high-skilled and professional jobs; in Sweden, the figure is 63 percent and in Germany and France 49 percent.[19]

---

[19] Organisation for Economic Co-operation and Development, *Education at a Glance, August 2004* (Paris: OECD, 2004).

Table 2.2. A Barometer of Aspiration: Percentage of 15-Year-Olds' Occupational Expectations by Age 30 in Selected OPECD Countries (2000)

OECD Countries	White-collar high-skilled	White-collar low-skilled	Blue-collar high skilled	Blue-collar low-skilled
Australia	65.0	11.7	10.4	12.9
Canada	70.9	10.2	7.1	11.8
Denmark	58.5	17.5	19.6	4.3
Finland	60.4	15.8	12.2	11.5
France	48.9	14.7	9.9	26.5
Germany	48.8	20.9	17.2	13.2
Italy	69.1	15.2	5.8	9.9
Japan	45.8	12.9	4.0	37.4
Spain	66.6	12.2	8.2	13.1
Sweden	63.2	10.3	8.1	18.5
United Kingdom	57.1	16.3	7.6	19.0
United States	80.5	8.2	5.1	6.2
Country mean	62.2	13.9	10.1	13.8

A close analysis of labor needs in postmodern economies like that of the United States indicates that the job expectations of America's youth are probably unrealistic. According to one perhaps conservative projection, only 21 percent of the U.S. job market in 2010 will require a bachelor's degree or higher. Only 13 percent of jobs will require sub-baccalaureate degrees and credentials. That leaves some 66 percent of the job market requiring a secondary diploma or less, although prospective employees can depend on employers for training.[20]

Yet we know, as discussed previously, that encouraging educational aspirations benefits the individual, society, and the economy in a variety of ways. Generally, estimates of the future educational needs of a national workforce outline minimum requirements. In an analysis of the difficulties of projecting the need for college graduates, economist John Bishop notes that the Bureau of Labor Statistics and other projections have a track record of underestimating market demand. "The task of projecting the number of jobs 'requiring a college degree' into the future is essentially impossible," he notes. Employers set out

---

[20] For an analysis of how the Bureau of Labor Statistics and others have estimated the need for college graduates, see Bishop, *Is An Oversupply of College Graduates Coming?*, National Center for Postsecondary Improvement, School of Education, Stanford University, 1997.

minimum requirements for a particular job but almost always desire the most educated and competent worker they can possibly hire.[21]

To be sure, there are dangers in creating a caste of overqualified (the term *overeducated* seems to relegate education to a strictly vocational purpose) workers in terms of an overinvestment in an individual's education and training and in the potential mismatch of personal ambitions with actual job possibilities. The archetypal example is the history or English Ph.D. who has invested in eight to 10 years of postbaccalaureate education, only to drive a taxi in the immediate aftermath of graduation.

We also know that the postmodern economies are constantly changing, and most workers will switch jobs numerous times during their careers; in the face of that fact, it's reasonable to assume that for most workers, the more education, the better. The old paradigm "once a factory worker, always a factory worker" or "once a plumber, always a plumber" no longer applies.

Education, and postsecondary education in particular, offers an avenue for general edification, with its own merits for the individual *and* the possibility of additional socio-economic mobility in the future. And from a purely economic viewpoint, it offers the best chances for improving worker productivity and for fostering the entrepreneurial ethos. And although there are limits in the job market for those with higher education degrees, there is also evidence that this cohort is more likely at least to be in the labor force. For example, in the United States, participation rates among 25- to 64-year-olds with upper secondary education are about 60 percent; among those with postsecondary education experience, the rate is 88 percent, and for those with university-level experience, the rate exceeds 90 percent.[22]

One might also argue that robust levels of postsecondary education, and the promise of access, are particularly important in postmodern economies that are experiencing or will experience a large influx of immigrants. The dynamic in relatively open societies and developed economies is that in-migration of foreign nationals correlates not only to job opportunities and improved standards of living; it also correlates with rising educational levels of native populations, and a corresponding expansion of high-skilled service and high-technology sectors.

Although some immigrant groups are highly educated and fill job needs in high-skilled and professional areas, more often they provide a labor force for low-skilled jobs that grows as the national economies of these countries grow. This is a dynamic long prevalent in the United States but relatively new in the European Union and other OECD countries. Robust mass higher education systems help in the assimilation of these new populations and other disadvantaged groups. They help mitigate a sense of permanent lower ethnic class or caste. As the process of globalization continues, marked by increasingly open markets and

[21] *Ibid.*
[22] National Center for Education Statistics, *Education Indicator: An International Perspective* (Washington, D.C.: U.S. Department of Education, 2004).

the flow of migration, education in all its forms will increase as a tool of creating a healthy, more equitable, and productive society.

Seeking a Structured Opportunity Market (SOM)

The command economy approaches to creating and regulating mass higher education in many parts of the world are withering. What is emerging is what I have called a "structured opportunity market" in higher education—essentially, a convergence, in some form, in the effort of nation-states to create a more lightly regulated and more flexible network of public higher education institutions.

The components of a structured opportunity market are not so much a reality in much of the world, but a powerful model that is slowly emerging, shaped by universal ideas on what works most effectively in the pursuit of both broad access and high-quality and productive universities and colleges. Reforms by governments and educational institutions adhere to local political and social cultures, but they are increasingly informed and shaped by powerful ideas on the successes, and failures, of other nations or by institutions such as MIT or Berkeley, or California's pioneering idea of the community college.

Some have called this the "Americanization" of higher education, in part because of the iconic and, dare I say, somewhat romanticized advantages of the U.S. model. But I would argue that that characterization is a misnomer, in large part because some of the most dramatic higher education reforms are occurring in other parts of the world, providing new models in key areas such as access and financing. What is emerging is a much more dynamic and global policy-transfer environment.

The structured opportunity market is my way of attempting to capture some of the seemingly universal aspects of this quasi-process of convergence in national approaches to higher education—always mindful that similar broad approaches will not result in a single international model. Political culture and socio-economic factors, along with the legacy of past institution building, are too powerful and important for that. At the same time, politically and economically unstable parts of the world will lag considerably, seemingly left out of the globalization process.

With those caveats in mind, I will say that increasingly institutions and developed and developing nations, and, in some cases, supranational entities such as the European Union, will move toward most if not all of the components of the structured opportunity market; those that don't will be compelled to offer in both domestic and international forums a rational reason why they are not adopting some aspects of the model.

In 10 years, I predict that most national systems will include the following —or will articulate why they are the exception to an emerging rule. It is a look into the future that, admittedly, is already partially fulfilled in many parts of the world, but certainly not all.

Shaping the Higher Education Market

What is emerging is a decidedly more consumer-driven approach to enroll-ment management, but with various budget and structural limits, usually includ-ing:

- Establishment or expansion of an *Open Access* provider.
- Fostering greater *Mission Differentiation* among existing and future higher education institutions.
- Market and government-induced *Mission Differentiation*, in turn,
  - o Helps to match student skills and interests to academic programs.
  - o Helps to keep the focus of institutions on their role in a larger system of higher education—in theory—and recognize that not all universities can or should be full-fledged comprehensive research institutions. There is a need for primarily teaching institutions with a liberal arts focus, or those that focus on an applied training program in engineering and the sci-ences, or those that provide vocational programs and language and encul-turation curriculums, or some combination of all of these. What is clear is that nation-states cannot afford this model, nor can the academy pro-duce across the board high-quality research that justifies such a large in-vestment of public funds.
  - o Mission differentiation, along with the transfer/matriculation function (see below), helps to rationalize the investment in highly selective public universities—that they are part of a logical larger and coherent mass higher education system.
- Providing significant *Institutional Autonomy* for public higher education insti-tutions to manage academic and financial affairs, and to determine which ways to best interact with society and the private sector will likely prove a de-ciding factor in which nation-states build universities of the highest quality.

    Even nation-states with a tradition of command economies and heavy government regulation of higher education are recognizing that nurturing the university sector, and the development of internationally productive and com-petitive higher education institutions, requires greater freedom for institutions to manage their own activities. This manifests itself in a number of ways in both financial and academic affairs, but a primary gauge of the quality of an institution is the degree of freedom afforded faculty, and the collective ability of those faculty and academic leaders to, for example, say yes to private sec-tor collaborations, and to say no if the arrangement infringes on academic freedom and management of the institution.

- Allowing for a well-regulated nonprofit and a for-profit *Private Sector*.

    Nations without quality nonprofit and for-profit institutions suggest they suffer from a lack of both flexibility and an understanding of the value of an array of higher education providers. On the other hand, nation-states that have a proliferation of for-profit higher education institutions generally indicate a lack of significant efforts to build their public mass higher education systems. Overdependence on generally high-cost and moderate- to low-quality for-profit institutions, which primarily seek profit by offering services as cheaply as possible, generally suggests a failure by nation-states to aggressively expand their public mass higher education systems.

- Supporting *Institutional and Regional Experimentation* is also a vital component for nation-states.

They must be ready to support innovative approaches to expanding access, new institution building, fostering high quality research, and greater levels of interaction with local, regional, national, and global businesses. This often requires a redefinition of the relationship of national governments and their ministries with regional governments, and with institutions. For example, allowing for greater regional experimentation—often a difficult political process—provides for a greater sense of competition among regions and, in turn, adoption of best practices as they emerge.

- Particularly at highly selective public universities, there is a growing effort at some form of *Affirmative Action*, with the purpose of accounting for socio-economic and racial factors in admissions, and expanding the number of disadvantaged students.

Simplistic approaches to expanding access to these groups include quotas; more sophisticated approaches look at the variety of factors that gauge not only the likelihood of a student succeeding and graduating from a university, but also: (1) their ability to overcome hardship, their motivations, and their academic and civic engagement once at a university; and (2) how a public university might best shape and influence the society it serves, including the goal of greater socio-economic mobility.

- Most nation-state efforts to build the vibrancy of their higher education systems will include a concerted effort to Enroll International Students and Seek Creative Ways to Retain the Best and Brightest in Their Own National Economies after Graduation.

Many components of the structured opportunity market relate to a concerted effort to not only generate native talent, but also to retain high-quality students who, increasingly, have international options and recognize quality institutions as having high levels of autonomy and academic freedom, or greater financial resources and international desires. At the same time, international talent, both in terms of students and faculty, will increasingly evaluate the vibrancy of not only selective research universities, but also the quality of national systems of higher education, as important in their decision where to go.

- As nation-states rapidly grow their higher education systems, there must be *Concerted and New Efforts at Institutional Coordination.*

This can be manifest in dual-enrollment programs, the sharing of facilities, and in larger policy realms such as the creation of shared admissions requirements or a single administrative unit for applying to multiple institutions, as in England.

Curricular Reform

As we have discussed, the academic and social abilities of students vary greatly. This requires different types of institutions and, to avoid socio-economic tracking, some curricular link that can help them come in and out of a higher education system, depending on their maturation and their aspirations. In part of these reasons, one sees:

- Efforts at some form of *Degree Compatibility, a la* the Bologna Agreement.

  Different national, and even institutional, approaches to the time to degree, and the meaning of a degree, are giving way to some form of international standardization. This is important for the student as it creates a larger understanding in a globalizing economy regarding the meaning of a degree; it is important for institutions as it usually includes a review of curriculum and its purpose.

- The ability for students to *Bank Credits*. Degree compatibility and banking credits, along with mission differentiation, provide for:

- Emerging schemes for a *Transfer/Matriculation Function* among different types of institutions (typically a two-year program to a three- or four-year university, but not exclusively).

- The revisiting of the curriculum and education program leading to a degree, including the need of some form of *General Education* even in three-year undergraduate programs focused on a specific field. Essentially, there is a growing need, and greater recognition by the academic community and private sector, for a more broadly educated engineer or scientist, for example, including training in business economics.

Higher Education Funding and Access

Increasingly relying on diverse funding sources, including a *Moderate Fee High Financial Aid Model*, will be a major determinant for pursuing both a high-access and high-quality higher education market. Creativity in the funding of higher education is extremely important and is, in fact, perhaps a determiner of the future vibrancy and efficiency of mass higher education systems, and all forms of postsecondary institutions.

- Seeking a greater *Diversity of Funding Sources*, and not simply relying on government to provide the vast majority of funds, as in the initial era of building most mass higher education systems, is already widely understood as a major new development vital for most higher education institutions—and in particular research universities.

  Government needs to be a consistent provider of a substantial portion of the costs, and make steady investments in both operating and capital costs, preferably in relationship to student enrollment workload and other factors. But vibrant higher education institutions will seek other sources; those that don't, or are restricted by governments and/or political cultures fixed solely on government sources of funding, will be much less competitive than in other countries or regions.

- Most nation-states will pursue or are pursuing a *Moderate Fee and High Financial Aid Model*, with the fundamental and vital concept that tuition and various fees form a means for income redistribution and supporting lower-income students and others from disadvantaged backgrounds.

Charging tuition is influenced by the idea of assessing the cost of education for the average student at an institution and the proper distribution of that cost to society, to institutions, and to individuals who benefit from access to this public good. For most institutions, fees will come to represent between 10 to 30 percent (or higher) of an institution's total revenues.

In many nations, there is vehement opposition to any form of fees for higher education, reflecting the values of a largely post–World War II culture in places such as Europe that view education as a public good that should be fully funded by governments. But that ethos is eroding; the pathbreakers include Australia, England, Germany, the Netherlands, and perhaps soon France—all nations where the support for university fees via legislation would have, at one time, been the effective end of a politician's career.

The key to any fruitful discussion of the role of fees is to clearly understand that it is not just about generating new revenue; any or all discussion and analysis of the introduction of fees, or their expansion, must be accompanied by their potential use to substantially defray costs for underprivileged students and other targeted populations. Indeed, clearly linking the goals of increasing funding, via tuition or other sources, with access is extremely important both for keeping the larger mission of institutions always in the forefront, and for political reasons: fees must equate, in some form, to a redistribution of wealth and privilege, a concept that helps expand the political viability of new forms or increases in fees and tuition.

- At the same time, nation-states must *Avoid Overly Complicated Admission and Financial Aid Policies*.

This returns us to the issue of institutional coordination and collaboration. If admissions policies, and most financial aid, are largely at the discretion of individual institutions, the result is a confusing tangle of requirements for students, and a path to higher education that has a larger negative effect on students from less privileged socio-economic backgrounds.

- With increased autonomy, including the introduction of new sources of funding such as tuition, comes a need for public universities and colleges to become *More Transparent in Most Academic and Financial Activity*.

The need to be more publicly accountable has led to an increasing array of regulations by nation-states, some of which are extremely interventionist —such as in England. Institutions themselves need to be more creative and collaborative with other like universities to expand the dialogue about accountability so that it is more a bottom-up process than, thus far, a largely top-down intervention by government.

- Finally, a key component for pursuing a greater diversity of funding sources, and an infusion of funds for enrollment and program growth, is more liberal *Tax Policies that Benefit Higher Education and Students.*

Many nation-states are just now seeing tax policies as not simply a tool for generating revenues for government-funded services, but as a major influence on markets and individual behavior. Tax credits for students and their families will grow as a method to support lower-income families, and to promote access to higher education. Many nation-states will also provide, or are beginning to include, tax credits for individuals and corporations for funding university-based research activities and capital costs, or for establishing and funding endowments. Beneficial tax policies will become increasingly a part of an expanded portfolio of funding sources for institutions.

Most governments in developed and, increasingly, in developing economies are moving toward most of these elements of this structured higher education opportunity market, or at least they are a topic of discussion, including supporting some grouping of postsecondary institutions open to all graduates of secondary schools. In much of the world, including Europe, the lack of a viable and culturally acceptable alternative to the university, and a one-size fits all mentality, means a negative drag on expanding access, and, in some cases, an overload of students in overextended and financially struggling universities.

Europe, for example, is arguably still too top-heavy in its higher education systems; meaning that the only major form of a higher education experience is to enter a university. In a growing number of nations, alternative postsecondary institutions are emerging, where a secondary diploma is not a requirement for an expanding array of postsecondary programs. There are, of course, constraints on the ability of students to enter specific universities or other institutions determined by admissions standards, financial aid, institutional financial resources, physical capacity, and other limits. But most nations are committed to broad access and are aggressively pushing demand. Why?

As noted previously, the reasons transcend immediate or even long-term job-market needs or the recognition that most workers will change jobs numerous times in the course of their working lives, often with the need for retraining under the rubric of *lifelong learning.* As important is the desire of most nation-states to promote a *culture of aspiration*, which in turn influences socio-economic mobility and creates a more talented and entrepreneurial population, global competitiveness, and the hope for a more prosperous and equitable society.[23]

This ethos is front and center for many E.U. member states in their conscious efforts to boost participation rates and refashion their national higher education systems, often battling the legacy of overt class distinctions and biases. "All those who have the potential to benefit from higher education should have the opportunity to do so," states an influential white paper issued by the Labour government in England in 2003. "This is a fundamental principle which lies at the heart of

---

[23] In his book *The American College and the Culture of Aspiration* (Ithaca, N.Y.: Cornell University Press, 1986), David O. Lavine discusses this theme.

building a more socially just society, because education is the best and most reliable route out of poverty and disadvantage."[24]

In effect, the goal of most postmodern governments, with only the tacit and sometimes reluctant support of the higher education community, is even larger in scope: to make broad access to higher education, or at least the opportunity at virtually any age, a part of citizenship. Just as compulsory education has moved from the elementary school level to the first two years of secondary school in most OECD countries, perhaps it will eventually include some form of postsecondary education. Alone, the economic arguments for such a policy shift are, in the contemporary era, not convincing because not all jobs require such an expansion. But the extension of compulsory laws to secondary schools in the early twentieth century was not explicitly formulated for economic reasons alone; rather, it related to broad ideas of citizenship, to fostering equality and socio-economic mobility, and to assorted other national priorities, including the integration of immigrant populations in America and restructuring labor markets. Such is the role of higher education in the contemporary world—real and imagined.

---

[24] Department of Education and Skills, England, *The Future of Higher Education* (Norwich: HMSO, 2003), 68.

II. Fees and Finance: The Conscious and Unconscious Restructuring of Markets

Size, Share, and Structure: The Changing Role of America's Public Research Universities

Irwin Feller[1]

There is an academic war story about a professor of religious studies who was known for asking the same question year after year on his course's final exam. The question was: Name the 12 tribes of Israel. Of course, the answer to the question was memorialized in the file cabinets of fraternities and sororities across campus. Finally, one year the department's head called the faculty member's attention to what was happening and advised him to change the final exam question. He did. His new final exam question was: Name the major and minor prophets of Israel. Obviously, most of the students were caught unawares, and did poorly. One creative student, a member of a fraternity, responded as follows: "Far be it from me, a mere student, to judge who were the major and who were the minor prophets of Israel, but as for the names of the 12 tribes, . . . " and so he proceeded.

This anecdote is relevant here for two reasons. First, it calls attention to how to characterize the current condition of America's public research universities and who is best positioned to make the call. Should current conditions be termed a crisis or a cyclical perturbation (Breneman 2002; Calhoun 2006)? Perhaps it

---

[1] Senior Visiting Scientist, American Association for the Advancement of Science, Penn State University.

should be termed something else, such as the early stages of irreversible senescence, or, alternatively, the onset of disadvantageous structural changes that yet permit reversal or redirection. Perhaps finally, given the recurrence of concerns of one form or another about the embattled nature of America's research universities, public and private, attendant with predictions of looming market shake-outs, the most appropriate descriptor might be that often used to describe the economic health of New York City's Broadway, namely that it is a "fabulous invalid."

Selected data elements, especially on state government appropriations to public colleges and universities as presented below, indeed do portray a stark picture. Rather than being conclusive, current discourse (and lamentations) based on these data cannot but bring to mind earlier symposia in which similar pessimism turned out to be unwarranted. Thus in 1994, a conference was held at the University of California, Los Angeles entitled, "Reinventing the Research University." The emphasis on reinvention reflected the then widespread pessimism about the health of America's research universities, a pessimism induced in large part by predictions of flat or slowing rising federal government funding for science (Greenwood 1994, 37). These predictions were made just before bipartisan congressional support led to a five-year doubling of appropriations for NIH, the single largest source of research funds for U.S. universities, which in turn helped fuel a 61 percent increase, from $23B to $37B in constant 2000 dollars, in total academic R&D expenditures between FY1994 and FY2003 (National Science Board 2006, vol. 2, Appendix Table 5–2).

For purposes of this symposium, what most clearly differentiates current from earlier concerns is that they are based on a dichotomy between the financial health of the full complement of America's research universities and its public research university component. To the extent that the research vitality of both public and private universities are each tied to the aggregate level of federal government funding of academic research, which provided 64 percent, or $29B of total academic R&D expenditures of $45.8B in FY2005 (current dollars) (NSF, 07–311, January 2007), each sector is better off as NIH, NSF, and DOE expenditures for academic research rises; each is worse off as they flatten or fall. Simmering concerns about the health of the U.S. academic enterprise indeed may already be felt as research universities adjust to disappointing levels of federal outlays for academic R&D for FY2007, and face even lower projected levels for FY2008 (AAAS 2007). But this is a separate topic.

In all, though, given the poor track record of past predictions about the future of America's research universities, far be it for me, like the above student, to pronounce such a weighty judgment about whether or not current and pending conditions warrant being termed a crisis.[2] Instead, I take the presence of a crisis, or some functionally equivalent description of ill health, as given, and proceed as the

---

[2] "[M]any previous prophecies of doom for American universities have proven to be false. Unfavorable events that were interpreted as trends turned out to be only a short-term dip in the long-term growth trend for all colleges and universities. The same could be true of the 1990s" (Noll 1998, 203–04).

student above to focus on listing a few issues that I perceive to require further analysis and research. These issues are:

- the nature of the crisis,
- roles of state governments,
- implications of the crisis.[3]

The Context

Since the following analysis is so heavily tied to the national context within which America's research universities function, I begin with a set of statements intended to highlight its salient characteristics (Clark 1995). I defer to symposium participants from other countries to assess the degrees to which these characteristics resemble or differ from their own.

- Historically associated with the emergence of private institutions established to specialize in research and graduate education—e.g., Johns Hopkins University; Clark University—the U.S. system of research universities is a "mixed" system comprised of both private and public institutions. The share of each sector as a performer of research varies according to the measures used. Employing here R&D expenditures as a measure of relative share, public research universities perform the larger portion of U.S. academic research. They occupied seven of the top 10, 13 of the top 20, and 33 of the top 50 places as performers of total R&D in FY2004 (National Science Foundation 2006, Table 27, p. 80). Private universities hold a more prominent position in rankings based on federal R&D expenditures. In FY2005, private universities occupied five of the top 10, 11 of the top 20, and 21 of the top 50 positions (NSF 2007, as reported in *Chronicle of Higher Education*, February 9, 2007; p. A24).

- The post–World War II expansion of the U.S. system of research universities largely reflected the creation of new public universities and the transition of many from undergraduate teaching to research-intensive-Ph.D. granting institutions. Using the longstanding if now discarded Carnegie Classification of Research I and Research II institutions, the total number of doctorate-granting

---

[3] This call for increased attention to these issues mirrors an observation made by Robert Zemsky, a member of the recent Commission on the Future of Higher Education (Spelling Commission), about how surprised he was "and more than a little disappointed to discover just how unimportant the research mission had become among higher education's would-be reformers" (Zemsky, January 26, 2007). A similar surprising lack of attention also characterizes the series of reports issued by the Kellogg Commission on the Future of State and Land Grant Universities. The commission's six reports address topics such as the student experience, engagement, and diversity. Only in passing though is the research role of public universities addressed, and then largely as a part of a broader discussion of teaching and discovery, with references made to historic missions and accomplishments.

institutions in the U.S. increased from 173 to 236 between 1970 and 1994. Considering only Research I institutions, their number increased from 52 to 88. The number of public universities increased from 30 to 59, representing 81 percent of the total increase.

- It is a competitive system. Public and private universities compete among themselves and between one another for inputs (faculty, students, external awards, gifts, etc.) and outputs (publications/citations; placement of Ph.D.s, reputation, rankings, etc.). As Geiger has noted, "Universities seek to hire the best possible faculty, *given the salaries they can afford;* and they admit the most qualified students, *given the students that apply.*" This competition requires universities to "continually seek improvement even to remain in the same relative position" (Geiger 2004, 15; italics in original).

The Nature of the Crisis

The nature and sources of concern about the current condition, or crisis, of America's public research universities are well known. For the most part, they relate to a combination of secular relative declines and periodic absolute constant dollar declines in state government appropriations for state-supported colleges and universities and the increased capital-intensity and rising constant dollar costs of leading edge research. The "revenue shortfall" side of this balance sheet has led public universities to shift more of the cost of education upon students in the form of increased tuition and fees (although still not removing substantial elements of public subsidization).

Etiology

Quantitatively, the crisis now besetting public research universities can be expressed in many forms and ratios their common element is a structural shift in state government expenditure priorities away from support of higher education. The percentage of state tax revenues allocated to higher education has declined steadily since the 1980s; concomitantly, although not in lock step, state appropriations have become a steadily declining percentage of the general operating budgets of public research universities.

The Pennsylvania State University is one such example. Even as the absolute level of state appropriations has increased, the Commonwealth of Pennsylvania's contribution to the university's operating budget has fallen from 54 percent in 1976–1977 to 9.7 percent in 2006–2007. UCLA is another example; it reports currently receiving only about 15 percent of its budget from state higher education appropriations (Carnesale 2006, B20). Comparably low, even lower, shares have been reported for other major public research universities (e.g., University of Michigan—10 percent; University of Colorado—9 percent). The overall pattern and trend in state government appropriations is summarized in the State Higher Education Executive Officers' 2006 review of state funding for FY2005:

> Despite an appropriations increase of 3.5 percent in fiscal year 2005, constant dollar per student and local funding for public colleges and universities was at the lowest point in 25 years. . . . Fiscal year 2005 state and local support per full-time-equivalent student in public institutions was $5,833; the high point since 1980 was fiscal 2001, when per capita support was $7,121 in constant 2005 dollars. . . . Between 2004 and 2005 average per student increases of 7.7 percent in net tuition offset the continuing slide in public funding. Total educational revenues (state and local support plus net tuition) grew by 0.2 percent, the first increase since 2001 . . . (SHEEO, March 22, 2006).

The impacts of this trend in state appropriations for higher education are many, including most obviously on tuition levels. Of especial relevance here, though, is the impact that these trends have had on a widening of salary differentials between public and private universities. A 2004 survey by the Association of American University Professors (AAUP) reported that the average salary of full professors at public doctoral universities measured 77 percent of those at private doctoral institutions (AAUP 2004). Evidence from other studies indicates that this gap has been widening since the 1970s (Ehrenberg 2003; Zoghi 2003).

Analytically, this is a good point at which to take stock of how these data might be interpreted. In a formal sense, to an economist, they may be seen as withdrawal/reduction of a government subsidy in the production of a commodity or service with the consequent incidence falling in part upon consumers (in the form of higher prices—tuition) and in part upon input suppliers (in the form of relatively lower faculty salaries). Neither impact, per se, directly affects the research function of public universities.

Body and Soul

For trends in state funding to create the reality or angst of a crisis in the health of America's public research universities requires the addition of the above cited characteristics of America's system of research universities—namely, a mix of public and private institutions and competitions between these two sectors (as well as among themselves) for inputs and outputs. Included as forms of competition in output markets are races for rank, position, or prestige. Viewed in this light, widening salary differentials between public and private universities reduces the ability of the former to retain their "best" faculty and to recruit the most promising cohorts of future researchers, "who, in turn, attract the brightest students and significant research dollars" (Yudof 2002, B. 214).

The increased capital-intensity of leading-edge scientific and technological research in both traditional and newly emerging research areas similarly requires additional resources, again if only to remain in the same relative position. An alphabet soup of high-end instruments—NMR spectrometers, PET scanners, MRI scanners, FT-ICR mass spectrometers—are now essential ingredients of world-class research. Acquisition of these instruments requires universities to make large upfront investments, reaching into millions of dollars in faculty start-up packages, physical plant, and equipment to compete for external awards to attract faculty and graduate students.[4] Fiscal straits associated with declining state support reduces the "slack resources" available to public research universities, causing or aggravating their competitive disadvantage in seeking externally funded, merit-based awards. Over time, time reduced competitiveness for competitively awarded external funds can diminish the scientific and societal significance of the research produced by their faculty and graduate students.

As articulated by leaders of U.S. higher education, the current crisis of public research universities appears in large part to relate to diminished competitiveness along these lines. Thus, according to Albert Carnesdale, UCLA chancellor, "Unless we change how we support great public universities, in the foreseeable future, they will be unable to compete with elite private institutions" (2006, B20). And according to David Ward, president, American Council on Education, "It may be that we're creating a superleague of very-well-endowed private institutions, and then a second level of public universities that will work out some partnership with the states, using endowment and federal money to create a firmer compact" (cited in Gose 2002, A21).

These statements represent relative deprivation, what Chubin has termed the institutional angst of the academic research community—in this case, public research universities—"when funding falls short of expectations" and "when the number of deserving researchers is such to deprive some of the chance to pursue promising opportunities (or pursue them as fast or as fully as one hoped) . . . (Chubin 1994, 122). The statements reflect concerns about a loss of position for historically top-ranked public institutions, augmented by a looming thwarting of the aspirations of upwardly striving institutions, such as the University of Florida, which according to its president seeks to become a top 10 university offering students "the same education they would get at Harvard or Yale" (as quoted in Lewin 2006).

Lest this interpretation seem dismissive, I too have advanced similar reasoning. Referring to the same above-cited bleak set of forecasts about trends in state government financing of higher education, I wrote the following for a 2005 symposium, "The Future of America's Public Research Universities," held at Penn State to celebrate its 150th birthday.

---

[4] A simple example based on a "comparatively" low-tech, low-cost instrument. A recent survey of Big Ten universities estimates the start-up costs of an fMRI, an increasingly essential research tool in the behavioral sciences, for equipment, modification of physical facilities, and core staff at $3.4 million of a 3 Tesla unit at $3.4 million and the costs of a 7 Tesla unit, a newer technology, at $11 million. At the same time, researchers in the physical sciences and biomedical fields are beginning to work with 12 Tesla and 15 Tesla MRI systems.

The above trends point to a sharper partitioning of national quality races in the near-term future. Elite private research universities will compete with other elite private institutions; a small number of historically strong public research universities will compete both with the elite privates and with other public research universities, strong and emerging, and many other public research universities will compete amongst themselves for position.

Thus, for all but a select few public research universities, such as the University of California, Berkeley, which historically have competed head-to-head with leading private universities, the future place of public research universities within the larger U.S. system of research universities is likely to be shaped mainly by competition among themselves, and less so with private universities. The race for most public research universities, including several of the more prestigious of them, will not be to become the next Harvard, Berkeley, or Stanford, but to be the new University of California, San Diego; Georgia Tech; or University of Alabama-Birmingham; while for the established public research universities, such as the University of Minnesota or Pennsylvania State University, the race will take on dimensions of running on a treadmill so as not to lose relative position. Movements upwards or downwards based on accepted ranking systems will occur, but they are more likely to constitute churning within the public sector system, than for any noticeable or systematic improvement of the position of public research universities related to private institutions (Feller, forthcoming).

As expanded on below, although my analysis is much the same as suggested by the above quotations, I draw a more open-ended set of implications from it. In part, it is because (1) I do not view churning of relative positions as necessarily a serious issue if viewed from a national perspective; (2) recent churning has involved relative gains on the part of several public research universities; and (3) self-imposed institutional limits on the part of several private research universities are likely to cap their aggregate level of academic R&D performance.

In part, too, this different slant arises from a personal concern that concentration on the crisis held to affect the (fiscal) body of public research universities may be muting attention to a crisis of their soul. At times ruefully and at times critically, many observers have stated that America's research universities, but especially its public research universities, are experiencing such a crisis. This crisis relates to the displacement of historic missions, values, cultures, and communities served by the transformation of academic research from a public good to a private good, the distortion of faculty and institutional incentives, cultures, and behaviors, and the unavoidability of systemic, not isolated, conflicts of interest and conflicts of commitment associated with the rise of the entrepreneurial university.

As stated by Duderstadt, the "key social principle" underlying America's public universities is "the perception of education as a 'public good' that is, the public university is established to benefit all of society and, hence, deserving of support by that society, rather than just by the individuals participating in its particular educational programs" (1996, 3). Treatment of how increased university and faculty involvement in patenting, licensing, and start-ups, and the panoply of issues associated with these and related trends have affected institutional and individual adherence to Duderstadt's social principle is too vast and complex a topic to be covered here. Two summary observations will have to suffice.

First, to the extent that a crisis of the soul exists in America's research universities, the malaise is not confined to the public university sector. The legal, legislative, scientific, and market factors propelling research universities into a different, if not entirely new, world of commercializing academic research are much the same, albeit not identical, for both public and private universities (Mowery, Nelson, Sampat, and Ziedonis 2004). Second, without gainsaying specific episodes of the "corporate corruption of higher education" documented in works such as Jennifer Washburn's *University, Inc.*, an accumulating body of empirical research on the impacts of industrial funding on faculty research agendas, the spread of university-industry-government (federal and state) research and development partnerships, the rise of academic patenting, licensing, and spin-offs, etc., suggest that some of the most deleterious impacts predicted in earlier exegesis, including my own (Feller 1990), have not occurred (Thursby, Thursby, and Mukhejee 2005; Hansen, Brewster, Asher, and Kisielewski 2006).

While a crisis for the public nevertheless may exist here, researchers and commentators may be looking for it in the wrong place. Its manifestation, according to observers such as Krimsky, is to be found less in measurable aspects of technology transfer than in the withdrawal of academic scientists from public interest science. He defines public interest science as "the rich tapestry of involvement that professors of universities have in providing expertise to government agencies and not-for-profit organizations in addition to the pro bono help that many of them offer to underrepresented communities" (Krimsky 2003, 215). According to Krimsky, the "greatest danger" of unrestrained commercialization by research universities is the loss of supportive venues in which public-interest science and public intellectuals can thrive" (*ibid.*). Although this danger applies to both private and public research universities, it would appear to be the greater, or the fall from a state of grace the larger, for public research universities, charged explicitly or implicitly by statute, mission, or tradition with responsibility for directing their research, teaching, and outreach activities towards the common good.

Indeed, it is distortion of mission rather than evidence of altered faculty research priorities, violation of Mertonian norms, or fiscally avaricious behavior that constitutes the gravamen of the criticism levied against the University of California, Berkeley for its participation in the Novartis agreement. As noted in the Busch et al. review of this agreement, the direct impacts of the agreement "have been minimal." Of concern, though, to the study's authors was the consistency of the agreement with the mission of land-grant universities; they write, "if university education and research are in fact needed to serve some public purpose, then it must be distributed in some manner other than solely via the market" (Busch et al. 2004, 21).

The crises of the body and of the soul are clearly connected: secular declines in the shares of public university budgets provided by state appropriations have propelled these institutions into increasingly more aggressive searches for supplemental forms of income, with the conversion of academic research findings into intellectual property being one alluring form. But again, much the same aggressiveness may be found on the part of private universities.

The point of distinguishing between crises of the body and crises of the soul affecting public research universities is primarily to mark the independent, if reinforcing, causes of the two maladies. If the causes are independent, so too can be the consequences of improved health. In particular, improvement in the fiscal health of public research universities by augmented state government appropriations, especially if as suggested below they arise in the form of targeted economic development programs will not necessarily address concerns about the loss of the public science/public service mission of public research universities. Nor for that matter will this latter crisis necessarily be resolved by augmented funds from other sources. Accumulating events over the past two decades may have produced institutional policies and cultures wherein faculty and university administrator understanding and appreciation of, and commitment to the social principle/public science values traditionally associated with and still claimed by public research universities have been so diminished that far more than simply a string of bountiful state budgets will be necessary to reverse direction and restore an earlier ethos.

The Role of State Governments[5]

The role of state governments as a cause or cure of the present competitive standing of public research universities is more complex than indicated by trends in appropriations alone. Indeed, their role is quite protean. Considered as part of the U.S. national innovation system, state governments are variously leading actors in selected fields of research, players with bit but well-acted parts, and players who may be reading from the wrong scripts or botching their lines.

Direct state government expenditures for academic research constituted a "small" portion, $2.9B, or six percent, of total academic R&D in FY 2005. (These amounts subsume that portion of state government general fund and capital budget expenditures for universities that wend their way into support of institutional academic R&D expenditures or otherwise contribute to the institution's research competitiveness.) State governments, however, are currently quite important in supporting selected areas of academic research. Given the Bush administration's opposition to relaxing restrictions of federal funding for embryonic stem cell research, several state governments, California most notably among them, have truly acted as "laboratories of democracy," funding research in this field in universities and other not-for-profit organizations, and thereby enabling the U.S. to remain active in a globally competitive area of scientific research.

Moreover, state governments can in no way be said to be unaware or unappreciative of the research function of their public universities. As gauged by gubernatorial state-of-the-state addresses, budgetary proposals and legislative actions, several may be said to be true believers in the arrival of the knowledge

---

[5] This section draws on Feller (2004).

economy. Beyond serving their historic "A&M" roles as sources of new products, processes and technical assistance to traditional, often resource-based industries, academic R&D has come to be viewed by state officials as an essential component of comprehensive "demand-side" economic development strategies. These strategies emphasize technological innovation and the associated creation of new products, processes, and services, often manifested in the launching of new firms and industries (Eisinger 1988). State technology development strategies vary in programmatic details and scale; their common core elements with respect to research universities are deploying state investments to attract ("leverage") federal, foundation, and industrial R&D funds and catalyzing and appropriating downstream economic benefits that arise as academic research findings are transferred, commercialized, spun-off, etc.[6]

States also are aware that their higher education systems operate within nationally competitive arenas. As one of many possible examples, in January 2007, Iowa Governor Chet Culver called upon his state to lift its ban on embryonic stem cell research, instituted in 2003, as well as proposing a $12.5 million appropriation for construction of an Iowa Center for Regenerative Medicine to be built at the University of Iowa. In announcing these plans, the governor also called attention to the harmful impact of the state's ban in allowing surrounding states like Wisconsin, Illinois, and Missouri to lure away Iowa's best researchers (Culver 2007).

The range of policies and experiences among 50 states over approximately a 20-year period rules out single-valued propositions. Still, as a general observation, it appears that states have exhibited both an overly optimistic and an unduly restrictive view of the contributions of public research universities to state economic development (and competitiveness). In particular, they seem to have an exaggerated belief in their ability to systematically "skim" off (that is, pay the marginal costs of) the economically relevant and spatially appropriable slice of a university's R&D program, leaving it to others (federal government, industry, foundations, etc.) to fund the remainder (of the fixed and other variable costs that sum to average cost), which, of course, is the larger share. In effect, at times and in selected states, the rationales, policies, and budgets for supporting public higher education and economic development have been dichotomized. The result, intentional or not, has been the substitution of targeted R&D support for general institutional support.

Again, this is not a blanket statement. Complementary, reinforcing win-win gains both in a state's first-mover advantage in entering newly emerging, economically significant scientific areas and maintenance and advancement of the academic quality of its resident higher education institutions are observable. The State University of New York-Albany's recent rise to national prominence as a

---

[6] The influence that the quality of a state's public universities or its comparative tuition rates has in retraining or attracting undergraduate and graduate students who remain in the state upon graduation, thus constituting the skilled labor force necessary to operate existing and new businesses or its pool of nascent entrepreneurs, tends to be receive far less attention in articulating or calculating the economic benefits that a state derives from support of higher education.

center of research in nanotechnology, in part funded by the state, may be an example here. Certainly, California's recent investments of $100 million in each of four California Institutes for Science and Innovation in quantitative biology, nanosciences, information technology, and telecommunications is widely viewed as a means of yoking together the state and its public research universities in their respective races for global economic competitiveness and international academic preeminence.

Nationally, though, the problem for public research universities from this state strategy and policy shift is that even though they may receive specific budgetary tranches, they appear to be net losers, at least in terms of their relative position to private research universities. They lose because (1) the funds appropriated for targeted R&D programs are less than the levels of additional general funds budgets they would have received if historic ratios of state support (as percentages either of state budgets or university general funds budgets) had been maintained, or even reduced at a slower rate; (2) funds from targeted R&D programs are allocated to private research universities and research institutes as well as to public research universities, thereby negating relative gains;[7] (3) state support for these programs has been volatile, both in terms of levels of funding and strategic orientation (Geiger and Sa 2005); and (4) funds are provided to selected scientific or technological fields with little attention to whether these funds produce general improvements across a campus or instead result in prosperous "enclaves" in otherwise economically depressed research institutions.

Moreover, even the positive impacts of this state strategy assumes that (1) the state has picked (or had the correct guidance from its industrial leaders, university leaders, or consultants) the right fields of scientific and technological research in which to invest, and (2) in fact has a comparative upstream research and downstream locational advantage in these fields relative to that of other states, whose targeted "clusters," if past history of state investments in microelectronics and biotechnology is taken as a guide, are likely to be much the same.

Making Sense of the Implications

To return to its opening, this chapter's objective has been to identify issues requiring further analysis and research; it has not been to either make predictions or to load them with normative judgments. Implicitly though to this point, in posing issues it has had an underlying thesis, namely, that whatever one chooses to term the current conditions of America's public research universities, statements about recent or projected loss of relative positioning for public research

---

[7] New York state currently supports 15 Centers for Advanced Technology at public and private universities. Six of these are at public research universities. The remaining 11 are at private universities. These include not only traditional research powerhouses, such as Columbia, Cornell, Rochester, and Syracuse, but also Alfred University and Clarkson University.

universities constitute the beginning, not the end of the analysis or research (or public policy).

Instead, I suggest framing the question as follows: Assume that the place of higher education in state appropriations priorities does not change—neither getting better nor worse—and that windfall gains from intellectual property remain as they are, highly skewed among a few universities, most of which are private and highly unpredictable, and that whatever successes public research universities have in their capital campaigns, private research universities do as well (or better). In short, the relative financial position of public research universities does not improve and possibly experiences further decline relative to private research universities. What would be the consequences of this scenario?

One consequence is built into these assumptions: the standing/performance of public research universities likely would decline relative to private universities by whatever set of metrics happens to be used—National Research Council "quality rankings," NSF R&D expenditure listings, *Times Higher Education Supplement* rankings, or whatever. (As a specific possibility, consider say the substitutions of Vanderbilt University [ranked 29th] and Emory [ranked 31st] for the University of North Carolina-Chapel Hill [ranked 21st] and the University of Minnesota [ranked 22nd] in NSF's table of top institutions in federal R&D expenditures, FY 2005.[8]

What societal objective underpinning federal government support of academic R&D would be adversely affected by such a substitution? Would it be the U.S.'s post–World War II preeminence in science and graduate education and/or its international economic competitiveness; the public interest; specific public research universities; states dependent on the performance of their public research universities; and/or undergraduate and graduate degree students unable for academic or financial reasons to be admitted to elite private research universities? Other, different answers would likely emerge relating to the severity of the crisis, its impacts, the principals and agents engaged in formulating and implementing various policies to prevent, ameliorate, or shift the incidence of these impacts, depending on which parts of the above compound question one chooses to address. Different analytical frameworks, methodologies, and types of data would also likely need to be addressed as these relate to different parts of this issue. America's public research universities do indeed confront serious problems. My hope is that this symposium will contribute to a more analytically coherent, empirically tractable, and yes, politically resonant way to state these problems. Recommendations about solutions are of course most welcome.

---

[8] In fact, public research universities seem to be faring quite well in recent positional races. Allowing for the volatility encountered in short-term movements in federal academic R&D expenditures, for FY2005 the University of Wisconsin broke into the top five for the first time in recent years, Arizona State University was the only new institution to break into the top 100 recipients, and Virginia Tech and the University of California, Santa Barbara made the largest advances—each moving up eight positions—of universities previously ranked among the top 100.

References

AAAS. 2007. *Research Funding Falls in 2008 Budget Despite ACI Gains; Development Hits New Highs.* Washington, D.C.: American Association for the Advancement of Science, February 7.

American Association of University Professors. 2004. "Don't Blame Faculty for High Tuition." <hptt:www.aaup.org/research/index.htm>.

Breneman, D. 2002. "For Colleges, This is Not Just Another Recession." *Chronicle of Higher Education*, June 14, B7.

Busch, L., R. Allison, C. Harris, A. Rudy, B. Shaw, B. Ten Eyck, D. Coppin, J. Konefal, and C. Oliver, with J. Fairweather. 2004. *External Review of the Collaborative Research Agreement between Novartis Agricultural Discovery Institute, Inc. and the Regents of the University of California.* East Lansing, Mich.: Institute for Food and Agricultural Standards, Michigan State University.

Calhoun, C. 2006. "Is the University in Crisis?" *Society* (May/June): 8–18.

Carnesale, A. 2006. "The Private-Public Gap in Higher Education." *Chronicle of Higher Education*, January 6, B20.

Chubin, D. 1994. "How Large an R&D Enterprise." In *The Fragile Connection*, ed. D. Guston and K. Keniston. Cambridge, Mass.: MIT Press, 118–44.

Clark, B. 1995. *Places of Inquiry.* Berkeley, Calif.: University of California Press.

Culver, C. 2007. Budget Address, Iowa General Assembly, January 30, 2007.

Duderstadt, J. 1996. "The Future of the Public University." Presentation to the Pennsylvania State University National Issues Forum, October 7.

Ehrenberg, R. 2003. "Studying Ourselves: The Academic Labor Market." *Journal of Labor Economics* 21: 267–87.

Eisinger, P. 1988. *The Rise of the Entrepreneurial State.* Madison, Wis.: University of Wisconsin Press.

Feller, I. 1990. "Universities as Engines of R&D-based Economic Growth: They Think They Can." *Research Policy* 19(4): 335–48.

———. 2004. "Virtuous and Vicious Cycles in State Government Funding of Research Universities." *Economic Development Quarterly* 18: 138–50.

———. 2007. "Who Races with Whom, Who Is Likely to Win (Or Survive); Why." In *Future of the American Public Research University,* ed. C. Colbeck, R. Geiger and C. Anderson. Rotterdam, Netherlands: Sense Publishers.

Geiger, R. 2004. Knowledge & Money. Palo Alto, Calif.: Stanford University Press.

Geiger, R., and C. Sa. 2005. "Beyond Technology Transfer: U.S. State Policies to Harness University Research for Economic Development." *Minerva* 43: 1–21.

Gose, B. 2002. "The Fall of the Flagships: Do the Best State Universities Need to Privatize to Thrive?" *Chronicle of Higher Education*, July 5, A19ff.

Greenwood, M. C. 1994. "Societal Expectations from Research Universities and the Higher Education System." In *Reinventing the Research University*, ed. C. Kumar Patel. Los Angeles, Calif.: University of California, Los Angeles.

Hansen, S., A., J. Brewster, M. Asher, and M. Kisielewski. 2006. *The Effects of Patenting in the AAAS Scientific Community.* Washington, D.C.: American Association for the Advancement of Science.

Krimsky, S. 2003. *Science in the Public Interest: Has the Lure of Profits Corrupted Biomedical Research?* Lanham, Md.: Rowan & Littlefield.

Lewin, T. 2006. "Public Universities Chase Excellence, at a Price." *New York Times,* December 20.

Mowery, D., R. Nelson, B. Sampat, and A. Ziedonis. 2004. *Ivory Tower and Industrial Innovation.* Stanford, Calif.: Stanford University Press.

National Science Board. 2006. *Science and Engineering Indicators 2006,* vol. 2. Arlington, Va.: National Science Foundation.

National Science Foundation. 2006. *Division of Science Resources Statistics, Academic Research and Development Expenditures: Fiscal Years 2004.* NSF 06-323. Arlington, Va.

———. 2007. *Industrial Funding of Academic R&D Rebounds in FY 2005,* NSF 07–311, January.

Noll, R. 1998. "The Future of Research Universities." In *Challenges to Research Universitie,* ed. R. Noll. Washington, D.C.: Brookings Institution, 201–06.

State Higher Education Executive Officers (SHEEO). 2006. "State Higher Education Finance FY 2005." Boulder, Co.

Thursby, M,, J. Thursby, and S. Mukherjee. 2005. "Are There Real Effects of Licensing on Academic Research: A Life Cycle View." National Bureau of Economic Research, Working Paper 11497. Cambridge, Mass.: NBER.

Washburn, J. 2005. *University Inc.* New York: Basic Books.

Yudof, M. 2002. *Chronicle of Higher Education,* January 11, B24.

Zemsky, R. 2007. "The Rise and Fall of the Spellings Commission." *Chronicle of Higher Education.* January 26, B6ff, B8.

Zoghi, C. 2003. "Why Have Public University Professors Done So Badly?" *Economics of Education* 22: 45–57.

Chapter 4

Market-Driven Trends in the Financing of Higher Education: What Can We Learn from Each Other?

Katharine Lyall[1]

One of the most thoughtful and sustained conversations about comparative international trends in higher education has occurred in the Glion Colloquium. Meeting annually since 1998, the colloquium has highlighted the most pressing issues facing European and American universities. As recently as five years ago, the key topic of the colloquium was "governance" of higher education institutions. University presidents and government education policymakers discussed how governing boards/authorities were appointed and what powers they had to effect change in university operations; whether faculty rights to participation in university governance strengthened or lessened responsiveness to societal needs; and whether higher education systems and the new imperatives of the European Union would assist or hold back necessary evolution. Very little attention was paid to questions of finance.

Since then, the colloquium has discussed changes affecting "the university at the millenium," the university in the digital age, trends endangering the research university, and the university and business, and (in June 2008) took up the effects of "globalization" on higher education. Each of these topics embodies underlying

---

[1] Carnegie Commission for the Advancement of Teaching; President Emeritus, University of Wisconsin System.

funding issues, and there is a growing literature analyzing the sharp changes occurring in both European and American funding for higher education, and the ways in which these are driving new approaches to dividing the financial investment in public universities among the state, the student, and the family.

Interestingly, many of the driving trends in higher education finance across OECD countries, including the U.S., stem from common roots, although approaches to dealing with these trends vary. Herein lies an opportunity for learning across borders, or what Chapman and Greenaway (2006) call "international policy transfer."[2]

Drivers of HE Policy Change

Common trends driving a reconsideration of national higher education policies include both changes in *economic* conditions and shifts in *political* values and perceptions. On the *economic* side: the maturing of European and U.S. economies, increasing global competition from countries formerly only weakly connected to international markets (especially China and India), expanding free trade policies, and the growth at home of competing social service claims on tax resources for health care, old age pensions, and homeland security all put pressure on public budgets and limit prospects for significant long-term increases in public investment in higher education. Nations recognize that economic growth requires broad and successful participation in higher learning but they cannot, or will not, commit the resources that a broad expansion of higher education opportunities requires.[3]

On the *political* side: a shift in perceptions about who benefits from higher education, from a societal gain to an individual benefit, makes it easier to justify policies that also shift costs to individuals and families. (This view is refined by economists who argue that "free tuition" policies are regressive since they apply revenues taxed from low- and moderate-income citizens to subsidize educational opportunities open mostly to middle- and upper- income students.) Similarly, as Richard Easterlin (1987) argued years ago, "demography is destiny" and many OECD countries will soon enter several decades of labor shortage. How they will cope with this exposes underlying political attitudes toward immigration,

---

[2] They assert that successful "international policy transfer" requires nations to have similar institutional and political preconditions, similar policy objectives, and similar antireform lobbies. The reader can make up his own mind about whether these requirements are met in any given situation.

[3] It might be argued that an efficient capital market would make *any* state subsidy unnecessary, by enabling students to match the timing of their educational costs with the earnings that education produces. However, if one concedes that there are any societal or collective benefits from higher education, it becomes apparent that a normal market-clearing price will underproduce the optimal amount of education. Subsidies fill the gap by enticing a larger output than the market alone can elicit.

issues about international study, and some very complicated questions about how long older workers will be retained in the workforce.

Finally, this change in political perspective is driven by growing skepticism about the basic competence of governments to handle 21st-century challenges, whether domestic, foreign, or environmental. As public institutions, universities fall under this same cloud and, as institutions dependent upon public support, universities are squeezed by the growing belief that "the market can do it better." In short, both economic and political shifts are driving public universities toward market opportunities and market discipline; in the U.S., this move towards "privatization" is well advanced.

Some Consequences of These Trends, to Date

The result of these trends in the U.S. has been to dramatically *reduce the share of government investment in higher education* from about 50 percent a decade ago to 25 percent or less today. (Some of the largest public universities, such as the University of Michigan, University of Colorado, and University of Virginia now receive less than 15 percent of their financial support from the state.) This, in turn, has *driven up tuition and fees* charged to students so that students and families are now often larger stakeholders (provide a larger percentage of the budget) than the public taxpayers. Public universities have worked diligently to *diversify their revenue sources* so that they now have multiple stakeholders (investors), each with a minority share of the enterprise and each demanding a share of university services: instruction for undergraduates, research and graduate training for businesses and states seeking economic development, public service and outreach for local communities in which universities are located, and training of requisite numbers of teachers, nurses, engineers, and other professions for local, state, and national needs.

New revenue sources, in turn, create new constituencies whose demands may or may not be well aligned with the traditional goals of public universities. As costs shift to students and families, there is concern about declining access for low- and moderate-income students and more pressure for new financial aid policies to sustain equitable access. Finally, in the U.S., these growing market pressures are driving wedges among the various *sectors* of higher education. Research universities are generally better positioned to diversify their revenues than comprehensive (mainly teaching) universities, which are less able to generate private support. Community colleges (and other two-year institutions) are the "safety net" for access, but have very little opportunity to raise additional revenue; as enrolment pressures rise, their quality is challenged and their choices are stark.

In addition, as these wedges move further into the public higher education system, the gap between public and private institutions expands. Private universities and colleges in the U.S. serve about 22 percent of postsecondary students and operate without many of the political pressures and regulatory constraints of their public counterparts. They are able to compete more effectively for top faculty and students and are generally more nimble in their ability to change policy direction. They are a critical slice of the American higher education landscape, but do not have the capacity to serve large numbers of students priced out of public universities using cross-subsidies from the rest of their students. (For perspective, a 10 percent reduction in the number of students served by public universities would require private universities to accommodate a 30 percent increase in enrollments, a level well beyond their current infrastructure capacity.)

These trends are not all bad, however. The discipline of the marketplace causes universities to choose their program array and their research agendas more carefully with a closer eye to what students and supporters want and somewhat less to what individual faculty may want. (That is, the cross-subsidies inherent in any university must be more carefully and explicitly chosen.) Shifting costs to students and families can sort out serious students from those just "killing time," and increase completion rates. And it enables some public institutions to buffer themselves from political intrusion and the volatility of government budgets by cultivating multiple sources of revenue.

But these trends also pose significant dilemmas of social equity; accountability (to whom, and for what); likely long-term economic viability, especially of smaller and more specialized institutions; the "commercialization" of the curriculum; and increasing public "regulation without investment."

It is my view that these moves toward marketplace management in the U.S. are more or less permanent, but that careful policymaking can preserve many of the most important public interest purposes of American universities. To accomplish this, the U.S. needs to learn from and adapt higher education finance experiments from other venues, using not only other states as laboratories but other countries as well.

Central versus Decentralized Control

In the U.S., public higher education is a creature of state (provincial) governments with the national government contributing support through financial aid to individuals and research grants to institutions. So the current pattern and location of American universities, as well as their missions, largely reflect state, not national, decisions and aspirations. A certain level of interstate (and interinstitutional) competition has always been a part of this process. Indeed, many observers would credit this competition for the excellence of American research development over the past 75 years (and some would blame it for "wasteful duplication" of institutions and programs across states). Unlike most European traditions, American universities have always charged students a portion of the costs of their education, but used state revenues to provide deep subsidies (on the order of 50-75 percent) to all students. Thus, the recent move to increase tuition and fees in the U.S. has been a difference of degree, not of bedrock philosophy.

This "federated" responsibility for higher education (states supporting institutions, national government supporting student aid and research) has recently become a matter of policy debate. Very mixed reactions (AGB 2007) to the recent national (Spellings Commission) report (U.S. Dept. of Education 2006) on challenges to American higher education highlight the tension between those national policymakers who would like to have central standards, central testing, and central accountability versus those who believe that in a competitive market model, diversity and accountability to clients (rather than to government) are the best solution. Because the national government has no coherent policy toward higher education,[4] nor do many states, universities are left to forge the best solutions they can in a rapidly changing financial environment.

U.S. Experiments of Possible Interest

The decentralized nature of American higher education provides an opportunity for individual states to experiment with different approaches to redesigning their higher education systems. Some experiments redesign the basic relationship between the university and the state; others simply make tuition costs easier to plan for; and some seek to realign the outcomes of higher education more closely with the needs of their states. Ongoing experiments include:

- *Charter Universities* (University of Virginia)—universities are separately chartered as independent entities in which the state uses public revenues to "buy slots" for students (usually limited to residents of that state). The number of slots bought can vary from year to year depending on state budgets, and universities retain the right to set their own operating policies, including tuition, personnel, and building matters as long as they enroll the number of contracted state students. Any excess capacity may be used to admit nonresidents at full cost. There may also be contract conditions concerning graduation rates or the number of graduates to be produced in certain specialties such as teachers, nurses, or engineers. The University of Virginia embarked on a charter experiment in 2004 and is carefully documenting its progress as a learning model for others (Courtier 2006). In effect, this model brings operating conditions into line with the de facto privatization of the university, which receives less than 10 percent of its revenues from the public.
- *Cohort Tuition* (University of Illinois)—maintains the legal structure of the university as a public institution but seeks to cushion the effect of rising tui-

---

[4] The Spellings Commission approached the question of a national higher education policy from the background of a controversial effort to establish national standards for K-12 education (the No Child Left Behind initiative.) Expensive and heavy-handed mandates for K-12 schools have failed to produce quick or significant improvements in learning outcomes. Ironically, the NCLB approach was designed to stimulate competition among states in K-12 education, while higher education institutions already have significant competition.

tion and fees on students by guaranteeing a specific tuition at entrance for the full four years of a student's undergraduate program. This enables students to plan costs in advance and to determine whether the level of borrowing that may be required is within their financial capacity to repay. This approach does not reduce overall costs to students or ensure continuing state investment; it simply reallocates the risks of future reductions in state support (and increases in tuition) to incoming student cohorts.

- A variation on this approach has been adopted by a number of states in the form of *prepaid tuition*. Prepaid tuition plans enable parents and grandparents to save for a child's education by purchasing "tuition units" or depositing funds in a tax-free savings account. The intent is to enable families to purchase tomorrow's college education at today's prices. Most state plans have limitations as to where the tuition credits can be spent and provide for taxability if the funds are withdrawn for noneducation purposes (Baird 2006). More recently, the maze of state plans has been overlaid by a national tax-free college savings provision called "529 accounts," which accumulate benefits that are portable across state boundaries.

- *Vouchers* (Colorado)—provides the state subsidy in the form of vouchers to individuals, rather than as operating grants to institutions. This changes the form of aid and the political perceptions of the taxpaying public but does not necessarily enhance access or stabilize funding for higher education institutions. In Colorado, vouchers have been instituted simultaneously with a large reduction in state support per higher education student. It is not yet clear whether administering vouchers for thousands of students each semester is more or less costly than the old method of processing budget allocations directly to universities (Thompson 2007).

- *Performance Funding* (South Carolina)—establishes certain threshold levels on a variety of performance measures (enrollments, graduation rates, etc.) and allocates public support to universities proportional to their achievement on each measure. One weakness of performance funding has been its history of broken promises: It takes several years for universities to gear up to meet the new requirements and when state budget cycles dip, states frequently decline to make the payments that university performance would justify. This ruptures trust in the "business approach" that performance funding is designed to foster and creates cynicism within the university about the ability of government to follow through on its commitments.

- *Zero Tuition Below Median Income* (Princeton, Harvard, Stanford)—richly endowed private universities have been criticized for charging high tuitions while amassing very large private endowments. Some of the most prominent private universities have recently announced that they will charge zero tuition to all students from families with incomes below the median income for the U.S. (about $45,000) (Foster, Selingo, Huckabee 2007). In effect, private revenues from present and past donors will subsidize low-income access. This defuses the political challenge to these institutions but creates a new challenge for competing public institutions whose endowments do not permit this.

These private universities will continue to be very competitive for admission and can admit only a fraction of those seeking a higher education opportunity nationally, so this approach does not significantly address the affordability challenge for a large number of potential students.

What U.S. Might Learn from Other Countries

Among experiments ongoing abroad, the experience of the U.K., Australia, and New Zealand with "income-contingent loans" may be the most interesting for the U.S. to consider. Unlike some of the experiments noted above, ICLs, rather than redesigning the entire university-state relation or trying to micromanage university operations, simply provide a financing mechanism that removes/reduces cost barriers to enrollment at an efficient administrative cost. As one writer put it, ICLs "match payments of principal and interest to the profits from an education" (Brody 1994).

Students' tuition and fees (and in some schemes, a portion of living expenses as well) are paid for them by the government while in school, and recovered through the tax collection system after graduation if and when their earnings exceed a specified threshold. This removes the "moral hazard" of default incurred with a conventional loan, makes students aware that they have an investment in their education, and provides a mechanism for government to direct subsidies (loan forgiveness) into targeted fields as a matter of social policy.

Published analyses of ICLs (Chapman and Greenaway 2006; Weko 2004) suggest that they can be efficiently administered by any country that has a reasonably reliable tax collection system, do not discourage low-income students from enrolling, and do not skew students' choice of program or field of study.[5] Compared to the more conventional student loans employed in the U.S., there are no credit checks and no administrative fees to banks and lending intermediaries. (In the U.S. until recently, banks were guaranteed a rate in excess of nine percent on student loans and protected from default losses. In 2006, Congress partially reduced this rate, saving more than $14 billion—which was not recycled into student aid! To put this in perspective, at the average public subsidy of $5,500 per student this $14B could have financed access for another 2.5M students). However, critics argue that ICLs do nothing inherently to restrain costs and may function regressively to discourage the amount of work effort undertaken by graduates if the repayments are large (Feldman 1976; Usher 2005). By breaking the link with a market rate of interest, ICLs may also obscure the real cost of higher education to consumers and policymakers.

What counts in considering a policy transfer? In thinking realistically about possible policy adaptations, what matters is the *scale* of current experiments and the ability to "scale up" (or down) to fit new circumstances (Australia has about 35 universities and the U.S. has 3,000+; how does this affect possible policy

---

[5] Although this effect depends critically on the specific design of the ICL program.

transfers?); the *goals* (and their priority) for a nation (access, diversity, completion, and efficiency are all important, but which are we willing to trade off, if necessary, to achieve the rest?); a *government's ability* to keep financial commitments on which higher education depends; a *university's ability* to sustain quality in the face of changing conditions; and the *political viability and perceived fairness* of financing arrangements that can facilitate or bar students from the most critical investment in human capital.

What to Do Next?

It is easy to become lost in the details of financing plans and lose sight of the real goals of higher education: maximizing access, ensuring quality, generating new knowledge, and producing successful learning for students. Sooner or later, it is necessary to come to some sociopolitical consensus on a "fair" and "effective" division of the costs of higher education among students, government, corporate third parties, and philanthropic donors if we are to stabilize higher education institutions and enable students to have realistic aspirations for postsecondary education. The longer it takes to reach this consensus, the more de facto adjustments will have been put in place and the fewer options there may be for preserving the vital public purposes of public universities.

In the interim, various financing innovations, whether vouchers, cohort tuition, income-contingent loans, or other tools can help students finance the rising share of higher education costs assigned to students and families. With this in mind, I suggest the following maxims for moving ahead in uncertain times:

- *Diversify, streamline, and audit revenues*—but focus accountability on learning and knowledge outcomes for those whose lives and futures depend on us.
- *Align governance structures with actual stakeholders*—governing boards should reflect the multiplicity of constituencies that finance the 21st-century university and not solely the government that legally "owns" it. The focus should be on finding an appropriate set of incentives and disincentives for operation in the public interest, not on grinding down public universities against the stone of one set of political interests.
- *Begin to think of higher education itself as an important "export industry"* in the global economy—in the U.S., higher education is the fifth-largest service export industry, attracting more than 550,000 international students who spend more than $1B annually in the U.S. The E.U. will undoubtedly have an equivalent or greater impact. Higher education is not just another social service or another government department; it is both a driver and beneficiary of national economic and social development.
- *Align the autonomy and management flexibility of public universities with desired levels of competition*—without this alignment, growing marketization will simply erode and eventually eliminate public universities as effective in-

struments for social equity and economic growth. Nation-states need to consider carefully how much market competition we want for higher education.

- *Adopt and adapt good ideas, wherever they originate*—consciously and with due consideration of differing social and political cultures. This will force us to be more aware of and more explicit about our real goals for higher education and more attentive to the actual costs and tradeoffs they require.

References

Association of Governing Boards of Universities and Colleges (AGB), < http://www.agb.org/wmspage.cfm?parm1=1193>.

Baird, Katherine E. 2006. "Do Prepaid Tuition Plans Affect State Support for Higher Education?" *Journal of Education Finance*, vol. 31, no. 3 (winter): 255–75.

Beatty, Jack. 2006. "The Insecure American." *The Atlantic Online*, Oct 4.

Brody, Evelyn. 1994. "Paying Back Your Country through Income-Contingent Loans." *San Diego Law Review*, vol. 31: 449–518, 199.

Brody, William R. 2007. "College Goes Global." *Foreign Affairs*, vol. 86, no. 2 (March/April): 122–33.

Carnoy, Martin. 2006. "Higher Education and Economic Development—India, China, and the 21st Century." Powerpoint presentation, <www.stanford. edu/School of Education>.

Chapman, Bruce, and David Greenaway. 2006. "Learning to Live with Loans? International Policy Transfer and the Funding of Higher Education." *The World Economy*, 1057–75.

Couturier, Laura. 2006. "Checks and Balances at Work." National Center for Public Policy & Higher Education, June.

Daniel, John, Asha Kanwar, and Stamenk Uvalic-Trumbic. 2006. "A Tectonic Shift in Global Higher Education." *Change* (July/August).

Douglass, John A. 2006. "The Waning of America's Higher Education Advantage." CSHE Occasional Paper #9.06, UC Berkeley (June).

Easterlin, Richard. 1987. *Birth & Fortune: The Impact of Numbers on Personal Welfare*, 2nd edition. Chicago: University of Chicago Press.

Feldman, Roger. 1976. "Some More Problems with Income-Contingent Loans: The Case of Medical Education." *Journal of Political Economy*, vol. 84, no.6 (December): 1305–11.

Foster, Andrea, Jeffrey Selingo, Charles Huckabee. 2007. "Princeton Freezes Tuition for First Time in 4 Decades, Escalating Elite Competition for Students." *Chronicle of Higher Education*, January 22.

Fulbright New Century Scholars. 2006. Report & Recommendations, UNESCO, Paris (October).

Hacker, Jacob. 2006. *The Great Risk Shift*. Oxford: Oxford University Press.

Ischinger, Barbara. 2007. "Post Secondary Education: The Challenges Ahead." OECD Director for Education speech, Ottawa, Canada, January 14–16.

Johnstone, D. Bruce. 2005. "Fear and Loathing of Tuition Fees: An American Perspective on Higher Education Finance in the U.K." *Perspectives, Policy and Practice in Higher Education*, vol. 9, no. 1 (January): 12–16.

Lipka, Sara. 2005. "15-Nation Study Finds That College Access and Affordability Are Not Always Linked." *Chronicle of Higher Education*, April 15.

Marcus, Jon. 2007. "The Celtic Tiger." National Center for Public Policy and Higher Education. *CrossTalk* (January 26): 1+.

Marginson, Simon. 2000. "Rethinking Academic Work in the Global Era." *Journal of Higher Education Policy and Management*, vol. 22, no.1: 23–35.

Oosterbeek, H. 1998. "Subsidizing Students, Families or Graduates?" <http://www.cmec.ca/ stats/quebec2004/vossensteyn.en.pdf>.

Osborne, Robert D. 2006. "Access to and Participation in Higher Education in Northern Ireland." *Higher Education Quarterly*, vol. 6, no. 4 (October): 333–48.

Thompson, Susan. 2007. "Is It A Shell Game? Colorado's Controversial New Way of Handing Out Its Higher Education Money." *CrossTalk*, National Center for Public Policy and Higher Education (Winter): 1+

U.S. Department of Education. 2006. "A Test of Leadership: Charting the Future of U.S. Higher Education." Report of the Commission on the Future of Higher Education. Washington, D.C., September 19—known as the Spellings Report.

Usher, A. 2005. "Much Ado about a Small Idea." Toronto, Ontario. The Educational Policy Institute <www.educationalpolicy.org/pdf/ICR.pdf>.

Weko, Thomas. 2004. "New Dogs and Old Tricks: What Can the U.K. Teach the U.S. about University Education?" *Atlantic Fellowship in Public Policy*, Higher Education Policy Institute (March).

Chapter 5

Australia's Experiment: Tuition Fees, Student Loans, and University Income Generation

Grant Harman[1]

Over the last three decades, Australian higher education has shown considerable capacity for policy experimentation, as it has coped with substantial expansion in student numbers, opportunities for major recruitment of international fee-paying students, the increased application of information and communications technology to higher education, and demands of new international trade patterns and the knowledge economy. This has included major mergers of institutions to reduce the number of public higher education institutions from about 65 universities and colleges of advanced education (CAEs) to 36 universities, abolition of the binary divide between universities and CAEs, a more selective approach to public research funding, and encouragement of private higher education. However, some of the most dramatic experimentation has occurred in the areas of student tuition fees, student loans, and incentives for universities to generate increasing proportions of their own revenue.

A decade and a half after abolition of tuition fees in 1974 by the Whitlam Labor Government, another Labor Government re-introduced tuition fees but under the innovative arrangements of the Higher Education Contribution Scheme

[1] Centre for Higher Education Management and Policy, School of Professional Development and Leadership, University of New England, Australia.

(HECS). This is an income-contingent government student loan scheme, with re-payments being made through the income taxation system but only after the an-nual income of graduates reaches a threshold that was originally set at average annual income. This scheme has been highly successful and has not adversely affected student participation in higher education to any major degree. Its strength is that fees need not be paid until after graduation and then only when annual in-come exceeds a specified threshold, thus largely overcoming the impact that tui-tion fees traditionally have had on participation by lower-income and disadvan-taged groups. Not surprisingly, this approach has attracted considerable interest internationally.

Universities have been strongly encouraged by the Commonwealth (or fed-eral) Government to generate increasing proportions of their own revenue, stimu-lating extension of links with industry and substantial increases in the enrollments of fee-paying international and domestic students. Fee-paying international stu-dents now constitute over 25 percent of total enrollments in public universities, while recently a number of universities have taken the opportunity under modified government policy to recruit full-cost fee-paying domestic undergraduate students in highly competitive disciplinary areas. This scheme is highly controversial, rais-ing important equity issues, especially as "full fee" students may be admitted to highly selective courses with lower "cut-off" scores than HECS-based students. To assist students enrolled in such courses and in private colleges, the Common-wealth Government has introduced a parallel loan system to HECS known as FEE-HELP that provides access to government income-contingent loans for courses other than HECS-based courses offered in both public and private institu-tions.

At First an Abolition of Tuition Fees and Its Impact

From the beginning of 1974, a Commonwealth Labor government led by Gough Whitlam abolished tuition fees in universities and CAEs in a bold move to in-crease student access and particularly provide for the less advantaged sections of the community. The Whitlam Government had been elected in December 1972 with a strong mandate for substantial social and education reform. At the same time, the government also assumed full financial responsibility for higher educa-tion that for more than a decade had been a shared Commonwealth and state responsibility, and introduced the Tertiary Education Assistance Scheme that provided means-tested student financial assistance.

While abolition of tuition fees and introduction of the Tertiary Education Assistance Scheme undoubtedly enabled some individuals to enroll in higher education who otherwise would have not been able to do so, it had relatively small effects on the overall composition of the student population. Student en-rollments increased substantially throughout the 1970s, providing increased op-portunities for students from disadvantaged backgrounds. Table 5.1 provides information on higher education enrollments from 1945 to 2005. However, the

Table 5.1. Australian Higher Education Students, 1945–2003

	Total Students	Percent Full-time	Percent Part-time	Percent External	Percent Female	Percent International
1945	15,586					
1950	30,630	62.7	28.1	9.2	21.6	NA
1955	30,792	62.3	27.9	9.8	21.9	NA
1960	53,633	58.7	31.1	10.2	23.1	NA
1965	110,250	55.4	38.2	6.4	24.0	NA
1970	161,455	57.9	36.1	5.9	27.1	NA
1975	276,559	63.4	30.3	6.4	40.6	NA
1980	329,523	54.5	34.7	10.8	45.3	NA
1985	370,016	55.2	32.5	12.3	47.6	NA
1990	485,066	61.7	27.4	10.9	52.7	5.2
1995	604,176	58.8	28.7	12.4	53.9	7.6
2000	695,485	58.6	27.6	13.7	55.2	13.7
2003	929,952	65.1	NA	15.1	54.4	22.6
2005	957,176	66.5	24.5	13.9	54.4	25.0

Source: Department of Education, Training and Youth Affairs (2001); *Higher Education Students: Time Series Tables 2000,* Canberra; Department of Education, Science and Training (2003, 2004, 2005, and 2006); *Selected Higher Education Statistics*, Canberra; and D. S. Anderson & A E. Vervoorn, *Access to Privilege: Patterns of Participation in Post-Secondary Education*, Canberra: Australian National University Press (1983).

expected increase in the proportion of students from low-economic backgrounds did not occur, partly because State Education Department teacher education scholarships were phased out from 1974. At one stage, these scholarships were held by some 50,000 tertiary students, many of them from modest backgrounds.

A major research study conducted in the late 1970s by Anderson and colleagues (Anderson et al. 1978) about the social composition of the student body before and after the change revealed no discernible difference in the social spectrum of higher education. But, as Anderson and Vervoorn later pointed out,

> Nevertheless this does not permit the conclusion that the removal of fees did not enable poor students to enrol who otherwise would have deferred; if there were such students—and common sense suggests that there must have been—either they were not sufficiently numerous to show up in statistical aggregates, or their poverty was not revealed by the [survey] questions directed at parental status, etc. When asked a direct question about the effects fees would have had on their enrollment, 20 per cent of the full time students said that they would have had to enrol part-time or not at all (Anderson and Vervoorn 1983, 172).

The relative lack of significant impact of the abolition of tuition fees was an important factor that encouraged the Hawke Labor Government in the late 1980s to reintroduce tuition fees in a new form in order to fund substantial planned expansion in enrollments and graduations.

Introducing the Higher Education Contribution Scheme

Curiously, just 15 years after their abolition Bob Hawke's Labor government reintroduced tuition fees in the form of HECS. Although often referred to as a graduate tax, perhaps more accurately it should be thought of as an income-contingent, interest-free student loan system, which contributes over time to the costs of tuition. HECS does not involve a uniform tax on all graduates in the community; rather, unless specifically exempted, all Australians who have undertaken higher education studies at a Commonwealth Government—supported institution since 1989 have been required to make payments to the extent of their particular indebtedness. Further, only when the income of graduates or students reaches a threshold level slightly below average weekly earnings are payments required to be made.

Students may pay up-front and enjoy a 25 percent discount, but those who are unable to pay in advance, or do not wish to do so, may defer payment until their personal income exceeds a minimum threshold income level. In just under two decades, HECS has become an important and well-accepted student contribution element in the financing of higher education in Australia. In 2002 it generated almost $1.8 billion and contributed about 28.3 percent of Commonwealth Government operating grant revenue to higher education institutions and 16 percent of total higher education funding.

The HECS scheme was introduced by the Hawke Labor Government in 1989 at a time when higher education in Australia had just entered a new phase of rapid expansion in student enrollments and substantial reform. In 1987, under the leadership of the newly appointed Minister for Employment, Education and Training, John Dawkins, the government took the view that, as part of major economic reform, higher education needed urgent redirection in order to contribute more effectively to economic and social reform, and to increasing Australia's competitiveness internationally. A Green Paper issued by Minister Dawkins announced proposed new directions, explaining that increased student enrollments, quality enhancement, and increased efficiencies were essential. However, this Green Paper also explained that the Commonwealth would find difficulty in funding enrollment expansion from its own resources alone and flagged that "additional sources of funding will need to be investigated, having regard to both the public and private benefits that higher education confers" (Dawkins 1987, 75).

Reintroduction of student fees in any form posed particular problems for the Hawke Government since substantial sections of the governing Australian Labor Party were strongly committed to the concept of free higher education; in fact, the Labor Party platform had been amended to forbid charging fees for higher education. Minister Dawkins, however, appointed a Committee on Higher Education Funding chaired by a former Labor premier of the state of New South Wales, Neville Wran, to investigate funding options, including possible schemes involving contributions from higher education students, graduates, parents, and employers. After careful analysis and with appropriate technical support, the Wran Committee became convinced of the need for substantial changes in the funding system. According to one of the technical experts who assisted the committee, the change to HECS came in response to two forces:

- One was the judgement that fiscal constraints meant that it was not possible to continue to finance a burgeoning higher education system almost solely from general taxation revenue.
- Second was the view that not having changes was regressive in a lifetime sense, given that students typically came from positions of socio-economic advantage and receive considerable economic benefits from being graduates (Chapman 1998, 43).

After consultations with key stakeholders, the Wran Committee in April 1988 came up with the idea of HECS and recommended its implementation to the government (Committee on Higher Education Funding 1988). This recommendation was relatively quickly accepted by the government after convincing the Labor Party national conference and the caucus to give support. Despite some initial protests from university students and academic staff associations, the idea of HECS attracted strong community support and the scheme was introduced with relatively little difficulty from January 1, 1989. Since then it has operated relatively smoothly, although there was some controversy in 1996 when the Howard Coalition Government made a number of significant changes to the scheme.

The essential idea of HECS as introduced was that students make compulsory contributions to the costs of their study, but such contributions are required only after taxable income exceeds average community income. Contributions are made via the regular personal income taxation system. The Wran Committee saw HECS as satisfying both the need to minimize financial barriers to access to higher education and to take full account of an individual's capacity to pay. The scheme gained wide community acceptance since it was seen as a more equitable arrangement than solely taxpayer funding of higher education, with those benefiting being required to contribute toward some of the costs. But it was also widely accepted because of its strong equity elements, with users being required to make their contributions only after their income reached the threshold of average weekly earnings.

While the Wran Committee recommended a three-tier contribution rate related to course costs, the Hawke Government decided on a single standard fee. Arrangements included mechanisms for the annual course contribution to be adjusted each year in accordance with inflation and for the income threshold level requiring payments to be adjusted in line with changes in average weekly earnings. While HECS began with the idea of including all Australian students enrolled in award courses at Commonwealth-funded higher education institutions, various exemptions were soon introduced, such as for research higher degree enrollments and schoolteachers funded under an exemption program for the professional development of teachers. From the start, it also was understood that HECS would not apply to fee-paying students and that HECS liabilities would be adjusted annually for inflation.

In August 1996, the newly elected Howard Coalition Government made important changes to HECS as part of a package of changes to the higher education system. In particular, it introduced a three-level system of contributions based on a combination of course costs and income levels upon graduation, and it reduced the repayment threshold significantly from AUD$28,495 p.a. to AUD$20,701 p.a., thus requiring graduates to commence repayment at an earlier stage. With regard to the three-level system, Band 1 applied to arts, humanities, social sciences, education, and nursing courses with the repayment amount set at AUD$3,300 p.a. for 1997, Band 2 to mathematics, computing science, sciences, engineering, agriculture, business, and economics courses with a repayment amount at AUD$4,700 p.a., and Band 3 to law, medicine, dentistry, and veterinary science courses with a repayment level of AUD $5,500 p.a. These changes generated considerable short-term controversy but this soon died away.

In 2004, following a major review, the Howard Government gave universities the choice to raise HECS fees by 25 percent. Initially, less than half the total number of universities decided to do so, but now only one university has refused to increase the HECS fee level. In addition, the government capped HECS fees for teacher education and nursing students on the grounds that these fields were national priority areas. Unfortunately, this has meant that universities receive less total funding per student unit in these areas, thus providing a disincentive to increase enrollments in these areas.

HECS is administered jointly by the Commonwealth Department of Education, Science and Training, the Australian Taxation Office, and universities. Unless specifically excluded, all students enrolled on the two specified census dates each year in higher education awarded courses funded by the Commonwealth Government must pay HECS. Students who withdraw after census dates because of illness may be granted reduction of all or some of their HECS liability for that semester (Australian Taxation Office 2000).

HECS eligible students who do not pay up-front must provide their university with their tax file number and each semester students must be advised by their university of their estimated tax liability for that semester. Up-front payments of amounts between $500 and the full semester liability are paid to the student's university. HECS liabilities are indexed to take account of changes in average weekly earnings but no interest is charged. Repayment amounts vary between three percent and five percent of salary. Most undergraduate students use the HECS system, either by paying up-front or deferring their payments. Total HECS debt in 2002 was AUD$8.0 billion, of which AUD$1.6 billion was regarded as being unlikely to be recovered.

Table 5.2 shows the HECS payment options chosen by different student enrollment categories. It will be noted that students studying part-time or externally

Table 5.2. HECS Payment Options by Type of Enrollment, 1998 to 2000, Equivalent Full-Time Students Units (EFTSU)

	1988			1999			2000		
	Liability deferred discount	Up-front with discount	Up-front with no discount	Liability deferred	Up-front with discount	Up-front with no discount	Liability deferred	Up-front with discount	Up-front with no discount
Full-time	246,736	61,164	808	250,860	58,863	1,158	242,549	56,013	1,286
Part-time	38,961	17,677	182	38,283	15,630	243	39,809	14,467	251
External	15,305	10,689	182	15,831	9,816	232	16,707	8,989	217
No information	8,250	2,253	61	9,122	2,385	74	14,013	4,298	131
Total	309,251	91,783	1,218	314,097	86,694	1,708	313,078	83,767	1,884

Source: Department of Education, Training and Youth Affairs (2001), *Higher Education Report for the 2001 to 2003 Triennium*, Canberra, p 101.

are more likely than full-time students to pay their HECS contribution up-front. In 2000, 19 percent of full-time students compared to 27 percent of part-time students and 36 percent of external students paid their contributions up-front.

Table 5.3 shows HECS liabilities as a proportion of Commonwealth operating grant funds to universities. HECS liabilities incurred by students in a particular year do not incorporate the substantial Commonwealth subsidies involved in HECS. In 1991, HECS liabilities represented around 21 percent of operating grant funds. This grew to 31 percent in 1999 and to 34 percent in 2003. Commonwealth subsidies involved in HECS include the 25 percent discount for up-front payments, a 15 percent bonus on voluntary payments, debt write-downs due to death, remission of HECS debts due to special circumstances, and the provision of doubtful debts. By taking these subsidies into account, the actual student contribution, on average, represents 24 percent of course costs. However, this does not include the subsidy to students that arises from the Commonwealth foregoing interest revenue on HECS debts.

Evaluating HEC's Success and Problems

How to evaluate the success and problems of Australia's great experiment in funding its higher education system? In the following I consider five major issues—public acceptance, administrative efficiency, the influence of the new funding scheme on academic activities, the role of students versus government in funding higher education, and perhaps most importantly the effect on student participation rates.

Public Acceptance

As already noted, despite some initial opposition, especially from university students and associations representing academic staff, HECS soon gained wide public acceptance. From the start, this method for students to make a contribution to their education was widely regarded as being fair and equitable. The concept that students need to begin repaying their indebtedness only when they are receiving a salary or wage equal to average weekly earnings or thereabout is widely understood and accepted.

Two other factors helped with winning public acceptance. First, at the time of the introduction of HECS, it was well known that various research studies had cast doubt on the value of the abolition of tuition fees for universities and CAEs in the mid-1970s. According to one of the experts who advised the Wran Committee, the arrangements without tuition fees that operated from 1974 to 1988 were "unfair, unjust, inequitable and inappropriate" (Chapman 1988, 35). Sec-

Table 5.3. How Students Pay HECS 1989-1990 to 2003-2004: Actual Figures and Estimates ($Million)

Financial year	Students' HECS liabilities	Voluntary repayments by students	Repay-ments through tax system	Up-front payments made to universities	Total payments	Accumulated HECS debt at June 30
1989–1990	527	2	9	82	93	N/A
1994–1995	888	17	304	157	478	3,354
1999–2000	1,605	73	530	269	872	6,243
2003–2004	1,861	100	672	304	1,076	9,721

Source: Department of Education, Training and Youth Affairs (2001); *Higher Education Report for the 2001 to 2003 Triennium* (Canberra, 2004), 102.

ond, many Australian families are used to paying high fees for their children to attend private schools. While overall almost 30 percent of Australian school students attend private schools, the proportion is much higher for the senior years of secondary education.

Administrative Efficiency

Overall, HECS works well in terms of administrative efficiency. While each university needed to spend substantial resources in converting their internal student administration systems to cope with HECS, the Commonwealth provided some compensation. Compulsory collection of contributions by the Australian Taxation Office (ATO) is handled in conjunction with annual income taxation assessments. No difficulties are now experienced in requiring students to provide individual tax file numbers since such numbers are required for many basic financial transactions including opening a bank account. Initially, when the Wran Committee was considering various options, the ATO opposed the introduction of HECS on the grounds that it was not a debt collection agency, graduates may emigrate, and since many individuals cheat on taxation some HECS debts would not be repaid. But once the government made its decision the role of the ATO with regard to HECS has not been an issue (Chapman 1998, 123).

Impact on Teaching and Academic Administration

The introduction of HECS had a number of unexpected effects, particularly on students and their expectations. Students soon became more conscious of their enrollment details and particularly the date each semester when they could withdraw from course units without HECS liability. They also soon became more concerned about securing value for money and more ready to complain about particular aspects of their courses and how they are delivered.

Administratively, there have been a number of consequences for handling enrollment procedures. Enrollment forms required revisions and particular care needs to be taken in ensuring compliance with legal requirements with regard to securing tax file numbers and reporting enrollment details. In a number of cases, universities found it necessary to introduce new student credit point systems in order to facilitate calculation of individual HECS liability.

Financial Contributions of Student versus Government

Student and graduate payments via the HECS system now make important contributions to financial support for higher education. However, it should be noted that the Commonwealth effectively provided in excess of $10 billion in loan funds in just over a decade to support HECS, and it has taken almost two decades for HECS contributions to reach their current level of contribution to total Commonwealth operating grants. These substantial contributions by the Commonwealth often are not fully recognized in discussions about HECS.

It should be noted, however, that instead of establishing an indentified loan fund the Commonwealth simply funded the introduction of HECS through its normal financial outlays to higher education. This relatively simple strategy was employed since at the time of the introduction of HECS there were no tuition fees and thus the introduction of HECS did not involve any increases in government outlays to higher education, except to take account of increases in student enrollments.

While HECS now makes major contributions to higher education funding, Australian higher education faces increasing financial problems each year with ongoing reductions in the Commonwealth's contribution to operating grants. Since coming to office in 1996, the Howard Government has continued the policy of the Keating Labor Government not to provide full, automatic supplementation for staff salary rises achieved through enterprise bargaining, requiring institutions to find the component above the general price adjustment index through internal efficiencies and external earnings. This has resulted in the nonfunded gap between operating grant indexation and actual salary average outcomes continuing to accumulate.

Impact on Student Participation Rates

It is widely believed that HECS has had only a minor impact on student participation rates and various research studies and official reports have largely supported this view. Certainly since the introduction of HECS, Australian higher education has enjoyed dramatic increases in enrollments, which places Australia today amongst the leaders of OECD nations in terms of participation of school leavers in higher and other postschool education. Between 1988 and the year 2000, total student enrollments increased from about 420,000 to about 695,000 while domestic (or nonoverseas) enrollments over the same period increased from about 400,000 to almost 600,000. Further, since a high proportion of research higher degree students have held HECS exemption scholarships, or for other reasons have not been deemed HECS eligible, the HECS scheme has had little direct influence on research training.

From the start, the main concern has been about the impact of HECS on low income and other disadvantaged groups, although since the 1996 changes there has been some concern about whether or not the introduction of three bands has tended to divert students away from disciplines in the more expensive bands, especially science, to disciplines in the least expensive.

Early assessments of the impact of HECS on students seeking entry to higher education in Western Australia (Bardsley 1989) and in Victoria (Robertson and Sloan 1990) focused particularly on the quantitative effects on overall enrollment patterns and found little evidence of major effects. One of these stud-

ies concluded that "if HECS has made any impact on decision making in relation to participation, it is largely at the postgraduate level, less so at the undergraduate level and hardly at all at the entry level" (Robertson and Sloan 1990,
72).

In 1991 a major national study sponsored by the Higher Education Council
looked particularly at compositional effects (National Board 1992). Samples of
Year 12 students and adults in four states were surveyed. For the Year 12 populations, the researchers found that, for those who had decided not to participate
in higher education, HECS was a low-ranking reason, while for those considering higher education HECS was perceived to be a middle-ranking factor (fourth
or fifth out of eight factors) that might frustrate intentions to enter higher education. However, HECS appeared to be more important in the perceptions of students from single-parent families and low socio-economic students from rural
areas, and of less importance to students from non–English-speaking backgrounds. For adult populations, HECS was a middle-ranking factor in decisions
whether or not to enroll, and it was marginally more important for single parents
and for adults from families with dependents.

Following changes made to HECS in 1996, Andrews undertook a study of
whether or not the changes had affected student demand or interest in undertaking higher education studies. He analyzed changes in the number of applications
for student enrollment made to state admission centers over a 10-year period and
concluded that the recent changes in HECS did not appear to have affected the
level of interest in undertaking higher education amongst school leavers, but
there may have been an effect on mature age applicants (Andrews 1997, v). Data
were analyzed to investigate the impact of differential HECS on the choice of
disciplines, and it was found that, while discipline choice varied considerably
from year to year, there appeared to be no relationship between these variations
and the HECS band within which a discipline was placed (Andrews 1997, 16).

Andrews and other colleagues in the Department of Education, Training,
and Youth Affairs in 1998 undertook work to identify what factors account for
low participation amongst low socio-economic status (SES) individuals and to
ascertain whether the introduction of HECS in 1989 and subsequent changes
have provided particular disincentives for such students. Each of the methodologies employed—attitudinal surveys, multivariate analysis, and quasi-
experimental analysis—pointed to HECS being only a minor factor, if a factor at
all, for the low participation of this group in higher education (Andrews 1999,
1). The study concluded:

> While students from low SES backgrounds are under-represented in higher edu-
> cation institutions, this is a long-term concern that has not worsened following the
> introduction and changes to HECS over the past decade. Survey findings indicate
> that HECS is not a main reason given by individuals for failing to participate in
> higher education. The financial returns to undertaking higher education remain
> high after the introduction and changes to HECS. HECS does not appear to have
> substantially affected the level of applications or enrollments of students in gen-

eral although little can be said concerning students from low SES backgrounds. Given HECS is a deferrable contribution towards students' education, it is not surprising that the demand response to the cost of increase associated with HECS is muted (Andrews 1999, 25).

More recent studies have suggested some modification to these conclusions. A study of demand for higher education as measured by applications through state admissions centers by Aungles, Buchanan, Karmel, and MacLachlan (2002) found that the introduction of HECS in 1989 did not deter interest in higher education among school leavers, but that 1996 changes reduced demand marginally by about 9,000 students per year. They also found that interest in higher education among "mature age" persons was not deterred by the introduction of HECS but that the 1996 changes substantially lowered demand amongst "mature age" by about 17,000 persons per year. In particular, older persons new to higher education and studying part-time or externally have been more responsive to HECS changes than other groups. This suggests the need for careful modelling of the likely impact of any further changes in HECS.

From "Government Funded" to "Government Subsidized"

Introduction of HECS was a key part of major reforms to higher education initiated by the Hawke Labor Government following its re-election in 1987. Despite strong opposition from students and academics, these reforms were implemented quickly and successfully and there followed a period of rapid expansion with total enrollments climbing to 485,066 by 1990 and 695,485 by 2000. However, during the second half of the 1990s rapid expansion in domestic HECS-based students levelled off.

In addition, under Minister Dawkins universities were strongly encouraged to generate additional revenue particularly by attracting international students on a full-cost fee basis, and enrolling postgraduate coursework students on a fee basis. Both initiatives proved highly successful, attracting large numbers of students and bringing into the more entrepreneurial universities substantial sums of discretionary income. International student numbers grew from 18,207 in 1988 to 95,607 in 2000 and to 239,495 in 2006, while by 2004 over 70,000 domestic postgraduate fee-paying students were enrolled. By 2002 international and domestic student fees totalled AUD$2.5 billion or over half the sum provided by the Commonwealth Government in direct subsidies to support teaching in universities.

These reforms were largely driven by economic reforms, which fundamentally changed the role of higher education to the extent that human capital investment came to be seen as being instrumental to economic reform. The 1988 White Paper on higher education expressed this as follows:

The society we want cannot be achieved without a strong economic base. In Australia, this now requires a greatly increased export income, a far more favourable balance of trade than at present and a considerable reduction in our external debt. It also requires a shift in the traditional profile of our economic activity. Our industry is increasingly faced with rapidly changing international markets in which success depends on, among other things, the conceptual, creative and technical skills of the labour force, the ability to innovate and be entrepreneurial (Dawkins 1988, 6).

Closely associated with changes in economic policy were new ideas in public sector management that became common in Australia from the mid-1980s. These ideas were quickly taken up in various government reports and in reform efforts at both federal and state levels. Election of a Liberal Party/National Party Coalition Government led by John Howard in 1996 essentially continued and somewhat accelerated previous trends, with achievement of an even more diverse student population associated with substantial increases in international student enrollments; a more market-oriented and competitive regulatory environment, with less institutional dependence on government operating grants and substantial increases in institutionally generated revenue; a more student-focused approach to course offerings and student learning; new access and equity initiatives; major expansion in research activity and research training, with closer university-industry research links; expansion of postgraduate studies and increased competition for resources; new quality assurance initiatives and a more international orientation; and, within universities, a more corporatist approach to institutional management and governance.

The first new public management ideas applied to higher education in Australia were simply ideas about efficiency and effectiveness, the application of improved management practices, and the use of performance indicators for accountability purposes. But from the early 1990s, the emphasis had changed with the introduction of the concepts of competition and contestability, or more commonly market forces. Under the Howard Government, contributions to University operating expenses fell and by 2003 only 35 percent of the costs of Australian universities were met by national government grants for teaching domestic students. Moreover, the official language changed for the public universities from being "government funded" to being "government subsidized."

In 2003, the Howard Government introduced further reforms providing additional funding for higher education of $1.5 billion over five years, but most of it was tied to particular projects. It also gave universities the freedom to increase HECS fees by up to 25 percent. The Labor Party opposed these measures in the 2004 general election campaign promising almost identical additional funding, but promising to roll back any increases in HECS and abolish full fee undergraduate enrollments (which had first been introduced by the Howard Government in 1997). Significantly, neither side of politics came up with sufficient additional funding to enable universities to reduce staff-student ratios, which have increased from about 1:12 in 1993 to about 1:22 today.

The Idea of Full-Fee Domestic Students

Full-fee domestic places were introduced in 1990 for domestic coursework post-graduate courses, prompted by a belief that in key professional areas either students or their employers would be willing to pay reasonably priced fees. Overall, this effort has been particularly successful in such professional areas of business management and IT, and to a lesser extent in education, nursing, and health management.

Full-fee undergraduate places that were in addition to HECS-based places were introduced in 1997. No more than 25 percent of the total number of places available in a given course could be offered to domestic fee-paying students, and universities faced penalties if they offered fee-paying places to Australian undergraduates but failed to fill their agreed number of Commonwealth-funded places. In 2005, the limit on full-fee places per course was increased to 50 percent. Initially full-fee undergraduate courses were limited to a few major universities, but more recently there has been a steady increase in enrollments and now a majority of universities offer such courses. Fee levels vary but in major universities fees are often at least AUD$20,000 p.a., with fees increasing for professional courses such as veterinary science to over AUD$30,000 p.a.

Full-fee undergraduate courses are highly controversial. Universities that offer such courses admit to concern about equity issues but justify their actions because of the relatively low levels of Commonwealth Government subsidies for HECS-based places. They also point out that would be somewhat inconsistent if domestic students were unable to access those fee-paying courses that are offered to international students. Opponents argue that since university education largely determines the life chances of young people, such courses should be offered on the basis on academic achievement and the likelihood to succeed, and should not depend on wealth. In its editorial of January 9, 2007, the *Sydney Morning Herald* well summed up the dilemma about full-fee undergraduate courses and community concern:

> Full fee-paying students are "buying" a better place than they deserve in the otherwise highly competitive university entry queue. By paying the full cost of a degree up front, rather than part of the cost through the HECS loan scheme, students can secure a place without a university admission index ranking up to 18 points lower than their HECS-paying peers. Up to a third of all places now go to those who can pay. The inequity is obvious. So, too, is the damage to national standards if money, not merit, determines Australia's student mix. But the real question is why funding needs these measures. Australia is the only OECD nation to have reduced spending on higher education since the mid-1990s, against an average increase of 48 per cent. And this at a time of unheard plenty (*Sydney Morning Herald*, January 9, 2007).

To assist fee-paying domestic students in both public universities and the growing number of private institutions, the Commonwealth Government introduced a parallel scheme to HECS, enabling students to defer fee payments until after graduation. With this FEE-HELP scheme, the upper limits for loans is AUD$80,000 for all courses except medicine, veterinary science, and dentistry, which attract a maximum fee loan of AUD$100,000. FEE-HELP operates in a similar fashion to HECS with graduates or students beginning to repay only when their annual income reaches a specified threshold, which in the 2006/2007 financial year was set at AUD$38,149 p.a.

The Promise versus the Result

A major difficulty today is that government support per student place has substantially declined over the past decade, despite a boom in the export of minerals that generates substantial budget surpluses. Increasingly universities are demanding either increased public financial support, or further deregulation to allow them to set their own tuition fee for all students. While the abolition of tuition fees could have been expected to have provided an important national experiment on the effects of zero tuition fees on access and participation, care needs to be taken in drawing conclusions because of limitations of data and the fact that at the same time state education departments ceased offering their teacher education scholarships that had in the past financed the university and college courses of large numbers of students preparing to teach in primary and secondary schools. While no clear effects were seen in the social composition of the student population, it appears that the removal of fees did enable some poorer students to enroll who otherwise would have not done so. But the effects were not strong or clear enough to stop fees being reintroduced in 1989 in the form of HECS.

HECS has been a highly successful experiment that works extremely well and is widely accepted. Its attraction is that lower-income students are not discouraged from participation since they are not required to pay fees at the time they enroll, and must commence repayment of their HECS debt only when their income reaches approximately the community average income level. At that stage, students from poorer backgrounds find it hard to argue that they are financially disadvantaged. Overall, the effects of HECS on participation have been limited, especially in the period up to 1996. However, more recent studies suggest that the 1996 changes did affect demand to some extent, particularly of "mature age" students and members of recognized disadvantaged groups. To date little evaluation has been conducted on the impact of recent 25 percent increases in HECS levels. One major concern is that unless government funding is increased universities inevitably will press for further increases in HECS levels.

To a surprising extent, government encouragement of universities' revenue raising has been highly successful. Many universities have displayed impressive entrepreneurial talent, particularly in attracting full-fee international and domestic students. The presence of large numbers of international students on university campuses has had many positive benefits. Domestic fee-paying undergraduate enrollments are raising large sums for an increasing number of universities, but this policy, understandably, is highly controversial. As already noted, a major dilemma for universities is that under the Howard Coalition Government, in power between 1996 and 2007, public subsidies per student continued to decrease. In 2003, the Commonwealth Government's spending on tertiary education as a share of gross domestic product was 0.8 percent, placing Australia in the bottom 20 percent of all countries in the OECD. Yet compared with comparable countries Australia does reasonably well internationally in university rankings. But a major worry is that the success of universities in their entrepreneurial activities may have been in part responsible for declining public financial support.

References

Anderson, D. S., R. Boven, P. J. Fensham, and J. P. Powell. 1978. *Students in Australian Higher Education: A Study of Their Social Composition Since the Abolition of Fees.* Tertiary Education Research Centre. Sydney: University of New South Wales.

Anderson, D. S., and A. E. Vervoorn. 1983. Access to Privilege: Patterns of Participation in Australian Post-Secondary Education. Canberra: ANU Press.

Andrews, L. 1997. *The Effect of HECS on Interest in Undertaking Higher Education.* Higher Education Division, Department of Employment Education and Training. Canberra.

———. 1999. Does HECS Deter? Factors Affecting University Participation by Low SES Groups. Department of Education, Training and Youth Affairs. Canberra.

Aungles, P., I. Buchanan, T. Karmel, M. MacLachlan. 2002. HECS and Opportunities in Higher Education: A Paper Investigating the Impact of the Higher Education Contributions Scheme (HECS) on the Higher Education System. Department of Education, Science and Training. Canberra.

Australian Taxation Office. 2000. *HECS: Your Questions Answered 2000.* Canberra.

Bardsley, N. 1989. Impact of the Higher Education Contribution Scheme Survey Report: Western Australia. Perth.

Chapman, B. 1988. "The Higher Education Contribution Scheme." In *Alternative Funding Strategies for Australia's Universities and Colleges,* ed. D. R. Jones, V. L. Meek, and J. Anwyl. Parkville: Centre for the Study of Higher Education, University of Melbourne, 33–43.

———. 1998. "Economics and Policy-Making: The Case of the Higher Education Contribution Scheme." *Canberra Bulletin of Public Administration* 90 (December): 120–24.

Committee on Higher Education Funding (Wran Committee). 1988. *Report.* Canberra: Australian Government Publishing Service.

Dawkins, The Hon. J. S. 1987. *Higher Education: A Policy Discussion Paper.* Canberra: Australian Government Publishing Service.

———. 1988. *Higher Education: A Policy Statement* ('the white paper'), Canberra: Australian Government Publishing Service.

Department of Education, Training and Youth Affairs. 2001. *Higher Education Report for the 2001 to 2003 Triennium.* Canberra.

National Board of Employment, Education and Training. 1992. *Assessment of the Impact of the Higher Education Contribution Scheme on the Potentially Disadvantaged.* Canberra: Australian Government Publishing Service.

Robertson, F., and J. Sloan, J. 1990. *Impact of the Higher Education Contribution Scheme Survey Report: Victoria.* Adelaide: National Institute of Labour Studies.

Sydney Morning Herald. 2007. "Duffers at University," Editorial January 9.

Chapter 6

England and an Evolving Student Fees Scheme: Implications of Raising the Cap

Juliet Chester[1]

The appropriate balance of funding in higher education between the public sector (the taxpayer) and the private sector (students or graduates) has become a particularly prominent policy concern for the English government over the past decade. Two developments over this period have increased the contribution from the private sector in different ways: first, the introduction of an upfront contribution toward tuition fees in 1998–99; and second, the introduction of variable deferred fees from 2006–07. Both of these developments were linked to a widely recognized need to increase the resources of English higher education institutions following many years of underfunding: between 1976 and 1996 the unit of public funding per student fell by more than 40 percent.[2]

In 1996 the Conservative government commissioned the National Committee of Inquiry into Higher Education, led by Sir Ron Dearing. The "Dearing Report" was published in July 1997 and included among its recommendations that graduates should make a contribution equivalent to a quarter of their tuition costs through income-contingent loans. In that year, the Labor government decided in-

---

[1] Higher Education Policy Institute, Oxford, England.

[2] See Chart 3.16 in the Report of the National Committee of Inquiry into Higher Education ("Dearing Report"), available at <http://www.leeds.ac.uk/educol/ncihe/>.

stead to opt for upfront tuition fees for which no loans would be available to students,[3] but to provide full or partial fee remission to those from low-income households, so that around a third of students paid no fees. The Teaching and Higher Education Act 1998 required all English universities[4] to charge full-time "home" (U.K.) and European Union (E.U.) undergraduates an annual fee of £1,315 ($2,600)[5] from 1998–99. According to the government, this fee represented around a quarter of the cost of an average higher education course.[6] The act also ensured that grants for these students would be replaced by larger government maintenance loans, which would be repaid by students on an income-contingent basis.[7]

The introduction of student fees at this level nevertheless left a substantial continuing funding gap for universities in the United Kingdom. Universities U.K., whose members are executive heads of British higher education institutions, estimated in 2002 that these institutions would need around £9.9 billion ($19.7 billion) over the following three years to achieve financial stability.[8] In 2003, a government White Paper, "The Future of Higher Education," set out new plans for reform of, and investment in, higher education in England. The paper included the proposal that variable or "top-up" fees, for which government loans would be available, should replace upfront tuition fees for full-time home and E.U. students. There was substantial debate both within and outside the political parties over this element of the proposed reforms, and a number of amendments were made to the original proposals, including the introduction of additional maintenance support to

---

[3] Except where specified, the term student is used throughout this chapter to describe full-time English domiciled and E.U. domiciled undergraduate students at English universities. This includes both students pursuing first degree courses and those pursuing other undergraduate courses (e.g., Higher National Diplomas or Foundation degrees). The English government is responsible for providing support in the forms of loans and grants to these students.

[4] Throughout this chapter, the term university is used to describe publicly funded higher education institutions in England, a list of which is available at <http://www.hefce.ac.uk/unicoll/HE/>.

[5] All figures in this chapter are uprated to 2010–11 prices, assuming an inflation rate of 2.5 percent per annum. In 1998–99 terms, the tuition fee was £1,000 ($1,977). Dollar conversions assume an exchange rate of $1.977 to £1 (exchange rate on 27 May 2008). Where figures are rounded in the text, the dollar conversion is based on the original figure, which is then rounded in the same way as the U.K. pound values.

[6] <http://www.direct.gov.uk/en/EducationAndLearning/UniversityAndHigherEducation/StudentFinance/FinanceAfterYourFirstYear/DG_070200>.

[7] This arrangement was modified in 2004–05, when the higher education grant was introduced. This is worth up to a maximum of £1,000 ($1,977) and is therefore significantly less generous than the maintenance grant introduced as part of the Higher Education Act 2004.

[8] <http://www.universitiesuk.ac.uk/Newsroom/Media-Releases/Pages/MediaRelease-326.aspx>.

help students from low-income households. In January 2004 the English Parliament, by a narrow majority, enacted the government's Higher Education Bill, which abolished upfront tuition fees for students and instead allowed universities to charge variable fees of between £0 and £3,300 ($6,524) a year from 2006–07.[9] Income-contingent loans are now available to all full-time home and E.U. students up to the value of their fees and are paid directly to the student's university. This means that although students may face higher overall costs, they need only pay their contribution toward tuition once they have graduated and are earning over the income threshold set by the government. These loans are offered at zero real rate of interest and any sum remaining unpaid after 25 years will be written off. In addition, the Higher Education Act 2004 introduced more generous support towards living costs—in the form of a government maintenance grant worth up to £2,980 ($5,891)—for English students from lower-income households. The 2004 reforms therefore also implied an additional commitment of public expenditure to student support. Since the enactment of these reforms, the other major political parties have published detailed alternative policies for the funding of universities and students. In September 2004, for example, the Conservative party announced it would abolish tuition fees and increase the value of maintenance loans, which would be offered by banks at market interest rates.[10] More recently, however, the Conservatives have indicated support for the continuation of student contributions through tuition fees.[11] Although universities have been free to charge fees between £0 and £3,300 to students starting courses since 2006–07 onwards, around 98 percent of first degree students are in fact paying the maximum fee.[12] In other words, there is essentially a new standard fee for most undergraduate courses rather than a market in fee levels.

Where universities differ significantly, however, is in the financial aid they provide to students from lower-income households, to offset the additional cost implied by higher fees. The government required all universities charging the maximum fee to offer minimum bursaries of £320 ($633) to students with a full government grant. But almost all universities have chosen to go beyond this

---

[9] In 2006–07 terms the fee was £3,000 ($5,931).

[10] Conservative Research Department, Funding the Future: A Conservative Policy for Universities and Students, 2004. These proposals were published in the run-up to the general election in May 2005. The other main political party in the U.K., the Liberal Democrats, also published proposals for higher education funding in January 2005: Liberal Democrats, *The Key to Life-Long Learning*, Policy Briefing no. 4, 2005, <http://www.ibdems.org.uk/media/documents/policies/04higherandfurthereducation.pdf>.

[11] See, for example, <http://news.bbc.co.uk/1/hi/education/4594836.stm>.

[12] In 2006–07 only eight universities charged less than the maximum fee for their full-time first degree courses. Based on current student numbers at each university, around 98 percent of first year home and E.U. first degree students were therefore charged the maximum fee. One university charging £2,750 ($5,437) in 2006–07 decided to charge the full fee of £3,300 from 2007–08.

minimum level, with many providing both significantly higher bursaries to the poorest students and additional bursaries to those in receipt of partial government grants. In the first year of the variable fee regime, universities spent 21.4 percent of their additional fee income[13] on financial support for lower income home and E.U. students.[14]

In 2009 the government will commission a review of the system of higher education funding and student support introduced in England in 2006. It is possible, although by no means certain, that the maximum fee that universities will be permitted to charge students (the fee cap) will rise following this review.[15] This chapter considers some of the implications of any such rise without a commensurate increase in commitment of public expenditure by the English government.[16] It does not discuss whether such a scenario would be the "right" one in future, but it acknowledges the arguments that are likely to be made in favor of an increased fee cap and the cost to the English Treasury of maintaining current arrangements for student support.

The current system of higher education funding in England is, taken as a whole, possibly the most progressive in the world. It recognizes that graduates have benefited from their higher education, and so should pay; it involves no fee payment upfront so none are excluded because of parental means; it ensures that no one is required to repay loans if they are not earning sufficiently to be able to do so; it protects the position of women and others taking a career break by writing off loans not repaid after a period; it provides maintenance loans for all, and it provides for generous cash grants for poor—and indeed now not so poor—English students.[17] In contrast to the United States, where detailed assessments of parental

---

[13] Additional fee income is defined as any income from home and E.U. tuition fees above the standard fee level set by the government

[14] This figure is based on data collected by the Office for fair access (OFFA), which was established in the Higher Education Act (2004) to safeguard access to higher education for underrepresented groups in the light of higher fees (see OFFA 2008/01, available at <http://www.offa.org.uk/about/publications/>). Lower-income students are defined as students with assessed household income of £52,330 ($103,456) or less (in 2010 terms). The vast majority of institutions offered financial support to U.K. students but not to E.U. students.

[15] Under the terms of the Higher Education Act 2004, the earliest possible date for parliamentary approval of any such proposal is January 1, 2010.

[16] Note that throughout this chapter references to the government and its expenditure relate to the English government only and not to the devolved administrations in the United Kingdom (Scotland, Wales, and Northern Ireland). This expenditure includes English-domiciled and E.U.-domiciled students only.

[17] The latest reforms to student finance, announced in July 2007, expanded the definition of the poorest students by raising the income threshold for receipt of the full grant by around £7,000 ($13,839). These reforms also indicate an increased concern with the financial needs of students from middle-income families (with annual income of

ability to pay are the bedrock of student finance, the English system is designed to keep assessed household contributions to a minimum. Household contributions are only assessed if students apply for means-tested support (part of the maintenance loans and other supplementary benefits). The maximum assessed contribution from a family living in England with two children and an income of £75,000 ($148,275) would be around £3,800 (around $7,500) per year.[18]

All this is admirable. However, it is expensive for the government to provide support at this level, and if fee levels increase, it would become more expensive unless some modifications are made to the current system.

Impact of the 2009 Review

Although the outcome of the 2009 review at the time of writing this essay cannot be predicted, there are likely to be influential voices in both the higher education sector and the government arguing for a rise in the maximum fee—the former to generate more revenue for their universities and the latter to encourage the variability in fee levels that does not exist at present, and which they have said is needed to stimulate improvements in the quality of the courses on offer. On the other hand it cannot be assumed that the government will increase the amount it provides to subsidize the provision of fee and maintenance loans at no real rate of interest. This will be a difficult circle to square.

Even if it agrees to an increase in current fee levels, the government is unlikely to sanction the operation of an entirely unregulated market by declining to set a fee cap. It is true that despite the concerns that some expressed when fees were first introduced in 1998, and again at the time of the 2006 reforms, the existence of fees has not had any noticeable impact on enrollment in higher education—by any social group (although it is still too early to form any definite conclusion about the 2006 reforms). Nevertheless, that does not mean that fees, whatever their level, would have no such impact in future. Part of the benign impact hitherto is undoubtedly due to the level at which the government subsidizes loans for fees—ensuring that they accrue a zero percent real terms rate of interest—and also the general repayment and grant and loan mechanisms. The government has to continue to be deeply concerned with the level of fees—to do otherwise, and

---

c.£40,000-c.£60,000 (c.$79,080-c.118,620), who from 2008 will become eligible for partial grants and enhanced loans.

[18] This figure assumes deductions are made for pension allowances and for one dependent child. A full explanation of the assumptions behind this calculation is available in Chester and Bekhradnia, "Funding Higher Fees," Annex A. The English system for calculating household contributions takes no account of assets, only of household income.

allow an unregulated market, would run counter to the direction taken by govern-ments in almost every other country with tuition fees.

Two levels of higher fee cap are therefore illustrated in this chapter—£5,000 ($9,885) and £7,000 ($13,839). Neither is thought to be the "right" level, but both are considered to be reasonable assumptions for the purpose of illustrating the policy options described here. The chapter also employs some working assump-tions about the average fee for full-time home and E.U. undergraduates in English universities under each of these fee caps.[19]

The Effect of Higher Fees:
Government Funding of Student Borrowing

The present arrangements for subsidizing student borrowing are expensive for the government. Its most recent published estimates suggest that the Resource Accounting and Budgeting (RAB) charge on tuition and maintenance loans for English and E.U. students—in other words, the cost of providing these loans at no real rate of interest, requiring repayments only at rates graduates can afford when working, and writing off unpaid debts after 25 years—is likely to exceed £1.4 billion ($2.7 billion) per annum in steady state. This is equivalent to at least 33 pence for every £1 of tuition fee loan—a 33 percent subsidy—and 21 pence for every £1 of maintenance loan.[20] When the cost of maintenance grants and hardship support is added to this, estimated taxpayer expenditure on student support for full-time English and E.U. undergraduates amounts to £2.6 billion ($5.1 billion) per annum in steady state. By way of comparison, £1.3 billion ($2.5 billion) was spent on student support in 2003–04. This means that finan-cial support for students is representing an increasing proportion of public spending on higher education in England. By 2010–11, the government expects

---

[19] Further explanation of these assumptions is available in Chester and Bekhradnia, "Funding higher Fees," 7.

[20] The latest published RAB figures from the U.K. Government's Department for Innovation, Universities and Skills (DIUS) are available at <http://www.publications.parliament.uk/pa/ld200506/ldhansrd/vo051110/text/51110-25.htm> "Education Finance." The RAB charge also includes deaths and defaults. DIUS has not yet published figures that reflect the estimated additional cost of the graduate repayment "holidays" announced in 2007. The cost of these is difficult to predict since it will depend on how many stu-dents take up the option of a repayment "holiday" and when they choose to do so, but may lead to RAB charges on fee and maintenance loans of 36 percent and 26 percent respectively. Given the purpose of this chapter, which is to illustrate the issue rather than to provide firm figures, and the uncertainty of these estimates, this chapter uses the latest published figures on RAB percentages, together with figures on the cost of maintenance loans and grants provided directly by DIUS.

24.7 percent of spending on higher education to be in the form of student loan subsidies, grants and hardship support, compared to 17.2 percent in 2003–04.[21]

Even under the current fee regime these costs would increase if, for example, the government were to reform the current system of funding for the growing number of part-time students in English universities, and offer them access to the same loans and grants on a pro-rata basis as full-time students.[22] The development of a system of funding appropriate to a changing landscape of higher education participation is a serious policy consideration. This chapter focuses, however, on a more specific issue: the implications for the current system of funding for students implied by raising the fee cap. For the purposes of this chapter it is assumed that the government would continue to commit current levels of public expenditure to student borrowing. The chapter does not, therefore, reconsider the arguments about the appropriateness of the current level of interest subsidy, which were, in any case, fully rehearsed at the time of the 2003 Higher Education White Paper, and which the government rejected.[23]

Future Options

The discussion so far has shown how expensive the present arrangements are for the taxpayer. The remainder of this chapter explores possible ways in which the Government could raise the fee cap without any increase in public expenditure beyond current commitments. Of course, it would be perfectly possible for the government to increase the provision of subsidized loans (although there are

---

[21] These figures are based on spending within Departmental Expenditure Limits, taken from the latest DIUS departmental report (May 2008) (Table 11, available at <http://www.dius.gov.uk/docs/about/21076_DIUS   percent20AR&A_Web_NEW.pdf>). Figures have been uprated where appropriate to 2010 prices. For the purposes of this chapter, the RAB charge on maintenance and fee loans, student support grants, and access (hardship) funds and bursaries are defined as student support, but the figures here exclude the cost of administering student support and the student loans management of provision.

[22] England's Secretary of State for Innovation, Universities, and Skills recently announced an overarching review of the English higher education sector, with a view to developing a 10–15 year framework for its expansion and development. Some consideration of the appropriate resources to support an increase in the proportion of part-time students is likely to feature in this review (see <http://www.dius.gov.uk/speeches/denham_hespeech_290208.html>).

[23] For a full explanation of these arguments see N. Barr, "Higher Education Funding," *Oxford Review of Economic Policy* 20:2 (2004): 264–83. It is recognized, of course, that this argument is likely to be restated in the run-up to the 2009 review and that there are a number of issues that are likely to be subject to further scrutiny (for example, where any money saved from removing the interest subsidy might be most appropriately targeted). A detailed review of these issues is, however, beyond the scope of this chapter.

strong arguments against even the present level of subsidy). The costs of this would, however, be significant: the RAB charge increases as the total debt rises, which means that the estimated 33 percent RAB charge on current student tuition fee loans would increase with a higher fee cap. Based on the assumptions made here about average fees across the sector, the RAB charge might increase by around £200 million ($390 million) per year with a fee cap of £5,000 and by £320 million ($640 million) with a cap of £7,000. That is effectively the base option, but it is not considered further here.

Putting on one side the possibility that the government would be willing to increase the subsidy of student borrowing, four possible approaches (Options A to D below) are considered, each of which entails different measures to try to ensure stability in taxpayer costs.

Option A

Option A would be for the government to continue to make fully subsidized loans available for the whole tuition fee (up to the maxima considered here of £5,000 and £7,000) but for part of the fee paid by students to be used to cover the cost of subsidizing additional loans. Any university charging average fees above the current maximum would pass to the government—possibly by a reduction in the HEFCE grant—a sum equivalent to the estimated RAB charge on additional borrowing. This would effectively mean that some of the additional income from students would be channeled to the government, and back to graduates via a higher loan subsidy.

Table 6.1 illustrates the effect of this option for a university of average size charging the maximum permissible fee on all its courses under the scenarios of £5,000 and £7,000 fee caps.[24] It shows the net increase in total fee income compared with the total under the current fee cap and the proportion of new fee income retained when the amount passed to the government is taken into account.

This arrangement would reduce the net benefit to a university charging £5,000 fees, from an additional 51.5 percent (compared to its income from fees of £3,300) to 35.2 percent. With fees of £7,000 the net benefit would decrease from 112.1 percent to 75.3 percent. Such a university would therefore retain 68.3 percent of the new fee income with a £5,000 fee cap and 67.2 percent with a £7,000 cap. This option could be attractive to students, as it would use a portion of the fee they pay to subsidize their loans. But it is safe to predict that universities would

---

[24] The calculations in the table are based on an assumed RAB charge of 41 percent on additional borrowing under a £5,000 fee cap and an RAB charge of 42.5 percent on additional borrowing under a £7,000 fee cap. These estimates are consistent with estimates provided by the DIUS, given the average fees assumed in this chapter under a £5,000 and £7,000 fee cap.

Table 6.1. Impact of Option A on Fee Income for Average University

Current fee cap

	£3,300 fees	£3,300 fees
Total fee income (£m)	23.5	23.5

Revised fee cap

	£5,000 fees	£7,000 fees
Total fee income (£m)	35.6	49.8
New fee income (£m)	12.1	26.3
Gross increase in fee income	51.5%	112.1%
Estimated additional borrowing (£m)	9.3	20.3
Amount passed to Government (£m)	3.8	8.6
Net increase in fee income	35.2%	75.3%
Proportion of new fee income retained by university	68.3%	67.2%

oppose such an arrangement, which would reduce the benefit they would derive from charging a higher fee.

Option B

Option B, which would allow universities to retain all of any new income from fees, would be to offer students unsubsidized loans to cover the cost of fees above £3,300 per year. A student on a three-year course might therefore, when they graduate, have up to three loans to repay at two different rates of interest: The first two would be the loan for the first £9,900 ($19,572) of the total fee and the total loan for maintenance, both of which would accrue interest only at the rate of inflation. The third would be a loan for the additional fee above £3,300 per year (a "top-up" loan), which would accrue a real rate of interest. The rate of interest on the top-up loan for students pursuing the most expensive courses might therefore be substantially higher than the rate of interest on the remaining loans.

This option would mean that graduates of courses charging higher fees could face both larger loan debts and additional interest payments. Because students from lower-income households would be more likely to meet the cost of any higher fee through the top-up loan rather than through household contributions, one disadvantage of this option is that it might reduce the likelihood of these students choosing courses for which the highest fees are charged. It might be necessary therefore to consider modifying the current mechanisms of student loan repayments—for example, by increasing the proportion of monthly income repaid towards the loan—to reduce the interest payable.

The introduction of differential terms for student borrowing would have other problems. For example, the taxpayer could end up paying more if financially literate students with a substantial institutional bursary or household contribution towards maintenance costs nevertheless took out additional maintenance loans, which would be available on more favorable terms, in order to cover the total cost of fees through subsidized loans.

Option C

Option C, which would prevent some students paying such high rates of interest on part of their loans, would be to spread the current level of subsidy across the whole of the higher borrowing that follows from a higher maximum fee—without making a distinction between loans up to £3,300 and those above this level. All students would take out all their loans—for fees as well as maintenance—on the same terms. Table 6.2 illustrates the effect this would have on the value of the subsidy (RAB charge) as a proportion of total borrowing and, therefore, the real rate of interest implied for any student borrowing.

Because the RAB charge increases with the level of debt, the reduction in the subsidy is more substantial with a £7,000 fee cap than with a £5,000 fee cap. Under the assumptions in Table 6.2, maintaining the current level of taxpayer subsidy on fee and maintenance loans (approximately £1.4 billion) with a fee cap of £5,000 would require the overall subsidy to reduce from 27.5 percent to 24.1 percent of the value of the total loan.[25] This is equivalent to a 12.6 percent reduction in the total subsidy. With a £7,000 fee cap the subsidy would reduce from 28.3 percent to 23.0 percent of the total loan, which is equivalent to a 19.2 percent reduction in the subsidy.

---

[25] As in Table 6.1, the calculations in Table 6.2 are based on an assumed RAB charge of 41 percent on additional borrowing under a £5,000 fee cap and an RAB charge of 42.5 percent on additional borrowing under a £7,000 fee cap.

Table 6.2. Impact of Option C on Student Borrowing

	£3,300 cap	£5,000 cap	£7,000 cap
FULL SUBSIDY			
Total combined fee & maintenance loan (£m)	5,160	5,640	5,920
Combined RAB charge on total fee & maintenance loans	26.3%	27.5%	28.3%
Cost of combined RAB charge on total fee & maintenance loans (£m)	1,360	1,550	1,680
REDUCED SUBSIDY			
Total combined fee & maintenance loan (£m)	5,160	5,640	5,920
Combined RAB charge on total fee & maintenance loans	26.3%	24.1%	23.0%
Cost of combined RAB charge on total fee & maintenance loans (£m)	1,360	1,360	1,360
Reduction in subsidy	0.0%	12.6%	19.2%
Estimated real rate of interest on any student loan	0.0%	0.3%	0.5%

This would mean that all students would pay a small real rate of interest, including those not paying a higher fee. On the assumption that a 100 percent reduction in the original subsidy would require a real interest rate of around 2.5 percent,[26] then a proportional real terms interest rate with fee caps of £5,000 and £7,000 and a reduced subsidy would need to be around 0.3 percent and 0.5 percent respectively.

---

[26] The discount rate on student loans is currently 2.2 percent but the rate of interest would need to take into account the longer period it would take graduates to pay off loans of equivalent value compared with current arrangements and the additional unpaid debt with an increased loan program (assuming repayment rates remained at their current level). Note that the use of a real terms interest rate of 2.5 percent above inflation to eliminate the taxpayer subsidy has been used in recent modeling by the Institute for Fiscal Studies (Dearden et al., *Higher education Funding Reforms in England*, 23–24).

This model would therefore entail those paying lower fees subsidizing those paying higher fees. This approach might well encounter some resistance from students, since it would result in increased costs for all students, including those opting for cheaper courses, in order to help pay for those on courses charging the higher fees. The additional borrowing associated with each above-inflation rise in the average fee charged across the sector would reduce the subsidy and increase standard interest rates for all students.

Option D

Option D is one in which the government allows the maximum fee level to rise but there is no government loan beyond the current fully subsidized maximum. This would mean that, in contrast to the previous three options, some students would no longer be able to defer all of their fee payments as they would not have access to sufficient loans to do so.[27] This option would certainly require substantial financial aid from universities to ensure that these students were not excluded because of financial constraints. Option D might therefore require more detailed assessments of a household's ability to pay or at least some evidence-based guidance as to what might constitute reasonable expected contributions from households at different income levels.

It might be thought that Option D has little to commend it. However, this option might be attractive to the government if it were felt that additional upfront payments, household contributions, and financial assistance from universities were more likely to gain parliamentary support than an increase in student borrowing and the changes to the present system that this might require.

Fee Waivers

The issues surrounding bursaries and maintenance support more generally are not addressed in this chapter. However, if part of the fee had to be paid upfront (Option D in the foregoing analysis) then some system of fee waivers would be necessary to ensure that potential students without the available means to pay part of the fee upfront were not prevented from attending those universities that charged higher fees. This could eat substantially into the benefit that universities derived from higher fees.

Unlike Option D, the other options for covering the higher fee that have been discussed (Options A through C), assume that the full fee would be covered by a

---

[27] Although as with Option B, some students might use maintenance loans to pay all or part of any additional fee. Again this would risk increasing taxpayer expenditure above current levels.

government loan of some kind. From a strictly logical perspective, therefore, it might be thought that there would be no need for students from lower-income households to receive fee waivers as part of a package of financial support, since the higher fee could be covered by additional borrowing, repayable only when the student had graduated and was working.

However, students from lower-income households would be taking a greater risk than their peers from better-off families: If their earnings after graduation were lower than anticipated they would have no family cushion, and even while they were at university they would have less prospect of family support. Government and universities would be concerned that such students might be deterred from applying to the most expensive courses by the additional cost incurred, even if this cost were deferred until after graduation.

One way of addressing this would be to provide fee waivers to students in receipt of substantial government grants. Table 6.3 shows what this would mean in terms of additional financial support for students at illustrative income levels, and with fees of £5,000 and £7,000, if English students in receipt of the full grant received a full fee waiver on any fee above the current maximum and those with incomes up to around £41,800 (around $82,600) received a partial waiver proportionate to their grant.[28]

Table 6.4 below shows the effect of these fee waivers on universities of average size charging the maximum permitted fee on all courses. The table shows the estimated cost of fee waivers with £5,000 and £7,000 fees and the proportion of new fee income retained by such universities once these payments to students are taken into account. The cost of these fee waivers would naturally depend on the distribution of incomes among the student body. Table 2.4.4 therefore illustrates the different effects on fee income for a university with a "standard" distribution of student incomes (an average proportion from low income households); a university with a significant number of students concentrated at the "high end" of the income distribution (and thus a small proportion of students from low-income households); and a university with a significant number of students concentrated at the "low end" of the income distribution (and thus a large proportion of students from low-income households).[29]

Table 2.4.4 shows that the estimated cost of the fee waivers described above might leave an average university with less than 60 percent of any new fee income. Even a university with relatively few low-income students would spend

---

[28] This income level is the current government threshold (in 2010 terms) below which no household contributions are assessed for any of the means-tested benefits available to full-time English undergraduates starting courses in 2008–09. An explanation of the methodology for determining these fee waivers can be found in Chester and Bekhradnia, "Funding Higher Fees," Annex B.

[29] A description of the distribution of student incomes for each of these models can be found in Chester and Bekhradnia, "Funding higher Fees," Annex C.

Table 6.3. Fee Waivers Proportionate to Government Grant

Residual household income (£)	Fee waiver (£5,000 fee) (£)	Fee waiver (£7,000 fee) (£)
26,270	1,700	3,700
27,500	1,581	3,441
30,000	1,340	2,916
32,500	1,098	2,390
35,000	856	1,863
37,500	703	1,530
40,000	635	1,381
41,800	585	1,272

Table 6.4. Cost of Fee Waivers to Average University

	Fee waivers with £5,000 fees (£m)	Fee waivers with £7,000 fees (£m)	Proportion of new fee income retained by university
"Standard" income distribution	5.0	11.0	58.3%
"High end" concentration	2.4	5.1	80.5%
"Low end"' concentration	6.4	14.0	46.8%

around 20 percent of any additional fees on these measures. It can be seen, therefore, that the level of student support that any post-2009 fee increase would require would substantially attenuate the benefit to universities charging a higher fee. In addition, of course, if Option A were the chosen approach for restraining the cost to government of increased student loans, then the benefit to universities would be reduced further.

Conclusion

The present arrangements for student contributions to the funding of universities are highly progressive, but expensive: Every £1 of fee loan costs the taxpayer at least 33 pence. So the greater the total amount of fee raised by universities, at present, the greater the government's financial commitment. It cannot be taken for granted that the government will be willing to increase this commitment, even if universities are permitted to charge higher fees in future.

This chapter has therefore examined how the system might be modified in ways that would allow for a higher fee cap but without increasing the public spending commitment to student support. The first option considered here would involve a portion of the income from universities charging higher fees being used to help pay for continued fully subsidized loans. The remaining three options involve some move away from the principle of a fully subsidized loan for students up to the maximum fee.

One of the options considered would require students to pay part of the fee upfront. This would represent a major break with the principles of the 2006 reforms, which established that no student would have to rely on their family for any part of the cost of tuition. Additional financial support from universities would therefore be vital to help ensure that no student is excluded from a course because of financial constraints.

In fact, it is suggested here that some form of fee waivers might be appropriate even if loans remain available up to the maximum fee permitted. This is because students from poor families are taking a greater risk than students from better-off families when they take on the commitments implied by going to university. For example, if future income is not realized at the hoped-for level, then that will hit students from poor families harder than others. They are taking a greater risk in a very real sense and it is not simply a question of attitudes to debt; it is real and differential risk. That, of course, is the case under the present fee regime, but would become more of an issue if fees rise. The chapter has therefore briefly explored the financial implications of providing fee waivers in proportion to the government grant on any fee above the current maximum to students from lower income households. It concludes that the benefit to universities that charge a higher fee post-2009 would be greatly attenuated by the level of fee waivers that would be required.

Chapter 7

The Big Curve: Trends in University Fees and Financing in the E.U. and U.S.

John Aubrey Douglass
Ruth Keeling Sobótka[1]

Globally, fees and tuition are growing as a source of income for most universities and with potentially significant influences on the market for students and the behavior of institutions. The current financial meltdown is, in fact, exacerbating this trend. Thus far, however, it is difficult to find comprehensive data on the fee rates of comparative and often competitive research universities, nor is there information on how these funds are being used by institutions. Research on tuition pricing has also focused largely on bachelor's degree programs, and not on the rapid changes in professional degrees. This chapter offers a brief scan of pricing trends among a sample group of 24 public and private research universities in the U.S., all with a wide array of graduate and professional programs, and a small sample group of E.U. universities. We trace a pattern of convergence

[1] John Aubrey Douglass, Center for Studies in Higher Education, UC Berkeley. Ruth Keeling Sobótka, Coordinator, European Education Policy Network, University of Cambridge. The authors wish to thank Jackie Bass, graduate student in political science at UC Berkeley, for her research assistance in the collection and organization of U.S. data for 2007. A version of this paper was published in the Center for Studies in Higher Education's Research and Occasional Paper Series, November 2008.

between not only U.S. public and private institutions, but also among E.U. universities (or at least an indicator that this is occurring).

We theorize that pricing among major research universities is increasingly influenced by a sense of what the market will bear, with a convergence in pricing driven in part by the perception that price equals quality for consumers, and hence prestige, and by perceived opportunity costs associated with not raising tuition and fees. This is all part of a big curve toward a restructuring of higher education financing, particularly among public universities, in which tuition and fees is becoming the largest single new source of money—much greater than corporate-generated research grants, gifts, and other private-sector sources. As we show here, this appears to be leading to the slow emergence of a global pricing system for higher education. The 2008 implosion in credit markets may seriously shake this emerging pricing model, in large part because it is increasingly dependent on students taking out sizable loans. But it is our sense that the long-term trends in pricing, including some level of convergence, will continue as institutions that are globally competitive look over their shoulder at what their perceived peer (or near peer) institution is charging for specific degrees and programs. This in turn will influence the entire higher education market.

The shifting focus on tuition and fees as a major component in expanding national higher education systems, and for fulfilling the ambitions of individual campuses, relates in part to a substantial shift in perceptions. A 2005 statement by the E.U. Commission on *Mobilising the Brainpower of Europe: Enabling Universities to Make Their Full Contribution to the Lisbon Strategy*, exposes the cultural shift among many nations that once adhered to a strict ideal of no-tuition higher education.

> The debate on social and private returns from higher education has highlighted its role as an investment benefiting both the individual (through higher income and status) and society as a whole (through higher employment rates, lower social costs and later retirement). It has been shown that free higher education does not by itself suffice to guarantee equal access and maximum enrollments. This casts the much-debated issue of tuition fees in a fresh perspective. In the consultation, those universities arguing for higher fees suggested that a major benefit would be higher quality education. Some analysts also point out that tuition fees could in practice provide better access for students from lower-income groups if the incremental funds were recycled into a sound student aid system. Given the differences between national systems, there can be no uniform response to this issue: each Member State needs to choose the approach best suited to its circumstances.[2]

This "fresh perspective" on the desirability of tuition fees is a worldwide trend and cultural shift of significant proportions. Increasingly, national systems

---

[2] Commission of the European Communities (2005). *Mobilising the Brainpower of Europe: Enabling Universities to Make Their Full Contribution to the Lisbon Strategy*, Brussels.

of higher education and their postsecondary institutions are adopting or increasing fees and tuition as a key funding resource. The reasons are multiple. For publicly funded institutions, still the dominant provider of tertiary education throughout the world, there are the unit costs related to expanding enrollment and services; there are generally rising costs related to academic research and the costs of funding highly paid professional labor. At the same time, there is increasing competition for public funds.

These factors are helping to create a new public university paradigm that includes four basic assumptions.

(1) At current tax levels, governments can no longer afford to be the primary or nearly sole source of revenues for public higher education, and market-related solutions to funding seem inevitable.

(2) Fee income will need to be an increasingly large component of the funding of higher education to replace declining government/taxpayer subsidization.

(3) The expanded responsibility of private/individual funding of public higher education assumes that there are both private and social benefits of higher education.

(4) More robust need-based financial aid programs and tax policies will mitigate economic barriers to a college or university education and avoid the current benefit transfer from low to high income families created by universal low tuition.

In the following, we explore the tuition pricing trends among a select group of U.S. public and private research universities, and a smaller sample of E.U. research universities—all with major and highly marketable graduate and professional school programs (see Table 7.1). In light of the dearth of analysis on the emerging curve toward fee income among public institutions, we see this as an initial set of data and observations that build on a previous study and article, and with the primary focus on pricing, rather than exploring what are now highly complex bursary systems and the net cost to a student. A focus on pricing provides a window into why and how universities are approaching financing, their market perception, and the political constraints faced by public institutions.[3]

Framing our discussion of pricing trends is a form of convergence among nations and their public universities in pricing, despite long political and cultural opposition. Increasingly, research universities throughout the world, and at different paces:

- Seek a greater *Diversity of Funding Sources*, rather than simply relying on government to provide the vast majority of funds, as in the initial era of building most mass higher education systems. This is already widely understood as

---

[3] We will expand our E.U. sample size considerably with the administration of a new on-line survey of universities this spring, starting with those institutions that are part of the League of European Research Universities. This online survey and further information about this transatlantic project is available at <http://cshe.berkeley.edu/research/fees-survey.htm>.

Table 7.1. Sample Group of Universities. Tuition and Fee Trends

U.S. Public	U.S. Private	E.U. Universities
Michigan State	Cornell-endowed	Oxford Univ.
Ohio State	Baylor Univ.	Cambridge Univ.
Pennsylvania State	Brown Univ.	University College London
SUNY at Albany	Harvard Univ.	Univ of Edinburgh
Univ. of Texas at Austin	MIT	Univ. of Amsterdam
Univ. of Alabama	New York Univ.	Univ. of Leuven
Univ. of California, Berkeley	Stanford Univ.	
Univ. of Illinois	Univ. of Chicago	
Univ. of Michigan	Univ. of Pennsylvania	
Univ. of Minnesota	Univ. of Southern California	
Univ. of Missouri, Columbia	Yale Univ.	
Univ. of Wisconsin, Madison		
Univ. of Virginia		

a major new development vital for most higher education institutions—and in particular research universities.

- Pursue a *Moderate Fee and High Financial Aid Model*, with the fundamental concept that tuition and various fees form a means for generating new resources for universities, and for facilitating income redistribution and the support of lower-income students and others from disadvantaged backgrounds. Most institutions charge students and their families, with these fees now representing between 10 to 30 percent (or higher) of an institution's total revenues. Discussion and analysis of the introduction of fees, or their expansion, should always be accompanied by their potential use to substantially defray costs for underprivileged students and other targeted populations.[4]

There will be exceptions; some nation-states may keep the older paradigm of a university education being an entitlement, subsidized primarily by the state. But they will increasingly need to rationalize their policies in the wake of global trends and limitations on government financing of higher education.

---

[4] These predictions on fees and access are part of a larger framework of predicted "Structured Opportunity Market," a convergence in higher education policy outlined in John Aubrey Douglass (December 2007), "A Look into a Possible Future: A Global Scenario for Higher Education Systems, Global University Network for Innovation, UNESCO, <http://web.guni2005.upc.es/news/detail.php?id=1141>.

Pricing and Objectives—A Few New Rules to the Game

The recent changes in tuition rates reflect a substantial change in the traditional understanding of how tuition fees relate to the overall objectives of universities and their many academic programs. The theoretical model often expressed in some form by public and private nonprofit universities that have been chartered or officially recognized by national and regional governments, and that receive substantial public funds, implies that tuition fees are or should be directly related to university costs. Under this model, fees and tuition contribute to the operating and capital costs of teaching, research, and community service programs. There is not only a link with the enrollment capacity and quality of programs benefiting from various funding sources, but also an assumption of a general balance between revenue and costs.

If revenue exceeds costs, there is the expectation that the excess funds will either be used in succeeding years to balance budgets or to pay for academic program expansion related to the social contract of institutions (such as expanding enrollment capacity or research capabilities related to socio-economic needs or institutional quality), or the funds might be used to lower costs to constituents (for example, student tuition rates or government expected rates of funding). This model defines a distinctly nonprofit venture.

Among the realities that presently tear at this model of public purpose and accountability are the following factors:

Bowen's Rule

All universities, and in particular major institutions with or seeking elite status, will use any and all funds they receive for the pursuit of perceived excellence and improvement. Research universities operate in a real and self-conceived environment of high competition—for undergraduate and graduate students, faculty, postdoctoral students, for high-level administrative staff (although this is often seen as a less decisive factor); in the domain of research expertise and productivity, and more generally for influence on society, on the economy, and the political sphere.

In one of the first systematic looks at the financing of higher education, economist Howard Bowen outlined this basic tenet of the academic enterprise: essentially, there is never enough money to seek sufficient prestige and simultaneously to fulfill the varied objective and subjective roles of universities.[5]

---

[5] See Howard R. Bowen, *The Costs of Higher Education*, Carnegie Council for Policy Studies in Higher Education (San Francisco: Jossey-Bass Publishers, 1980).

Financial Insecurity Rule

All public and private institutions face a fundamental degree of uncertainty about their total funding for coming fiscal years, which influences their behavior in setting tuition and fee rates. In the public sector this is a more recent phenomenon with the overall decline in the willingness of governments to fund higher education via previously fairly stable systematic methods—usually related to enrollment workload or some form of basic funding covering most operating costs.

As governments have adopted more market-driven approaches to funding of some government services while simultaneously facing rising costs for entitlement programs (e.g., pensions, health care) and a general reluctance to raise revenue (deemed antimarket in the U.S.), the uncertainty facing public universities has grown considerably. Government and university leaders assume that the old funding paradigm is dead and that the answer is for universities to seek a more diverse portfolio of revenue sources. Tuition and fees have emerged as the largest single and marginally acceptable stopgap measure. The volatility of the funding picture, combined with political constraints on setting tuition levels for in-state students (or in the case of Europe, E.U. members), and significant concern and lack of knowledge about the possible impact on middle- and lower-income student access, make the setting of tuition rates a complex political activity.

Where possible, public universities seek to maximize tuition increases—because of budgetary uncertainty, and because of Bowen's Rule—while governments tend to want to minimize rate increases because of their fear of political retribution by voters and interest groups who still largely see public higher education as an entitlement, and perhaps to a lesser extent, because of real concern over access rates.

Private universities in the U.S. face a similar set of uncertainties, but with far fewer constraints. For one, they operate as separate corporate entities and they set their price independently (thus far) without political constraint or need for government sanction. They are in competition with public research universities for student tuition income and for federal and privately funded research grants (a large source of operating expenses for both publics and privates). But they also have no need or compulsion to grow and meet enrollment demand by society and, generally, have a highly valued market position that allows them to charge higher tuition rates. In the U.S., population growth and increasing overall demand for higher education means that high- and medium-prestige privates are finding increased demand for their limited enrollment capacity. Scarcity leads to the ability and desire to increase overall tuition rates—indeed at a rate higher than available for publics, according to the data we present in this chapter.

Pricing Equals Prestige Rule

Net pricing (ignoring for now scholarship and grant off-sets) is increasingly being influenced by what institutions and consumers see as its correlation with quality and prestige—often irrespective to its actual link. (This was one of the major findings of the previous Ward and Douglass study.) At the undergraduate level, selective privates have long disassociated the cost of actually enrolling a student with tuition rates and have engaged in a regular increase in these rates well beyond inflation and, most importantly, these privates have increased tuition in unison. There is very little variance in the tuition rates, including the cost of room and board, among private research universities and their private liberal arts counterparts.

One reason for this is that any setting of fees well below a group of real or perceived peers translates to lower quality *and* prestige to the respective institutions and consumers (students and their families)—a basic market phenomenon in many consumer products whether they be soap or cars. Another related reason: it means an unnecessary loss of revenue in a market that continues to experience rising demand. While the private university sector in the U.S. has long been subject to this phenomenon, the relatively new tuition framework of the Labor government in England and the reaction of higher education institutions again demonstrate this basic market impulse. In 2006, British universities were allowed to raise their tuition rates from £1,000 *up to* £3,000—a range that was supposed to encourage market pricing that depended on the student constituency, cost and quality of programs, and prestige. But instead of implementing a range of pricing, virtually all institutions set their tuition rate at the maximum allowed under government policy.

This "Pricing Equals Prestige" factor is now the major influence shaping pricing for graduate programs and, in particular, professional degree programs in both public and private institutions. Where there once was a general pricing scheme for undergraduates as well as graduates (circa 1960s), there now is a growing array of pricing schemes that depend not only on the program, but also on a relatively new desegregation of student clients—as more fully described below—and with an eye toward the pricing by real or perceived higher education competitors.

Student Client Differential Rule

While the pricing of programs in such fields as business and law appear increasingly related to "market price" and/or to "market value" than to institutional costs, another factor influencing public universities is the relatively new concept of differential pricing for students depending on their residency—or more exactly, depending on whether they are a *protected or nonprotected* client.

In the U.S., the states continue to be the key determinant of fees at public universities. They chartered all public higher education institutions, remain their single largest source of funding, and generally retain legal control or significant influence over tuition rates. There has been long been an understanding that public universities are to provide access primarily to state residents, and specifically students who are state taxpayers.[6] Public funds thus are intended to subsidize the educational costs for students from the state, placing a constraint on tuition rates charged to these *protected* students. Consequently, out-of-state students are deemed nonprotected, and tuition rates are to approximate the actual cost of educating the student—a difficult cost to determine as universities engage in such a wide variety of activities and cross-subsidization via different funding sources.

The net effect is that public universities in the U.S. have been given sanction by governments to set out-of-state fees for undergraduates on a relatively independent basis, in ways that are increasingly shaped by the market price of perceived competitors in other states. The primary reason governments have allowed this to occur is the general consensus for the need to enhance institutional revenues.

As part of the commitment to establish a European Higher Education Area (a goal of both the Bologna Declaration and the Lisbon Agreement), most, but not all, E.U.-member nations differentiate pricing for E.U. and non-E.U. students—in particular, a number of the Nordic countries. According to E.U. law, member states can no longer charge differential fees for domestic and foreign students, if these are also members of the E.U. (a *protected* constituency). But non-E.U. members may pay a much higher rate, again largely set independently by institutions according to perceived market price. Continental European universities are beginning to follow a pattern established by the United Kingdom, which has charged international students higher fees since the early 1980s (U.K. Education Fees and Awards Regulations 1983).

Hence, pricing for in-state students in the U.S., or for E.U. members in the U.K.,[7] is subject to different constraints and political considerations than for out-of-state and non-E.U. members. The nonprotected cohort is largely deemed as part of a larger world market of students, and pricing between public and private institutions, particularly in high-demand programs like in business administration, in medicine, in law, and in engineering, are subject to the "Price Equals Prestige" rule.

Further, and perhaps as a harbinger for other programs, many U.S. and some E.U. major public research universities have successfully asserted that their MBA programs are part of a world market and that there should be little or

---

[6] Indeed, most public universities have limited the number of "out-of-state" students; at the University of California, out-of-state and international students represent only five percent of all undergraduate enrollment.

[7] Unless otherwise stated, U.K. in this document refers to the U.K. higher education system of England, Northern Ireland, and Wales. Supported by parliamentary devolution, higher education developments in the U.K. (Scotland) have followed a slightly different path.

no distinction between protected and nonprotected clients. Gaining the authority from governments or governing bodies for this authority rests on now familiar rationales: one, the private benefits to students (on average), in the form of subsequent high average salaries for graduates; and two, that the costs for running programs, primarily in the form of higher faculty salaries to attract and retain top talent from the more lucrative private sector, require greater revenues.

Differential rates have another and relatively new wrinkle: While some countries cling to a "no tuition" policy, an increasing number of countries are charging tuition fees at some level. Some are experimenting with deferred tuition fees (including Australia, Scotland, New Zealand, Ethiopia, England, and Wales), many others (in 2007 including Australia, Egypt, Ethiopia, Hungary, Kenya, Poland, Romania, Russia, Tanzania, Uganda, and Vietnam) also offer "dual-track" tuition fees.[8] This last innovation includes offering a designated quota of students free tuition, based on criteria such as high entrance exam scores, and then offering the remaining enrollment spots at a designated nationally set tuition rate.

Privatization (Program Desegregation) Rule

Differential fee structures for programs within a university, and now also within programs themselves, are contributing to significantly new dynamics for setting tuition rates. Both private and public institutions are undergoing an erosion in the concept of single tuition rates and broad revenue sharing, shifting to an organizational structure in which a set of primarily professional schools desire to both independently raise tuition to perceived market prestige prices, *and* attempt to claim all or most additional resources as their own.

Disassociation of Price and Institutional Cost Rule

The net effect of all of these trends is a significant and growing disassociation between pricing and the actual costs of an educational program, a movement led by the U.S. privates, but now being mimicked throughout the public sector in the U.S., and now increasingly within the E.U. and other nations. Very new pricing schemes introduced at Harvard and Stanford and a few other selective privates, have, for the first time, set "progressive" pricing schemes that offer significant price discounts for students with family incomes of $60,000 or less, and with a lesser but still substantial discount for those under $120,000. Thus far, only eight elite privates have created progressive pricing schemes (Colum-

---

[8] For a survey of fee and tuition policies at the bachelor's level by various nations, see Pamela Marcucci and D. Bruce Johnstone, "Tuition Fee Policies in a Comparative Perspective: Theoretical and Political Rationales," *Journal of Higher Education Policy and Management*, vol. 29, no. 1 (March 2007).

bia, Harvard, Stanford, Yale, the University of Pennsylvania, Brown, MIT, and Duke) in addition to two selective publics (North Carolina and Virginia, with free tuition for students with family incomes below $40,000—the current federally designated poverty level).

The goal is to encourage more low-income *and* middle-class students to attend college by softening the financial blow of rising prices—costs that have caused Congress to launch investigations into the financing of what are often very wealthy institutions with large endowments. Essentially, this is a recognition by private elite institutions that they have very few low-income students and that, despite the claim of significant resources made available via bursaries for students once they enroll, pricing does influence the sense of affordability and ultimately access for students. In fact, most selective privates have only about ten percent or less of their students from low-income families, and there is a downward trend among Ivy League institutions. A similar trend exists among many, but not all, major public universities.[9] The University of California, for example, has around 30 percent of its undergraduate students with Pell Grants (a widely used indicator of low-income status), and the Berkeley campus alone enrolls more Pell Grant students than all the eight Ivy League institutions combined.[10]

Nearly unaffordable pricing for middle-class students may increasingly lower their access rates and lead to a political backlash. Private universities, as well as public institutions, are heavily reliant on largely federally funded financial aid, thereby providing an indirect subsidization of the privates.

Such progressive pricing schemes may well be a good policy response for both private and public universities, by essentially recognizing that pricing should relate to a student's ability to pay, and not simply relying on often complicated financial aid grants and loan packages which are, arguably, difficult to navigate for all potential students and their families, but in particular for lower-income groups. But this trend also means that pricing, and ultimately tuition and fee income, is not pegged to costs for educating a student—fee income is simply one source among many that funds the overall operation of a university.

Most of these trends can be seen in the U.S. and in an increasing number of E.U. countires; but they also are an expanding and perhaps permanent component in most other nascent and growing higher education systems.[11] The following provides a brief analysis of market changes and trends, again based on a sample group of major public and private research universities in the U.S., and a small sample group of E.U. institutions, that reflect the diversity of ap-

---

[9] Gerald Danette and Kati Haycock, *Engines of Inequality: Diminishing Equity in the Nation's Premier Public Universities*, The Education Trust, 2007.

[10] John Douglass and Gregg Thomson, "The Rich and the Poor: Economic Stratification among Undergraduates at the University of California," CSHE Research and Occasional Paper Series, CSHE 15.08 (October 2008).

[11] Marcucci and Johnstone "Tuition Fee Policies in a Comparative Perspective," (2007).

proaches—from a single tuition price for all programs, to a growing array of differential tuition rates.

Gauging the Change in U.S. Market Price: 2003–2007

National and supranational governments and agencies (such as the U.S. Department of Education and the OECD) collect and report data on undergraduate tuition in fees in aggregate form, mixing institutional sectors and with no information on the rapidly changing variable tuition and fee rate for graduate and professional programs. In the previous study (Ward and Douglass), the authors focused on a specific higher education market in 2003–04: a group of 24 (13 public and 11 private) comprehensive and generally high prestige research universities in the United States, which included both undergraduate and graduate program tuition rates.[12] These institutions are influencing the market price. At that time, we chronicled only the in-state rate for public universities.

Among the findings of that previous study was a still significant difference between public and private tuition pricing for undergraduate (UG) and major graduate and professional degree programs. On average, the differential at the UG level was $22,280 and slightly less at the graduate level. The differential within most major professional programs was smaller: dentistry at the high end at just over $25,000, pharmacy at $18,000, MBA programs at $17,480, and law at just over $15,000. An important variable is that public universities tend to offer a greater variety of professional programs with the specific purpose of meeting societal needs, in fields such as nursing, veterinary medicine, and optometry (no private institution in the sample group offered optometry). Often these are relatively high-cost programs that privates avoid—in part, because publics fulfill the market, but also because privates tend to have fewer academic degree programs and are wary of high costs and perceived low-prestige professional fields and programs. Table 7.2 provides a summary of the differential pricing.

One of the conclusions of the previous study was an assumption of near convergence over time of public and private fees at the graduate and professional level. "The privatization movement," it was noted, "and the relatively new market thrust of public universities means that the differential fees between public and private institutions, and at the undergraduate and graduate and professonal levels, will likely decrease in coming decades. The push by institutions to increase revenue via tuition will be significant." Yet our comparison of the

---

[12] David Ward and John Aubrey Douglass, "Higher Education and the Specter of Variable Fees: Public Policy and Institutional Responses in the United States and United Kingdom," *Higher Education Management and Policy* (OECD), vol. 18, no. 1 (2006): 1–28; see also John Aubrey Douglass, "New System of Top-Up Fees: Brief on English HE Market Response," CSHE Research and Occasion Papers Series, CSHE 12.05 (October 2005).

Table 7.2. Public In-State and Private Research University Tuition Rates (Sample Group): 2003–04

	Public In-State Sample Average	Private Sample Average	Public/Private Differential 2003
UG	$5,914	$28,191	$22,278
Graduate	$7,086	$28,107	$21,021
Dentistry	$17,462	$42,708	$25,247
Medicine	$20,542	$31,779	$11,238
Optometry	$11,865	$0	-
Pharmacy	$11,347	$29,420	$18,073
Veterinary Medicine	$14,537	$23,153	$8,616
Law	$16,629	$31,765	$15,136
MBA	$14,876	$32,058	$17,182
Master's Nursing	$4,945	$22,425	$17,480
Theater & Film	$7,666	$29,611	$21,944

Source: IPEDS

2003–04 pricing of the sample group with 2007–08 tuition rates provides a more nuanced outcome. Tuition and fee data were collected via the Integrated Postsecondary Education Data System (IPEDS) and by consulting institutional postings of fees and programs.

Within the public universities, in-state tuition and fees rose on average $2,208 between 2003 and 2007, a 37 percent increase. Penn State and the University of Texas–Austin had the largest increases (see Figure 7.1). The average in-state price among our sample public universities was $8,122—about $2,000 more than the national average for all four-year public universities in the U.S.[13] Similarly, graduate programs (non-professional) rose by an average of $2,281, a 32 percent increase (see Figure 7.2). At the undergraduate and graduate level (including arts and humanities, social sciences, and science and engineering) differential fees have yet to emerge – although there are some marginal differences charged at institutions such as the University of Michigan's flagship Ann Arbor campus.

When comparing public in-state pricing with privates over the five-year period, the total dollar increase was higher for privates in most programs. As shown in Figure 7.3, at the undergraduate level, the sample group of private institutions rose by a total of just over $4,600; at the graduate level by $2,650. The largest increases, however, occurred in dentistry, pharmacy, nursing (only

---

[13] College Board, *Trends in College Pricing: 2007,* Trends in Higher Education Series, College Board, 2007a.

Figure 7.1. UG Public University In-State Student Tuition by Campus 2003–04 and 2007–08 Rates

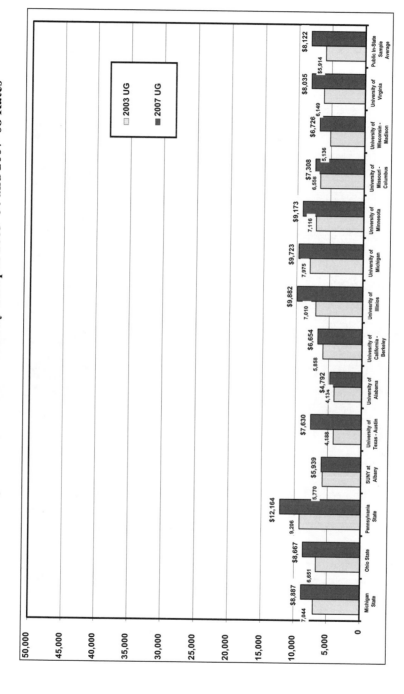

Figure 7.2. Graduate School Public University In-State Student Tuition by Campus 2003 and 2007 Rates

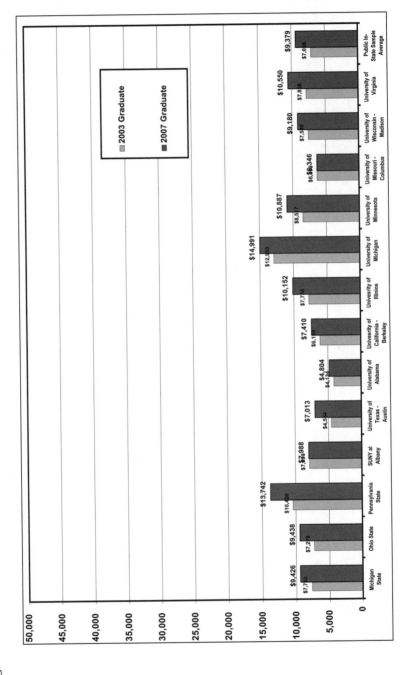

Figure 7.3. Public University In-State Student and Private Tuition by Program: Total Increase in 2003 and 2007 Rates

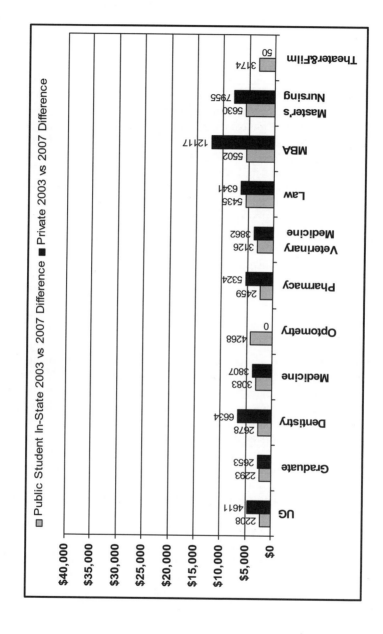

three privates in the sample group offer nursing programs), and most spectacularly in MBA programs, with a jump of just over $12,100.

Public universities also rose in all of these professional programs but at much smaller total increases. The largest increases were in nursing, followed by the MBA, law, and optometry (none of the private sample groups offer optometry programs). Theater and film programs held largely flat in pricing among the privates, which were, at an average of nearly $22,000, already highly priced programs—there is also more variability in the degree programs among both publics and privates that makes comparison more difficult.

The net effect among most academic programs is that the difference in the price charged by publics for in-state students and those charged by privates has grown, and not converged (see Figure 7.4). At the UG level and marginally within graduate programs in dentistry, pharmacy, law, and the MBA, the difference grew. In medicine and nursing it declined, however. Veterinary programs provide the exception to the rule: privates actually declined in their price differential. There are very few veterinary schools in the U.S. and within our sample only two privates (the University of Pennsylvania and Cornell, a quasi-public private) offer the program at a lower tuition rate than the six publics (Michigan State, Ohio State, the University of Illinois, Minnesota, Missouri, and Wisconsin).

Relatively New Pricing Markets in the U.S.

An even more illuminating variable in the curve toward higher pricing is out-of-state tuition pricing by public universities where political restraints are far fewer, and where the "Pricing Equals Prestige" and other rules of the game are more at play. Thirty years ago, most public universities in the U.S. had relatively similar and relatively low tuition and fee pricing for all degree programs, undergraduate, graduate, and professional. Public universities also generally charged either the same or nearly the same tuition rate for out-of-state and international students. This has all changed over the past decade or more. State governments have given greater freedom to institutions to increase fees, particularly for out-of-state students and in professional fields in which operating costs are relatively high and that promise, on average, high rates of personal return.

Figure 7.5 provides a glimpse of the two-tier tuition rates among the sample group of public research universities for 2007–08. The ethos professed by universities is that out-of-state pricing is based on an assessment of the actual cost to educate a student in their chosen program; but, as discussed, pricing probably has more to do with a sense of what the market will bear—informed, in part, by what private counterparts are charging.

Differential pricing is evident in comparing our sample group of private and public universities, demonstrating an evolving market. Figure 7.6 provides the private sample average, along with in and out-of-state pricing among our public sample. Out-of-state (nonprotected) students in the publics generally face an up-

Figure 7.4. Difference in Public University In-State Student and Private Tuition by Program: 2003 and 2007 Rates

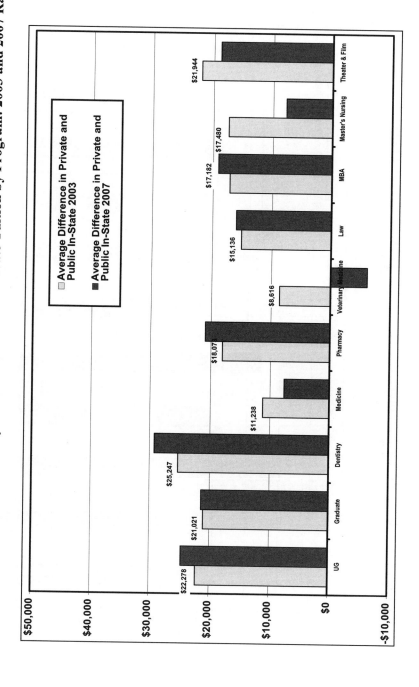

Figure 7.5. Difference in Public University In-State Student and Market/Out-of-State Tuition by Program: 2007 Rates

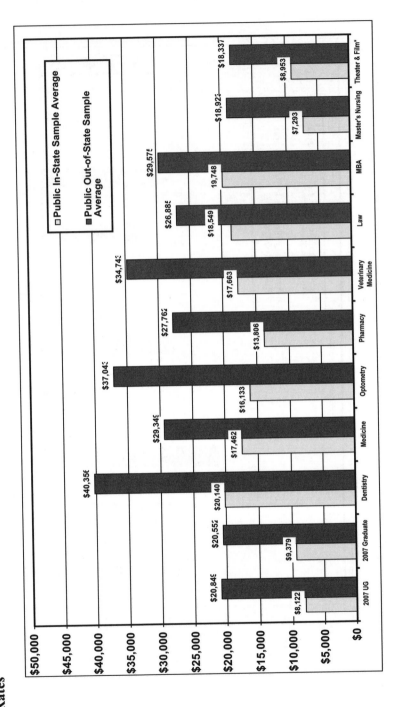

Figure 7.6. Private and Public In-State and Market/Out-of-State Tuition by Program: 2007 Rates

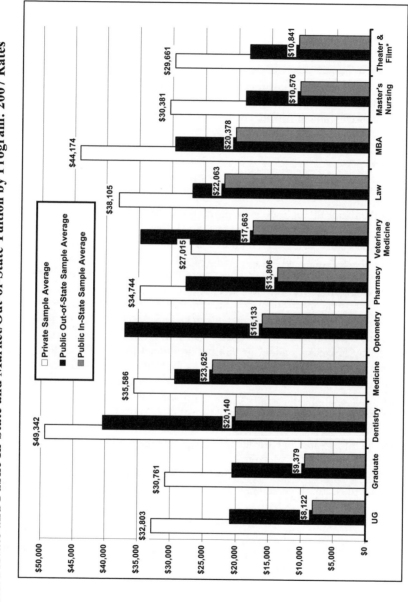

front price of a quarter less than if they enrolled in a private counterpart—at least at the undergraduate and graduate level, in law and theater/film. In dentistry, medicine, and pharmacy that public rate is closer to the private price. Veterinary medicine remains the anomaly.

Figure 7.7 provides the same out-of-state and private university data in a different logarithmic pattern and identifies clusters of university pricing. Some institutions have clustered pricing for most of their professional programs and are consistently at either the high or low end of the spectrum, including most of the privates, and public institutions such as Michigan and Virginia. These public institutions have the most significant interest in privatization and see their competitors largely as the private elites. Other publics have more scattered pricing, such as Ohio State.

The Emergence of a Price Market in the E.U.

The U.S. is not the only country moving toward differential pricing for designated groups of students and programs. Some three decades ago, most nations in Europe had a singular national approach to tuition: either no direct fees for enrolling in a publicly funded university (by far the dominant provider of higher education), or rather modest fees that were the same for all students and all programs. Many countries did not have policies that encouraged international students, other than those students who came from former colonies or who otherwise held some form of favored status. The general concept of charging tuition in any meaningful amount was seen as an infringement on citizenship, and discussion by lawmakers about generating additional income for rapidly growing tertiary institutions was generally seen as a form of political suicide.

A cursory recent sample of a small number of E.U. institutions provides a window into contrasting approaches to pricing. Institutions in the U.K., led by the Russell group of leading research universities, have been the most aggressive at differential pricing. Following the reintroduction of tuition in 1998 (previously, in the 1950s and earlier, Oxbridge charged tuition), certain limits remained on fees charged for the bachelor's degree—at first the £1,000 required fee, then *up to* £3,000 in 2006 and inflation-adjusted after that (now £3,415).

Oxford, Cambridge, along with the London Business School and a number of other European universities such as the University of Amsterdam, were allowed by lawmakers to charge a higher fee for the MBA. Advocates for MBA programs, a relatively recent import from America, successfully argued for its status as a distinct degree program with a global, or at least European, market. The introduction of global market rate fees was a vital component in the 1996 establishment of the new Said Business School at Oxford—it would not have gained the already reluctant approval of Oxford's academic leadership without the promise of fiscal independence. Oxford, like Cambridge's Judge Business School established five years earlier, originally sought to charge a differential

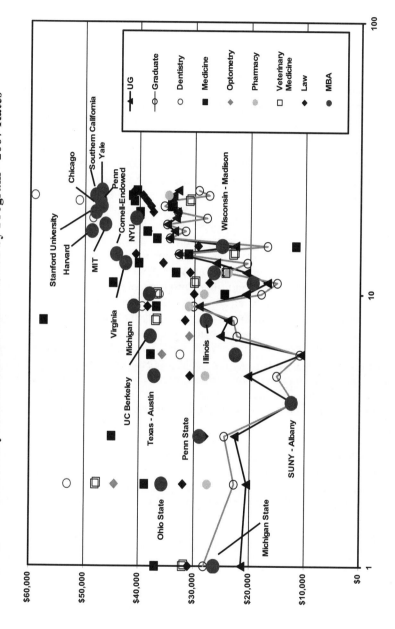

Figure 7.7. Private, Public University Market/Out-of-State Tuition by Program - 2007 Rates

fee for non-U.K. students, later making no differentiation and now charging among the highest fees in the world for the MBA.

Political acceptance of MBA programs as an exception to the rule throughout much of Europe, along with increasing acceptance of tuition as a legitimate income source for public universities, provided an opportunity for other differential fees for professional programs. Heightened mobility within the E.U., and the increased emphasis on attracting talent from throughout the world, are factors encouraging increased coordination, harmonization (and even possible standardization) among European higher education systems. While the Bologna Declaration makes no mention of fees, the development of the European Higher Education Area, and more generally the expanding role of universities in the European Union, has led to a broadening discussion of the possible role of tuition and fees for resource-deprived universities. One European Commission report in 2005 (quoted in the opening of this chapter) noted two general reasons why tuition might be embraced by member nations. For one, "It has been shown that free higher education does not by itself suffice to guarantee equal access and maximum enrollments." It was also argued that university fees would not only improve the quality of education offered by universities, but it might "provide better access for students from lower income groups if the incremental funds were recycled into a sound student aid system."[14]

An important legal decision at the European level helped to frame the development of differential fees analogous to the differentiation of in-state (protected) and out-of-state (nonprotected) students in the U.S. In 1985, and in reaction to a suit from a French student charging discrimination for differential fees charged in Belgium for a program in art, the European Court of Justice ruled in the *Gravier Case* that no E.U. nation could charge differential fees to legal residents of other E.U. member states. Whatever fees were charged to U.K. citizens living in Britain were the maximum that could be charged to any and all E.U. residents as well; to do otherwise would be a violation of Article 12 of the European Union's principle of the free movement of labor between E.U. member states.[15]

In a 2006 scan of tuition and fee structures, Oxford University had the most elaborate differential pricing scheme—indeed, much more complex than that of any American research university. Figure 7.8 provides a sample of 14 different degree programs and their differential pricing in euros at Oxford in fall 2006.[16] Cambridge offered a much more simple pricing scheme, built around "bands" of

---

[14] Commission of the European Communities, *Mobilising the Brainpower of Europe: Enabling Universities to Make Their Full Contribution to the Lisbon Strategy*, Brussels, 20.4.2005, <http://ec.europa.eu/education/policies/2010/doc/comuniv2005_en.pdf>. COM (2005) 152 final.

[15] Judgment of the Court of Justice, Gravier, Case 293/83 (February 13, 1985), <http://www.ena.lu/judgment-court-justice-gravier-case-293-83-13-february-1985-030002987.html>.

[16] Currency conversion in Figures 9–12 based on March 14 2008 conversion: 1.57 dollars = 1.00 Euro; 1.29 Euro = 1.00 Pounds.

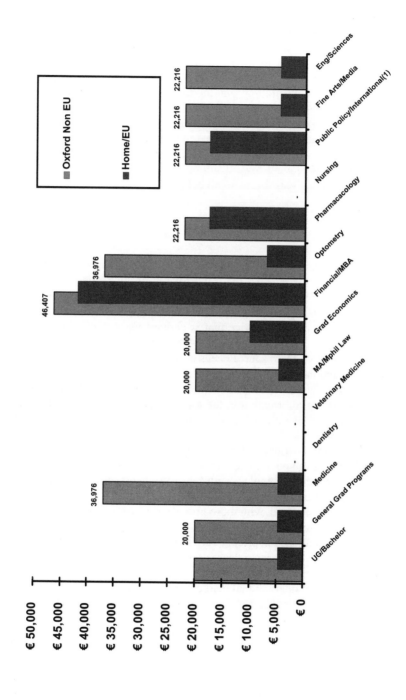

Figure 7.8. Oxford Non-EU and Home Sample Tuition Rates: Bachelor, Graduate, and Professional School 2006

programs: for example, medicine, dentistry, pharmacology, and law all at the same price for non-E.U. members.

On the other end of the pricing spectrum is the Universiteit Leuven (Flemish-speaking community of Belgium). Amsterdam shows more variance, providing an example of an institution in transition, essentially in between the high cost of the U.K. institutions and the more moderately priced Leuven. Figure 7.9 provides pricing among four institutions as a sample of variance: Oxford, Cambridge, Amsterdam, and Leuven. A large proportion of European universities retain either no-fee policies, or charge a standard university fee for all students. Yet all regions of Europe (with perhaps the exception of Scandinavia) show indications of moving toward tuition and differential fees, and have begun to introduce higher fees for international (non-E.U.) students.

Patterns of Convergence

It has been generally understood that U.S. higher education institutions, led by the privates, have created the trend for setting high prices (again, ignoring for now the complexity of bursaries and costs for room and board) for professional and academic degree programs. Private, prestige programs such as a Harvard MBA have a published price that is perhaps tangentially related to operational costs, and have everything to do with markets. Now we see that this model, based in part on the resource needs of major research universities, and in part on markets and the "Price Equals Prestige" rule, is growing rapidly globally.

Figure 7.10 provides U.S. out-of-state, E.U. member, and U.S. private university pricing information in the graduate programs of law, MBA/finance, and medicine in a logarithmic scale and in 2008 U.S. dollars, this time including the University of Edinburgh. The greatest variation occurs within medicine, which remains tied to national labor needs (at least more so than law and finance) and comes with large operational costs. The pricing of degree programs in medicine is inherently more complex, with fewer providers and heavy influence from national health care systems and the demands of the medical profession. Law is more market oriented, with more providers generally, but also with strong ties to national and regional legal systems and professional requirements. Yet we see a general convergence in pricing between our U.S. and E.U. sample group.

The MBA and related degree programs in business and international finance areas also generally grouped in the range of $35,000 to $50,000. In what is surely a sign of international market trends, both Cambridge and Oxford have by far the highest price tag for their MBA-related programs, even allowing for currency and cost-of-living factors

There is significantly less divergence and, of course, much lower prices, for *protected* student groups (in-state and E.U. member), as shown in Figure 7.11 (and not including U.S. privates). What is evident is the convergence in the price among public universities in the U.S. and E.U. in degree programs leading to the bachelor's degree, graduate programs, medicine, and law. Once again indicative

Figure 7.9. Non-E.U. Member Sample Tuition Rates: UG, Graduate and Professional School 2006

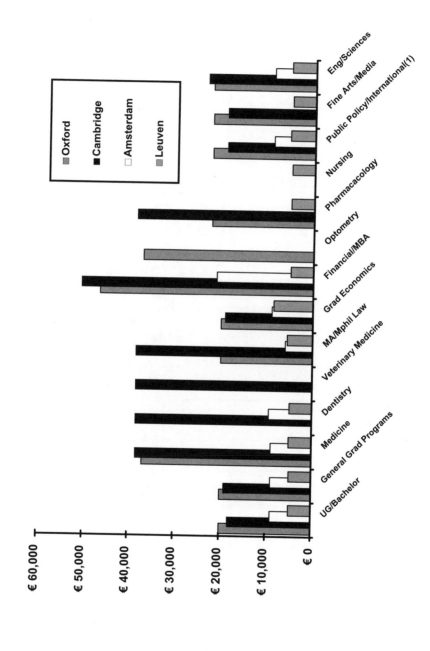

Figure 7.10. U.S. Private, Public Out-of-State, and Non-E.U. Sample Tuition Rates: Law, MBA/Finance, and Medicine

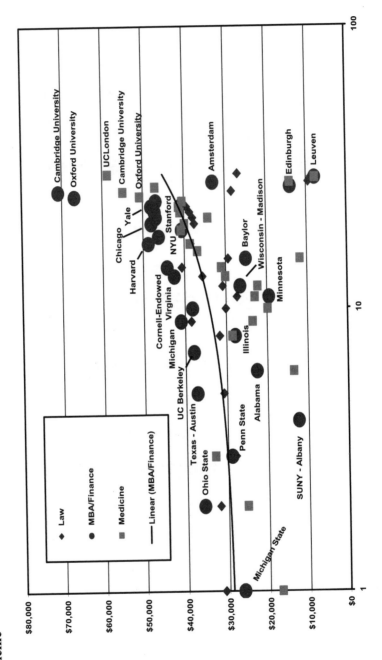

Figure 7.11. US Public In-State and EU Member Sample Tuition Rates: UG, Graduate, Law, MBA/Finance, and Medicine - 2007

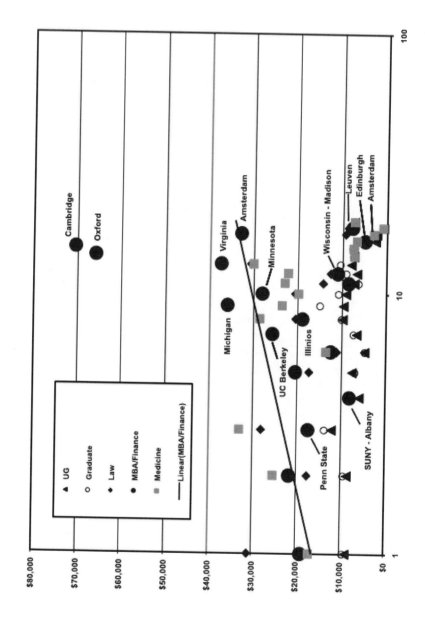

of the world market for MBA programs, many (but not all) publicly oriented institutions charge one price for all students. Cambridge and Oxford offer only a very minor break for E.U. members (around 500 Euros); Amsterdam and Leuven none. Edinburgh did offer a significant price break, reflective of Scotland's current focus on keeping fee levels low for Scottish students, including a decision in 2006 to eliminate fees for bachelor's level programs—a decided break from patterns in most of the E.U.. The University College of London, one of our sample E.U. institutions, offers no MBA program.

Among the U.S. publics, there remains wide variance in the in-state and out-of-state fee level (see Table 7.3). On average among the sample group, the difference is around $9,100, with the University of Texas, the University of Wisconsin, Ohio State, and Berkeley with the greatest difference. Reflecting the increasing market orientation of the University of Virginia and the University of Michigan, which have the highest priced MBA programs among the publics, each offers a discount of only $5,000 for in-state residents.

It is our intention to continue to track trends in tuition and fees, with the expectation that the differential in-state and out-of-state, and E.U. and non-E.U. member prices, will erode, and probably become nonexistent among a cadre of public institutions that see themselves increasingly drawing from a global market of students.

Concluding Comments—A Trend Not Yet Complete

What patterns in pricing will we see over the next decade among research universities in the U.S., the E.U., and elsewhere? As we state, there is a process of convergence in pricing, with the elevated sense that tuition and fees represent the key new source of revenue for public universities in particular. But in following this path, public universities need to contemplate a number of questions:

- What should be the relative role of tuition and fees in funding the higher education enterprise?
- What is the elasticity in pricing when *combined* with a financial aid program that can maintain or possibly enhance affordability for lower- and lower-middle-class students?
- What would a socially responsible moderate fee and high financial aid model look like?
- How will new fee revenue be used?

It is our impression that pricing is arguably being set and influenced by government underfunding of higher education, and by a process of incremental policymaking, generally lacking a coherent policy approach. There are a number of models that might guide pricing.[17] These include the following.

---

[17] Models originally outlined in Ward and Douglass, "Higher Education and the Specter of Variable Fees."

Table 7.3. U.S. Public Universities: In-State and Out-of-State MBA Price 2007

	In-State	Out-of-State	Difference
Michigan State	$18,878	$26,328	$7,450
Ohio State	$21,660	$35,814	$14,154
Pennsylvania State	$17,390	$28,992	$11,602
SUNY at Albany	$8,188	$12,428	$4,240
Univ. Texas, Austin	$20,418	$37,222	$16,804
Univ..of Alabama	$12,500	$22,625	$10,125
Univ. of California, Berkeley	$25,705	$37,950	$12,245
Univ. of Illinois	$18,910	$27,860	$8,950
Univ. of Michigan	$35,989	$40,989	$5,000
Univ. of Minnesota	$28,072	$38,160	$10,088
Univ. of Missouri, Columbia	$8,601	$19,494	$10,894
Univ. of Wisconsin, Madison	$11,098	$26,536	$15,438
Univ. of Virginia	$37,500	$42,500	$5,000
Public Sample Average	$20,378	$29,575	$9,197

Model 1—Tuition Fees Relate Directly or in Some Measure with the Costs of Academic Degree Programs

This has been a basic principle in the effort to set prices for nonprotected groups (out-of-state and non-E.U. members) and provides a logical base for setting fees—full cost, or partial cost, depending on students and their backgrounds. But full-cost accounting for teaching programs is a difficult proposition in major research universities, which are highly reliant on cost-sharing: e.g., teaching supports research activities; research activities support teaching and mentoring functions, etc.

Model 2— Public vs. Private Benefits

Contemporary fee increases in the U.K. and the U.S. are based, in part, on a simple proposition. Since the private benefits of higher education will continue to grow, students and their families should bear a larger burden of the educational costs. As early as 1973, the Carnegie Commission on Higher Education, led by Clark Kerr, offered a structural approach to the funding of public HEIs. By estimating the proportionate public and private benefits of public higher education, the commission proposed a threefold division of costs: students and their families; state government; and institutional sources, including federal financial aid support.[18]

At that time, around 15 percent of all operating expenses at four-year public institutions were covered by fees. Today it is around 20 percent. The actual public and private benefits of higher education are of course difficult to determine, but this model provides an equitable and negotiable solution to setting fee rates.

Model 3—What the Market Will Bear

An alternative model for public institutions is to charge what the market will bear, while staying mindful of the need to generate funds sufficient for a robust financial aid program that also draws on institutional, state, and national sources. HE finance reforms in the U.K. essentially followed this model, but placed an artificial ceiling on tuition: up to £3,000 beginning in 2006. Generally, the increased acceptance of the market model among public institutions, including differential fees, has prompted government policies that limit the total amount that can be charged—either as a ceiling as in the U.K., or as a percentage change per year.

A true market model, of course, would set no limits. There are many variables influencing the systems to which both the U.K. and the U.S. are apparently drifting. In the U.S., fees (sticker prices) are set at the state system or multicampus level, but usually with campus variability, while in the U.K. they are to be set at the institutional level. Differential fees have also crept into graduate and professional degree programs. The market model tends to focus on institutional revenue generation, but with little understanding of its influence on student choices and affordability.

Model 4—National/International Comparative Norms

Another model would calibrate tuition and fees based on what a comparable group of institutions (within a state, within a country, and perhaps internationally) charges. This is a competitive model devoid of any larger sense of the relationship of revenue generation to the specific financial needs of an institution, or to its influence on affordability and access.

Yet in the U.S., fee policies currently in place at public and private institutions reflect the influence of this model. In the public sector, as state subsidies have declined, decisions on corresponding fee increases are sensitive to the overall percentage increase in fees and the overall decline in total resources generated on a per student basis. They also actively look at the price charged at

---

[18] Carnegie Commission on Higher Education, *Higher Education: Who Pays? Who Benefits? Who Should Pay?* (New York: McGraw-Hill, 1973).

other institutions outside of their state—particularly in the New England and mid-Atlantic States, where there is greater student mobility.

This sensitivity explains the limited variability of fees charged by similar public institutions. Institutions with tuition levels outlying this average (whether higher or lower) often argue that their fees should be closer to the norm for all institutions. This argument is not based on an actual analysis of revenue needs, affordability, and access suitable for their mission, but rather is simply one of the few political tools that has some saliency with lawmakers.

Model 5— Fees Pegged to Economic Indicators or a Percentage Limit

Another model widely discussed but rarely applied sets fees in relation to economic indicators, primarily the cost of living. Fees would rise only in relation to what people could afford. Many lawmakers and critics of higher education in the U.S. are partial to this model. They sense that university operating costs and fees at public and private HEIs have been rising too fast, but they also ignore the effects of significant declines in state subsidies for the public sector.

Percentage limits of course ignore the realities of the actual revenue needs of higher education and make large assumptions regarding affordability. The tendency is to start with a base fee range that, as we have seen, already bears the marks of instrumentalism. The rationality of the model requires at least an initial fee level based on institutional mission, revenue needs, and affordability. Percentage limits also have another disadvantage: a percentage increase in the relatively small fees of community colleges would generate very little additional revenue, while the same percentage increase in the relatively high fees of an elite private institution would generate large sums. It all depends on the base.

None of these models are necessarily mutually exclusive, but they all raise serious questions about the interconnectedness of HE institutions and the need to identify some simple systematic relationships of tuition between and among both similar and different kinds of HE institutions. Should new fee regimes focus simply on improving the competitive financial position of individual institutions or, in the case of the U.S., multicampus systems (such as the University of California and the State University of New York)? Or should they also have as an objective some level of revenue-sharing among all or some public higher education sectors in order to subsidize less-affluent institutions, or to help fund national and state financial aid programs?

The sense of collective interest is, we think, not (yet?) an influential factor in the fast-paced world of pricing higher education degree programs. Government constraints, and political repercussions from increases deemed too rapid and damaging to the public good, restrict the ability of most publicly dependent institutions[19] to increase their fees for tuition, let alone to explore new models of "tuition sharing." However, there is evidence of a potential paradigm shift with the emergence of a global pricing system.

In confronting the world of differential pricing, and the efforts of major research universities to both improve their fiscal position and seek prestige and quality, national governments have a special responsibility to see that the larger socio-economic needs of society are not ignored in the resulting equation. Here are a few of the policy areas that need to be raised and addressed.

- Robust financial aid programs that are adequately funded at a level that reduces the net cost to targeted populations.
- Gradual increases of tuition and fee prices in relation to a schedule of long-term financing of public higher education.
- *Student Choice—UG and graduate levels*: Particularly at the UG level, differential pricing may skew student choices, creating market forces that would be heavily influenced by a student's economic background.
- *Financial Aid and Interinstitutional Revenue Sharing*: Within state public HE systems (U.S.) and national systems (U.K.), a natural question is how new fee-generated revenue might work into a general scheme of revenue sharing specifically for financial aid.
- *Campus Revenue Sharing, Or Will the Rich Get Richer?* Public universities have only recently adopted differential fees. They are often making choices without clear norms or well-scrutinized goals beyond the search for new revenues. Without a strong commitment to revenue sharing from the outset, increasingly powerful academic units will resist allocations based on shared revenues in their own individual quest for quality and prestige.

The language of E.U.-commissioned study quoted at the beginning of this chapter is telling. Charging fees has long been a delicate political issue in Europe, one that has only been broached carefully and diplomatically in earlier European Commission studies. This political hesitancy continues: "Given the differences between national systems," notes the report, "there can be no uniform response to this issue: each Member State needs to choose the approach best suited to its circumstances."[20]

Despite the careful reference to continued public subsidization and national governments' continued responsibility for higher education management, the fact is that these national frameworks are increasingly influenced by the actions of partners and competitors both inside and outside the European Higher Education Area. Barring a revolution in the funding predilections of governments in E.U. member states, diverse fee rates for university studies will become ever more a part of the higher education landscape in Europe, and European universities will

---

[19] This includes universities that still get substantial operating funds from public coffers, have their origins in state charters and have state public purposes, as well as universities under more direct public control.

[20] Commission of the European Communities, *Mobilising the Brainpower of Europe,* 2005.

be confronted with fee models, pricing decisions, and distribution dilemmas that have long been familiar to their U.S. counterparts.

References

Barr, Nicholas. 2004. "Higher Education Funding." *Oxford Review of Economic Policy*, Oxford University Press, vol. 20, no. 2 (summer): 264–83.

Bowen, Howard R. 1980. *The Costs of Higher Education.* Carnegie Council for Policy Studies in Higher Education. San Francisco: Jossey-Bass Publishers.

Carnegie Commission on Higher Education. 1973. *Higher Education: Who Pays? Who Benefits? Who Should Pay?* New York: McGraw-Hill.

Chapman, Bruce. 1997. "Conceptual Issues and the Australian Experience with Income Contingent Charges for Higher Education." *Economic Journal*, Royal Economic Society, vol. 107, no. 442 (May): 738–51.

Carneiro, Pedro, and James J. Heckman. 2003. "Human Capital Policy." IZA Discussion Papers 821, Institute for the Study of Labor (IZA).

Chapman, Bruce. 1996. "Conceptual Issues and the Australian Experience with Income Contingent Charges for Higher Education." Discussion Papers 350. Centre for Economic Policy Research, Research School of Social Sciences, Australian National University.

———. 2005. "Income Contingent Loans for Higher Education: International Reform." Discussion Papers 491. Centre for Economic Policy Research, Research School of Social Sciences, Australian National University, revised.

College Board. 2008a. *Trends in College Pricing: 2008.* Trends in Higher Education Series, College Board.

———. 2008b. *Trends in Student Aid: 2008.* Trends in Higher Education Series, College Board.

Danette, Geraldine, and Kati Haycock. 2007. *Engines of Inequality: Diminishing Equity in the Nation's Premier Public Universities.* The Education Trust.

Douglass, John, and Gregg Thomson. 2008. "The Rich and the Poor: Economic Stratification among Undergraduates at the University of California." CSHE Research and Occasional Paper Series (October), CSHE 15.08.

Douglass, John Aubrey. 2007. "A Look into a Possible Future: A Global Scenario for Higher Education Systems." Global University Network for Innovation, UNESCO.

Epiney, Astrid. 2007. "The Scope of Article 12 EC: Some Remarks on the Influence of European Citizenship." *European Law Journal* 13(5): 611–22 doi:10.1111/j.1468-0386.2007.00386.x

Commission of the European Communities. 2005. *Mobilising the Brainpower of Europe: Enabling Universities to Make Their Full Contribution to the Lisbon Strategy*, Brussels.

Ehrenberg, Ronald G. 2002. *Tuition Rising: Why College Costs So Much.* Harvard University Press.

Greenaway, David, and Michelle Haynes. 2003. "Funding Higher Education in The U.K.: The Role of Fees and Loans." *Economic Journal*, Royal Economic Society, vol. 113, no. 485 (February): F150-F166.

Heckman, James, and Pedro Carneiro. 2003. "Human Capital Policy." NBER Working Papers 9495. National Bureau of Economic Research, Inc.

Horn, Laura J., and Chris Chapman. 2003. *Getting Ready to Pay for College: What Students and Their Parents Know about the Cost of College Tuition and What They Are Doing to Find Out*, U.S. Department of Education, National Center for Educational Statistics.

Johnstone, D. Bruce. 2005. "Fear and Loathing of Tuition Fees: An American Perspective on Higher Education Finance in the U.K." *Perspectives: Policy and Practice in Higher Education*, vol. 9, no. 1: 12–16.

Marcucci, Pamala, and D. Bruce Johnstone. 2007. "Tuition Fee Policies in a Comparative Perspective: Theoretical and Political Rationales." *Journal of Higher Education Policy and Management*, vol. 29, no. 1 (March).

Ward, David, and John Aubrey Douglass. 2006. "Higher Education and the Specter of Variable Fees: Public Policy and Institutional Responses in the United States and United Kingdom." *Higher Education Management and Policy* (OECD), vol. 18, no. 1: 1–28.

III.   Access, Quality, and Accountability:
A Postmodern Race to Expand Educational
Attainment and Research Evidence

Chapter 8

Treading Water: What Happened to America's Higher Education Advantage?

John Aubrey Douglass[1]

The U.S. was the pioneer in the movement toward mass higher education. But for a variety of reasons discussed in this chapter, the U.S. has stopped innovating and is arguably losing its first-mover advantage Overall, national educational attainment levels remain torpid.[2] While the U.S. largely treads water in the race for human capital, dependent increasingly on foreign skilled labor in key economic sectors, other parts of the world are making major changes in their higher education systems, largely focused on expanding tertiary access, achieving more robust graduation rates, and competing more effectively for talent in the global market. The net result is a very different trajectory from that of the U.S.

International comparisons are fraught with difficulties, in part because there have been differing national views on what constitutes higher education, with the United States being the most liberal. Europeans, for example, tend to think of a

---

[1] Center for Studies in Higher Education, UC Berkeley.

[2] This essay is in part based on analysis first offered in "The Waning of America's Higher Education Advantage: International Competitors Are No Longer Number Two and Have Big Plans in the Global Economy," CSHE Research and Occasion Papers Series, CSHE.9.06. (June 2006), and since reiterated in a number of national studies.

distinct class of universities as constituting higher education, whereas in the United States, anything after secondary school is deemed tertiary education. Yet a host of national higher education reforms throughout the world and efforts to improve international data collection by agencies such as the OECD are beginning to offer a better picture and a better sense of trajectories.

The contemporary story of American higher education is also one of peaks and valleys, with many groups, particularly those with high economic and educational capital, finding their way to top-quality universities and colleges. As discussed here, the valleys are getting wider, and deeper for many groups, with increasing numbers of students failing to gain reasonable access to higher education, a fact that reflects larger disparities in American society. In short, the U.S. has now become a bit better than mediocre in getting students into higher education, and not very good relative to competitors in actual tertiary degree attainment—a malady that is finally garnering national attention with the Obama administration.

The Global Race for Access

Overall, the United States still retains a lead in the number of people with higher education experience and degrees. But at the younger age cohort, a different story emerges. On average, the postsecondary participation rate for those aged 18 to 24 in the United States has fluctuated between approximately 35 and 38 percent over the last decade, ticking up in the last few years.[3] There is substantial variation among the states. In 2002, Rhode Island had the highest rate at 48 percent, and Alaska had the lowest at 19 percent. California, Florida, and Texas—states with large and fastest-growing populations—had approximately 36 percent, 31 percent, and 27 percent, respectively, attend some form of postsecondary education. In the majority of states, these participation rates have flattened or marginally declined over the last decade. More students today are part-time, and more are in two-year colleges; the wealthiest students are in the four-year institutions, and students from lower- and even middle-income families are now more likely to attend a two-year college, less likely to earn a bachelor's degree, and now take much longer to attain a degree than in the past.[4]

In contrast, within a comparative group of fellow OECD countries, many nations are approaching or have exceeded 50 percent of this younger age group participating in postsecondary education, and most students are enrolled in programs that lead to a bachelor's degree. Between 1995 and 2006, access rates into higher education among all OECD countries were an average of 20 percent, with a few countries, such as Poland and Finland, doubling the size of their university systems. Some 65 percent of young adults in Australia, Finland, Hungary, Ice-

---

[3] See *Digest of Educational Statistics: 2006*, table 189.

[4] Sandra Ruppert, *Closing the College Participation Gap*, Education Commission of the States, 2003; William G. Tierney, *State of College Admissions,* National Association for College Admissions Counseling, January 2005.

land, New Zealand, Norway, Poland, the Slovak Republic, and Sweden enter programs leading to the bachelor's degree.[5] These are truly large increases that are largely due to two factors: major national government reforms to expand national higher education systems, and rising demand by students and growing markets for not only skilled labor, but also for workers who are knowledgeable about the world.

What would the U.S. need to do to increase educational attainment levels? It is not an exaggeration to say that the socio-economic health and vitality of the U.S. relies to a large extent on the future of the nation's public universities and colleges—where nearly 80 percent of all students are currently enrolled. America's population has continued to grow, reaching 300 million in 2006. A study by the Education Commission of the States estimates that some 2.2 million additional students will enter accredited public and private colleges and universities between 2000 and 2015 if national participation rates hold steady.

Yet current rates of participation within the traditional age cohort (18- to 24-year-olds) and older students (25 and older) are arguably too low. If the participation rates nationally were to reflect the best-performing states, the result would be 10.3 million additional students in accredited postsecondary institutions by 2015. This large difference in projected enrollment demonstrates how poorly many states, particularly heavily populated ones, are doing in their participation rates.[6] It appears that this is not a short-term trend.

The United States still affords a much more dynamic higher education system than most nations. Students in the U.S. often transfer from one institution to another or delay entry into a postsecondary institution, coming in and out of higher education in the course of their lives. This system is much more forgiving than in the vast majority of other countries where young adults are often tracked into a university or nonuniversity path very early in their student careers, although this is also beginning to change. But many Americans and the growing number of immigrant groups are not getting their degrees.

The U.S. is one of the few OECD nations in which the older generation has achieved higher tertiary education rates than the younger population.[7] A recent study looked at the tertiary degree attainment rates of the high school graduating classes of 1972 and 1992. On average, those who graduated from high school in 1972 were more likely to gain a bachelor's degree over a 12-year period. This fact held true for both Euro-Americans and Asian Americans. There were, however, increases in degree attainment rates for Latinos and African Americans— evidence of a rising middle class and perhaps the benefits of affirmative action. Women also increased their degree attainment. A similar pattern is evident for those achieving a master's or professional degree or a doctorate: declines for

---

[5] The Organisation for Economic Co-operation and Development, *Education at a Glance 2008* (Paris: OECD, 2008).

[6] The Organisation for Economic Co-operation and Development, *Education at a Glance 2006* (Paris: OECD, 2006), 42, 50.

[7] OECD, *Education at a Glance 2006*, 32.

Euro-Americans and Asian Americans and, generally, increases for African Americans and women but, interestingly, a decline for Latinos.[8]

In some states, such as California, access to higher education for the traditional age cohort has declined significantly over the past two decades. In 1970, some 55 percent of all public high school graduates in California moved directly to tertiary education, among the highest rate in the nation; in the year 2000, the rate was a mere 48 percent, with the vast majority going into community colleges, most as part-time students and most destined never to attain a two-year degree, let alone a bachelor's.[9] Since 2000, the college-going rate of high school graduates has probably declined further, influenced in part by the large number of high school dropouts. This has occurred in an economic environment in which demand for a labor pool with postsecondary training and education is expanding. A 2006 study estimates that by the year 2022, one in three new California jobs generated will require an associate's degree, bachelor's degree, or higher. Jobs requiring higher education are already growing faster than overall employment in the state.[10]

There is some good news. In the United States, there are healthy increases in the participation rate of older students over the past decade—important for lifelong learning in the postmodern economy and for facilitating socio-economic mobility. The United States also has among the highest rate of the labor force participating in some form of continuing education and training, such as non-degree and usually short programs often funded by employers. But even in this regard, a number of OECD countries are attempting through national policies to expand participation of older students with the goal of meeting or, better yet, exceeding the rates found in the United States.[11]

Within the European Union, the push to increase participation rates in higher education transcends national borders. So important is the expansion of universities for E.U. nations that many countries are now integrating degree standards (like the American model) under the 1999 Bologna Declaration. That year, European ministers of education convened in Bologna to voluntarily seek common higher-education reforms, including creating comparable degrees, programs to ease student mobility between countries, and efforts at reviewing and improving the quality of academic programs. The objective of the declaration is to "ensure that higher education and research in Europe adapt to the changing

---

[8] Clifford Adelman, *Principal Indicators of Student Academic Histories in Postsecondary Education: 1972–2000* (Washington, D.C.: Institute of Education Sciences, U.S. Department of Education, 2004), 20.

[9] John Aubrey Douglass, "Investment Patterns in California Higher Education and Policy Options for a Possible Future," CSHE Research and Occasional Papers Series, CSHE 5.02, April 2002.

[10] Robert Fountain, Marcia Cosgrove, and Petra Abraham, "Keeping California's Edge: The Growing Demand for Highly Educated Workers," Campaign for College Opportunity, Oakland, California, April 2006.

[11] OECD, *Education at a Glance 2005*, (Paris: Organization for Economic Cooperation and Development, 2005), Indicator C6, 50.

needs of society and advances in scientific knowledge" and to "increase international competitiveness of a European system of higher education."[12]

Since the initial adoption of the Bologna Declaration in 1999 by 20 European countries, additional countries have joined the process, demonstrating the willingness for Europe's universities to work together to create a common higher education and research area. As of May 2005, the total number of signatory countries in the Bologna Process was 45.

Although the rhetoric of markets and deregulation pervades much of the talk in Europe about how to promote higher participation rates, it is largely governments that are forcing reforms and creating bureaucratic regulatory regimes focused on access, productivity, and quality. Government wields a heavier hand in Europe than in the United States, in part because of historical and cultural differences: The development of public higher education in America has been a largely organic process of building institutions and creating self-regulated systems over a long time, whereas in Europe and most of the world, higher education was until the 1960s (and, arguably, later in many countries) an elite function forcibly transformed by governments. E.U. members seek their own "social contract" built around their cultural and educational institutions while looking to the American model for ideas.[13]

European integration is a complicated political process with many conundrums, obstacles, and no clear end result. But it is also a powerful force that, along with the rise of China and India as economic powerhouses, will significantly alter the world economy and the flow of skilled labor. What is clear is that proactive national policies of E.U. members have produced a surge in participation rates, particularly over the last two decades. To some extent, the higher education community in each country has been a reluctant or ambivalent partner in these government-initiated attempts to increase access. The results, however, are astounding. Higher education enrollment has grown by over 30 percent in England over the past two decades and in France by a staggering 72 percent.[14]

One indicator of the differences between the U.S. and E.U. higher education markets is illustrated in Figure 8.1, which provides data on enrollment increases by major continents in the previous decade. Even with significant population growth in North America (dominated by the United States), overall postsecondary enrollment grew by only 2.6 percent between 1990 and 1997—this at a time when immigration has contributed to an 11.4 percent overall increase in the number of

---

[12] European Higher Education Area: Joint Declaration of the European Ministers of Education, Bologna on June 19, 1999.

[13] For a comparative look at European mass higher education and the influence of the American model, see Ted Tapper and David Palfreyman (eds.), *Understanding Mass Higher Education: Comparative Perspectives on Access* (London: Routledge Falmer, 2005).

[14] Organisation for Economic Co-operation and Development, *Education at a Glance* (Paris: Organization for Economic Cooperation and Development, 2001).

Figure 8.1. Percentage Change in Student Enrollment by Area of World: 1990–1997

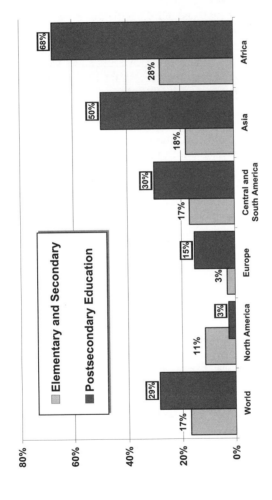

Source: Education at a Glance (OECD 2001).

students in elementary and secondary schools. In sharp contrast, European higher education enrollment has increased 15.2 percent over this short seven-year period, while growing at only 3.1 percent at the elementary and secondary levels, On the one hand, this reflects relatively slow population growth, and on the other, the significant emphasis on expanding access to tertiary education.

One sees even greater increases in Africa, Asia, and Central and South America. Such growth in these parts of the world reflects relatively recent large-scale increases in schooling in "developing" nations *and* the building of nascent higher education systems. Few regions of the world currently match the postsecondary participation rates in the United States, the European Union, and a collection of economies like Canada, Korea, and Japan. But this may slowly change.

Another glimpse into the race for access is shown in Figure 8.2, which contrasts the overall change in population among select OECD countries and the change in enrollment rates between 1994 and 2004. Many countries within Europe and parts of Asia face declines in the overall population—and many are seeking, or will seek, a greater infusion of immigrants to make up for labor needs. This is the case in Hungary, Greece, the Czech Republic, Korea, Sweden, Denmark, Portugal, Spain, Belgium, Norway, Germany, and France. But in each of these countries there has been a substantial increase in the enrollment in tertiary institutions. The U.S. is not shown in this chart, but if it were it would show a relatively significant increase in general population and virtually no change in enrollment rates. Comparing countries like Iceland or Sweden, or even Germany, to the relatively huge population and economy of the U.S. can be misleading. But the important point for this discussion is the trajectory of a large swath of countries with developing, or rapidly developing, economies. Collectively, they paint a picture that gives a sense of the global race for access.

The Global Race for Degree Attainment

While there are impressive increases in access among most OECD member states (and in other parts of the world including China and India), an important question relates to the quality of the educational experience and efficacy of institutions. This is difficult to answer in light of the major differences in the socio-economic composition of various nations, and the quality and mission of their various higher education institutions. One aspect is to simply look at degree completion rates. The quality and efficiency of higher education systems in Europe are not uniform, with many students in France, Spain, and Italy, for example, never completing a degree.

But reforms are being undertaken in places such as Italy and Germany, Portugal and Spain, to radically change degree structures, in part to address high attrition rates. As a consequence, many OECD countries are approaching or exceeding degree productivity rates found in the United States. Figure 8.3 offers a glimpse at data on actual graduation rates of those who enter tertiary institutions.

Figure 8.2. Changes in Population and Tertiary Enrollment Rates Among Select OECD Nations: 1995-04

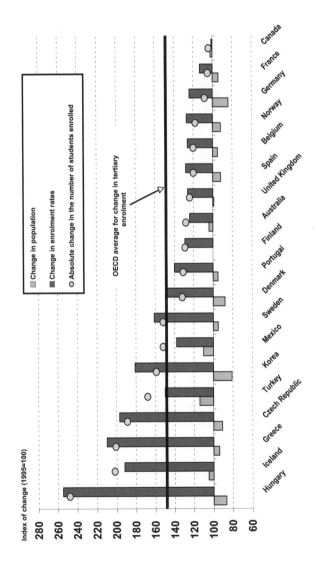

Source: Education at a Glance (OECD 2006).

Figure 8.3. Tertiary Graduation Rates among OECD Nations, 2004

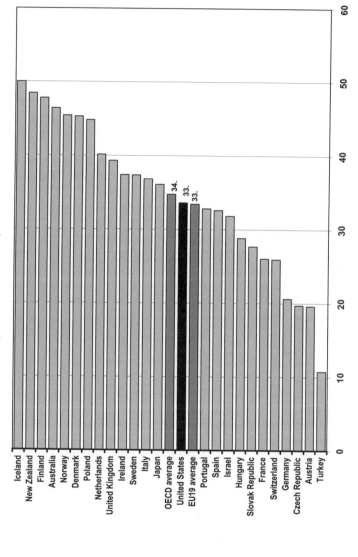

Source: Education at a Glance (OECD 2006).

The OECD estimates the role of education in increasing labor productivity, measured as GDP per person employed. One important cause of rising economic productivity, economists argue, is educational attainment of the working population—a correlation embraced by national governments. In 2004, the United States ranked sixth in the role of educational attainment in productivity growth, behind Portugal, the United Kingdom, Italy, France, and Finland. In previous decades, it had ranked number one. "By many measures, since 1980, the quality of the U.S. workforce has stagnated, or its growth has slowed down dramatically," note economists Pedro Caneiro and James J. Heckman.[15]

There are other indicators that America's leadership position is faltering. Relative to most other nations that are economic competitors, significantly smaller proportions of college-age students are entering scientific fields. In 2005, it is estimated that China had nearly three times and India over two times the number of college graduates in engineering, computer science, and information technologies as the United States.[16] The Chinese national government is engaged in a large-scale effort to expand higher education through building both native institutions and cleverly created limited partnerships with foreign providers—partnerships in which the national government retains significant institutional control. In the midst of its rise as a major economic player in the world, China also has stated an intention to eventually create 20 MITs—a mighty task, to be sure.

At the same time, many high-technology-based conglomerates, including IBM and Nokia, have started new research and development centers in major Chinese cities and in other developing economies where higher education is growing, such as in India, and where academic programs are largely focused on science and technology. A 2006 study by the National Academies (a consortium that includes the National Academy of Sciences and the National Academy of Engineering in the United States) notes that in 2005 chemical companies closed down 70 facilities in the United States and planned to close 40 more; at the same time, 120 chemical plants were being built around the world with price tags of $1 billion or more, with some 50 in China and only one being built in the United States.[17] More lax environmental regulations play a part, but so does the availability of skilled labor and technical knowledge.

There is increasing evidence that the quality of these academic programs in other parts of the world, and the clusters of research expertise that entice international companies, are growing and becoming increasingly competitive with U.S.

---

[15] Quoted in Jack Cassidy, "Winners and Losers: The Truth About Free Trade," *The New Yorker*, August 2, 2004.

[16] Committee on Prospering in the Global Economy of the 21st Century, National Academies, *Rising above the Gathering Storm: Energizing and Employing America for a Brighter Economic Future* (Washington, D.C.: National Academics Press, 2006); original estimates in this publication were revised; see "The Disappearing Chinese Engineers," *Inside Higher Education*, June 13, 2006.

[17] National Academies, "Broad Federal Effort Urgently Needed to Create New, High-Quality Jobs for All Americans in the 21st Century," press release, October 12, 2005.

institutions and research centers. This has led critics of shrinking state and federal funding for higher education in the United States to argue that the nation is at the edge of losing its long dominance in basic science.[18] For example, of the articles in the world's top physics journal published in 1983, some 61 percent were authored by scholars in American universities; in 2003, that proportion dropped to 29 percent.[19] As a percentage of GNP, federal funding for basic research in the U.S. in the physical sciences and engineering has been declining for the past 30 years, to less than 0.05 percent in 2003. Asia's developing economies are placing increasing percentages of their GNPs into science and technology. The payoff? Their share of global high-tech exports rose from seven percent in 1980 to 25 percent in 2001. According to National Science Foundation figures, the U.S. percentage fell from 31 percent to 18 percent.[20] The U.S. is still competitive; it is just that others have become more competitive.

Others see benefits in what appears to be the edge of a sea change. The increased quality and concerted efforts of governments to build their higher education sectors mean a richer global market for scientific and technological expertise, much of which will be drawn to the United States. Some even predict a "glut of technical[ly] sophisticated human capital," or at least a large enough surplus of talent that will fill high-skilled labor needs in U.S. economic sectors.[21] But few policymakers, thus far, would view growing and significant reliance on the international market for scientific and technical labor and innovation as sound long-term national economic policy, and few would, in essence, turn their backs on producing native talent. Investing in native talent and attracting and seeking skilled labor in the global market are not mutually exclusive objectives.

Further, recent studies point to the net job creation benefit of a well-educated society. Across the OECD, increases in the educational attainment level of a national population have been matched by the creation of high-paying jobs. Further, "OECD countries with the fastest growth in tertiary attainment had close to or negative growth in unemployment among the highly educated." This means that worries about a potential oversupply of tertiary degree holders—meaning a possible overinvestment by government and by families—are generally not relevant.[22] Greater supply generally does result in a lower wage premium (benefit) for those with, for example, bachelor's degrees over those who gain only high school diplomas, but the premium remains and compounds over the length of a person's life.

As the global production of scientists and engineers grows, the rise of new high-technology industries and research clusters outside the traditional hegemony

---

[18] See National Academies, *Rising above the Gathering Storm.*

[19] Cassidy, "Winners and Losers."

[20] National Science Foundation, *Science and Engineering Indicators 2006* (Washington, D.C.: National Science Foundation, 2006).

[21] See Robert B. Freeman, "Is a Great Labor Shortage Coming? Replacement Demand in the Global Economy," National Bureau of Economics Research, working paper 12541.

[22] OECD, *Education at a Glance 2008.*

is altering the flow of talent. Some worry that the U.S.'s and Europe's attractiveness for global talent will decline in relative terms. As a recent OECD report notes, how can the United States retain "a strong knowledge economy without a stronger education system?"[23] As emphasized throughout this book, higher education is not just a tool for meeting immediate labor needs and for promoting economic innovation, although that is an important role; it also is a vital route for socio-economic mobility, for creating a more inclusive society, and for promoting democracy itself.

Explaining the U.S. Stagnation

Beyond the rise of concerted competitors who are expanding access and graduation rates, what factors contribute to this erosion in America's once-dominant position in higher education? There is no one domestic cause but, rather, an array of interrelated causes. However, they can be boiled down to four main factors. One is the stagnation and, in many states, significant *declines in high school graduation rates*, which in turn erode the demand for higher education. A second cause is *declining political interest and government investment in public higher education* (where, again, some 80 percent of all American students are enrolled). This factor helps generate a third cause: *increased fees without adequate increases in financial aid.* And a fourth cause is the possibility that all mature higher education systems, such as that of the United States, may reach *a point of equilibrium*—a leveling-off of participation rates, reflecting in some measure a point of saturation. The following focuses on two of these causes— secondary graduation rates and increased fees.

Secondary School Attrition Rates

A major variable in explaining the relatively weak performance of the U.S. higher education system relates to major problems in the educational pipeline. Rising skill demands in OECD countries have made qualifications at the upper secondary level the minimum credential for successful labor market entry. "Secondary school dropouts experience much longer periods where they are neither employed nor in post-school education or training," observes one OECD publication.[24]

---

[23] Barry McGaw and Andreas Schleichler, "OECD Briefing Notes for the United States," *Education at a Glance 2005.*

[24] *Education at a Glance 2008*; See also their study on U.S. and Australia secondary school dropouts, Russell W. Rumberger and Stephen Lamb, "The Early Employment and Further Education Experiences of High School Dropouts: A Comparative Study of the United States and Australia," OECD Paper, May 1998: <http://www.oecd.org/dataoecd/40/37/1925643.pdf>.

Whereas less than two decades ago the United States had the highest secondary graduation rates, it is now among the lowest within the OECD, ranking 19th. See Figure 8.4. Based on U.S. Department of Education reports, the OECD reports a 75 percent completion rate in 2004. A 2005 study by Paul E. Barton, however, estimates that the percentage is possibly as low as 66.1 percent, down from an estimated peak of 77 percent in 1969. Burton and others insist that previous and current estimates by the Department of Education, and in turn by state governments, of high school completion rates are too high.[25] Federal data for 1970 through 2001 show only a marginal decrease in the number of 18- to 24-year-olds who have completed high school.[26]

But because of disparities in data collection among the thousands of school districts and the 50 states, there are good indicators that federal data artificially inflate the nation's claimed high school graduation rates—a reality just recently officially recognized by the U.S. Department of Education. Perhaps most importantly, and as noted earlier, there are huge peaks and valleys in the secondary graduation rate between regions, and between racial and socio-economic groups. One recent study, for example, shows that in many of California's poor urban areas the high school graduation rates are a tragic 39 percent.[27]

In more optimistic times, it was thought that the United States might reach a high school completion rate of 90 percent, which was a goal set by President George H. W. Bush and the nation's governors in 1990. However, according to Barton's analysis, between 1990 and 2000, the completion rate declined in 43 states, and in 10 states, it declined precipitously—by more than eight percent. Only seven states experienced increases.[28] There are few indications that this trend has bottomed out. Among the causes cited by a growing body of literature are not only significant socio-economic shifts in the American population, but also in the overall vitality and focus of America's high schools.

Many argue that increased high school dropout rates, and hence the declining pool of potential college students, relate to inadequate curricular demands among a large proportion of the nation's secondary schools, particularly, but not exclusively, in lower-income communities. One assessment is that 40 percent of American high school graduates are not prepared for college work. A 2004 survey of all 50 states by Achieve Inc. reports that no state "requires every high school student to take a college- and work-preparatory curriculum to earn a diploma. While some states offer students the option to pursue a truly rigorous course of study, a less

---

[25] Paul E. Barton, *One-Third of a Nation: Rising Dropout Rates and Declining Opportunities* (Princeton, N.J.: Educational Testing Service, 2005).

[26] U.S. Department of Education, National Center for Education Statistics, *Dropout Rates in the United States: 2001*; see also NCES, *Digest of Educational Statistics: 2003*, Table 102.

[27] See Cal Dropout Research Project: <http://www.lmri.ucsb.edu/dropouts/about.htm#1>. Also "Which California Schools Have the Most Dropouts?" <http://www.lmri.ucsb.edu/dropouts/pubs_statbriefs.htm>.

[28] Barton, *One-Third of a Nation*, 4.

Figure 8.4. Secondary Graduation Rates among OECD Nations: U.S. Official and Low Estimate

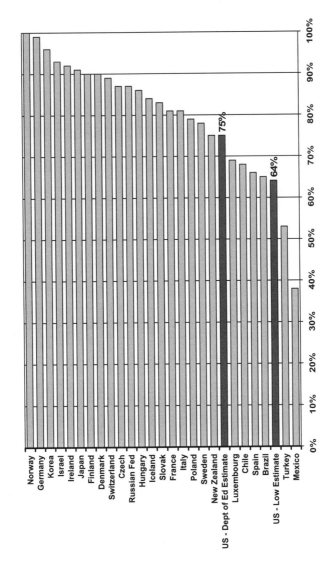

Source: Education at a Glance (OECD 2006).

rigorous set of course requirements remains the standard for almost every state."[29] Before a meeting of the nation's governors in early 2005, Microsoft Chairman Bill Gates claimed that the American high school system is "obsolete" compared with education abroad. America's system, he stated, was undermining the workforce of the future and "ruining the lives of millions of Americans every year."[30]

The high attrition rates of male students are yet another wrinkle in the story. Males are more likely than females to drop out of high school. They tend to get lower grades and take fewer college-preparatory courses. Females are now the majority in chemistry and advanced math courses. In 1960, males represented 64.1 percent of all college and university students; they now represent less than 43 percent. A similar trend can be seen among the other OECD countries.[31] There is some evidence that this phenomenon reflects pent-up demand and the opening of the job market to females. But increased enrollment by the female cohort is more exaggerated in the United States and correlates with rising levels of poverty, the complexities of growing immigrant populations, and other social factors not clearly understood.

High school attrition rates are tied to socio-economic trends and public investment patterns. There have been significant demographic changes in the United States over the past four decades, along with a significant increase in the gap between the rich and the poor and, arguably, erosion in the financial position of the middle class. "Economic inequality in the United States is higher today than at any time in the past sixty years," notes a 1999 study by economists Claudia Goldin and Lawrence F. Katz. "One would have to return to the period just before our entry into World War II, still during the Great Depression, to find inequality measures comparable in magnitude to those at the current time."[32] In 1999, some 34 million people, or 12.4 percent of the population, lived below the federally determined poverty line, and that figure is creeping upward.

Shifts in demography and income have influenced the socio-economic mix and in turn the college-going rates of various subgroups. Some immigrant groups have fewer real and perceived opportunities and expectations of entering postsecondary institutions; other immigrant groups lack the *cultural capital* but also exhibit a substantial drive to enter public higher education; most notably, recent Asian immigrant groups. Most significantly, blacks and Mexican immigrants and their children have extremely low high school graduation rates relative to the general population. In border states such as Florida, Texas, and California, the low participation rates of the fastest-growing minority group, Chicanos/Latinos, pose a

---

[29] Achieve, Inc., *The Expectations Gap: A 50-State Review of High School Graduation Requirements* (Washington, D.C.: Achieve, Inc., December 2004), 4.

[30] Microsoft Chairman Bill Gates before the National Governors' Educational Summit, March 1, 2005.

[31] Robert A. Jones, "Where the Boys Aren't: for Young Males, the Drift Away from Academic Achievement Is a Trend," *CrossTalk*, vol. 13, no. 3 (Spring 2005): 6–8.

[32] Claudia Goldin and Lawrence Katz, "The Returns to Skill in the United States across the Twentieth Century," National Bureau of Economic Research, April 11, 1999.

major problem. And for reasons even more complex, African-American high school and college participation rates correlate even more directly with economic status. Nationally, only 14.7 percent of Chicanos/Latinos have earned either an associate's or higher degree; for African Americans, the number is 20.0 percent, and for Asian Americans and Euro-Americans, the numbers are 50.5 percent and 33.6 percent, respectively.[33]

Fees and Access

Public institutions have attempted to make up for a portion of a substantial decline in government investment relative to costs by raising fees. In 1980, fees and tuition made up approximately 15 percent of public university operating costs; they grew to about 28 percent by 2000. At the same time, student debt has increased. In the face of rising fees at both public and private institutions, the policies of governments and colleges and universities have perhaps made things worse. The federal government has moved precipitously toward loans over grants, most recently raising the interest rates in a move largely calculated to reduce the federal debt. Many institutions, particularly the privates, have also devoted more of their own institutional financial aid to "merit" over "need-based" grants and loans.

As a result of the combination of these forces, two-thirds of the students graduating from college now have student loans, carrying an average debt of close to $20,000, an increase of 60 percent in just seven years. Graduate students carry an average debt of $45,000. Almost every college-qualified, high-income high school graduate enrolls within two years, but more than 20 percent of qualified low-income students do not go at all.[34] Not surprisingly, the net cost of attending a college or university is taking a larger share of family income at a disproportionate rate. One estimate indicates that the net cost of attending a college or a university (fees minus financial aid) absorbs 38 percent of the total income of families and individuals in the lowest income quintile, and that figure is 45 percent in the second-lowest quintile. The lower figure for lower-income groups reflects in some form more readily available financial aid, yet both are arguably large percentages with deleterious influences on access. Families in the middle, fourth, and highest income quintiles devote 30 percent, 20 percent, and 14 percent of their family income to college costs.[35]

Criticism of increased tuition has stressed the impact on middle-income families of a reduced entitlement, prompting various congressional hearings. But arguably, the biggest influence is on the growing number of low-income Americans.

---

[33] Ruppert, *Closing the College Participation Gap*, 16.

[34] Donald E. Heller, "Trends in Public Colleges and Universities," in *The States and Public Higher Education Policy*, ed. Donald E. Heller (Baltimore, Md.: Johns Hopkins University Press, 2001): 11–38.

[35] *Ibid.*

Rising fees, for example, appear to be accentuating the tendency for students from more affluent families to congregate at the higher-priced and most prestigious colleges and universities, both publics and independents.[36] "At a time when the financial payoffs of a college education have risen," notes Rupert Wilkinson in his study of the history of financial aid in the United States, "widening the economic gulf between college graduates and others, many qualified young people are not going to college because of lack of money and fear of debt."[37]

It has long been assumed that higher tuition fees in public and private institutions will negatively influence access among lower-income groups. As fees at public institutions began to creep up in the 1980s, one study published in 1987 indicated that for every increase of $100 at a four-year institution, one might postulate an almost one percent decrease in participation among 18- to 24-year-olds.[38] A 1995 study on price sensitivity indicated that a $1,000 increase at four-year institutions resulted in a decline in demand by lower-income students of 1.4 percent.[39] Both studies indicated the obvious: Lower-income students are the most sensitive to price changes. As a group, part-time students, many of whom are from lower- or middle-class backgrounds, are also heavily influenced by price increases. In the United States, part-time students are now the majority and the fastest growing higher education population.

Rapid and unpredictable increases in fees at public universities, as opposed to gradual and planned increases, may be the biggest culprit negatively influencing access. Private colleges and universities can establish a funding plan and keep to it; publics are subject to political and economic vacillations. After severe state budget cuts to most public universities in the early 1990s, an improved economy caused lawmakers in a number of states to force fee reductions largely for political gain and not as part of a long-term plan for financing higher education. Virginia, California, and Massachusetts all followed this path. Previously, rapidly rising fees helped to suppress demand; after the fee reductions, demand then grew. But the effects appeared temporary—more an indicator of price sensitivity and confusion about the availability of financial aid. Marginal fee increases in subsequent years resulted in relatively stable demand for higher education. In short, students and their families could better plan for educational services and their cost.

There is a great need for expanded research on the relationship between tuition levels, affordability, and access in public colleges and universities. There are very few good studies focused on micro-economic questions related to pricing and

[36] See Alexander W. Astin and Leticia Oseguera, "The Declining 'Equity' of American Higher Education," *The Review of Higher Education*, vol. 27, no. 3 (Spring 2004): 321–41.

[37] Rupert Wilkinson, *Aiding Students, Buying Students: Financial Aid in America* (Nashville, Trnn.: Vanderbilt University Press, 2005).

[38] L. L. Leslie and P. T. Brinkman, "Student Price Response in Higher Education," *Journal of Higher Education*, 58, 181–204.

[39] Tom J. Kane, "Rising Public College Tuition and College Entry: How Well Do Public Subsidies Promote Access to College?" Working Paper Series No. 5164 (Cambridge, Mass.: National Bureau of Economic Research, 1995).

student (consumer) choices in higher education within the modern context. For example, might an overall decline in resources for public institutions, and resulting reductions in academic staff and the number of courses offered, be a bigger threat to access than moderate increases in fees over time? Might access and equity be achieved best by raising the costs for the affluent to attend selective public universities and redirecting the resulting augmented resources to expand financial aid for the needy? It is a complex problem with many social and economic variables; nonetheless, there are economic models that could provide guidance. It is perhaps not an overstatement to say that we are entering a new era of moderate or high fees at public institutions without a strong sense of what may transpire.

The Future and the Vital Role of the Publics

In 1960, John W. Gardner, then president of the Carnegie Corporation, insisted on the centrality of creating a culture of aspiration. "If the man in the street says, 'Those fellows at the top have to be good, but I'm just a slob and can act like one'—then our days of greatness are behind us. We must foster a conception of excellence that may be applied to every degree of ability and to every socially acceptable activity. A missile may blow up on its launching pad because the designer was incompetent or because the mechanic who adjusted the last valve was incompetent. The same is true of everything else in our society. We need excellent physicists and excellent mechanics, excellent cabinet members and excellent first-grade teachers. The tone of our society depends upon a pervasive, an almost universal, striving for good performance."[40]

Economists and sociologists are increasingly interested in the question of how one accounts for societies characterized by high levels of social aspiration, actual socio-economic mobility, and economic growth and technological innovation. How can we account for economic growth, social progress, and the differences among nations? One widespread interpretation, building on the work of economist Gary Becker and earlier work on human capital, is that political cultures that build and expand institutions over time, such as higher education but also democratic legal frameworks, are the key factors that account for historical differences in the economic performance of nations. Further, investment rates in these institutions (politically and economically) will influence future performance and the competitive position of nations and regions. That is, particular political cultures both create social and economic institutions and are fundamentally shaped by them over time. It is a long-term and cumulative investment.[41]

---

[40] John W. Gardner, *Excellence: Can We Be Equal and Excellent Too?* (New York: Harper & Row, 1961).

[41] Among the growing body of literature on this topic, see G. Glaeser, R. La Porta, F. Lopez-de-Silanes, and A. Schleiger, "Do Institutions Cause Growth," National Bureau of Economic Research Working Paper No. W10568, 2004; D. Acemoglou, S. Johnson,

Globalization, supranational entities, and international frameworks, such as the European Union and the General Agreement on Trade and Services (GATS), are tugging at the once-dominant role of nation-states in shaping political culture and institutions. Yet nations remain the most significant influence on the extent and vibrancy of educational institutions, particularly in more advanced economies that owe much of their present position to previous investment rates in education. The nation-state is not dead yet; indeed, its resilience or transformation into regional alliances may surprise globalists.[42]

With the exception of political battles in America over admissions to a few selective public universities and concerns over cost containment, American higher education remains a second-tier political issue. The crisis of the publics—the underinvestment in public colleges and universities, which are the primary providers of postsecondary education—is not a mainstream political concern. For this and a variety of other reasons, the United States has become relatively complacent in maintaining its higher education advantage.

A full discussion of policy options for bolstering America's already mature mass higher education system lies beyond the scope of this book. Instead, I present only a few thoughts on a difficult problem. Although this and earlier chapters have outlined many maladies of the U.S. system, there are many strengths. Arguably, America's brand of higher education is not in need of the kind of top-down regulatory reforms recently and currently pursued in European and other nations. What is needed is the interest and attention of national and state governmental leaders and some consensus in the higher education community on how to improve the nation's school system, how to create a national agenda focused on increasing higher education participation and degree-attainment rates, and a sustainable financial model for public universities and colleges.

America's population continues to grow, reaching over 300 million in 2006. Revised projections by the U.S. Census Bureau issued in the summer of 2008 estimates that the nation will have 490 million people by 2050—up from a previous projection of 420 million. The U.S. is among a small group of developed economies with significant growth in population with a record of some 4.3 million births in 2007.[43]

How might that translate into growing enrollment in higher education in the U.S.? The answer depends on whether the U.S. expands access to keep pace with competitors, or simply treads water or makes only marginal gains. A study by the Education Commission of the States estimates that some 2.2 million additional students will enter accredited public and private colleges and universities between 2000 and 2015 if national participation rates hold steady. Yet current rates of participation within the traditional age cohort (18- to 24-year-olds) and

---

and J. A. Robinson, "The Colonial Origins of Comparative Development: An Empirical Investigation," *American Economic Review*, 91 (2001): 1369–1401.

[42] John Aubrey Douglass, "How All Globalization is Local: Countervailing Forces and their Influence on Higher Education Markets," *Higher Education Policy*, vol. 18, no. 4 (December 2005): 445–73.

[43] "The Population Gap," *Science Magazine*, vol. 321 (August 29, 2008): 1139.

older students (25 and older) are arguably too low. If the participation rates nationally were to reflect the best-performing states, the result would be 10.3 million additional students in accredited postsecondary institutions by 2015 (see Figure 8.5). That large projected difference demonstrates how poorly many heavily populated states are doing in their participation rates.[44]

Most past projections have significantly underestimated demand, in part because the population has grown faster than projected, job-skill requirements have escalated, and perhaps most importantly, individual aspirations have grown. Whether there are 10 million additional students seeking entrance into higher education or a higher figure, the most likely scenario is that public universities and colleges will take the bulk of them if they have the funding, political desire, and capability to meet that demand. The number and type of providers, including for-profits, will undoubtedly increase, further diversifying the nation's higher education system. But in no small part, educational attainment in the United States will depend on the vibrancy of its public higher education sector. In my view, it is also critical that, as the higher education sector grows over time, selective public universities retain in some major form their historical role in society as broadly accessible agents of social change; as a corollary, they must avoid near convergence with their private counterparts, which is the possible outcome of privatization. Hence, they must uphold their historic social contract.

Most contemporary pundits agree that there are significant problems with access to and financing of public colleges and universities. In the United States, as noted, these are second- or third-tier national policy issues. In many E.U. countries, they are first-tier issues, with concerted efforts to, in the words of the Bologna Declaration, "increase international competitiveness of a European system of higher education." They have formed supranational forums for debating and forming policies to assess and reposition the E.U. Arguably, the U.S. federal government has a greater historical and contemporary role in supporting higher education than in supporting K-12. Although such a suggestion cuts against the current political ethos of free markets and less government and raises the danger of another stifling round of accountability bureaucracy, one might reconsider how a national strategy could strengthen American higher education.[45]

On their own, states in general lack a broader understanding or concern regarding the issue of national competitiveness and the larger problems of growing social and economic stratification. Individual states may seek increased participation rates and recognize the need for additional resources for public higher education, but most are financially incapable (because of competing needs, political gridlock, and legal restrictions on generating revenue) of launching a rate of investment similar to the post–World War II and 1960s eras. Indeed, the resources and political commitment in that period that significantly expanded access re-

---

[44] Ruppert, *Closing the College Participation Gap.*
[45] John Aubrey Douglass, "Higher Education as a National Resource," *Change Magazine*, vol. 37, no. 5 (Sept./Oct. 2005): 30–38.

Figure 8.5. Projection of U.S. Postsecondary Participation, Steady State and Benchmark: 2000–2015

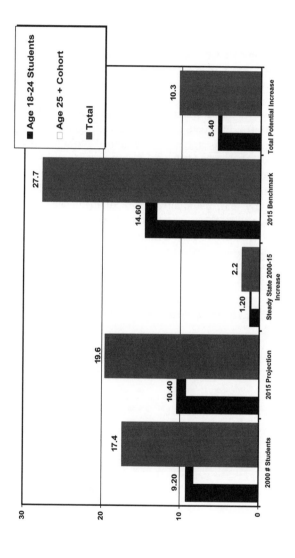

Steady State = U.S. average participation rate for Age 18-24 Students (34.0 percent) and Age 25+ (4.5 percent)
Benchmark = Top State U.S. participation rates for 18-24 Students (47.7 percent) and Age 25+ (6.5 percent)
Source: Closing the College Participation Gap, Education Commission of the States, 2003.

quired a collaboration of state and federal government—neither could do it on their own. Certainly, those political eras and policy approaches could not and should not be directly replicated. However, the specter of privatization and market models will probably not generate the investment rates and political commitment needed to adequately bolster American education and to retain its leadership position.

Or perhaps the world economy and priorities of competitor nations have permanently eroded America's once-distinct higher education advantage. Even if this is the case, a new sense of resolve by political and higher education leaders in the United States is paramount, both as a key route for economic development *and* socio-economic vitality. What would it mean for the United States to continue its downward trajectory relative to other developed economies in secondary graduation rates, in access to higher education and degree production, and the resulting ramifications for socio-economic mobility? How will the growth of new science clusters and the shift in the production of science and engineering degrees to new areas of the world shape future economic activity? The answers to these questions will profoundly influence the future development of the nation's economy and, eventually, political influence. America should look across the oceans and to other continents for ideas, inspiration, and a pragmatic sense of the globalizing and increasingly competitive world.

Chapter 9

Widening Participation in Sweden: Expanding Access to Nontraditional Groups

Kerstin Eliasson[1]

One of the great challenges facing national systems of higher education is to expand access and academic positions to nontraditional groups. In the case of Sweden, these groups include women and those with a working-class or foreign background. As discussed in this chapter, national policymaking has led to significant expansion in access and the beginning of a concerted effort to include all segments of Swedish society.

Two contextual factors help in understanding higher education policymaking in Sweden. First is Sweden's overall economic health and links with a greater Europe, having been a European Union member since 1995—although, like the U.K. and Denmark, the nation has not adopted the Euro. Compared to the European average and to the U.S., economic growth in Sweden has been higher than the European average and higher than in the United States. This has resulted in an increased interest in the Nordic or Scandinavian "model" of combining economic growth with a strong welfare state, i.e., high taxes and a broad array of social services, including health care. Productivity growth in Sweden during the last 10 years has been stronger than in the U.S. and in Western Europe.

---

[1] Former State Secretary for Higher Education and Research in Sweden.

Second, and related, is the political culture of Sweden. The Social-Democratic Party had been in power in Sweden since the Second World War with a few exceptions: during 1976–1982 and 1991–1994. At the last election in September 2006, the Social-Democratic government lost power and now there is a coalition of four parties from the right of the political spectrum, the Conservative Party being the biggest. During the last 12 years of Social-Democratic rule this party did not have an absolute majority and had to lean on the Green Party and the Left Party to get proposals through Parliament. When working out bills on research or higher education in the ministry, negotiations had to take place with representatives of those parties in order to make sure that the government's proposals would pass in Parliament. Negotiations also had to take place with other ministries, particularly with the Ministry of Finance.

A Growing System

Within this political and economic context, the structure of the nation's system of higher education mirrors that of other European countries. There is homogeneity, uniformity, and centralization. Most postsecondary education in Sweden belongs to the higher education sector, including, for example, different health care professions, schoolteachers and preschool teachers, and the art colleges. There are some 50 institutions of higher education, most of them public. Both public and private universities and colleges are, to varying degrees, supported by the state, i.e., taxpayers' money. Resources for education and research are granted separately. For undergraduate education, resources are granted based on the number of students and their accomplishments, but the government also sets a maximum total amount that each university or college can obtain (as the total grants for higher education are always limited).

Resources for research are given either through direct faculty grants or via research councils and other government agencies and from private sources; i.e., business and industry. The external funding has steadily increased over the years, a fact that many institutions of higher education complain about. External funding amounts to some 50 percent of the research income but in some areas, such as technology and medicine, it may be around two-thirds.

There are general eligibility requirements, but for admittance to most programs and courses there is also special eligibility. *Numerus clausus* is used for all study programs. The government decides what degrees may be awarded and the goals of these degrees. The content of courses and programs, however, is decided by the institutions of higher education themselves. There is no tuition, not for Swedish students and not for foreigners. Sweden also has a fairly generous system of study finance in undergraduate education. The support consists of a grant and a loan. Students may go abroad to study and bring their study assistance with them. In research training, the student can obtain either a postgraduate post or a study grant.

The number of students in undergraduate education has increased from 14,000 in the mid 1940s to 330,000 today. Research training has also expanded markedly. There is at least one college or university in each county in Sweden. The number of women has increased from 20 percent to 60 percent in undergraduate education. There are big differences among different programs in the proportion of women. The proportion of women who finish a doctoral degree has increased from 15 percent in the 1970s to 45 percent today. Since the beginning of the 1990s, participation in undergraduate education has widened. The proportion of students with a working-class background has increased from 18 to 24 percent.

So what has driven this enormous expansion? What is the ideology behind it? There are several factors.

- A belief that knowledge is the key to the future, to economic growth and prosperity of the country, but also to the well-being of the individual. Both higher education and research have benefited from this belief (Sweden spends around four percent of its GDP on R&D).

- A conviction that access to higher education should be possible for everyone regardless of family background, gender, or ethnicity. This is facilitated by having no tuition fees, geographic closeness to the institutions of higher education, and a generous system of study assistance.

- An idea that education and research belong together, that research benefits from the input of students. Therefore, most research is carried out at the universities and colleges; there are few research institutes outside of higher education.

Reflecting similar goals in other E.U. nations, including England, the Social-Democratic government set a goal that 50 percent of an age cohort should go on to higher education before the age of 25. The figure now is now about 45 percent. The new government has not adopted this goal, partly because it has felt that it is more important to increase the quality of higher education; i.e., to grant more resources per student, partly because it has been difficult for some with certain higher education diplomas to get employment. Generally speaking, though, the more education individuals have, the less likely it is that they will be unemployed. There has been a diminished interest in higher education among young people, so that fewer have applied. This decrease happened for the first time in the spring semester of 2006 (by nine percent compared with the spring of 2005) and continued for the fall semester of 2006 (by another eight percent). Also for the first time in 2005, the number of students in higher education diminished by 2.4 percent.

It may be that the media's focus on those unemployed after higher education has contributed to the diminished interest in pursuing an academic program. However, there are still more applicants than can be accommodated in undergraduate education. During the fall of 2005, for example, the number of new applicants was 117,000, compared with 57,000 admitted. The size of the age cohorts of young people is increasing dramatically. From 2003 until 2010 the number of 20-year-olds in the population is expected to increase by 30 percent—from 100,000 to a bit more than 130,000. This means that there is a need to expand higher education if the transition rates from upper secondary education to higher education are not going to decrease.

In spite of Sweden's positive economic development, the labor market did not really catch up until after the election. If the demand for jobs continues to grow as it has for the last year, this may also negatively affect the demand for higher education, if students can find jobs immediately after upper secondary education. Another difference between the former government and the present one concerns who should be eligible for higher education after upper secondary education. The present rules of admittance to higher education give general eligibility to anyone who has completed upper secondary education, even to those who have completed a vocational program in upper secondary education. The new government wants to separate the students in upper secondary school so that mainly theoretical programs will grant general eligibility to higher education. Those in vocational programs in upper secondary education would be able to update their theoretical knowledge later on, in municipal adult education.

According to a recent study by the National Agency for Higher Education, there will be a surplus of people who have pursued studies in the natural sciences, in upper secondary teaching, architecture, the arts, journalism, and library science. A severe lack of teachers in the lower grades and preschool, doctors, dentists, and engineers will result if present trends continue. How the present government chooses to address these problems is not yet clear. This is understandable as this government has only been in power for six months. The problem will have to be addressed, no doubt.

Women in Higher Education

Equality between the sexes has been high on the political agenda in Sweden for decades. Not least, the very comprehensive and generous system of child care and parental leave is well-known abroad. This system has no doubt contributed to the fact that there are more children born in Sweden than in most Western European countries. For example, the government in Germany has been looking at the Swedish system of child care and parental leave as a possible solution to the low birth rate in Germany. The debate in Sweden now is about how many of the months of parental leave presently allowed should be divided between the man and the woman.

In political life women are well represented—in government, parliament, in the political assemblies of county councils and municipalities, and in the political party organizations. The focus now in Sweden is on the lack of women in corporate structures. The situation of women in academia, however, is not given much attention in the media.

The opportunities for women in academic life have no doubt improved since the mid 1990s. At that time some much-debated measures were taken by the government to improve the situation of women in research. Money was provided for the establishment of 32 professorial chairs and some 70 postdoctoral research appointments for the underrepresented gender (read women). In addition, there were new funds for research training posts to increase the number of women. The academic world reacted in a very negative way, with a few exceptions. What these measures created, however, was a much greater awareness of the situation of women in academia.

Other measures have followed since then. Today the universities and colleges have to always pay attention to equality between the sexes in whatever that they do. This is a regulation by law. Since 1992, the universities and colleges are supposed to actively promote and broaden participation in higher education.

The government yearly asks the universities and colleges to present measures undertaken to obtain a better balance between the number of men and women in education programs, including research training. Since 1997, the government sets recruitment goals for all categories of employees, such as professors, and defines targets for the other teaching and research categories, where the gender balance is uneven.

In terms of personnel, the government sets recruitment goals for professors, and encourages the universities and colleges to set their own recruitment goals for the other teaching and research personnel. The universities and colleges will have to report to the government on what they have done in order to achieve a better gender balance when recruiting personnel to posts such as deans, provosts, and other categories. All the research councils, such as the Research Council of Sweden and Vinnova (a government agency promoting technological research and innovation) will have to promote equality between the sexes in their activities of promoting science and research.

Finally, knowledge about gender issues can promote a more gender-balanced society. There are special funds for gender research, which have doubled in recent years, even if sums still are small. In 2004 women made up 60 percent of the student population in higher education. Among newcomers to research training they were 50 percent, up from 45 percent in the year 2000. Among those obtaining doctorate degrees, women constituted 45 percent in 2004 compared to 39 percent in 2000. Women held 40 percent of postdoctoral research appointments, 34 percent of senior lecturer positions, but constituted only 16 percent of professors. One-third of the vice-chancellors in Sweden are women, up from 17 percent in 2000. These figures show that measures taken have had an effect, as it is unlikely that this positive development would have taken place otherwise—at least the development would have been much slower. However, what has to change is the number of women who go into male-dominated educational programs and make careers within these areas. The number of women at the top of the academic ladder will have to be greatly increased. Without a constant focus on the issue of women, there is a risk that the positive development will be reversed.

Widening Participation of Nontraditional Student Groups

In a recently published study[2] the authors argue rightly that the key elements of the goal of widening participation in Sweden have been:

- liberal entrance requirements (only necessary qualifications should be required)
- recognizing informal learning and nonacademic qualifications
- equality of treatment (strict rules and centralized admission procedures)
- increasing geographical accessibility (at least one college or university in each county)
- expanding intake capacity to both pre-HE and HE
- upgrading of nonuniversity HE (vocationally oriented tertiary education)
- giving adult students not able to benefit from earlier education reforms a second chance

An important feature of the Swedish policy for widening participation has been to integrate new groups of students into the system of higher education without special treatment for them. Mainstreaming is the notion, as it is also when it comes to equality between men and women. To allow access by adult students, the general eligibility rules were changed in the late 1960s so that adults aged 25 or older with at least five years of work experience would be able to enroll in certain "open" fields of study at the universities and colleges. (This rule is likely to be changed by the new government). Likewise, the student support scheme was made more uniform for all students regardless of parental income, family situation, children, etc. A continuation of those policies was to consider student grants as pensionable income and to let students work part-time during the semesters.

The inclusion of postsecondary education, such as nursing, teaching, and shorter engineering programs often pursued by students from working-class backgrounds was also a way to widen participation in higher education, as was the general expansion of higher education into all regions of the country. It is a fact that geographic closeness to an institution of higher education has contributed to the recruitment of nontraditional student groups.

An important difference between Sweden and many other European countries that the authors of this report point to is that general eligibility for admission to higher education in Sweden does not guarantee admission, only the right to compete for admission. There is a word in the Swedish language that is used when discussing widening participation—"socially imbalanced recruitment" (to higher education). This occurs when young people with a certain social background attain more often than others a higher level of education. Statistics of students' background in terms of parental occupation and level of education are available every other year.

---

[2] ("Bridging the Gap: Widening Participation in Sweden and England" by Johansson, Kim, Storan, and Sörlin) Stockholm, Sweden: Swedish Institute for Studies in Education and Research.

Socially imbalanced recruitment was decreasing for the first time since the mid-1990s. Between the academic years 1993–94 and 2003–04 the proportion of students from a working-class background among new higher education students increased from 18 to 24 percent in the 18–34 age group. If, however, recruitment to higher education were to reflect the social composition of the population at large in these age brackets, one-third of the students would come from working-class backgrounds. The number of newcomers to higher education under the age of 35 has since 1993–94 increased in all social groups. In terms of individuals, the increase is from 62,000 to 83,000 persons. The increase has been the greatest for those with a working-class background, where the numbers have doubled in 10 years.

The differences in students' social background are bigger between programs than between institutions. In medicine and dentistry there are fewer students with a working-class background, but in (for example) nursing there are small differences in the backgrounds of the students at different higher education institutions. What is interesting to note is that in terms of the success rate there are no significant differences between students from different social backgrounds, but they vary according to the programs.

Middle-class students more often opt for the highly competitive programs in higher education whereas students from working-class backgrounds tend to pick shorter and more vocationally oriented programs. This reflects the choice of students in upper secondary education, where pupils can choose between theoretically or more vocationally oriented studies. Also, the upper secondary school reforms in the 1990s made the vocationally oriented courses more theoretical than before, which may have led to a higher dropout rate from upper secondary education.

Among nontraditional student groups are students with a foreign background (exchange students not included). Foreign background is defined as where both parents were born abroad or where the student was born abroad. The number of students with a foreign background has increased by almost 50 percent between 1994–95 and 2001–02. In 2003–04 those students constituted some 14 to 17 percent of all newcomers to higher education, which reflects the composition of the population at large. There are, however, great differences between nationalities. For example, students with an Iranian or Polish background were well represented, whereas students from Africa were very few. The number of students with disabilities has also increased. These students can obtain special pedagogical support. The number of students who received such support increased from 2,000 students in 2002 to 3,400 in 2004. The universities and colleges have to set aside 0.3 percent of their basic funding for this support.

All in all, the information presented above points in a positive direction when it comes to widening participation. And it was in the mid 1990s that things started to change. It reflected in part that the Swedish society was becoming a multicultural society, and that the notion that diversity was an asset had gained ground. A special commission on diversity in higher education was appointed in the late 1990s. The commission proposed a number of measures to broaden access to higher education through (for example) preparatory courses of different kinds, language courses, and more flexible admission procedures. As a result a new commission on recruitment was set up to stimulate various kinds of activities at the universities and colleges and 120 million SEK was allotted to this commission between 2002 and 2004. Another commission of equal size in terms of funds was set up to stimulate regional cooperation and increased enrollment in higher education.

For many years some universities and colleges have arranged an introductory year to higher education to give students the qualifications they need to enter regular higher education. This started in science and has since been broadened to other areas. The regulations are such that these courses can be arranged in areas where there are fewer applicants than number of places. Universities and colleges can also arrange a so-called college education of one year in cooperation with municipal institutions of adult education. The latter programs have only attracted a few students, whereas the introductory courses enroll several thousands of students. Around 70 percent of those students continued their studies in higher education after the introductory courses.

The Swedish Net University was established in 2002. Some 30 universities and colleges cooperate to develop courses in distance education with the help of IT. The government provided almost half a billion SEK over a three-year period as an extra allowance for each full-time student admitted to such courses. An evaluation by the National Agency for Higher Education has shown that distance education with IT support has been able to recruit more students with working-class backgrounds than campus courses have.

The Challenge of Demographic Change

Widening participation for women and nontraditional student groups in higher education has been a political objective for decades. Many of the educational reforms that have taken place in the last 40 years have affected participation by women and nontraditional student groups in a positive way, even if there were also other objectives of these reforms. Particularly since the 1990s, changes have taken place when it comes to women and nontraditional student groups, including those of foreign descent. Few changes would take place without government intervention, and government measures to promote these groups' participation can help and have helped. And, in a system that is largely financed by the state, many of the achievements would not have taken place without additional resources.

A special challenge in the years to come is demographic development. Age cohorts will be much bigger and unless funds are provided for an additional number of students, a smaller proportion of young people will be able to pursue studies in higher education. If higher education is not expanded and special measures to widen participation are not continued, fewer students from working-class homes and from the immigrant population will enroll in higher education.

Chapter 10

Fostering Competition and Creativity in German and European Higher Education

Wilhelm Krull[1]

Since the late 1990s we have been witnessing enormous changes in the higher education and research landscape of Europe. Declarations and agreements named after cities like Bologna (1999), Lisbon (2001), and Barcelona (2003) are just publicly acknowledged signposts of new policies and approaches that more or less simultaneously affect institutions at various levels of decision-making within the European Union (E.U.). Creating European Higher Education and Research Areas (EHEAs, ERAs) is by no means a straightforward endeavor. Indeed, it forces us to thoroughly rethink and subsequently realign our hitherto quite stable institutional concepts and approaches, in particular when it comes to meeting the requirements of up-to-date and sustainable undergraduate and graduate education, but also in creating a stimulating and inspiring environment for achieving breakthroughs in research and technological development. Ultimately, each institution has to live up to the challenges of increasing global competition and of establishing its own culture of creativity.

It is against this background that this chapter addresses some of the most significant shifts in the policymaking, financing, and governing of higher educa-

---

[1] Volkswagen Foundation.

tion and research in Germany and the E.U., as well as the challenges involved in reconfiguring enrollment policies, management processes, and institutional research structures. Last, but not least, it also comments on the rapidly changing public-private interface in higher education, research, and technological innovation.

Changes and Challenges

Change and talking about change and the challenges that go with it are as old as European thinking. The Greek philosopher Heraklitos once said, "Change is the only thing in the world which is unchanging." And yet, when we look back at the fundamentally new developments of the past 10 to 15 years, we cannot help but recognize that the speed as well as the impact of change has increased quite dramatically. This not only applies to the European political landscape and its restructuring since 1990, but also to the public and private infrastructures that so deeply affect our daily lives. Gradually, we have come to realize that we live in an increasingly interdependent, basically science- and technology-driven world that requires a thorough rethinking and subsequent realignment of traditional approaches.

As far as the higher education and research system itself is concerned, I foresee six major developments. The first one is the growing impact of electronics and information technology on the creation, distribution, and absorption of new knowledge. The second one is an increased emphasis on inter-, or transdisciplinary approaches; and the third one is the move from bi- or trilateral internationalization toward network approaches and strategic alliances, setting up for example joint graduate schools or virtual research centers across the globe, and thus linking up with elite institutions in other countries. The fourth major development is the changing public-private interface and its consequences for the division of labor, particularly in the research and technology sector, as well as the need to mobilize more private resources for public purposes like basic and strategic research.

The fifth major development is on the research side itself, which has to come to terms with integrating evaluation, foresight approaches, and priority-setting processes, thereby trying to find new ways of assessing performance while at the same time avoiding solutions that are too technocratic. And finally, of course, there is the growing public concern about recent scientific and technological developments, particularly in areas like stem cell research or nanotechnology, but also in other areas, where the research community has to consider discussing openly which kind of programs and which kind of approaches we develop.

During the next 20 years, Europe's economic paradigm will change fundamentally. While the manufacturing base will continuously shrink, future growth and social welfare will rely increasingly on knowledge-intensive products and services. And we can also observe that, particularly with our demographic development in Germany and more or less in the whole of Europe, we are faced with a completely new challenge of how an aging society can actually innovate. In this respect—as well as with respect to the overall financial situation—priority-setting will become even more important in the future.

Strengths and Weaknesses

When we try to position Europe's performance on a global scale, it is interesting to see that the picture is not as bleak as it is often perceived and also reported in the press. As we know, the E.U. countries have agreed to a goal for 2010 of spending three percent of the GDP for research and development. It is an ambitious goal, and thus far only the Nordic countries have reached the three percent threshold or are even far beyond it. With respect to the total number of graduates, the figure for the E.U. is considerably larger (roughly three million) than for the United States (2.2 million). Also, the number of Ph.D. graduates (85,000) is almost twice as large as the number for the U.S. (44,000). When we look at the numbers of scientific papers published in the different parts of the world, we also see that Europe has overtaken the United States in the mid-1990s and is currently the largest producer of scientific publications (with a 38 percent share compared to 33 percent for the U.S.). But in the meantime we have to recognize that the Asia-Pacific region (with a share of 25 percent) is catching up quite fast. This rapid growth of scientific output in Asia-Pacific nations is in stark contrast to slow growth in Europe and stagnation in the United States. If this trend continues, the Asia-Pacific nations will be the biggest research community in about 10 years' time. In a number of other relative indicators—such as publications per inhabitant, per scientist, or per million Euros spent in our universities—the E.U. is also ahead of the United States and Japan; and in triad patents per millions spent in business R&D, some European countries—Germany, Sweden, and the Netherlands—clearly outperform Japan and the U.S.

With respect to top-ranking elite institutions, Europe is not in such a good position. For example in a ranking of the best universities published by Shanghai Xiaotong University in 2005, only two of the top 20 universities were European, while 17 were American. On the other hand, in the top 500 of the same ranking, Germany comes second with 46 universities, compared with 38 British and 168 American universities. Of course, we could discuss the basis for these rankings and the explanations for these results at length, but it seems to me that the results basically reflect the fact that we have tried to develop good universities in the various parts of Europe, but over the last three decades we have largely considered higher education as a tool for regional development, and have not really focused on creating high-class, internationally competitive universities. The result is reflected in not only these rankings, but also in many other benchmarking studies.

In particular, Europe has been losing ground in the field of basic breakthroughs. Fifty years ago, European scientists dominated the lists of the Nobel

Prize awardees and other prestigious prizes as well. Today, Nobel Prizes and similarly renowned awards are mainly won by scientists working in the U.S. And the gap in R&D investments per capita between the E.U. and the U.S. is steadily increasing. Apart from a few research areas such as astrophysics, space research, nuclear physics, and molecular biology, Europe suffers from an almost total lack of transnational support of basic and strategic research. In particular, risky, open-ended frontier research is not supported sufficiently, and it still remains to be seen whether the newly established European Research Council (ERC) will be able to change this.

The message for European higher education and research in an environment of global competition seems clear: We really have to make an effort if we want to develop competitive breeding grounds for new talents and ideas, as well as attract some of the most competent researchers to our institutions. However, as the relative indicators show, we are not doing as badly as is publicly perceived, we are doing quite well in some respects, and we still have a very strong research base—I believe it is important to keep this in mind when analyzing the overall situation. But we really have to do something to establish new creative milieus in order to achieve more breakthroughs.

New Contracts between Universities and Governments

With the exception of the United Kingdom and the Netherlands (where the principles of accountability and new public management were already applied to the higher education sector in the 1980s), the relationship between European governments and universities, even in the early to mid-1990s, was still characterized by political and financial patronage. Based on input-related facts and figures, in most cases just the sheer numbers of students, professors, assistants, etc., meant the respective institution was more or less entitled to a certain amount of government subsidies. In many respects, the related processes and procedures put the universities, in particular their leadership, in a quite comfortable position. Without almost any pressure to demonstrate the efficiency and effectiveness of its operations, often more money would flow into the institution solely based on mutually agreed upon quantitative increases (more students = more professors = more money).

By and large, this system of political and financial patronage came to an end in the course of the 1990s. With the implementation of new budgeting procedures, performance indicators, evaluation and benchmarking exercises, an explosion in the area of institutional as well as subject-related rankings, and an increased emphasis on successfully raising money from other sources, e.g., from research councils, private foundations, and from industry, the relationships between governments and universities were transformed into contractual partnerships. Usually, the university had to commit itself to achieving mutually agreed upon goals in teaching and research (occasionally also in technology transfer) within the next four or five years, and in exchange for its endeavor the government committed itself to secure budgetary continuity for the respective period of time.

Due to the fact that European universities were neither organizationally nor administratively equipped to manage their affairs by objectives—particularly not with respect to the necessary personnel development and technical infrastructure—the transformation of the contract relationship with the government into its internal decision-making structures and processes turned out to be quite a cumbersome learning process. With a few exceptions, mostly those supported through specifically designed programs such as "Efficiency through Autonomy" by the Volkswagen Foundation, or similar initiatives of the German Donors Association (Stifterverband für die Deutsche Wissenschaft) and the Bertelsmann Foundation, hardly any university was aware of its own strengths and weaknesses. Strategically relevant reporting systems and medium- to long-term planning procedures were practically nonexistent. They were often introduced on request of the newly established governing boards whose members helped to transfer know-how from other institutions as well as the private sector.

Despite the many difficulties encountered in the late 1990s and the numerous controversies, even in the early years of the 21st century, about the adequacy and usefulness of the new governance structures, decision-making processes, and financial operations, it can rightly be said that at least all those universities that proactively made use of the new opportunities for increased self-regulation and enhanced transparency nowadays feel no desire to return to the old system. Last, but not least in view of the enormous speed of change and the widely felt need to quickly adapt to an ever more competitive environment, it has become clear that the necessary degree of efficiency and effectiveness can only be achieved by unbureaucratically, interactively, and flexibly governed institutions that are fully aware of their strengths and weaknesses, and know how to make the best possible use of newly emerging opportunities.

Reconfiguring the Public-Private Interface

In many European countries, citizens are used to carrying a high tax burden, and expect governments to cover the costs of public institutions. However, the interface is becoming blurred between domains that have been publicly financed, and those that hitherto have been part of the private sector, and over the past decade there has clearly been a shift toward a stronger involvement of private persons and institutions. Higher education and research policymakers as well as university rectors are increasingly stressing the need for new "public private partnerships," and are practicing new modes of financing. Meanwhile there is a wide spectrum of private involvement in funding public universities. These range from newly introduced tuition fees and donations by alumni, increased funds raised from foundations all the way through to contract research and newly established linkages between publicly financed universities and privately run research laboratories and companies. This has by no means been a straightforward development; rather, it has turned out to involve a difficult process of mutual learning and trust-building. Nevertheless, it seems a necessary, if not inevitable step for both sides.

Well into the 1980s, there was to be a dividing line between publicly financed universities dedicated to the creation of new knowledge as a public good, and industry, which was to produce marketable goods financed by private capital. Today, the borders between the two domains have lost importance. In many areas, the distinction between the results of basic research, and their contribution to the advancement of the knowledge base as well as the development of new solutions to practical problems that can be transferred into new products and processes is no longer valid. Especially in generic technologies, such as computer science, materials research, and biotechnology, innovation has turned into a simultaneous, interactive process. Private investment in publicly funded research laboratories, joint ventures between universities and major companies, the outsourcing of long-term research activities by industrial R&D divisions, the establishment of joint professorships for entrepreneurship—these are just a few of the changes occurring at the public-private interface that require not only more flexible regulatory policies, but also more effective approaches to the production, absorption, and distribution of new knowledge.

Also with respect to infrastructures there are now a number of initiatives and concrete examples in which the interface between the public and private areas of responsibility has shifted far into the field of commerce, and this does not just apply to the construction and management of real estate, the provision of high-power computers, and so forth, but also to joint training courses. In addition, there are by now in Germany alone more than 30 private higher education institutions, most of them small-scale, often single-subject institutions, e.g., law schools and business schools, the only exception being the International University at Bremen, which recently joined forces with the Swiss-based Jacobs Foundation. It provides more than 1,200 student places in a wide spectrum of different disciplines encompassing undergraduate as well as graduate courses. On the other hand also some of the technical universities such as Karlsruhe, Munich, and Hamburg-Harburg have developed private arms in order to market their training and research capacities at an international level, in particular to students from outside Europe.

Higher Education and Research Policy Making in the E.U.

Despite the wide variety of different higher education and research systems in Europe as well as the quite diversified and often multifaceted structures within each country, we can nevertheless observe a growing trend toward converging policies, similar reconfigurations, and subsequent realignments across the continent. This is due to the impact of the new currents of globalization. The "Bologna Process" and the creation of a common "European Higher Education and Research Area" proposed by the commission and endorsed by the Council of

Ministers must also be seen in this context. Based on similar student workloads, bachelor's and master's degrees will in future be conferred by universities all over Europe, and the implementation of a European Credit Transfer System (ECTS) has enhanced mobility while at the same time diploma supplements allow for a high degree of flexibility. Competition and cooperation across borders are no longer mutually exclusive. On the contrary, networking and establishing strategic alliances in competing for the best students and the most prestigious research grants at the European level are of greater importance than ever before.

However, this does not imply that at the end of this restructuring process there will remain only a few "global universities" (Peter Scott). Growth in size of staff and student numbers, mergers and campus acquisitions, or an expansion of one's campus across the globe do not seem adequate responses to the changes and challenges outlined above. What is needed is not a megalomaniacal approach, but rather a careful selection of aims, strategies, and structures that can help the respective institution to fully realize its potential. In this respect, proactively minded, small- to medium-scale universities may well be better equipped to successfully weather the storms to come than larger tankers. In particular, research-active universities with a clear focus on creating a strong community of researchers, lecturers, and students will through international linkages of their research centers and graduate schools probably have a competitive advantage. It could come as a surprise to many policymakers and university leaders on the current scene that Wilhelm von Humboldt's basic ideas will yet again survive another revolution in higher education and research in a quite triumphant manner.

This process of realignment within the university sector coincides with a wide array of attempts in several European countries to assess and subsequently reconfigure the existing funding agencies, or to establish new ones (like in France and Ireland). Although in recent years more and more national funding agencies have been moving toward providing new incentives for medium- to large-scale inter- and transdisciplinary centers as well as toward international collaboration, it has become increasingly clear that there is a lack of pan-European funding structures that could help to establish both a cooperative climate for the development of new ideas, and an institutional environment that will encourage competition among Europe's best researchers to produce more cutting-edge results.

Crucial to the process of ultimately establishing a European Research Council (ERC) was a redefinition of "European Added Value," which until recently was confined to the collaboration of research teams from different countries. With the advent of the 7th Framework Programme we now have a broader definition that incorporates the principle of allowing a researcher in any European country to compete with all other researchers on the basis of excellence. Competition in order to achieve real excellence in research will thus become an essential part of a new, forward-looking definition of "European Added Value."

The ERC is designed to be a funding body for basic research and will cover all fields of science and scholarship. Initially, there will be two types of grants available. First, the Starting Independent Researcher Grants ("ERC starting grants") will provide support to the independent careers of excellent researchers, whatever their nationality, located in, or moving to the E.U. and associated countries, who are at the stage of establishing or consolidating their research team or program. The ERC starting grants will amount to a lump sum of up to two million Euros for up to five years. It is envisaged that 200 such starting grants will be made annually. Due to the fact that the ERC's funding will increase substantially over the period 2007–2013, there will also be a second scheme for so-called "Advanced Grants" that will support excellent research projects led by established top research leaders, working in or moving to work in Europe, whatever their nationality. Both schemes are designed to foster Europe's traditional scientific excellence and in particular to stimulate transformative research.

On its homepage, the ERC clearly emphasizes the goal of supporting "frontier research." It stresses as "the secret of success": "The ERC will offer the long-term support that can provide top research leaders the freedom and flexibility they need to succeed. As a result, it will boost Europe's research performance by helping to attract and retain the best researchers; stimulating creativity; encouraging risk-taking; promoting discovery and high-impact research."[2]

Facilitating Creativity

Europe can only be successful in establishing and maintaining a globally competitive knowledge-based society if it continuously strives to enhance the quality of its research base, to strengthen the structural dynamics of the various research and innovation systems, and to support frontier research in carefully selected areas. Each institution will have to review its own processes of quality assurance, and to respond to the question whether it provides a stimulating training and research environment that encourages risk-taking and enables its members to break new ground.

Achieving and maintaining such a culture of creativity is not at all straightforward. On the contrary, it is full of paradoxes and contradictions. Whilst every institution, not least for securing its own survival, has to insist that its members adhere to its rules, quality standards, etc., the creation of new ideas ultimately is about breaking the rules and about being tolerant to errors made. Epistemologically speaking, radically new ideas can often not be phrased in terms of the initial question, and the openness to "fresh thinking" is not only required by those who produce new ideas, but also by those who are expected to pick them up. The readiness to listen to independent voices inside and outside of one's own institutional network, to encourage risk-taking in "off the beaten track" areas,

---

[2] European Research Council (2009) <http://erc.europa.eu/index.cfm>.

and to foster a climate of mutual learning are prerequisites for successfully establishing a true culture of creativity. They have to be complemented by an innovation-friendly human resource policy.

In view of the increasing complexity of knowledge production, many universities and research institutions have tried to expand in size and diversity, and subsequently created an increase in hierarchic structures and bureaucracy. More and more, it has become clear that such increases in size and diversity have negatively affected performance, and produced a great deal of unproductive heterogeneity, a decrease in interdisciplinary interaction, or transdisciplinary integration, and ultimately led to great losses in innovation-friendly experimentation and flexibility.

When it comes to establishing a true culture of creativity, there are at least seven aspects that have to be considered:

- *Competence*—Train or hire competent researchers and enable them to develop their skills as freely as possible.

- *Courage*—Not only on the side of the researchers, but also at the level of institutional leadership and on the side of funding organizations, in particular endowed foundations. The readiness to take risks must be complemented by a high degree of error tolerance.

- *Communication*—Thought-provoking discussions are essential for achieving progress in research, in particular cross-disciplinary and transcultural exchanges, but also interactions with the outside world.

- *Diversity*—New knowledge is usually formed at the boundaries of established fields, so the interfaces between these areas of expertise must be activated. To be successful it is essential to provide ample opportunities for all the researchers to interact intensively so that new paths can be developed and breakthroughs achieved.

- *Innovativeness*—Academic leaders as well as heads of foundations must appreciate unconventional approaches and encourage risk-taking by providing incentives such as additional funding and long-term commitments.

- *Persistence*—To forge new paths in a barely known territory often takes longer than two or three years, the usual lengths of project funding. Mistakes must be allowed as well as changes of direction.

- *Serendipity*—It is impossible to plan the precise moment at which a radically new idea emerges or a major scientific discovery occurs. But there are numerous examples in the history of university-based research that prove that it is possible to establish a particularly stimulating environment more conducive to scientific breakthroughs than others. Although there is no one-size-fits-all kind of recipe we can apply, it is certainly worthwhile to try and try again.

With respect to fostering creativity I consider these aspects as preconditions. It is important to focus on small teams of five to seven researchers embedded in an adequately enriched environment, and supported by modes of funding that provide medium- to long-term financing of some seven to 10 years. Such time and space for some thorough rethinking of common wisdom is urgently needed and has to be expanded. This also calls for a reconfiguring of the review process, including personal presentations and interviews, and last, but not least, the actively communicated readiness of the leadership of the institutions involved to take risks.

If Europe wants to meet the challenges involved in the increasing processes of globalization, it must act swiftly and at the same time take a long view. It must also be prepared to make long-term commitments whilst maintaining the flexibility to respond to new challenges. The most important prerequisites for performing successfully at the global level clearly are new, Europe-wide arenas of competition for some of the most prestigious grants, more coherent approaches to higher education and research policymaking at the national level, and at the institutional level an innovation-friendly governance and decision-making structure.

Universities and research institutions have to constantly tap their resources and realize their potential, ensure efficiency in their spending practices, accelerate and simplify their processes, and intensify communication within the organization and beyond it. Ultimately, we should not feel overwhelmed by the complex and sometimes quite complicated issues involved. Rather we should take an optimistic view, just like Albert Einstein, who once said, "Amidst all the difficulties, there is also room for opportunities."

Chapter 11

China and India:
A Steep Climb to World-Class Universities

Philip Altbach[1]

Although the booms of China and India have been fueled by cheap labor and inexpensive low-end manufacturing, the economic future of these countries relies on a better-educated workforce. Both countries lack sufficiently educated personnel to meet demand for employment in the expanding and increasingly sophisticated sectors of manufacturing and service. Universities are central in the race to arm these countries' respective workforces with skills to make them competitive in the global knowledge system. However, neither China nor India is well equipped to face their common challenges in improving the quality of postsecondary education and increasing access to these institutions. The two countries are taking widely different approaches to their education dilemmas, with China working hands-on to build world-class institutions, while India appears to turn a blind eye to the urgency of increasing education funding.

Today, neither country is an academic powerhouse, although China may be moving in that direction. According to the London-based Times Higher Education Supplement's 2006 ranking of the top 100 universities, two are in China (Peking

---

[1] Center for International Higher Education, Boston College. A version of this article appeared in the *Far Eastern Economic Review* (January-February, 2007).

and Tsinghua universities), three are in Hong Kong (Hong Kong University, the Chinese University of Hong Kong, and Hong Kong University of Science and Technology), and one is in India (Indian Institutes of Technology).

For both countries, the last 50 years have not been kind to traditional ideas about learning. Each has a long tradition of respect for knowledge and academic learning. China, after all, created the civil-service examination system, and Confucian values stress education and learning. India invented the concept of the guru. However, both China and India eventually jettisoned established educational institutions and adopted western models. India, after several centuries of colonialism, inherited the British university ideal and English as the main medium of instruction. China adopted western education models even prior to the establishment of the People's Republic in 1949, although it subsequently turned to Soviet models and then rejected higher education altogether during the Cultural Revolution, before returning to western patterns of higher education development in the 1980s. Like many developing countries, China and India have looked to the West for academic guidance.

China and India have huge higher education enrollments, yet still struggle to meet growing demand for access to postsecondary education. China has 23 million students in postsecondary education—the largest enrollment in the world—although it educates 21 percent of the age group, still low by the standards of industrialized nations. India has the third-largest postsecondary enrollment in the world with 16 million students, but this accounts for only 13 percent of the age group.

The world has only seen the development of mass higher education systems in the past half-century or so. For developing countries, the advent of "massification" is even more recent. It is estimated that total worldwide demand for higher education will more than double in the next 18 years, from around 100 million today to 263 million by 2025, with the majority of new demand coming from developing countries.

In both countries there is a stark shortage of globally competitive researchers, scholars, and managers to staff world-class universities or other institutions. Employers in both countries complain that the graduates of the bottom levels of the higher education systems are not sufficiently well trained to be productively employed in the new high-technology and service sectors. There is too much reliance on rote learning in the university selection process and in the academic curriculum, and too little creativity from graduates.

As a percentage of GDP, neither country spends enough on higher education; both are well under the international average for investing in higher education. India spends 0.37 percent and China 0.50 percent of GDP on higher education, compared to the U.S. at 1.41 percent and the United Kingdom at 1.07 percent.

Further, both countries export a high proportion of their "best and brightest" to the U.S. and other developed countries. India and China rank first and second with regard to number of students studying in the U.S., accounting for a total of 142,000 students together, about a quarter of all international students in the U.S. And these countries send at least that number to the rest of the world. A large percentage of foreign-educated graduates from China and India do not return home after their studies—some estimate that between 70 percent and 80 percent remain abroad. But as the economies expand and offer stimulating and remunerative jobs, return rates will increase.

One new development in higher education that China and India face is the rapid growth of a private higher education sector. In common with other developing countries, China and India see the private sector as a way of absorbing rapidly expanding demand for access to higher education without much additional public expenditure. Very few private universities have aspired to the top of the academic hierarchy, however. A primary goal of the schools is to make money for their owners and managers, and thus the private sector largely serves those who can afford to pay tuition costs, excluding students from lower socio-economic backgrounds. Both countries have realized that an unregulated private sector is an invitation for chicanery of all kinds, and they are moving to enhance scrutiny and regulation. Ensuring that the private higher education sector serves broad public interest is a significant challenge.

What Would Confucius Do?

China has had a commitment to build a few internationally competitive universities for almost two decades now. Its "985" and "211" projects have identified a small number of universities for significant funding by the central government. This continuing infusion of funds, combined with government pressure to merge universities in some cities and guidelines to stress research and improve standards, have led to the marked improvement of a number of Chinese universities. The traditional "flagships" such as Peking and Tsinghua universities and a few others such as Shanghai Jiaotong and Fudan are now internationally competitive. However, pedagogy throughout Chinese higher education is lecture-based. Little discussion is encouraged, and building creativity has been recognized as a problem.

The top of the system faces some significant problems, though. Building a viable research and self-regulating academic culture is not easy. Continuing cases of plagiarism, favoritism in appointments and admissions, and other corrupt practices are evidence of the challenges. Academic freedom is not yet guaranteed, especially in the social sciences and humanities. While efforts have been made to create a stable career path for professors, further work is needed. World-class universities need more than fine laboratories, state-of-the-art information technology, and good libraries—they require a unified academic culture built on meritocratic values, competition, collaboration among faculty and students in research and teaching, and a commitment to honesty. The top Chinese universities have made major strides in these areas but still have a long way to go, as evidenced by the recent firing of a prominent professor, Chen Jin at Shanghai Jiaotong University, for academic dishonesty.

At the bottom of the system, things are less rosy. Demand for access has led to the rapid expansion in the number of universities and enrollment growth in many. Student-teacher ratios have deteriorated. Tuition has been increased to pay for the expansion since public funding for these institutions is inadequate. Public universities have turned to a variety of money-making schemes, including adding students who have lower entrance exam scores but who pay high fees, or opening semiprivate branch campuses that charge high tuition. Student riots have taken place over the name on the diploma granted by at least one of these "branch" campuses. Universities have started consulting firms, and have urged their faculty to moonlight at private schools—all to earn needed income. These efforts generally detract from the educational mission of the university, and lower the standards.

Some of the new private universities are of questionable quality. The majority of these institutions are not fully recognized by China's Ministry of Education, and therefore their degrees and certificates do not have full legitimacy. Provincial and municipal authorities establish or authorize universities and colleges, often without adequate resources. These schools provide access but often deliver an inferior product.

There is widespread criticism in China about higher education standards and an oversupply of university graduates. The two issues are directly related. Graduates of the small number of "name brand" universities have an easier time finding employment. A recent survey by the American Chamber of Commerce in Shanghai notes that a skills shortage has emerged as the top challenge for U.S. companies operating in China as they find that local graduates do not have the required knowledge or skills. Graduates are having an increasingly difficult time finding jobs—in 2005 almost half of the four million graduates could not find satisfactory jobs.

Chinese authorities have recognized the problem, and are starting to loosen some of the overly rigid controls over the universities, while at the same time trying to rein in expansion. However, until there is a fundamental rethinking of how students are admitted to higher education and how teaching and learning is organized, major improvement is unlikely. Further, higher education needs more adequate funding if it is to provide both quality and access.

India Struggles to Pass

India's large and diverse higher education system is a paradox. On the one hand, it produces a modest number of highly competent graduates who readily find employment in the nation's burgeoning high-tech industry and are competitive in the international job market. On the other, the large majority of India's colleges and universities are well below international standards. Indian employers complain about the low quality of most university graduates, including those in engineering and management. The high-tech industry has even been hiring small numbers of Americans and other foreigners to work in India because of a shortage of sufficiently competent local applicants.

This paradox is based on several factors. At the top of the Indian higher education system there are only a small number of institutions that have high standards, innovative curricula, and competent and committed faculty. While these institutions are not lavishly funded—by international standards they have modest budgets—they have had fairly consistent public support. Some institutions have considerable autonomy to set their own curriculum, and they are rigorously meritocratic in hiring and promotion. Examples include the Indian Institutes of Technology, Tata Institute of Fundamental Research, the All-India Institute of Medical Sciences, and the Indian Institute of Science, among others. These schools are extraordinarily competitive—thousands of applicants sit for national examinations each year, and only the cream of the crop is accepted. But total student enrollment at top institutions is still only about 50,000 students out of 16 million nationwide.

The higher education system in India is based on more than 18,000 colleges —amazingly half of the world's total postsecondary institutions—many of which are too small to take advantage of economies of scale and to have adequate libraries and laboratories. Most of these colleges are affiliated to some 250 public universities that have the responsibility for setting and grading examinations, approving the curriculum, and determining a variety of rules for the colleges. This structure is a legacy of British colonialism and ensures a straitjacket of bureaucratic rules and regulations. Supporters of the status quo point out that the propensity for academic corruption and caste or ethnic politics requires strong controls. However, innovative ideas typically require the creation of a new institution outside of the structure of the existing universities. The structural impediments to reform are strong, and the traditional universities have not changed much.

The main sources of public funding for higher education are the state governments, which have differing policies and commitments to higher education. It is fair to say that none of the governments provide adequate support. The central government gives funding for a small group of nationally prominent institutions as well as research and academic innovation, including curricular reform. Most of the 18,000 colleges are privately managed. Traditionally, the majority of these colleges had public financial support, but by 2006, more than half were "unaided" and received no direct government support—they are dependent on tuition charges and other fees levied on the students.

India does have several higher education advantages. The use of English as the medium of instruction and research in a significant part of the system makes international links easier. A tradition of academic freedom is also important. Many top Indian scholars and scientists already have strong ties to the international academic community. However, many in India recognize that higher education is in crisis and is not contributing to economic development. The establishment by Prime Minister Manmohan Singh in 2006 of a Knowledge Commission to recommend ways of improving higher education and linking it better to development is a sign of this concern. The fact that several members of the commission have resigned in frustration does not bode well for its future. The challenge of numbers is overwhelming: India now educates only a small proportion of the age group and needs to increase coverage. The demand for access combined with the need for a few high-quality universities of international standards seem insurmountable challenges in the context of inadequate public funding and entrenched bureaucracy and inertia within the system.

Internationalization

Both China and India are beginning to pursue international strategies in higher education. While both countries are mainly exporters of students, they also host significant numbers of students from abroad. In 2004–2005, 110,800 international students studied at Chinese universities, while 17,500 studied in India. The large majority of students coming to both countries are from developing countries. While China sees its internationalization strategy as a projection of its "soft power" as well as a way to earn income, India seems mainly concerned with the commercial advantages of international higher education. While statistics are unavailable, it is likely that a significant proportion of these international students are from the large Chinese and Indian diasporas.

Both countries are also major targets for the international strategies of other countries and their universities. The U.S., the United Kingdom, Australia, the Netherlands, Germany, and others are establishing links with Chinese universities and are moving toward establishing branch campuses in China. They are also looking at India as a location for branches and linkages, but a changing regulatory environment and lack of clarity about how programs might work have been impediments. Most industrialized countries heavily recruit students from China and India to study in their countries. A majority of international students in Japan, for example, are from China. The same is true for New Zealand and some other host nations.

While China and India seek to establish themselves as forces in international higher education, they are so far the subjects of other countries' international initiatives. In the long run, China and India can become international players. There is already a growing interest in studying the cultures and languages of these two key countries. As universities improve and become more integrally linked to the world higher education system, they will become more attractive to overseas students and scholars, mainly from the developing world. It is unlikely that they will become major international destinations on the scale of the United States or some of the major European nations.

Who Is Ahead?

Comparing these two giants is not easy. Both are large and complex academic systems with multiple problems and great potential. World-class institutions in both countries are absolutely necessary for future social and economic development. Clearly, China is currently ahead in the knowledge race: It educates a larger proportion of its age group, it has a few universities that have achieved international standards of quality, and it has made investments, while spotty, that contribute to continued development. It benefits from the ability to focus resources and policies, although the danger of overly centralized government direction in higher education is significant. India, on the other hand, has a very few small specialized postsecondary institutions that operate at international standards. Even with these exceptional institutions, a handful of productive academic departments in some universities, and some high-quality undergraduate colleges, Indian higher education suffers from bureaucracy, inertia, and a scarcity of resources. There are few, if any, current government efforts to build world-class higher education capacity in India.

The two Asian giants will dominate their region's—and perhaps the world's—economic future. If they can build world-class higher education systems that serve demands for mass access, the needs of a sophisticated economy, and active participation in the world knowledge system, their development will be quicker and better sustained.

Chapter 12

An Upward Trajectory: Doctoral Education and Scientific Research in China

Wanhua Ma[1]

In the past 30 years, higher education in China experienced a remaking process. System expansion, diversification, and massification of Chinese higher education are the concepts used frequently to describe the changes. The establishment of graduate education is one of the key elements for leading Chinese universities in academic development and scientific research. Higher education system expansion helps the development of graduate education in China. In 1978, there were only 405 higher learning institutions in China, including three-year vocational training colleges. By 2006, there were already 1,867 public universities and colleges, with 444 public adult higher-learning institutions as well. System diversification also provides the possibility for high school students to get a tertiary education in the private sector.

Now in China, there are 278 private (Minban in Chinese) colleges and universities that have already been certified by the ministry of education, with 994 more institutions that are ready for certification, and 318 independent colleges that have some kind of affiliation with public universities. Now, China has about 3,901 higher-learning institutions with a gross enrollment rate of 22 percent. The total number of students is 23 million, making the higher education system one

---

[1] Peking University.

of the largest in the world. The massification of higher education in China provides an opportunity for the development of graduate education in China. Before 1978, there was virtually no graduate education with academic degrees in the country.

Generally speaking, graduate education with academic degrees in China only has a history of 30 years. In 1980, the state council issued a document on the regulation of graduate education and graduate degrees, which is most important for the development of graduate education. It states that Chinese academic degrees include bachelor's, master's, and doctoral degrees. Those students who have a bachelor degree or its equivalent could take the exam for entering a master's degree program, and those who have a master's degree or its equivalent could be admitted into a Ph.D. program. In 1978, a few universities had already started to establish graduate education programs by enrolling a few master's degree students. By the time the regulation was issued, these students were ready to get master's degrees. And in 1981, Peking University enrolled three Ph.D. students.

Due to the higher education system's expansion, there was a growing need for qualified professors and researchers. Especially in the middle 1980s, when university research became an important part of China's scientific research system, there was a great need for highly educated and well-trained professors and researchers. But due to limited access to graduate education in China, many Chinese students and scholars rushed to the United States and other developed countries for advanced knowledge and graduate education. Statistics shows that in 1983, only 19 Ph.D. degrees were conferred in China. In 1987, the total number of students in Ph.D. programs was only 8,969.

After two decades of development, the situation improved greatly. In 2002, 14,706 students got Ph.D. degrees.[2] In 2005, the total enrollment of graduate students was 364,800. Of this number, 54,800 students were in Ph.D. programs. In the same year, 27,700 students got Ph.D. degrees.[3] Now there are 766 institutions offering master's and Ph.D. degrees. These 766 institutions consist of 450 public universities and 316 research institutes. Currently, China's Ph.D. education is the third largest in the world after the United States and Germany. The quick development of the Ph.D. programs and large growth in number of students are the result of great societal demand.

The Reform of Student Recruiting Strategies

Though China has adopted the three-degree system according to the U.S. model, the student recruiting procedure or method is quite different. In the United States, the application and recommendations are the most important elements for

---

[2] *Report on the Development of Academic Degrees and Graduate Education in China* (Beijing: Higher Education Press, 2002), 24.
[3] *Education Statistics Yearbook*, 2005. (2006) Beijing: People's Education Press.

student recruiting. In China, examination and test scores are the most important criteria. Theoretically, if a student passes the examination, he cannot be turned down. Superficially, this is considered to be the only recruiting strategy that is fair to every applicant. But the problem of using examinations for the selection of students is obvious, and this practice has been criticized for many years because it is hard to tell which applicants are the most creative and intelligent just making reference to test scores. Many cases prove that examination is not the best method for recruiting students, especially for the selection of creative students, but so far there does not seem to be any other better substitutive method. The situation now has been improved a bit by adding interviews and student profile reviews in the selection.

In global competition, Chinese universities face great challenges, even in retaining the best graduate students. At Peking University, there used to be a popular saying to describe the quality of the Ph.D. students it recruited: "The undergraduate students are first rate, the masters students are second rate, and Ph.D. students are third rate." How do we understand this? During the 1990s, at Peking University, the top third of its undergraduates went abroad for graduate education. In most cases only the middle third went to domestic graduate schools or professional training for master's degrees. After they got their master's degrees, the top third of master's students went abroad either to pursue a Ph.D. degree, or for professional training. Research in 2000 shows 76 percent of the students in high-tech fields at Peking University and 82 percent of the students in the same field at Tsinghua University went to the United States.[4] From these descriptive percentages, one can see that for China, the brain-drain issue is already happening from the beginning of graduate education.

The cause of the problem is complex. Many reasons contribute to the situation, and one of them is the problem of recruiting. In China, a student who wants to get a Ph.D. degree, as mentioned above, has to take three exams. The first exam he must take is the national examination for university admission in order to get undergraduate education for a bachelor's degree; the second is for admission to master's degree programs; and the third is for admission to Ph.D. programs. These examinations not only require a lot of preparation time for students, but also create a lot of anxiety and psychological stress. It is obvious that no student would like to take such tedious, memorization-based exams. Now, people can understand why so many students in China want to go abroad for graduate education. To avoid psychological stress is one of important reasons.

Many researchers show that Chinese universities have no autonomy, and this makes them less competitive. And many Chinese university presidents complain that because of the lack of autonomy they cannot do things better, including recruiting Ph.D. students. In reality, the issue is far more complicated. Concerning the problem of recruiting graduate students, new strategies have been put in place. In order to make sure the best students have a chance to get master's and Ph.D.

[4] Zhaokui Feng, "How Could China Win the Global Competition for Talent?" *Liaowang*, no. 32 (2000).

education inside the country, in 1985, 169 universities received the privilege of having students directly entering the graduate education program by application and recommendation. In Peking University, the strategy of combining recommendation and examination has been adopted for many years. Table 12.1 shows the number of Ph.D. students the university recruited in different years with different strategies.

Of course, there are debates over the fairness of recruiting students by recommendation. And just recently, Peking University was challenged again for having more than half of its graduate students recruited by recommendations. The major concern is public fairness or academic accountability for putting more of its own students into Ph.D. programs. The criticism is largely concerned with equal opportunities for students at other universities who want to get into Peking University.

The intention of adopting recommendation strategies is to keep the best students in the university or at home, though there is a danger of student inbreeding in Ph.D. education. In fact, faculty inbreeding has been a serious problem in Chinese universities. And in order to encourage graduate students with international perspectives and to avoid serious academic inbreeding, Peking University has used many strategies. Sending students abroad for short-term study is one of the strategies recruited. And just earlier this year another project was launched by the ministry of education: The universities in the 211 and 985 projects are given more opportunities to send their graduate students to study abroad for one or two years as visiting scholars with government financial support. This policy provides Peking University an opportunity to send three to five hundred graduate students abroad every year.

Scientific Research in Chinese Universities

Most Chinese students abroad in Ph.D. programs have fellowships as RAs and TAs. This not only provides opportunities for them to assist their advisers and get financial support, but also for them to provide valuable insights for research. In Chinese universities, there is also an effort to bring research and academic training together. But China's scientific research system is different from that of the U.S. In 1952, China adopted a scientific research system that separates scientific research from teaching. Serious scientific research is mostly conducted in specialized research institutes in the Chinese Academy of Sciences. University research was considered important only for the promotion of teaching and learning. In August 1977, Deng Xiaoping, vice chairman of the CCP Central Committee, published his speech "A Few Suggestions on the Work of Science and Education." He pointed out that if China wants to catch up with the world, the country needs to develop science and education. Universities, especially key universities, should be one of the major forces for scientific research. To begin

Table 12.1. Ph.D. Students Recruited with Different Strategies at Peking University (2002, 2004, and 2006)

	2002	2004	2006
Direct recommendation to Ph.D. program	107	255	225
Masters and Ph.D. combined recommendation	354	526	413
By examination	799	645	726
Total number of Students	1,250	1,426	1,364

Source: the Website of Graduate School, Peking University

with, China should build key universities. It was only after this speech that scientific research in universities started to get more attention.[5]

Afterwards, universities started to develop graduate programs. But it took quite a few years for universities to get into the country's scientific research system. In the "Decision for the Reform of Chinese Higher Education" issued in 1985, leading universities were identified as "the center for student training and the center for scientific research." In 1986, the first national key research laboratory was established at Peking University. This marked the beginning of university research with R&D funding in nationally sponsored laboratories on university campuses.[6] And it also marked the beginning of university research as part of the nation's basic scientific research system. The idea of establishing key national laboratories at universities actually came from the model of research universities in the United States.

The American federal government's financial support for university research was very influential concerning the scientific research system reform in China during the late 1980s and early 1990s. The most commonly used examples are the Lawrence Berkeley National Laboratory, the Lawrence Livermore National Laboratory, and Los Alamos National Laboratory in the University of California system. But the national key laboratories at Chinese universities are mostly discipline-based, with the goal of creating centers of excellence in related areas of study.

---

[5] Deng Xiaoping, speech made on "Symposium on the Work of Science and Technology," August, 4–8, 1977.

[6] Wanhua Ma, "The Flagship University and China's Economic Reform" in *World Class Worldwide: Transforming Research Universites in Asia and Latin America*, ed. Philip G. Albtach and Jorge Balan (The Johns Hopkins University Press, 2007).

Based on information provided by the China Education and Research Network, up to 2002, there were 91 key national research laboratories at the leading universities. Peking University alone now has 13 such national laboratories, whose research projects are closely linked to the country's most urgent problems in development. To administer the country's R&D fund, the Chinese National Science Foundation was established in 1985 as a sponsoring organization for research in science and technology, both in universities and in the Academy of Sciences. In 1986, a famous national scientific research project, the "863 plan," was established. The plan was intended to help pursue advanced research in such areas as information technology, automation, energy, new materials, and biotechnology by using the country's R&D fund, and it was also intended to bring scientists in the Chinese Academy of Sciences and university professors together in these areas.

The establishment of key national laboratories at universities has increased university research capacity and the quality of Ph.D. training in science and technology. Statistics show that in 1998/99, nine leading universities awarded 2,465 doctoral degrees; 5,891 research papers were indexed in SCI in 2000; and in 2002, those nine universities had 295 key research disciplines. In the same year, university research received 78 percent of national technology invention awards and 49 percent of national technology progress awards. Among the 6,118 patents, 32.4 percent came from the nine leading universities.[7]

But in comparison, one can easily find that university research and Ph.D. education in China are not well funded because the amount of the national R&D fund in basic research itself is very small. Figure 12.1 shows the exact percentage of national R&D funds in basic research.

The figure shows that most of China's national R&D fund is used in development and applied research, and the national R&D fund used in basic research is much smaller than the other two parts. Between 1999 and 2003, funds for basic research only increased 0.7 percent. According to a report from the National Statistics Bureau in 2004, the proportion for the three categories changed, and the situation for basic research was not much better. The fund for basic research increased slightly to 6.0 percent, while applied research took 20.4 percent and experiment under development 73.6 percent.[8]

And even with the small basic research fund, universities have to compete with the Chinese Academy of Sciences. As to the allocation of the research fund, the following table shows that in 2003, university research used only 10.5 percent of the national R&D fund, while research institutions in the Chinese Academy of Sciences used up 25.9 percent, and enterprises or industries used up

---

[7] Y. Zhao, editor, "Annual Report on China Torch Program 2002." Beijing: Ministry of Science and Technology Torch High Technology Industry Development Center (2003).

[8] <http://www.ilib.cn/Abstract.aspx?A=qqkjjjlw200505013>.

Figure 12.1. Distribution of National R&D Funds, 1999–2003

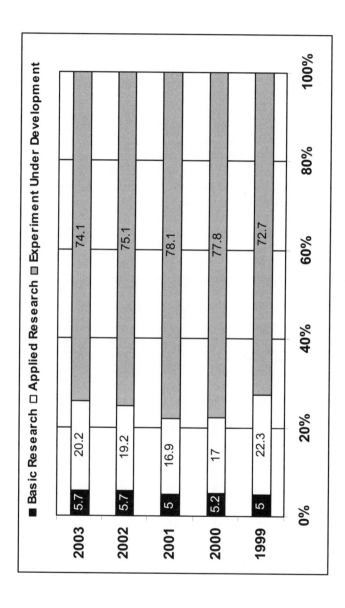

62.2 percent. But comparatively speaking, the percentage of annual R&D funds devoted to university research kept increasing: In 2000, it was only 8.6 percent, and in 2005, it increased to 10.5 percent.[9]

Figure 12.2 shows how the country's R&D fund was distributed among three categories of research organizations from 1999–2003.

To convert the 10.5 percent of the research money that went to universities into U.S. dollars, it was only 1.06 billion, while in the same year in the United States, it was 47.7 billion, and in Japan in 2002 it was 17.2 billion.[10] There is a large difference among those countries. In China, investment in basic research is far behind in comparison with the speed of economic growth.

For basic research in the Chinese Academy of Sciences, the situation is not much better. In 2005, the Chinese Academy of Sciences had a total operational research fund of 10.656 billion RMB (around 1.3 billion dollars). Of this amount, basic research took 34.3 percent, applied research 58.41 percent, and experiments 7.3 percent.[11] This set of figures also reveals that currently the Chinese Academy of Sciences mostly focuses its attention on applied research, not on basic research. As a result, most of the degrees conferred are in applied fields. Figure 12.3 shows the disciplinary distributions of Ph.D. degrees awarded by universities, the Chinese Academy of Science, and the Chinese Academy of Social Science between 1982 and 2003. From 1982 to 2003, more Ph.D. degrees were awarded in engineering, mathematics, and medicine than in any other field. This reflects China's emphasis on scientific research and economic development needs.

And even now the situation does not seem to have changed much; most of the national R&D fund goes to the Chinese Academy of Sciences, though the importance of university research has been emphasized frequently. Less funding means fewer Ph.D. students in the field and fewer research opportunities for Ph.D. students. The problem of separate graduate education and scientific research may provide an explanation for why Chinese Ph.D. students are less productive in knowledge creation and research. A lack of creativity in Chinese Ph.D. students is a common phenomenon in comparison with the United States and Japan. And that is one of the reasons why Chinese students still prefer to go abroad for Ph.D. education, especially to the universities in the United States with good research facilities and more research opportunities.

Graduate Education Financing in China

Since China's economic reform, its economic structure has changed greatly; the market-oriented economy pushes both the government and universities to pay

---

[9] *Report on the Development of Academic Degrees and Graduate Education in China* (Beijing: Higher Education Press, 2002), 35.

[10] <http://www.ilib.cn/Abstract.aspx?A=qqkjjjlw200505013>.

[11] The Chinese Academic of Sciences, Annual Report 2006, 12.

Figure 12.2. Distribution of National R&D, 1999–2003

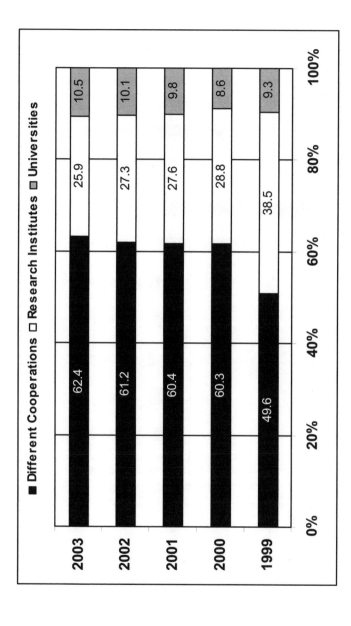

Figure 12.3. Distribution of Awarded Master and Ph.D.Degrees, 1982–2003

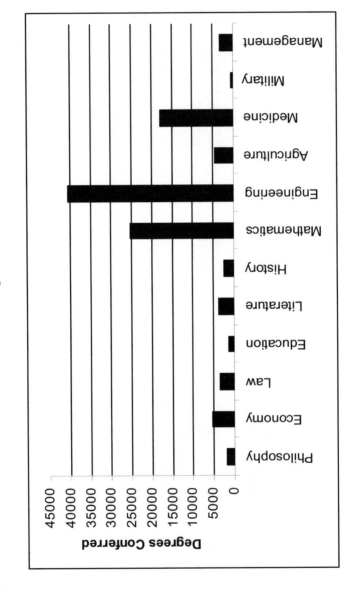

Note: The numbers in the table only refer to research Ph.D degrees, and do not include professional degrees.

more attention to the quality of Ph.D. education. Quality control of graduate education in China is highly centralized. Originally even the selection of doctoral student advisers had to be approved by the ministry of education. Now a few universities are given opportunities to set the criteria for Ph.D. students' advisors. At Peking University, all of the full professors could direct Ph.D. students, under the condition that the professor holds a Ph.D. degree. But even now, if a university wants to recruit one more Ph.D. student, the university still has to report to and get approval from the Bureau of Graduate Education in the Ministry of Education, because the ministry controls the financing of the student.

The governance of graduate education in China is very complicated. In December 1980, an academic committee was established under the state council, and was charged with setting standards for graduate education and providing guidelines for the quality of graduate degrees. Any policy change related to academic degrees has to be reported to this committee. In 1983, the ministry of education established the Bureau of Graduate Education to coordinate implementing degree-regulation activities between universities and the state council's Academic Committee. Also, for quality assurance, universities are allowed to establish graduate schools to regulate student and faculty activities in Ph.D. education. The graduate school at Peking University is one of the first graduate schools in China.

Thus, for quality control of Ph.D. education, the state council takes care of quality and makes guidelines for conferring the degrees, and the National Development and Reform Commission decides the number of students admitted each year. Based on the number of students each university is allowed to admit, the ministry of education allocates graduate education funds to universities.

Roughly, for each master's student, the university gets 10,000 RMB ($1,300), and for each Ph.D. student, the amount is 12,000 RMB ($1,400). This amount will cover student tuition and provide a living stipend. The money goes to the university directly, and then the university provides each student a minimum of 290–300 RMB ($40) a month for living expenses. In the 1980s and 1990s, the graduate student's financial support was considered to be enough for the student's basic living expenses. But in recent years, that amount seems not to be enough for students' monthly bills, and many students have to either work for their advisers or do other part-time jobs in order to make a living. Some students from well-to-do families may still be dependent on their parents during their studies.

Government allocation of funding for graduate education follows a flat scheme, without considering the regional or disciplinary differences between Ph.D. programs, and a graduate student in a provincial university in a less developed area costs much less than a graduate student in a large city. That is one of the reasons why top universities in Beijing and other economically developed cities tend to have smaller and stronger Ph.D. programs, and provincial or local universities tend to have larger Ph.D. programs. Different top universities adopt different strategies for supporting their Ph.D. programs. In China, universities are allowed to open enterprises to translate university research and inventions into financial productivity. This way, universities are supposed to get a certain percentage back in order to support basic research. By 2005, Peking University had 10 large companies, as did Tsinghua University. These university enterprises serve as extensions of university research and teaching by providing graduate students with internship opportunities. Statistics show that in 1997, about 520,000 students worked or carried out their research in university enterprises—among them, 1,419 students earned their doctoral degrees and 2,817 students earned their master's degrees.[12]

University enterprises are not trouble free. Due to a lack of control and regularity in auditing, nobody knows what amount of these resources have gone to university enterprises from universities and vice-versa. And what is worse is that nobody knows what has been used for private benefit. In June 2006, a top CEO in one of the Nankai University enterprises disappeared with 110 million RMB (14 million USD) from the enterprise, and because of his misconduct, the enterprise also lost 300 million RMB through misinvestment. In total, the enterprise lost over 400 million RMB. And just a few months before this incident, Tianjin University, Nankai's next-door neighbor, came across a similar problem. The seriousness of the problem has caught a lot of attention. It seems that in the near future, there will be some kind of legislation to regulate universities' and university enterprises' financial conduct.

Commercialization and the Effect on Ph.D. Education

In China, there is severe competition among universities for establishing Ph.D. programs in order to raise the academic status of the university. However, there is less quality assurance. Many universities pay more attention to developing continuing education and nondegree professional training programs. Commercializing knowledge and training programs for higher fees and tuition is a common choice for many universities hoping to relieve financial pressure.

The appearance of "independent colleges" is one resulting phenomenon of universities' commercializing behavior. In China, private institutions appeared during the 1980s. Since the concept of "private" has some connotation with capitalism, the term "Minban" was used as a substitute. For quite some time, Minban colleges and universities were allowed to exist, and some even made a good profit. But due to ideological differences, it took a long time for those colleges and universities to be legally accepted. Since there was money to make, some public universities started to establish independent colleges. They are

---

[12] Wanhua Ma, "From Berkeley to Beida and Tsinghua: The Development and Governance of Public Research Universities in the U.S. and China" (Beijing: Educational Science Press, 2004).

called "independent," because in theory, they are independent from the mother institution in student admission, quality control, and degree granting practices, but they pay back to the mother institution for using its name and prestige. In many cases, such institutions are the result of cooperation between public institutions and private education enterprises. Now there are 295 such colleges, with a student population of 1.05 million.

People might ask why public universities should take the trouble to work with private ones. In most cases, independent colleges in China are allowed to collect higher fees and tuition. While resources are limited, some public universities considered this the fastest way to make money. At first, opening an independent college was seen as an aspect of the mother university's investment behavior. And many parents seemed to like the idea of paying higher fees and tuition to send their children to such colleges because of those independent colleges' affiliation with their mother institutions. What they did not know is that the independent colleges have nothing to do with the mother institution in terms of academic quality control. They are independent academically from the mother institution, though graduate students and faculties from the mother institutions might be able to teach in those independent institutions.

It was only after four years that parents and students felt they were cheated, when they found out that students could not get a degree from the mother institutions, and that they had difficulty being recognized as college-educated students on the job market. The student riot in 2005 at one university in Zhengzhou, the capital of Henan Province, was such a case.

For top universities, instead of developing "independent colleges," they develop professional training programs. The training programs include part-time, short-term, and long-term degree programs; and schools or departments can themselves charge tuition and fees directly to students. In most cases, those programs are much more expansive than regular programs. The fees and tuition go directly to the university and school. Now the proliferation of training programs on campus or off campus are a common phenomenon. And often those programs are clearly targeting those who have the means. Though the current discussion in China about access and equality mostly deals with post secondary education, these are also issues that need to be addressed at the graduate level.

Private and Public Benefits?

In 1996, Chinese universities started to collect tuition and fees for undergraduate students. Government loans, work-study programs, and part-time work programs seem to play a very important role in helping those students who could not pay for an undergraduate education. But it has long been considered whether to charge tuition and fees for graduate education, since the budget from the government does not guarantee the quality of graduate education. Why not charge tuition and fees? A very important argument is that whoever benefits from the education should pay. So a policy has been adopted that starting this year, whoever joins a graduate education program needs to pay their share of the cost. It seems to be fair to everyone, to universities and the students themselves. Then comes the question of how much students should pay and what to do about those who could not afford it. In the past 10 years, there was a constant increase in the number of students taking part in the national examinations for graduate education, but this year, the number of participants has gone down. Some critics have said that students become more rational about graduate education because they can no longer enjoy the "free party" and they worry if they could really pay out of their own pocket, which might partly be true.

In China, on the one hand, universities and colleges are considered to be the engines or locomotives for the country's economy, and policies and strategies have been adopted to enforce and reinforce the university's function in the country's economic transitions. Graduate education is considered to be an important part in contributing highly qualified personnel to aid in the country's social and economic transition. On the other hand, the universities become targets for criticism. Last year a survey asked people to express what were the three most important issues that concerned them. It was found out that higher education is the number one issue people are not satisfied with, because of higher tuition, lower quality, lack of equity, academic corruption, and all of the other criticisms Chinese higher education faces. Some critics then started to call for attention from the central government and demanded that related organizations pay attention to the problem, because it is seen as an important factor for influencing the "social and economic stability" of the country. Now, no matter whether it is in the economy or in education, maintaining "social stability" is the number one concern, including reforming graduate education financing.

To conclude, Chinese graduate education is still in its developing stage and faces many challenges. There is a need to increase enrollment and to improve quality, especially with regard to the ability of students to conduct scientific research. When one looks at statistics, one can find that the number of foreign graduate students in Chinese universities is increasing, but most of them are in language programs and the humanities. In Chinese universities, graduate students in science and technology seldom have the opportunity to study with foreign students. In this case, most Chinese graduate students do not have much multicultural experience. The governance of graduate education in China is highly centralized and lacks flexibility. The problem has been consistently discussed, and now universities are given more freedom in student selections and have more opportunities to explore different resources for financing graduate education. The question is how and by whom should universities' commercial activities be regulated, in order to ensure equality, access, and quality in graduate education?

IV.   Science and Technology:
      New Growth Theory Meets the University

Chapter 13

Evolution of the University's Role in Innovation and the New Asia Model

Henry Etzkowitz[1]
Chunyan Zhou

Almost three decades ago, Swedish social scientist Gunnar Myrdal's *Asian Drama: An Inquiry into the Poverty of Nations* (1968) painted a bleak picture with pessimistic prospects for Asia. Myrdal held that the chances of economic take-off were slim unless Asian countries enforced the discipline that was needed to implement development plans. His prescription was the centralization of government power accompanied by the decentralization of its functions. More recently, Razeen Sally has argued that the emerging influence of Asian countries in globalization constitutes a New Asian Drama, precisely the opposite of the old (Sally 2006). In the interim, many Asian countries took a path to development, i.e., beginning with manufacturing enhanced by high-tech processes to accumulate capital and then developing high-tech industries. The increased salience of knowledge to development through higher education reform is the next act of the New Asian Drama of development.

Despite progress, there are significant gaps in the research ability of universities and the innovation capacities of industry in many Asian regions. Since most enterprises lack a sufficient R&D base, it is difficult for them to take the initiative

---

[1] University of Newcastle; and Chunyan Zhou—Shenyang University.

to establish cooperation with universities. Moreover, most enterprises typically do not have enough funds to pay universities for R&D activities. In addition, excellent graduates often prefer to work for the government as civil servants rather than for private firms in some countries. Also, many universities do not have first-class experimental facilities, excellent researchers in their employ, or the organizational capacity for knowledge transfer. Thus, research results from these schools may not be either attractive or available to industry.

Nevertheless, Asian universities are increasingly drawn into the innovation picture as the need for advanced technology becomes a higher priority in the quest for a knowledge-based economy. Since Asia is in a follow-on mode, the approach to an entrepreneurial university is quite different from that in the U.S. Asians may revise and reformulate experience from developed countries in order to collapse the time frame and take a short cut to realizing the university's role in economic development, using their government-led advantage. Universities are increasingly encouraged to serve regional innovation, using their administrative and human resources to create new economic activities, without necessarily having yet developed the research capabilities to sufficiently lead this strategy. In this chapter, we use the university-industry-government triple helix as a lens to explore the growing role of university participation in regional innovation in Asia, with a special focus on China.

The Triple Helix Thesis

Interaction among university-industry-government is the key to improving the conditions for innovation in a knowledge-based society. Industry is a member of the triple helix as the locus of production; government as the source of contractual relations that guarantee stable interactions and exchange; the university as a source of new knowledge and technology, the generative principle of knowledge-based economies. An industrial penumbra arises around universities as they become involved, often in a leadership role, in regional coalitions for economic and social development. Even as the entrepreneurial university retains the traditional academic roles of social reproduction and extension of certified knowledge, it places them in a broader context as part of its mission to promote innovation.

The triple helix model comprises three basic elements: (1) a more prominent role for the university in innovation, on a par with industry and government in a knowledge-based society; (2) a movement toward collaborative relationships among the three major institutional spheres in which innovation policy is increasingly an outcome of interactions among the spheres rather than a prescription from government or an internal development within industry; and (3) in addition to fulfilling their traditional functions, each institutional sphere also "takes the role of the other," operating on a vertical axis of their new role as well as on the horizontal axis of their traditional function (Etzkowitz 2008).

Three variants of the triple helix model provide a framework to compare innovation systems and analyze the convergence among them. First, there is a statist triple helix, in which the state encompasses and controls academia and industry and directs the relations between them. A *laissez-faire* or remote triple helix consists of separate institutional spheres where government, university, and industry operate apart from each other, with interaction typically arranged by intermediary organizations across strong boundaries. An interactive triple helix consists of relatively autonomous yet overlapping institutional spheres; each taking the role of the other, with hybrid organizations emerging at the interfaces. We identify the beginnings of a change from a statist to an interactive triple helix model in Asia, based upon signs of administrative separation of university and industry from government.

The Entrepreneurial University

Entrepreneurial universities have arisen from strikingly different academic missions, even with the "first revolution," research, occurring simultaneously with the "second revolution" of economic and social development. An entrepreneurial mode is typically an overlay on a research university, but it can also be a strategy for development from a teaching university, with the phases accomplished simultaneously or even in reverse order from the usual progression. For example, the State University of Rio de Janeiro Friburgo campus began with a Ph.D. program in IT, accompanied by an incubator, in an innovative academic and regional development strategy.

Beyond serving as a source of new ideas for existing firms, universities are combining their research and teaching capabilities in new formats to become a source of new firm formation. While the entrepreneurial university originated at MIT early in the 20th century, it is still at a relatively early stage of development. Classically, the second academic revolution, the assumption by the university of economic and social development missions, followed from the first academic revolution, the internalization of a research mission. Recent developments in Asia suggest that an alternative path to an entrepreneurial university may be nonlinear, with academic economic development initiatives providing the base for the expansion of research, and vice versa.

Most universities orient themselves to serve regional innovation in order to ensure government and public support, but various types of higher education institutions make their contribution in different ways. (See Figure 13.1.)

Higher education institutions have different missions: The teaching university is based on education and dedication to the personnel market; the research university engages in production of knowledge, as well as teaching; the entrepreneurial university encompasses teaching, research, and service to society. In practice, any university has the potential to advance economic development, irrespective of level and mission. Only the entrepreneurial university has the capacity to complete a circulation of trilateral cooperation.

Figure 13.1. Higher Education Institutions' Orientation to Regional Innovation

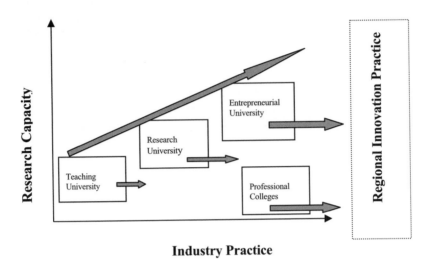

Industry Practice

An entrepreneurial university can continually participate in society's technological innovation through its five primary characteristics:

- Significant resources for S&T research or knowledge innovation;
- Entrepreneurship is widely accepted as a value and is supported systematically;
- There are organizational mechanisms in university-industry interface, e.g., a technology transfer office, and/or an industry-university collaboration committee;
- A considerable number of staff and students is available to form firms;
- Sufficient funds can be received to support campus research and entrepreneurial activities.

The characteristics can also be used as criteria to assess universities' entrepreneurial abilities.

University-Pushed Triple Helix

Founded in the mid-19th century, MIT was the first entrepreneurial university. It drew for its development upon various streams of academic formats (polytechnic, research, and land grant university) imported to or invented in the U.S. during the early and mid-19th century. The overall objective was to establish a close relationship among the university, technology, and the local economy, initially in agriculture and then in industry. In the 1930s, MIT, led by President Karl Compton, proposed a strategy of forming new firms and pushing technology, industry, and the economy forward by using university research as a basis for economic development (Etzkowitz 2002).

According to a World Bank report in 1997, if the companies founded by MIT graduates and faculty formed an independent nation, the revenues produced by the companies would make that nation the 24th-largest economy in the world. The 4,000 MIT-related companies employ 1.1 million people and have annual world sales of $232 billion. That is roughly equal to a gross domestic product of $116 billion, which is a little less than the GDP of South Africa and more than the GDP of Thailand (Bank Boston 1997).

The MIT model was introduced by Frederic Terman to Stanford, encouraging the rise of another entrepreneurial university and Silicon Valley. These two universities exemplify how the university has initiated regional innovation and development, with government and industry support following on. Such a regional innovation model is a "university-pushed triple helix" since the university is not only a source but also an organizer of innovation.

Cognitive changes in a growing number of scientific fields open up possibilities for scientists to meet two goals simultaneously: the pursuit of knowledge and profit (Viale and Etzkowitz 2005). Accordingly, the norms of science that traditionally condemn profit-making motives are beginning to change to allow for entrepreneurship; and varying institutional structures are experimented with to fit these new cognitive and normative patterns. Multiple uses of knowledge is likewise emphasized by Asian countries, especially rapidly developing ones.

Government-Pulled Triple Helix

A "government-pulled" triple helix occurs when the state compels university and industry to undertake innovation projects for the national interest. Government is the most important actor through direct investment and indirect policy support. It is a "head" that directs and the other spheres are "wings" that realize the project. Industry is predominantly influenced by government, including those firms that have changed to private ownership. Under the leadership of government, universities help enterprises to upgrade technology through collaboration with universities. Moreover, the government provided market protection and incentives for the adoption of domestic products when indigenous Chinese firms started to compete directly with joint ventures (Mu and Lee 2005).

A government-pulled triple helix has the following characteristics: (1) government initiates and controls significant projects for innovation; (2) all or most research universities, key research institutes, and large-scale enterprises are affiliated with (central or local) government; (3) the top leader's thought gives direction to all of the country (party and government), and government policy and resolutions are the instruments for realizing objectives; and (4) government organizes and directs primary innovation agents, such as high-tech development zones (including science parks and incubators), markets for technology and intellectual property, and an information network. The ministry of education decides the status and goal of each higher education institution.

A government-pulled model has advantages and disadvantages. The advantages include: the ability to achieve large-scale innovation projects; the capability to reorganize the regional innovation process and fill gaps; the power to create a consensus in regional innovation; establishing industry-university links by government authority; protecting universities' interests in entrepreneurship by policies and administrative measures; and more easily organizing activities and creating platforms for innovation.

The disadvantages include the fact that industry-university joint projects tend to be "shows" rather than a real venture in order to get support from government, since personnel, equipment, and funds nominally from the two parties are actually both from the state; the fact that university and industry might lose the flexibility to deal with problems in the innovation process; and the danger that the two parties might rely excessively on government, resulting in passivity and inertia.

Since the 1980s, China has created policies and laws to promote the development of science and technology, knowledge industrialization, and high-tech industry. However, the policies may lack stability and continuity. Moreover, there is often a lack of foresight in policymaking. Policies and laws in China are often *ex post facto*, used as tools to remedy mistakes. Current officials' ideas are often critical. Every official who has taken an important action is typically followed by another person who has his or her new ideas to put forward in order to demonstrate achievement in the post. This leads to less-consistent policies, but is a commonplace of policy and politics everywhere. Neither universities nor industry are strong enough to become the organizer of regional innovation. On the other hand, the ownership relationship among universities, industry, and government, with the government controlling university and industry, leaves only the government to organize collaborations.

Government-Led Reform in Asia Higher Education

Enhancing science and education has become a national economic growth strategy in many Asian countries. As Ischinger observes: "Today, countries like China or India are starting to deliver high skills at moderate cost and at an ever-increasing pace" (2006). Playing an important role in the reform, governments have become concerned with the development and delivery of high skills. For example, during the past two decades, the Indian government made an investment in education beyond three percent of its GDP, increased this to four percent in the early 21st century, and raised the current objective to six percent. The Indian government also set a strategy to develop IT technology and industry through the development of higher education.

As developing countries in Asia shift from a dependent to an independent innovation strategy, their higher education institutions increasingly emphasize the research and service missions of the university. It has become critical to foster talent by enhancing educational quality, even as professor Changlin Tien (the former president of the University of California, Berkeley, and academician of the National Academy of Engineering) reminds us that originality and talent are competitive advantages in the economy of the new century.[2] A "Strategy of Flourishing China through Science and Education" is being implemented, while other countries such as Singapore and Japan inaugurate similar policies. In "hard state" Asian countries, the government's ability to rapidly reshape university policy, including the transition to an entrepreneurial university model from teaching and research formats, represents a comparative advantage (Etzkowitz and Zhou, 2007).[3]

Most Asian countries have undertaken double objectives: to meet both the domestic human resources market and global competition. In countries such as China, Japan, Singapore, and India, reform of higher education increasingly concentrates on developing research universities and educating the entrepreneurial elite in order to achieve innovation and intelligent economic growth. China's government role includes the appointment of university leadership; governance of recruitment procedures; command of common curricula; and regulation of the assessment process from relevant departments. The centralization of government power is reflected in university mergers and quality evaluation, whereas the decentralization of government functions to local authorities opens up opportunities for increasing the autonomy of the university.

University Merger or Recombination?

Just as various specialized universities, focused on particular industries, were established under the plan of national development in the early 1950s, government plays an important role in organizing public university mergers. The source of the merging phenomenon is a dream to establish "world-class universities" in a global era. The purpose of constructing a broad-based university is to create a better reputation, combining strong + strong or strong + weak or weak + weak = stronger. The advantages are expected to be the enhancement of critical mass, discipline upgrading, and interdisciplinarity. Moreover, university mergers are expected to amend the waste in human capital and material resources from previous overspecialized universities.

Since 1990, "university recombination" has been an important aspect of China's university development. For example, Sichuan University merged with Chengdu Science and Technology University in 1993. The present Shanghai University, a leading school, was the result of a merger of Shanghai Industry University, Shanghai Science and Technology University, Shanghai S&T Senior School,

---

[2] President Tien's speech in Global Young Leaders Conference II in Taiwan.

[3] See the theme paper for Triple Helix VI International Conference in Singapore at <www.triplehelix6.com>.

and the original Shanghai University in May 1994. Shandong University was created from Shandong Medical University, Shandong Industry University, and the original Shandong University. Jilin University, located in Changchun City, emerged from Jilin Industry University, Bethune Medical University, Changchun S&T University, Changchun University of Post and Telecommunications, and the original Jilin University on June 12, 2000. The former Quartermaster University of PLA was also merged into Jilin University on August 29, 2004.

According to the report by the Ministry of Education (MoE), up to May 15, 2006, 1,084 universities were involved in the merger movement; they were merged into 431 "new" universities (MoE 2007).[4] In recent years, the "merger movement" encountered obstacles from university administration and faculty. Since early 2005, Liaoning Province Government has struggled to join Northeastern University and China Medical University, but it was not arranged until August 2007. The key argument is whether China Medical University should remain independent, for it is the one and only university with "China" in its title in Liaoning Province. The important reason for supporting the merger is to allow Northeastern University to compete with its regional competitor, Dalian University of Technology.

A Shift from Quantity to Quality

Rapid scale-up is a basic characteristic of higher education development in the past half century in Asia. Japan and Singapore took the early lead as "education developed countries." In the 1950s, the enrollment rate for four-year institutions was 10 percent; however, it reached 30 percent in the 1970s, 40 percent now, and 70 percent if other higher education institutions are counted. China, India, and Indonesia are engaging in a similar strategy. India has made a considerable achievement relative to its one billion population. In China, since 1998, universities increasingly recruit undergraduate and graduate students (Figure 13.2). The gross enrollment rate of higher education in China was 9.8 percent in 1998, 15 percent in 2002, and 21 percent in 2005. Higher education enrollment has reached over 50 percent in Beijing and Shanghai.

This strategy has resulted in the rapid development of China's higher education since 1998. Nevertheless, the lack of sufficient skilled workers is a gap in China's higher education reform and development strategy. The traditional belief in social hierarchy, which implies that the "white collar" has a higher social class than the "blue collar," is still strong despite socialist ideology. On one hand, society needs highly skilled workers, but lacks sufficient high-quality vocation-

---

[4] The practice of the government also brings about some discontent. Recently, some proposed that Beijing University and Tsinghua University, China's two leading universities, should merge into one in order to make a world-class university. Some observers have commented on the intensity of the merger phenomenon, saying that continuing unification might lead to only one university, the "Chinese University."

Figure 13.2. Change in the Number of Recruited Students (1998–2004)

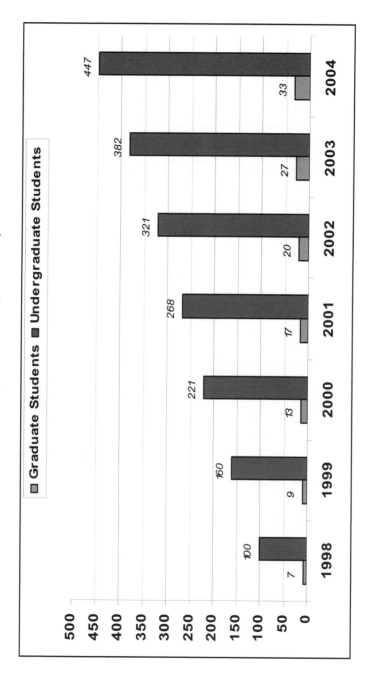

Source: Binglin Zhong, 2007 <http://www.pgzx.edu.cn/upload/files/yuanxiaopinggu/ZhongBL2.pdf>.

technical colleges to train them. On the other hand, the rapid expansion of universities has made the issue of graduate unemployment increasingly more serious.

The dilemma of quantity versus quality seems inevitable due to limited educational resources. The student-teacher ratio in Chinese universities has increased sharply since 1998 (Figure 13.3). In some science and engineering teaching labs, several students are often crowded at one device, even though the investment in teaching hardware has increased and many experiments are arranged in the evening or weekend. Previous teaching lectures for 30 people have expanded to over 100 or 200 students in some universities. University presidents such as Qingshi Zhu of China Science and Technology University have expressed concern about how to protect teaching quality. Moreover, as graduate education expanded rapidly, administrators are worried that graduate education will be degraded to the undergraduate level.

The attempt to generate higher quality merely through quantitative expansion has proved a failure. The assumption was that an increase in quantity must naturally improve quality, allowing selection of the best students from a larger pool of candidates. In India, university students reached 10.5 million in 2005 from 0.1 millions in 1947, but the average public investment per student declined 30 percent during 1991 and 2003 (Johnson 2006b). Many of China's universities will also face a financial crisis. The bank debt of higher education institutes so far has reached over ¥200 billion. An insufficiency of expenditure will inevitably influence the output quality. In the Eleventh Five Year Plan of China, upgrading the quality of higher education was suggested. It will become a core task in the coming five years. Expansion has slowed down for next year, with only a 5% undergraduate growth rate in comparison to 26.1% annually from 1999 to 2004 and 28.6% at the graduate level.

To enhance the quality of higher education, the Chinese and Indian governments have organized quality assessment exercises. In China, every other year, each university has to undergo an "undergraduate teaching assessment" to prove its qualification to provide a higher education. If the university in question cannot pass the assessment, its enrollment authority will be cancelled, stopping the recruitment of students. Alternatively, improvement may be requested within a limited time. A similar assessment process exists in graduate education. Universities that want to provide a master's degree or Ph.D. in some discipline are assessed to achieve the right to enroll students.

Mobilizing Higher Education Resources for Innovation

Since most Asian countries face both development and employment issues, they generally emphasize upgrading research universities and developing various vocational-technical colleges simultaneously to meet needs in the domestic human resources market and deal with international competition. Although India

Figure 13.3. Change in Student–Teacher Ratio in Chinese Higher Education

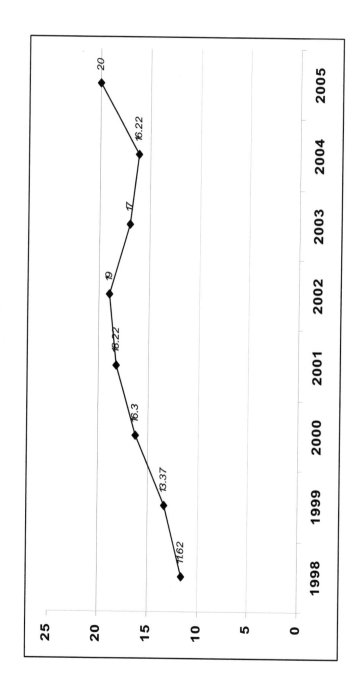

Source: Binglin Zhong, 2007 <http://www.pgzx.edu.cn/upload/files/yuanxiaopinggu/ZhongBL2.pdf>.

produces millions of graduates annually, the raw numbers, as company after company finds in its recruitment drives, are a misleading metric for employable skills. While 3 million students graduate from Indian universities each year, only about 25 percent of engineering graduates and 10-15 percent of general college graduates are considered suitable for employment in the offshore IT industry, according to a recent study by Nasscom. Kiran Karnik, the Nasscom president, said, "Our education system is not producing enough people with the skill-sets our economy needs. This could seriously stymie India's economic growth" (Johnson 2006a).

At the 1997 Fifteenth Congress of the Central Committee of the Communist Party of China, a "Strategy of Flourishing China through Science and Education" was announced. The potential of higher education to promote the economy has been recognized in *The Educational Action Plan Toward 21st Century* in 1999, which proposed training for innovation excellence, enhancing scientific research and developing a university high-tech industry to foster new growth poles of economic development. Government support enhances university research and entrepreneurship activities through direct investment and indirect policy support.

Since the 1990s, government has also supported university science park development to accelerate academic entrepreneurship and technology transfer. These science parks have made a significant contribution to local economic growth. For example, Zhongguancun Science Park in Beijing achieved a gross income of 360.09 billion China yuan in the first half-year of 2007, representing 76.6 percent of the gross income of development zones in Beijing.[5] Table 13.1 reflects the situation of national science parks in 2002–2005. To date, the Ministry of Science and Technology and Ministry of Education have approved 63 "National University Science Parks."

A wave of science park development is spreading rapidly across Asia, supported by government policies and funds. Science parks become key high-tech entrepreneurial centers, incubating thousands of start-ups. They include Tsukuba-Agency of Industrial Science and Technology-Research Center in Japan, Software Technology Parks in Bangalore, India, Zhongguancun in Beijing, China, Xinzhu Sci-tech Park of Taiwan, etc. Since the mid to late 1980s, South Korea has combined science parks with industry parks. For example, 38 joint ventures have been built in Daeduk Science Town, including 21 universities, 13 research institutes and design institutes, over 80 production enterprises, and more than 100 experiment and production workshops.

Some of these parks are merely new locations for government research institutes and R&D units of large firms that have been incentivized to relocate to science parks in order to make the projects appear to be a success. Science parks by themselves rarely incubate new firms unless they are also closely associated with universities or other sources of technological innovation.

---

[5] See <http://news.zgcsd.com/Article/2007/7-30/20077301557295443.html>.

Table 13.1. 2002–2005 General Situation of National Science Parks (Incubators)

	2002	2003	2004	2005
Incubator number	58	58	46	49
Possessing ground area (million m^2)	1.450	5.784	4.853	5.005
Incubating enterprises number	2380	4100	5037	6075
People's number in incubating enterprises	51576	70855	69644	110240
Number of new incubated enterprises	867	1099	1156	1213
Accumulative total of graduated enterprises	720	584	1256	1320

Resource: Analyzed Report on National Science Parks, <http://www.chinatorch. gov.cn/yjbg/200610/102.html>.

Note: Data from 2004 all came from National Science Parks.

Case Study: Evolution of NEU's Role in Regional Triple Helix

Chinese universities have been a major source of new enterprises since the mid-1980s when government started to reduce university funding, forcing schools to make up the shortfall, allowing them to use their remaining resources to engage in business activities. Utilizing campus resources and available teachers and students, enterprises were initiated as part of the academic structure as University-Run Enterprises (UREs), rather than as spin-off firms, since there were no sources of venture capital at the time to set up independent units. Nor, for the most part, was research spill-over available to set up high-tech enterprises. Instead, some UREs began a marketing operation selling consumer electronics and other goods from stores located in university science parks in order to accumulate capital. Others began as low-tech producers. In the 1980s, most UREs were low-tech, traditional, and service enterprises. Since the early 1990s, UREs have become a mixture of low and high tech, traditional and modern, joint venture and independent enterprises in service, marketing, and production industries.

UREs generally have three characteristics: (1) the university takes ownership of its UREs; (2) university staff or students (alumni) typically raise UREs and run them by themselves, especially at their very beginnings; (3) UREs mainly rely on the R&D in their mother universities. Therefore UREs actually are "enterprises possessed by universities," although recently a few tend to be public through stock exchange. At the end of 1980s, in order to support UREs and establish a consensus atmosphere for university entrepreneurship, NEU proposed its "123 guideline";

that is, one fundamental point: fostering excellence; two centers: teaching and research; and three functions: dissemination, production, and application of knowledge.

Case Study: Neusoft Group Co. Ltd. and Entrepreneurship and Rapid Growth

Neusoft Group Co., Ltd (Neusoft) generated from the NEU campus, is a leading software and computer consulting enterprise, with three core businesses: medical treatment systems, IT education, and training. In 1989, three young professors who returned from the US, Canada, and Japan, along with several Ph.D. candidates, started their entrepreneurial dream in two classrooms with ¥30,000 and three computers in NEU's recently founded Software and Network Workshop of the Computer Department. The original idea was to build an advanced lab in network and software technology to continue their research that they had started abroad. However, financial problems compelled them to undertake consulting projects for clients to get the capital to realize their academic objective.

The principal founder of Neusoft, Jiren Liu (1955–) is the first Chinese Ph.D. in computer applications. He is the president of Neusoft, a vice president of NEU, and director of the National Engineering Research Center of Computer Software, simultaneously holding academic, business, and governmental positions. Neusoft exemplified again that, in the process of university entrepreneurship, some individual heroes played a key role, for example, V. Bush at MIT, F. Terman at Stanford, and Xuan Wang at Peking University. They are typically not "bookworms," but excellent scholars who acknowledged that research should have the best application.

NEU Administration of Government Support

At their inception, Neusoft and similar firms were conducted as part of the university's operations. In recent years, the strengthening of the legal system has made producers liable for their products. In response, the MoE commands universities to establish the "group company" to separate UREs from their academic source. Thus S&T Enterprises Group of NEU was established in August of 2005. The University-Enterprise Cooperation Committee of NEU was established in 2001, constituted by the Economic and Trade Committee of Liaoning Province Government, and includes representatives of the Educational Department, NEU, and 35 firms.

The latter comprises most relevant large-scale state enterprises in the province. According to the agreement between the university and member companies, NEU must offer its newest research achievement to the membership enterprises. Its technologies should transfer to those enterprises primarily; second, in the selection of research projects and training of excellent students, NEU should consider the needs of membership enterprises first. On the other hand, membership enterprises should first make their technology needs known to NEU to be resolved.

The university is expected to serve local innovation in three ways: providing entrepreneurship education; helping industry resolve problems or jointly establish some R&D centers with it; and supporting UREs. Industry is encouraged to rely on university research to renew existing products and achieve new technological innovations and products. The province government also tries to build a platform for enterprises to have access to universities, to directly support university and industry through making financial resources available to them, including those from the Ministry of Science and Technology, the Ministry of Education, China Academy, and China NSF. In the first year of the committee's establishment, over 500 industry-university contracts were signed; the total amount reached ¥270 million, creating an economic interest of ¥2 billion.

Another important factor is the transformation in the criteria of academic assessment by university administration. Market success has become a criterion to assess the academic level as well as the value of technology results. In the past, the number of publications, awarding of prizes, and patents decided the academic level of a professor. More recently, contribution to product improvement is taken into account as well. In 2002, a fundamental research "to achieve grain refinement in rolling of new-generation steel material" and "advanced manufacturing technology of 500 MPa carbon steel" took the lead in producing the 2050 product line of hot rolling of steel in Shanghai Baosteel Group Corporation. Moreover, the No. 2 production line of Fushun Steel Corporation, with the help of "production process of clean steel" offered by the faculty of NEU, increased the sales income of 2002 to ¥215 million. These achievements led to the promotions of their originators.

Evolution of the Role of Universities

The Asian triple helix, characterized by government-pulled plus industry-university collaboration, can be expected to evolve toward the coexistence of industry-university and university-industry collaboration first, respectively forming corporate-led and university-pushed innovation; and then move toward a triple helix interaction of university-industry-government. The essential difference between university-industry and industry-university collaboration is whose goals are the top priority. The former considers the goals of the university first, whereas the latter concerns itself solely with industry needs. Indeed, U.S. universities always try to find university-industry collaboration, rather than industry-university collaboration.

Universities in some countries such as China and Japan are typically asked to serve industrial development through collaboration. They passively work as government's tools to promote industrial innovation and regional economic growth. In the Asian triple helix, which mainly contains industry-university collaboration, the proportion of university-industry collaboration is increasing as the university's role evolves and its ability to conduct research and innovation increases. In the course of the evolution, entrepreneurial universities will be formed that participate in innovation in the regions where they located and also at the national level. Utilizing their knowledge base and research activities, they help renew firms, upgrade older industries, start joint ventures together with enterprises, form firms, and participate in the process of regional policy and decision-making, making a more direct economic contribution.

Although the Asian triple helix starts from a government-pulled model, government dominance will gradually reduce to promote more bottom-up innovation activities. The roles of university and industry will be incrementally strengthened and become equivalent to government in regional innovation. This is a process of social democratization, also an innovation in triple helix formation. In the end, a cooperative interest in innovation will result in symbiotic university-industry-government interactions.

China exemplifies an evolution from a government-pulled plus industry-university collaboration model in which the university plays a role as a helper, from a passive position. The objective of industry-university collaboration is to meet needs from industry. The motives of universities here focus on taking industrial funds and applying knowledge to resolve problems in practice with industrial enterprises, the organizers and designers of these innovation activities. The university's previous role is to respond to state needs as its first priority.

As an Asian triple helix develops, the university's role in regional innovation strengthens. From the NEU case study, we conclude that the university's development relied predominantly on generating its own resources. As China's economy strengthened, the government was able to allocate resources to further spur academic development. Thus, a tri-evolutionary process was initiated among university-industry- government, each supporting the others' development. Conversely, the university can make additional contributions to the economy as its resources increase. Moreover, the role of the university in regional innovation developed as industry's need for innovation increased.

The Neusoft case suggests the beginning of a change from a government-pulled triple helix to a model in which the university gains some independent freedom of action. As its industrial research ability develops, China will also rely on a corporate-led model. The Collaboration Committee, with the leadership of government, bridges between university and industry to precisely meet industry's needs to renew and upgrade its technology. The university plays its economic role under the direct leadership of government, in contrast to the U.S. where government influence takes place indirectly. An entrepreneurial university with research and entrepreneurship capacities augurs a future innovation triple helix, together with industry and universities, as an independent institutional sphere, not only in Asia, but the entire world.

References

BankBoston Economics Department. 1997. "MIT: The Impact of Innovation." Boston: BankBoston.

Chatterji, S. K. 1970. "Some Aspects of Myrdal's 'Asian Drama.'" China Report 6: 33.

Davis, Hugh G., and N. Diamond. 1997. The Rise of American Research Universities: Elites and Challengers in the Postwar Era. Baltimore: Johns Hopkins University Press.

Elsevier. S. 1989. "Motivations and Obstacles to R&D Cooperation." *Technovation* 9: 161–68.

Etzkowitz, H. 1994. "Knowledge as Property: The Massachusetts Institute of Technology and the Debate over Academic Patent Policy." *Minerva* (Winter).

———. 1998. "The Norms of Entrepreneurial Science: Cognitive Effects of the New University-Industry Linkages." *Research Policy* 27: 823–33

———. 2002. MIT and the Rise of Entrepreneurial Science. London: Routledge.

Etzkowitz, H., and Chunyan Zhou. 2007. Sixth Triple Helix International Conference Theme Paper (Singapore), <http://www.nus.edu.sg/nec/Triple Helix6/SingaporeConferenceThemePaperChinese.pdf>.

———. 2008. The Triple Helix: University, Industry, and Government in Action. London: Routledge.

Geisler, Elizer, Autonio Furino, and Thomas J. Kiresuk. 1991. "Toward a Conceptual Model of Cooperative Research": Patterns of Development and Success in University-Industry Alliances." *IEEE Transactions on Engineering Management*, vol. EM-38, no. 2 (May): 136–45.

Hughes, Kirsty, and Ian Christie. 1995. *U.K. and European Science Policy: The Role of Collaborative Research*. London: Policy Studies Institute.

Ischinger, Barbara. 2006. "Asian Nations Move to Head of Class: Report Shows U.S., European Students Lose Ground Despite Spending." Arkansas Democrat-Gazette Press Services, Wed., Sept. 13.

Johnson, Jo. 2006. "Engaging India: Demographic Dividend or Disaster?" *Financial Times*, November 15.

———. 2006. "Are India and China Up to the Job?" *Financial Times*, July 19.

Liu, Jin-Long. 1983. "How Corporations Cooperate with the Academic Organization for R&D." Tsong-Te Industrial Research Foundation, Chinese Taipei.

Lowen, Rebecca. 1997. *Creating the Cold War University: The Transformation of Stanford*. Berkeley: University of California Press.

Merton, R. K. 1973 [1942]. *The Normative Structure of Science in the Sociology of Science*. Chicago: University of Chicago Press.

Ministry of Education. 2007, <http://gaokao.chsi.com.cn/gkxx/gxmd/200705/20070517/904802.html>.

Mu, Qing, and Keun Lee. 2005. "Knowledge Diffusion, Market Segmentation and Technological Catch-Up: the Case of the Telecommunication Industry in China." *Research Policy* 34: 6 (August): 759–83.

Myrdal, Gunnar. 1968. Asian Drama: An Inquiry into the Poverty of Nations. New York: Pantheon.

Roessner, D., C. P. Ailes, I. Feller, and L. Parker. 1998. "How Industry Benefits from NSF's Engineering Research Centers." *Research-Technology Management* 41, 5: 40–44

Peterson, John, and Margaret Sharp. 1998. *Technology Policy in the European Union.* Basingstoke: Macmillan.

Sally, Razeen. 2007. "The New Asian Drama: Globalisation and Trade Policy in Asia." *Economic Affairs* 27,1: 87.

Smilor, R. W. 1987. "Commercialization Technology through New Business Incubators." *Research Management* (Sept./Oct.): 36–41.

Viale, R. and H. Etzkowitz. 2005. "Third Academic Revolution: Polyvalent Knowledge; the 'DNA' of the Triple Helix." Paper presented at 5th Triple Helix Conference, Turin, May 18–21.

Zucker, Lynn, and Michael Darby. 1998. "Intellectual Capital and the Birth of U.S. Biotechnology Enterprises." *American Economic Review* 88, 1: 290–306.

Chapter 14

A World of Competitors: Assessing the U.S. High Tech Advantage, the Role of Universities, and the Process of Globalization

John Aubrey Douglass[1]

New growth theory has become a ubiquitous part of the lexicon of international business and university leaders, and, perhaps most importantly, ministries and political leaders of almost all political persuasions. The shared axiom essentially states that postmodern economies, and increasingly developing economies, are growing in their dependence on "knowledge accumulation." Promoting knowledge accumulation locally, via knowledge-based businesses and entrepreneurial universities working together and supported by government, leads to technical innovation, new products, robust local economies, and ultimately greater national productivity and global competitiveness. That is the axiom of the modern era.

In part, the growing political acceptance of new growth theory relates to a number of highly touted regional success stories, what I call for the purposes of this chapter Knowledge Based Economic Areas (KBEAs). The United States, in

---

[1] Center for Studies in Higher Education, UC Berkeley. An earlier version of this essay was published in *Higher Education Management and Policy*, vol. 20, no. 2, 2008.

particular, continues to be viewed as the most robust in creating KBEAs, providing in some form an influential model that is visited and revisited by business and government leaders, and some academics, who wish to replicate its wonders. But with significant efforts by regional and national governments to pursue the edicts of new growth theory, and to create KBEAs on their own political and cultural terms, one might ask what are the current advantages, and disadvantages, of the American model? Does the U.S. retain a substantial global advantage, in part by being one of the first movers in creating vibrant KBEAs? With growing global competition in creating strong high-technology clusters in regional areas, what policy innovations are being pursued in the U.S.?

The following essay attempts to place universities within the larger political and policy environment by discussing market factors that have influenced knowledge accumulation and HT innovation in the U.S., an assessment of their current saliency in the face of globalization, and the growing market position of competitors, such as the E.U. The article also provides observations on major U.S. state-based HT initiatives to create KBEAs as a follow-up on a previous HEMP article on that topic, and discusses the prospect of a major new federal initiative to increase national R&D funding.[2]

The Status of the U.S. HT Advantage[3]

One widely understood challenge centers on how to create the conditions and circumstances for knowledge-based economic areas (KBEAs) that are not simply regionally or nationally competitive, but globally competitive. Universities, and the educational attainment of a population generally, play a critical role— perhaps as important as any other major policy and investment variable. Indeed, the first major U.S. KBEAs focused on nondefense HT sectors, including the San Francisco Bay Area (including Silicon Valley), Boston, the Austin area in Texas, and a number of others, that benefited from the presence of major and high-quality research universities. But there is, obviously, much more complexity underlying the factors required to both generate KBEAs, as well as the HT sector in general, and sustain them.

The U.S. remains highly competitive as a source of HT innovation because of a number of market positions, many the result of long-term investments in institu-

---

[2] This section builds on a previous analysis of U.S. state-based HT initiatives in an earlier publication by the author. See John Aubrey Douglass, "The Entrepreneurial State and Research Universities in the United States: Policy and New State-Based Initiatives," *Higher Education Management and Policy* (OECD), vol. 19, no. 1 (2007). This chapter is based on John Aubrey Douglass, "A World of Competitors," *Higher Education Management and Policy* (OECD), vol. 20, no. 2 (2008).

[3] Significant portions of this section of the brief rely on data and analysis provided in the most recent edition of Science and Engineering Indicators (2006) published by the National Science Foundation. For more information, see: <http://www.nsf.gov/statistics/seind06/c4/c4h.htm#c4hl7>.

tions (such as research universities) and R&D funding, more broadly influenced by a political culture that has tended to support entrepreneurs and risk-taking. In essence, the U.S. was the first to understand and pursue the nexus of science and economic policy. The following narrative outlines a number of the market factors that have historically influenced knowledge accumulation and HT innovation in the U.S., along with a brief assessment of their current saliency in the face of globalization.

Political Interest and Support for HT—The Mantra of the Postmodern Economy

Among the general public, and most importantly among major political leaders in the U.S., the tenets of new growth theory, as noted previously, are growing in influence. With declines in older manufacturing and consumer goods industries, high technology and service industries are widely viewed as the sources of near- and long-term economic competitiveness.

This worldview is, of course, shared by many other developed economies, such as the E.U. The difference is that the U.S. has had a longer history of essentially believing (rightly or wrongly) that HT innovation and economic activity will, in some form, be the crux of its future economy, and this belief influences R&D investment rates. There is, of course, abundant empirical evidence of the central importance of HT innovation, including highly productive regional economic areas such as Silicon Valley and the San Francisco Bay area for IT, San Diego in communications, and Boston for biotechnology. But there has also emerged a political rhetoric influenced by these success stories, including the desire to replicate in some form their seemingly universal formulas for success, and by an optimistic enthusiasm and sense of political competition that often drives policymaking.

The major change in the U.S., and the similar trend in other parts of the world, is the movement of policymaking and public investment intended to promote HT innovation and encourage university-business collaboration, to the regional (or state) and local level, with state governments increasingly becoming active. However, there are peculiarities to the dynamics of policymaking in the U.S. For one, the source of public R&D funding has historically been the federal (national) government. State- and local-based initiatives to build university-business collaborations two decades ago, for example, were in large part pursued to capture federal funds. This motivation remains, but increasingly states are simply investing their own money in basic research efforts in areas such as stem cells —an area that, for political reasons, the Bush administration refused to fund via federal coffers.

Political interest, enthusiasm, and the sense of political competition (to borrow the practices of competitor states or local regions, or to beat them to new policy initiatives), are in some form prerequisites to building KBEAs. Arguably, although with many nuances, the U.S. has a high political interest and desire to promote KBEAs, and HT innovation, the same as anywhere in the world. At the same time, the U.S. has its own peculiar ironies in how citizens view science and technology. For example, less than half the American population accepts the theory of evolution. Whether and how the theory of evolution is taught in public schools remains one of the most contentious issues in science education. A recent U.S. survey has not shown much change over time in the public's level of knowledge about science.

At the same time, the most recent Eurobarometer does show an increase, with marginal change occurring in almost all countries surveyed, although there is considerable variation in science-knowledge across countries in Europe. Belgium, Germany, Ireland, Luxembourg, and the Netherlands recorded double-digit increases between 1992 and 2005 in the percentage of correct responses to science literacy questions. These political and cultural factors hinder development of a more scientifically educated population and workforce, and ultimately the number of native-trained scientists and engineers.

University and Private Sector Interactive Vibrancy—High-Quality, Elite HE Institutions and Growing Partnerships

In the course of creating the world's first mass higher education system, the U.S. built a large array of public and private universities that have found merit and success in interacting with and supporting private enterprise and local economies. The public universities that emerged in the mid-to–late 1800s in particular had as part of their charters the responsibility of providing research and training in agricultural fields and emerging areas of industrial engineering that catered to local and regional needs. From their founding, the governing boards of these public institutions reflected these important components of their charge, with the majority of their members usually representing business and farming interests.

The result was a culture that promoted applied uses of scientific and engineering research that, by the early 1900s, became a major cultural component in most major American research universities, public and private, and particularly in engineering fields. In addition, federal funds, the initiatives of state and local governments, and the efforts of sectarian communities and private benefactors, helped to create a vast array of public and private institutions that, essentially, supported the emergence of a cadre of high-quality research universities. One indicator of the concentration of high-quality research universities is the high ranking of U.S. institutions in a variety of studies, including the highly publicized study based at Shanghai's Jiao Tong University. (See Table 14.1.)

The idea of using mass higher education to service, at least in part, the broad and ever-expanding needs of local and regional economies in the U.S. stood in sharp contrast to most other nations (such as most of Europe), and gave the U.S. a significant market advantage. The tradition of public-private partner-

Table 14.1. Regional Distribution of Top World Universities Shanghia Ranking 2006

	Americas	Europe	Asia/Pacific	Africa
Top 10	8	2	0	0
Top 50	39	9	2	0
Top 100	57	35	8	0
Top 500	198	205	93	4

Source: DG Research; ed.sjtu.cn/ranking 2006.

ships and other cultural and legal factors (such as intellectual property laws) continue to significantly shape HT innovation in the U.S. Foremost, there is a relatively strong building of alliances and flow of funding. Since 1993, R&D expenses paid to other domestic R&D performers outside their companies have increased as a proportion of company-funded R&D performed within firms. In 2003, companies in the United States reported $10.2 billion in R&D expenses paid to other domestic R&D performers outside their companies, compared with $183.3 billion in company-funded R&D performed within firms. The ratio of contracted-out R&D to in-house R&D was 5.6 percent for the aggregate of all industries in 2003, compared with 3.7 percent in 1993.

Participation by federal laboratories in cooperative research and development agreements (CRADAs) increased in FY 2003 but was still below the mid-1990s peak. Federal laboratories participated in a total of 2,936 CRADAs with industrial companies and other organizations in FY 2003, up 4.3 percent from a year earlier but still below the 3,500 peak in FY 1996. At the same time, U.S. companies continue to partner with other American and international companies worldwide to develop and exploit new technologies. New industrial technology alliances worldwide reached an all-time peak in 2003 with 695 alliances, according to the Cooperative Agreements and Technology Indicators database. Alliances involving only U.S.-owned companies have represented the largest share of alliances in most years since 1980, followed by alliances between U.S. and European companies.

Relatively High R&D Investment Rates —Investment in Basic Research

Absolute levels of R&D expenditures are important indicators of a nation's innovative capacity and are harbingers of future growth and productivity. Indeed, investments in the R&D enterprise strengthen the technological base on which economic prosperity increasingly depends worldwide. The relative strength of a particular country's current and future economy and the specific scientific and technological areas in which a country excels are further revealed through comparison with other major R&D-performing countries.

Since 1953, U.S. R&D expenditures as a percentage of GDP have ranged from a minimum of 1.4 percent in 1953 to a maximum of 2.9 percent in 1964. Most of the growth over time in the R&D/GDP ratio can be attributed to steady increases in nonfederal R&D spending. Nonfederally financed R&D, the majority of which is company-financed, increased from 0.6 percent of GDP in 1953 to an estimated 1.9 percent of GDP in 2004 (down from a high of 2.1 percent of GDP in 2000). The increase in nonfederally financed R&D as a percentage of GDP is indicative of the growing role of S&T in the U.S. economy. (See Figure 14.1.)

Yet much of the R&D expenditures in the U.S. are concentrated geographically in about 10 states, and these states vary significantly in terms of the types of research performed within their borders. In 2003, the top 10 states in terms of R&D accounted for almost two-thirds of U.S. R&D. California alone accounted for more than one-fifth of the $278 billion of R&D that could be attributed to one of the 50 states or the District of Columbia. Over half of all R&D performed in the United States by computer and electronic products manufacturers, for example, is located in California, Massachusetts, and Texas, while the R&D by chemical manufacturing companies is particularly prominent in two states, accounting for 61 percent of New Jersey's and 49 percent of Pennsylvania's business R&D. Together these two states account for almost one-third of the nation's R&D in this sector.

The United States remains one of the biggest investors in R&D with the highest relative investment in basic research, most of which is conducted in its network of research universities. For example, in 2000, global R&D expenditures totaled at least $729 billion, half of which was accounted for by the two largest countries in terms of R&D performance, the United States and Japan. Worldwide, there remains a heavy concentration of R&D in seven major economies. The U.S., Canada, France, Germany, Italy, Japan, and the United Kingdom performed over 83 percent of OECD R&D in 2002. At the same time, more money was spent on R&D activities in the United States in 2002 than in the rest of the G-7 countries combined.[4]

R&D intensity indicators, such as R&D/gross domestic product (GDP) ratios, continue to demonstrate the advantages enjoyed by developed, wealthy economies in the global HT economy. Yet there are signs that competing nations are beginning to push R&D investment rates in both the public and private sector that match or exceed the rates in the U.S. Overall, in 2004 the U.S. spent 2.7 percent of its total GDP and ranked fifth among OECD countries in terms of reported R&D/GDP ratios. Israel (not an OECD-member country), devoting 4.9 percent of its GDP to R&D, led all countries, followed by Sweden (4.3 percent), Finland (3.5 percent), Japan (3.1 percent), and Iceland (3.1 percent).

---

[4] See Science and Engineering Indicators 2006, National Science Foundation, <http://www.nsf.gov/statistics/seind06/c4/c4h.htm#c4hl7>.

Figure 14.1. R&D as a Percentage of Gross Domestic Product, 1953–2004

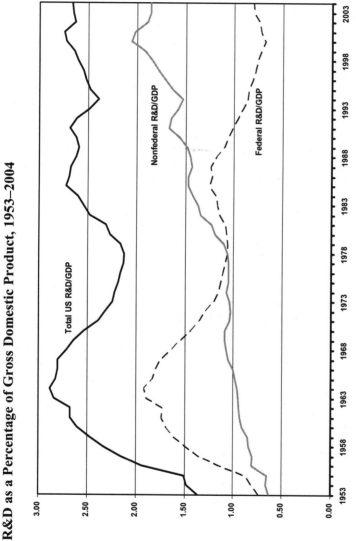

Source: Science and Engineering Indicators 2006, National Science Foundation

But there are two major market advantages for long-term economic growth for the U.S. relative to other economies. First is the high proportion of R&D investment by the private sector. R&D performed by the business sector is estimated to have reached $219.2 billion in 2004. The business sector's share of U.S. R&D peaked in 2000 at 75 percent, but following the stock market decline and subsequent economic slowdown of 2001 and 2002, the business activities of many R&D-performing firms were curtailed. The business sector is projected to have performed approximately 70 percent of U.S. R&D in 2007.

The second market advantage is the relatively high investment rates in basic research and the way that funding is dispersed. The United States expends approximately 18 percent of its total R&D portfolio on basic research; a little more than one-half of this research is funded by the federal government and performed in the academic sector. (See Figures 14.2 and 14.3.) The largest share of this basic research effort is conducted in support of life sciences. Yet that advantage is beginning to wane as other nations have begun to re-allocate their total R&D portfolio, which was once heavily invested in development and applied research toward blue-sky research. For example, the Russian Federation now spends 16 percent of all its R&D expenditures on basic research; in South Korea, which is currently the sixth largest R&D-performing member of OECD, the figure is 14 percent; in Japan 12 percent.[5] Indicating the growing emphasis on promoting scientific research and HT innovation in the E.U., basic research now accounts for more than 20 percent of total R&D performance reported in Italy, France, and Australia.

In the postmodern world, however, national rates of R&D expenditures, and the role of public and private sector funding, fail to capture significant global shifts in research activity. With the growth of HT clusters and research expertise worldwide, U.S.-based multinational corporations (MNCs) continue to expand their investment in R&D activity overseas. In 2002, R&D expenditures by affiliates of foreign companies in the United States reached $27.5 billion, up 2.3 percent from 2001 after adjusting for inflation. By comparison, total U.S. industrial R&D performance declined by 5.6 percent, after adjusting for inflation, over the same period. Cross-country R&D investments through MNCs continue to be strong between U.S. and European companies. At the same time, certain developing or newly industrialized economies are emerging as significant hosts of U.S.-owned R&D, including China, Israel, and Singapore. In 1994, major developed economies or regions accounted for 90 percent of overseas R&D expenditures by U.S. MNCs. This share decreased to 80 percent by 2001. The change reflects modest expenditures growth in European locations, compared with larger increases in Asia (outside Japan) and Israel.[6]

---

[5] Compared with patterns in the United States, however, a considerably greater share is funded for engineering research activities in each of these three countries.

[6] *Science and Engineering Indicators 2006.*

Figure 14.2. US R&D by Character of Work, 2004

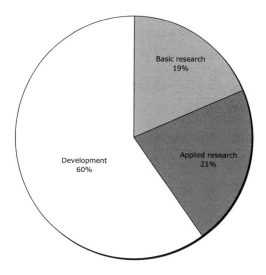

Source: Science and Engineering Indicators 2006, National Science Foundation.

Figure 14.3. US Basic Research by Performer, 2004

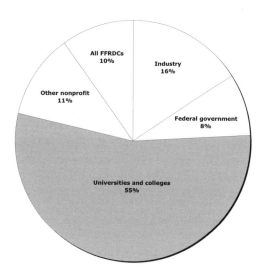

Source: Science and Engineering Indicators 2006, National Science Foundation.

Venture Capital—U.S. Still Most Robust

Venture capital is a primary source of funding for HT businesses. The U.S. remains the single largest source of venture capital, representing a major market advantage unmatched by any other major developed nation. The lack of an equity investment culture, information problems, and market volatility are factors that hinder the development of early-stage financing in many OECD countries.

In the United States, a continuum of capital providers, e.g., business angels and public and private venture funds, helps diversify risk and ensures a steady flow of quality deals. These networks—together with the use of staged financing instruments linked to performance, provision of technical and managerial support, and easy exits on secondary stock markets—have contributed to the survival and growth of portfolio firms. The number of venture capitalists with financial and technical expertise is limited in many countries and has not generally matched the rapid growth in risk capital supply across the OECD. Some countries, including Canada and Sweden as well as Israel, fill this experience gap by attracting venture investors from abroad.[7]

In many countries, structural, regulatory, and fiscal barriers act to constrain the development of a dynamic venture capital market and business environment. A 2007 study on venture capital notes that, around the world, almost 20 percent of all venture deals take place across national boundaries, an increase of 250 percent over the preceding five-year period. The authors observe that this trend has been accelerated by the practice of "venture licensing," the replication of proven business models in new markets.[8] Though the U.S., Europe, and Israel remain key in the industry, practices like this are expected to lead to even more focus on emerging markets in the coming years.

Not everyone agrees, however, that national borders are disappearing as a factor in venture investment. U.S. firms are merely dabbling in overseas markets. Although many U.S. portfolios include foreign companies, most of the time these firms make up less than five percent of total firm investment. Instead, U.S. venture firms appear to be taking a different approach to capitalizing on emerging markets. About 88 percent of respondents to one recent survey indicated that their portfolio includes companies with a significant portion of their operations overseas, mostly in India and China. This figure is almost twice the number reported last year. One conclusion is that venture capital firms remain cautious about expanding their global portfolios and that, although the pace of global investment will continue to grow in the next few years, it will do so slowly.[9]

---

[7] Science Technology Industry—Venture Capital: Trends and Policy Recommendations, OECD 2004.

[8] Ernst & Young's Acceleration: Global Venture Insights Report 2007, <http://www.ey.com/global/content.nsf/International/SGM_-_Venture_Capital_ Insight_Report_2007>.

[9] Deloitte, Global Trends in Venture Capital 2007 Survey, <http://www.nvca.org/pdf/U.S._Rpt_Global_VC_Survey_7-25-07.pdf>.

Yet despite the small amount of portfolio space dedicated to investments in China and India, the sum of all of these smaller investments from around the world has made China a major presence in the industry. The report also provides a number of new models for global investment, including "international joint funds, strategic limited partners, local funds with a global brand, local teams under one global fund, or a hybrid of these models" that may ease some of the reservations of U.S. firms about investing globally. These types of partnerships, which are already changing the face of global venture investment, may create an industry in which international investment is common, but a local presence is necessary.

Intellectual Property (IP)—U.S. as the First Mover

In part because it has been one of the most prolific generators of intellectual property, the U.S. has created a relatively elaborative and generally protective set of laws that, in turn, has significantly influenced economic development. Two major developments help to decipher the proliferation of IP and its influence on the American market.

First, in 1980 the federal government revised patent and licensing law. The Bayh-Dole Act of 1980 opened the doors for universities and their faculty and researchers to own patents and issue licenses developed through federally funded research. Previously, by allowing universities and research staff to jointly own discoveries supported by federal research grants, Bayh-Dole is credited with providing an important market force for creating the entrepreneurial university and for bolstering activity in a key economic sector, a model later replicated by other national governments, beginning with the U.K. during the Thatcher Administration. Bayh-Dole generated a revised worldview for both the university and business sectors by encouraging tech-transfer, arguably an exaggerated sense of potential profits for researchers, universities, and business partners alike. This national initiative, along with the funding of new federally funded university-business centers in engineering, had another effect: State governments, and to a lesser extent municipal governments, looked for new ways to harness their universities to support and grow their tech-based businesses and to compete for growing federal funding.

Another major shift in IP laws was shaped by the legal system, and specifically what was liberally determined to be a patentable discovery or idea. Remarkable discoveries in the life sciences, fed in part by long-term investments in basic research, created unique requests for patents and licenses. In 1980, the same year the Bayh-Dole Act was passed, the U.S. Supreme Court upheld a lower court decision providing an extremely broad definition of "patentable material," including the patenting of organisms, molecules, and research techniques related to new biotechnology fields.[10]

Arguably, the growing focus on patents and licensing by universities, and by industry, has had a deleterious effect on the sharing of information and discoveries that previously bolstered scientific inquiry. But this new focus has also encouraged greater investment by capital markets and resulted in research collaborations in the U.S. to a degree not yet replicated in similar developed economies. Within the U.S. domestic economy, a record number of patents (more than 169,000) were issued in the United States in 2003, although the rate of growth in U.S. patenting has slowed since 2000.[11] Nonetheless, U.S. patents have enjoyed a period of nearly uninterrupted growth since the late 1980s.

The U.S. also retains a strong market position in the number of international patents held and marketed to other nations. In 2003, U.S. receipts totaled $48.3 billion and its trade in intellectual property produced a surplus of $28.2 billion, up about five percent from the $25.0 billion surplus recorded a year earlier. About 75 percent of transactions involved the exchange of intellectual property between U.S. firms and their foreign affiliates. Exchanges of intellectual property among affiliates grew at about the same pace as those among unaffiliated firms. These trends suggest both a growing internationalization of U.S. business and a growing reliance on intellectual property developed overseas.

Yet another indicator of changing markets is the growing number of U.S. patents held by foreign sources. In 2003, U.S. residents accounted for about 55 percent of all successfully granted patents, while foreign inventors accounted for about 45 percent of the total. (See Figure 14.4.) A decade ago, businesses based in Japan, Germany, the U.K., France, and Canada, and a few other developed economies, were the largest source of U.S. patent applications. This has changed. Since 1997, Taiwan and South Korea replaced France and Canada in the top five foreign sources of inventors seeking U.S. patents. In 2003, Taiwan accounted for nine percent of foreign sources of U.S. patent applications and South Korea for close to seven percent. Canada and the United Kingdom accounted for five percent and France for four percent. If recent patents granted to residents of Taiwan and South Korea are indicative of the technologies awaiting review, many of these applications will prove to be for new computer and electronic inventions. Also impressive is the growth in patent applications by inventors from Israel, Finland, India, and China.

Foreign firms now account for about 36 percent of all U.S. biotechnology patents. These patents are more evenly distributed among a somewhat broader number of countries than that for all technology areas combined. (See Figure 14.5.) Another evident pattern is the more prominent representation of European

---

[10] David C. Mowery, Richard R. Nelson, Bhaven N. Sampat, and Arvids A. Zeidonis, *Ivory Tower and University-Industry Technological Transfer Before and After the Bayh-Dole Act* (Stanford, Calif.: Stanford University Press, 2004).

[11] National Science Foundation, Science and Engineering Indicators 2006, see figure 6–22 appendix table 6–12.

Figure 14.4. US Patents Granted by Country of Origin, 1990–2003 (Patents in Thousands)

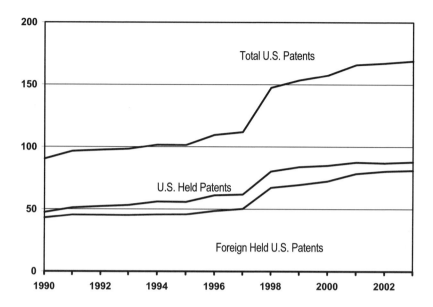

Source: Science and Engineering Indicators 2006, National Science Foundation

countries in U.S. patents of biotechnologies and the smaller representation by Asian inventors. Japan and Germany are not only the leading foreign generators of U.S. patents overall, they are the leading foreign sources for U.S. patents granted that are related to biotechnologies. Recently, however, Germany's share of U.S. biotechnology patents granted has been rising while Japan's share has been falling. In 2003, Germany was still the leading foreign source, accounting for 6.5 percent of U.S. biotechnology patents granted, up from around four percent in the late 1990s, while Japan's share was 6.4 percent, about half the share held by Japanese inventors in the early 1990s. These patenting trends indicate that while the U.S. remains a leading source of patents, and offers a liberal business environment, there are concrete signs of significant technology innovation in Asia and in a transitioning Europe.

Tax Policy—U.S. Most Advanced and Long-Term

One major U.S. advantage in shaping investment patterns and promoting risk taking relates to tax policy at the federal, state, and, increasingly, local level aswell. The U.S. has long engaged in using tax structures not simply to generate

Figure 14.5. U.S. Biotech Patents by Foreign Inventor, 1990–2003 (Number of Patents)

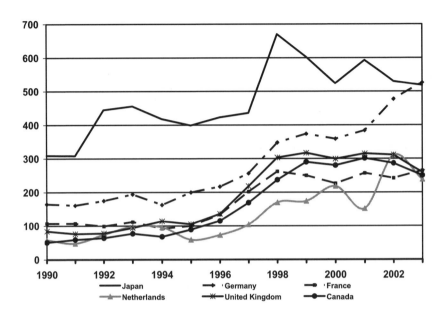

Source: Science and Engineering Indicators 2006, National Science Foundation

revenue, but to shape economic behavior—a characteristic relatively new to most other economies including the E.U. that have focused on relatively simple tax structures. For example, bankruptcy laws in the U.S. have been the most liberal of any major developed economy, reflecting a political culture that essentially promotes entrepreneurship, recognizes the high rate of failure among all types of businesses, and spreads the risk so that a business failure does not mean permanent ruin. The complexity of the tax system has also long included "tax credits," encouraging businesses to invest in technology and increasingly in R&D. At the same time, the U.S. tax code is so complex, and easily amendable, that it is also subject to major political influence, largely by corporate interests, including the growing HT sector. State and local taxation systems, historically, varied significantly and were rather simplistic, including a sales tax in some states, or an income tax model like the federal system, or both.

But over the past three decades, states and local government have become much more engaged in shaping tax policy to attract desirable businesses, including HT, and in generating investment in both university and business-based research. From 1990 to 2001, for instance, research and experimentation (R&E) tax credit claims by companies in the United States grew twice as fast as industry-funded

R&D, after adjusting for inflation, but growth in credit claims varied throughout the decade. R&E tax credit claims reached an estimated $6.4 billion in 2001. From 1990 to 1996, companies claimed between $1.5 billion and $2.5 billion in R&E credits annually; since then, annual R&E credits have exceeded $4 billion. However, in 2001 R&E tax credit claims still accounted for less than four percent of industry-funded R&D expenditures.

Talent Pool and Mobility—Attractiveness and Openness for Skilled Labor and Foreign Students

The U.S. has reaped tremendous advantages from its early commitment to mass higher education. Over most of the last century, more Americans went to college and graduated, with many entering graduate programs, than did residents of any other nation in the world. Adding to the nation's supply of talent has been a relatively open market approach to attracting academics and researchers. In the 1930s, the U.S. provided a haven for preeminent scientists escaping Nazi Germany and World War II. The emergence of a large network of high-quality, sometimes prestigious, universities that would hire foreign nationals as professors and researchers contrasted sharply with many if not most nations where university faculty held or hold civil service positions, and in which national governments limited the hiring of non-native talent.

Particularly after World War II, and beginning in earnest during the 1960s, the presence of foreign students in U.S. universities also grew dramatically, supported sometimes by their national governments, and increasingly by offers of student financial aid in graduate programs such as engineering where, today, foreign nationals are often more than 50 percent of the total students in a given program.

In previous decades, students who came to the U.S. for both undergraduate and graduate programs stayed largely in the U.S. and entered the job market. Their presence has influenced HT innovation dramatically and the growth of that sector in the U.S. economy. For example, one study indicates that nearly one third of all the successful start-ups in the Silicon Valley were started by foreign nationals, most of who gained their training in American universities. As shown in the Figures 14.6 and 14.7, foreign nationals from Asia became the largest single source of talent coming to the U.S. for their education, largely in graduate programs in science and engineering. Bolstered by Chinese national government initiatives, students from China became the largest single source of foreign students in the U.S. beginning in the early 1990s. The overall growth in all foreign nationals entering U.S. graduate degree programs in that period also reflected a significant shortfall in the training of "native" U.S. students in STEM fields, and the push by HT economic sectors to get the talent they needed

Figure 14.6. Geographic Origin of Foreign Graduate Students Enrolled in US Universities, 1960–2000

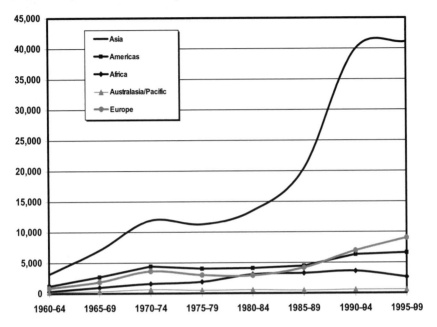

Source: Science and Engineering Indicators 2006, National Science Foundation.

via U.S. universities, and by successfully advocating more liberal visa policies for highly educated immigrants.

This pattern of attracting and then retaining talent is beginning to erode for two general reasons. First, the U.S., along with other developed economies with mature higher education systems, is finding that a growing number of foreign nationals educated in science and engineering fields, and professionals that have long contributed to S&T innovation and businesses, are beginning to return to their native economies as they mature, buttressed by national policies to attract top scientific talent. Second, the overall market for higher education, one of the primary means of attracting talent, is both growing and shifting with the maturity of university systems in the E.U. and elsewhere.

Since 2000 and 2005, the number of international students in national higher education systems (defined as those students with citizenship or residency from another country) has grown from around 1.8 million to 2.7 million. Over that short period, most E.U. nations have either retained or expanded their market share of international students, as shown in Table 14.2; countries such as Australia and New Zealand have also grown in their market share. Meanwhile, and in the midst of a significant expansion in the number of students seeking higher education out-

Figure 14.7. National Origin of Foreign Graduate Students from Asia Enrolled in US Universities, 1960–2000

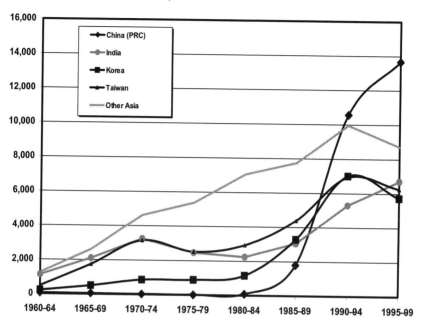

Source: Science and Engineering Indicators 2006, National Science Foundation

side of their home country, the share of international students attending U.S. universities and colleges has declined from just over 26 percent to 21.6 percent.

Much is made in the media and elsewhere about the U.S. being the number one single destination for foreign students to study in a tertiary institution. But his is not a fair comparison as the size of the U.S. in 2009, at just over 306 million people, is bigger than five of the largest E.U. nations combined—Germany at approximately 83 million, the U.K. and France at 61 million, Italy at 59 million, and Spain at 41 million, for a total of 305 million. Table 14.2 provides data on the international student enrollment among a sample group of 9 E.U. nations plus Switzerland, all with the highest percentage of international students in Europe, and with a combined population approximately the size of the U.S. While the overall world market share has dropped slightly between 2000 and 2005, this is in the midst of a boom in the overall number of students. Over that period, the U.S. grew by some 115,000 international students; the sample group grew by some 310,000 students. The sample group also significantly grew in the percentage international students represent of overall national enrollment. In the U.S., only about 3.4 percent of all enrolled students are international. In the E.U. sample group the percen-

Table 14.2. International Student Enrollment in National Systems of Higher Education: Sample Group 2000 and 2005*

	2000	2005	% Foreign Students of Total HE Enrollment 2005	
	# Enrolled	# Enrolled	All Enrolled	Ph.D. and Res
Europe Sample				
U.K.	222,798	318,396	17.3%	41.4%
Germany	186,968	259,787	11.5%	nd
France	136,953	236,344	10.8%	34.4%
Italy	24,917	44,979	2.2%	4.3%
Spain	40,740	45,527	2.5%	18.9%
Belgium	40,558	45,252	19.9%	30.8%
Sweden	25,468	39,254	9.2%	20.3%
Switzerland	26,008	36,801	18.4%	43.2%
Austria	30,373	34,620	14.1%	20.2%
Netherlands	1,455	32,712	5.6%	nd
Sub-Europe Total	736,234	1,093,670	10.6%	26.7%
E.U.-19			6.3%	17.5%
U.S.	475,242	589,906	3.4%	24.1%
Total OECD	1,545,945	2,295,289	7.6%	17.5%
Total Globally	1,818,759	2,725,996	nd	nd

* Largely defined as students with citizenship outside of the national HE system they are enrolled in. Note that Switzerland is not part of the E.U.
Source: OECD Education at a Glance 2007 tables C3.1 C3.8.

tage is 10.6 percent, with the highest percentage in the U.K., Germany, and France.

An important caveat is that much of the growth in international students within the E.U. relates to the Bologna and Lisbon Declarations, and the creation of an evolving European Higher Education Area. These policy reforms and the general concept of E.U. citizenship have resulted in much greater mobility within the E.U. for tertiary-bound students. Yet a clear pattern is emerging in which the international attractiveness of major E.U. higher education centers, along with the entrepreneurial effort to enroll international students in Australia, New Zealand, and even Japan, marks, in some form, the shifting of the market. Most E.U. and many OECD countries have conscious national policies to draw talented international students to their home universities. There is no strategic approach at the national or even state level of government in the U.S., which remains largely de-centralized in its approach to the structure and goals of higher education.

The U.S. does retain a strong international draw for the graduate level, and particularly in engineering, the sciences, and business management. Most Chinese students wishing to study abroad still come to the U.S. Nearly 30 percent of all international Chinese students enroll in a U.S. university or college. And globally, some 24 percent of all doctoral level students in the U.S. are foreign nationals. But as an indicator of shifts in the global talent pool, there is now an even a higher percentage in the E.U. sample group (nearly 28 percent); in Australia the percentage is 28 percent. There is then the question of the relative quality of the international student pool, and the quality and reputation of the graduate programs they enroll in—all rather difficult factors to evaluate. The U.S. remains a world leader in the prestige and, arguably, the quality of its advanced graduate programs. Yet there is growing evidence that students throughout the world no longer see the U.S. as the primary place to study, that in some form this correlates with perceived quality and prestige in the E.U. and elsewhere, and further that the trajectory of growth in international students may mean a continued decline in the U.S. market share of international students.

Attracting talent from abroad is an important component of the U.S.'s HT advantage. Educating a more robust native population should be an equally, if not more, important goal. A significant factor that will influence the U.S.'s market position, and the general socio-economic health of the nation, is the significant relative decline in higher education attainment rates of Americans when compared to other developed economies.

Although the United States still retains a lead in the number of people with higher education experience and degrees, at the younger ages a different story emerges. On average, the postsecondary participation rate for those aged 18 to 24 in the United States is approximately 33 percent according to a 2005 study, down from around 38 percent in 2000. In the U.S., more students today are part-time than in the past, and more are in two-year colleges; the wealthiest students are in the four-year institutions, and students from lower and even middle-income families are now more likely to attend a two-year college, less likely to earn a bachelor's degree, and now take much longer to attain a degree than in the past.[12]

In contrast, within a comparative group of fellow OECD countries, many nations are approaching 50 percent of this younger age group participating in postsecondary education, and most are enrolled in programs that lead to a bachelor's degree. According to 2004 data, the U.S. has slipped from first to 14th in the higher education participation rate. Without a major effort by states and the federal government, and by higher education institutions, it is likely that this ranking will go down further over the next decade. The U.S. will undoubtedly remain a leader in

---

[12] For an analysis of the decline in the U.S. advantage in higher education access and degree production, see John Aubrey Douglass, *The Conditions for Admission: Access, Equity, and the Social Contract of Public Universities* (Stanford, Calif.: Stanford University Press, 2007).

HT and will continue to draw talented graduate students and scientists to its un-matched network of research universities. Already the initial negative influence of the Patriot Act has ebbed and foreign applications to U.S. graduate schools have begun to increase once again, although perhaps the numbers will grow at a slower pace than in previous decades.[13]

Because of concerted policy efforts and investment in education, however, particularly in science and technology programs at universities, and the corre-sponding growth of S&T sectors, new competitors for faculty, graduate students, and more generally talent will continue to grow in number and quality. America's once-dominant competitive advantage will diminish. Universities in the E.U., for example, have grown significantly in their ability to attract graduate students (out-side of Oxbridge), and many are becoming more liberal in their willingness to hire foreign nationals as faculty. The Bologna Agreement and other policy initiatives seek great mobility of talent and jobs, influenced at least in part by the American model. Moreover, the emergence of English as the dominant language in academia and business once had, and remains, a market advantage for the U.S., the U.K., and other English-speaking countries. But the use of English in non-English speaking nations, and the growing number of graduate programs (particularly pro-fessional programs) offered in English throughout the world is also diminishing the market advantage of U.S. universities.

An emerging body of research largely produced by the scientific community and economists worries about the ability of the U.S. to continue its market advan-tage in both attracting and retaining talent from abroad. A congressionally re-quested report by a preeminent committee of scientists and S&T leaders, chaired by the former CEO of Lockheed Martin Marietta, Norman Augustine, recently argued that "a comprehensive and coordinated federal effort is urgently needed to bolster U.S. competitiveness and pre-eminence in these areas."[14] The political traction of such analysis, however, has proven marginal, thus far.

Labor economist Robert Freeman has observed that a diminished comparative advantage for the U.S. in high tech will "create a long period of adjustment for U.S. workers, of which the off-shoring of IT jobs to India, growth of high-tech production in China, and multinational R&D facilities in developing countries, are harbingers." The U.S. will need to adjust, he notes, reflecting the observations of many others, by developing "new labor market and R&D policies that build on existing strengths" and that recognize scientific and technological advances in other countries.[15]

---

[13] Council of Graduate Schools, "Findings from the 2006 CGS International Gradu-ate.

[14] Committee on Science, Engineering, and Public Policy, *Rising above the Gather-ing Storm: Energizing and Employing America for a Brighter Economic Future* (New York: National Academies Press, 2006).

[15] Freeman, "Does Globalization of the Scientific/Engineering Workforce Threaten U.S. Economic Leadership?"

A Comparative Assessment of the U.S.'s Competitive Advantage

The U.S. remains a productive environment for S&T and will remain so in the short run not only because of the excellence of its research universities and the growth of new business sectors like biotechnology. There is also the availability of venture capital, relatively high rates of R&D investment, and tax incentives and legal precedents that, thus far, are not matched in other economies.

With the exception of the dot com bust, university research and HT economic growth remain robust in the U.S. For example, the science and engineering workforce in the United States has grown rapidly, both over the last half-century and the last decade. From 1950 to 2000, employment in S&E occupations grew from fewer than 200,000 to more than 4 million workers, an average annual growth rate of 6.4 percent. Between the 1990 and 2000 censuses, S&E occupations continued to grow at an average annual rate of 3.6 percent, more than triple the rate of growth of other occupations. Between 1980 and 2000, the total number of S&E degrees earned grew at an average annual rate of 1.5 percent, which was faster than labor force growth but less than the 4.2 percent-growth of S&E occupations. S&E bachelor's degrees grew at a 1.4 percent average annual rate, and S&E doctorates at 1.9 percent.

On average, American companies spend three times as much as those in Europe on R&D, and they have access to some 10 times as much debt financing. This is one reason why many S&T firms in Europe and other parts of the world set up offices in the U.S.—not to gain access to scientific expertise, but to capital markets. Because of the high cost for an initial public offering on the stock market, many international firms are merging with existing, and often fledgling, U.S. firms.

The question is how long these American advantages will remain. The global environment is changing rapidly, with individual countries growing significantly in their R&D abilities, in part via government policies and in part because of expanding investment by the private sector. The European Research Area and the emerging 7th Framework are intended to significantly boost R&D investment *and* to help shape tax policies and the availability of capital.[16]

Table 14.3 offers an unscientific assessment by the author of the major factors that promote and sustain national and regional HT economies. Most of these advantage factors have, in some form, been discussed previously. Added to our list are factors such as the overall quality of the science and tech workforce, mobility within a region or nation for these workers, the concept of a relatively

---

[16] A recent E.U. report states that Europe's lagging R&D intensity results from structural characteristics, including tax incentives and an improved environment for entrepreneurship among small firms, not underinvestment in R&D by individual and usually large European firms. See Petro Moncada-Paternò-Castello et al., "Does Europe Perform Too Little Corporate R&D? Comparing E.U. and non-E.U. Corporate R&D Performance," European Commission Joint Research Centre, Institute for Prospective Technological Studies (IPTS), Seville, 2006.

Table 14.3. National and Regional Factors for Knowledge-Based Economic Area

(10-point scale: 1 = low; 10 = high; improving = +; declining = -)

	U.S.	Bay Area	E.U.
1. Vitality of research universities	8	10	7+
2. R&D investment – public	8+	9+	7+
3. R&D investment – private	8	9	4+
4. Access to venture capital	10	10	6+
5. Intellectual property laws/protection	9	9	8+
6. Concentration of knowledge intense companies	8	10	8
7. High quality workforce	6-	9	7+
8. Workforce mentality	9	10	6+
9. Access to global labor/immigrant factor	9-	10-	7+
10. Supporting risk taking – culturally, legally	10	10	6+
11. Open business environment	8	9	7
12. Quality of life: housing, transportation	8-	7-	8
13. Political support/government inducement	8	8	8

open business environment (e.g., collaborations between universities and business, and between different business enterprises, and the sharing of workforce and knowledge, which is widely perceived as one ingredient in the success of Silicon Valley), and the overall quality of life offered to that workforce, including housing, local schools, and transportation. Increasingly in cities and in regions with successful HT sectors, housing costs are rising with the real or potential threat of diminishing the attractiveness of the region for employees. Also, in the U.S., urban area schools are generally declining in quality and there is poor public transportation and the increased division of rich and poor, all of which add strain to the quality of life.

The objective of Table 14.3 is to offer an assessment of the general status of these various advantages in supporting KBEAs in the U.S., in the San Francisco Bay Area (including Silicon Valley and biotech corridors in San Francisco and around Berkeley), and in the E.U. (particularly among the E.U. top five) on a 10-point scale—10 being the most favorable. In addition, the author's sense of the trajectory of each advantage factor is indicated by a plus (going up) or minus (going down).

Americans are generally not looking across the Atlantic or Pacific, or across their borders, for ideas on HT policymaking. Lawmakers and other policymakers are concerned about being competitive in the global marketplace, but the U.S. remains largely isolationist in its leanings despite the fact that the HT sector is increasingly an international endeavor. The focus of government and much of the business sector is on protecting or expanding foreign markets, intellectual property rights and tax incentives, buttressing venture capital markets, and reducing restrictions on immigrant/visitor visas.

U.S. political culture retains a sense that it is a nation that remains the most productive and innovative home for science and technology, and that, for instance, the cure for cancer or the breakthroughs promised by stem-cell research will be homegrown. Thus far, this seems to ignore the significant knowledge centers in Europe and emerging S&T centers in countries like China, India, and other parts of the world.

An important indicator of the research gains and HT productivity of Europe and other parts of the world is a relatively little-known fact, at least among Americans. The U.S. no longer has a trade surplus in HT advanced products (thus not counting mass consumer items such as electronics). A major bright spot in the overall trade imbalance has been its relatively strong export of HT goods and services. Maintaining and, indeed, enhancing this market position was one of the major reasons for the concerted policy efforts beginning in the early 1980s with the passage of Bayh-Dole and other federal initiatives that formed a formal transition of science policy as a major component of national economic policy.

For some two decades, the U.S. enjoyed a substantial surplus in HT products. However, as shown in Figure 14.8 and 14.9, between 2001 and 2002 the U.S. moved from a $6 billion surplus to a $15 billion deficit in these goods and services. In 2004, the deficit was more than $25 billion. Within the various categories of HT products, aerospace and electronics retained surpluses; the largest single deficit was in information and communications. It is important to note, however, that these shifts reflect the process of globalization and the international nature of many HT businesses. American-controlled HT firms, for example, have products being created and manufactured throughout the world, as do other major international conglomerates. The blurring of national boundaries in terms of business activity, including finance, makes the story line of surpluses and deficits increasingly complicated.

Yet another indicator of the shift in America's HT advantage is the growth of international patent activity (see Figure 14.10). The widely perceived U.S. hegemony does not accurately reflect recent data. The accompanying chart demonstrates that among OECD countries the U.S. retains a major market position.[17] The growing E.U. has an actual larger total number of patents, with a significant portion generated by individuals and HT businesses in Europe's top five economies. The trajectory indicates that Europe, and many other parts of the world, are making sizable and relatively fast gains as global players in HT markets. Even in the area of R&D investment, as noted earlier, the market is shifting.

As a percentage of GNP, federal funding for basic research in the U.S. in the physical sciences and engineering has been declining for the past 30 years, to

---

[17] Patents applied for at the European Patent Office (EPO), the Japanese Patent Office (JPO) and granted to the U.S. Patent & Trademark Office (U.S.PTO), estimations for priority year 2001. The priority date corresponds to the first international request for protecting an invention.

Figure 14.8. US Trade Balance in Advanced HT Products, 2000–04 $b

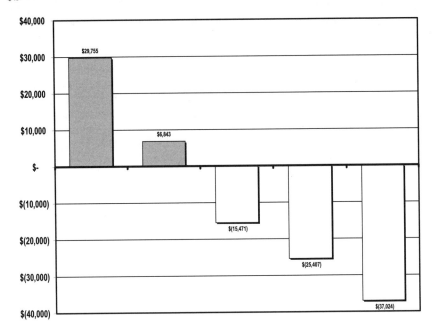

Source: Science and Engineering Indicators 2006, National Science Foundation.

less than 0.05 percent in 2003. Asia's developing economies are placing increasing percentages of the GNP into science and technology, and they are on the edge of a payoff, with their share of global high-tech exports rising from seven percent in 1980 to 25 percent in 2001. According to National Science Foundation figures, the U.S. percentage fell from 31 percent to 18 percent.[18]

Cluster Theory—The Geographic Dispersion of U.S. HT

While the U.S. remains a major source of HT innovation and job growth, among the various states there are significant differences in the geographic dispersion of mature KBEAs, particularly in the generation of new HT businesses and centers of venture capital. A recent study indicates that larger firms with over 1,000

---

[18] National Sciences Foundation, Science and Engineering Indicators 2006 (Washington, D.C.: National Science Foundation, 2006).

Figure 14.9. US Trade Balance in HT Categories, 2004 $b

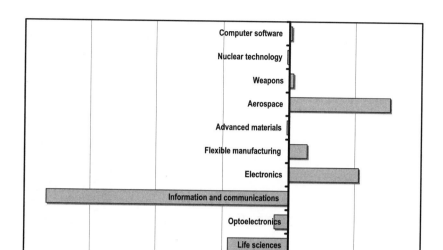

Source: Science and Engineering Indicators 2006, National Science Foundation

employees are the most likely to collaborate with universities and other public research institutes (nonprofits).

Further, most if not all of these firms are already engaged in R&D activity, sometimes via contracting research activity, and have therefore successfully built a capacity to absorb and use publicly generated research.[19] Another study indicates, not surprisingly, that university-based start-ups are largely concentrated in states with the largest economies and with the largest levels of venture capital.[20] Table 14.4 shows that the total amount of U.S. venture capital investment in 1996 was $11.3 billion, and rose to $26.0 billion in 2006. Most states retained their market share of that venture capital investment portfolio, with California the only state that significantly increased its share from just over 40 to 48 percent.

---

[19] Robert Fontana, Aldo Geuna, and Mirrell Matt, "Factors Affecting University-Industry R&D Collaboration: The Importance of Screening and Signaling," Research Centre in Economics and Management, Strasbourg, 2005.

[20] Celestine Chukumba and Richard Jensen, "University Invention, Entrepreneurship, and Start-Ups," National Bureau of Economic Research, Tech-Based Economic Development Research Center, 2005.

Figure 14.10. US and EU International HT Patents: 2003

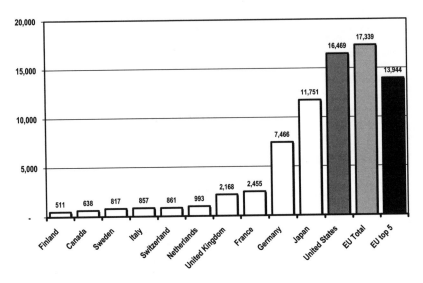

Patents applied for at the European Patent Office (EPO), the Japanese Patent Office (JPO) and granted to the the US Patent & Trademark Office (USPTO), estimations for priority year 2001. The priority date corresponds to the first international request for protecting an invention.

Source: Science and Engineering Indicators 2006, National Science Foundation.

A recent study by Martin Kinney and Donald Patton illustrates the geographic concentration of firms that grow from being start-ups into public companies listed on the New York Stock Exchange (initial public offerings of stock, or IPOs) and also the concentration of new HT activity in sectors such as semiconductors and biotechnology. IPOs indicate the maturity of the industry. Data is from the period 1996 through 2000.[21] As the accompanying two charts indicate (Tables 14.5 and 14.6), in the biotechnology sector, there is a heavy concentration of new firms in specific regions: the states of Massachusetts (the Boston area), New York, and the East Coast corridor down to Maryland, along with California's San Francisco Bay Area and San Diego. These regions accounted for approximately half of the 65 HT businesses going public. New IPOs emerged also in North Carolina, Georgia (Atlanta), Michigan (Ann Arbor), Texas (Austin and Houston), and the state of Washington (Seattle).[22]

---

[21] Martin Kenney and Donald Patton. "Entrepreneurial Geographies: Support Networks in Three High-Tech Industries." Economic Geography 81, 2 (2005): 201–28.
[22] *Ibid.*

Table 14.4. Top 10 U.S. States Receiving Venture Capital Investment: 1996 and 2006

	1996	2006
All states ($ billions)	$11.3	$26.0
States % share	100.0	100.0
California	40.4	48.0
Massachusetts	9.6	10.9
Texas	4.7	5.3
New York	3.6	4.9
Washington	3.6	3.9
New Jersey	3.6	3.1
Pennsylvania	2.7	2.9
Maryland	1.2	2.6
Colorado	2.7	2.56
North Carolina	1.6	1.8
All others	26.3	14.0

Source: Science and Engineering Indicators 2008.

Table 14.5. Cluster Theory: The U.S. Example
Location of Biotechnology IPOS (65 firms going public 1996-2000)

	Percentage
Bay Area – Northern California	42
Los Angeles/San Diego – Southern California	8
New York Corridor – New York, New Jersey, Connecticut	12
Massachusetts	17
Pennsylvania	6
District of Columbia Region – Maryland, Virginia	6
Other	32

Source: Martin Kenney and Donald Patton 2005.

Semiconductor IPOs in that period of four years were even more concentrated, with the vast majority in the Bay Area and San Diego, followed by Boston and the New York to Maryland corridor. A similar pattern of concentration is found in the telecommunication sector. In all three HT sectors—biotech, semiconductors, and telecommunications—there is a general recurrence of HT business activity. In each of these geographic areas, there is a link between existing and high-quality research universities and the existence of an urban environment that has built, over time, a robust and talented workforce and research environment.

Table 14.6. Cluster Theory: The U.S. Example
Location of Semiconductor IPOS (44 firms going public 1996-2000)

	Percentage
Bay Area – Northern California	61
Los Angeles/San Diego – Southern California	11
New York Corridor – New York, New Jersey, Connecticut	7
Massachusetts	5
Oregon	5
Colorado	5
Other	7

Source: Martin Kenney and Donald Patton.

There is also evidence that this workforce, including a significant number of HT business professionals, scientists and engineers, often with immigrant backgrounds, are mobile, moving from one KBEA to another. Further, there is a distinct pattern in which the vast majority of venture capital investments are focused in these areas, specializing in making bets within an HT research and business environment that appears to offer the best potential payoff. Even then, one recent study estimates that some 70 percent of venture capital investments in U.S. HT businesses fail.

At the same time, data collected by the U.S. Bureau of Labor on the number of employees in HT businesses in both the public and private sectors indicates a much more dispersed geographic distribution. In this case, employment numbers include all those in businesses and industries classified by the U.S. government as HT, including financial services and industries such as automobile manufacturing and aerospace—a wide swath of activity in the economy. Figure 14.11 shows the total employment in HT businesses by state and as a percentage of all workers—unfortunately, not by major regions within a state. The employment numbers indicate that while states such as Massachusetts, California, Texas, Michigan, and Maryland (where there is a high concentration of federal and private research laboratories) have many HT businesses, many other states have relatively high employment in HT industries as well. The chart also indicates the concentration of university R&D as a percentage of the gross state product (GSP). Again, these data provide a more nuanced illustration of the role of university-based R&D in relationship to a state's entire economy. Some big HT states, such as California, which has the highest number of HT employees of any state and secures the most federally and privately funded R&D investments, have economies that are extremely diverse. Or, in other words, HT is important, and the role of research universities is a major factor in their economies, but neither is a dominant player now or for the foreseeable future in most states.[23]

---

[23] For a further discussion on the differences among the states in HT activity, see John Aubrey Douglass, "The Entrepreneurial State and Research Universities in the

Figure 14.11. Dispersed Pattern of HT Employment: 2000

50 State Comparison: HT as a Percentage of All State Employment and University R&D Per $1,000 of Gross State Product

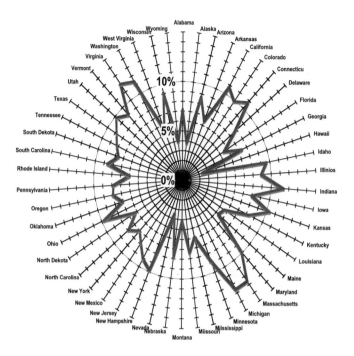

Source: US Office of Technology Policy, State Science and Technology Indicators, 2004.

One possible implication of the dispersed HT employment in the U.S. is that as this sector continues to mature, the traditionally dominant KBEAs may continue to create innovation and businesses, but actual employment may end up in other geographic areas—effectively helping to create competitors. Further, innovative HT businesses, as they grow, seek other locales, whether in the U.S. or increasingly in other nations, in which to locate part or all of their operations —one obvious example is the tremendous dispersal of the software industry. Efforts by governments to build and support KBEAs may reap significant local economic and social benefits, but they might not keep the investment locally as jobs are dispersed to other regions. These benefits are national and international.

United States: Policy and New State-Based Initiatives," Higher Education Management and Policy (OECD), vol. 10, no. 1 (2007).

In total, in 2000 some 8.8 percent of the workers in the U.S. were employed in the HT sector. In comparison, the 15 largest European Union economies averaged for that year 7.6 percent working in HT industries and universities, with Germany having the highest percentage at around 11.2—according to data collected by CORDIS. The problem is that this data is already old, although it is the latest data I could secure. The probability is that there is significant growth of nascent KBEAs in the U.S. and E.U., and elsewhere, building on the formula of university and private sector coordination and, increasingly, government-based initiatives.

The Politics of High Tech

The politics of HT, and the devotion to new growth theory, yields a growing sense of competition and a remarkable new era of policymaking, driven in part by a sense of urgency and by the natural laws of interest group politics. In the U.S., this has created a remarkable level of effort by states and regional governments to make targeted investments that are relatively new, and to enter policy arenas once largely reserved for the federal government—the traditional source of publicly supported R&D. Some investments are attempts to leverage federal funding, or to create new funding streams, for example to create public-funded venture capital in states that lack private investors, or in the case of stem cell–related research, to fill a void left by the Bush Administration's edict effectively severely limiting federal funding for research thought improper by neoconservatives.[24] Even with recent advances in alternatives to embryonic stem cells, the unprecedented limits set by President Bush have, essentially, led to a entirely new pattern of basic science funding, largely by already high-tech and more liberal states such as California and New York.

Over the last decade or so, lack of leadership at the federal level in science and technology funding, where funding levels to date have been relatively stagnant except for the National Institutes of Health, has resulted in state political leaders being active policymakers in areas thought vital to the socio-economic health of their respective state. This has occurred not only in S&T, but also in health care, immigration, and in issues related to global warming and energy.

There is a prospect of a significant consensus on the need for a new infusion of federal funding largely intended to bolster basic research and support the nation's HT efforts with innauguration of a new presidential administration, depending, in some form, on the health of the national economy. Even with renewed federal leadership, it is likely that states and local governments will continue to be the most prolific generators of new HT initiatives, based on rational assessments of best practices, new ideas, and increasingly the sense of competition and devotion to new growth theory. In the course of a growing era of state initiatives, the respective role of federal and state governments, and therefore the attention of the

---

[24] *Ibid.*

S&T community, will continue to be substantially altered. The perceived wonders of a high-tech-driven society, and the political culture it has bred, are a driving force that is creating new policy regimes and players, and has reshaped the sources of funding.

Yet numerous initiatives to bolster science and technological prowess remain, as I noted previously, myopic. There is a huge disconnect in U.S. policy related to promoting KBEAs and national competitiveness. Few policymakers, or even the higher education community, are aware of stagnant and, in some states, real declines in higher education access *and* graduation rates relative to economic competitors.[25] Combined with global changes in the market for S&T talent, and the significant and increasingly successful efforts of competitors to increase the educational attainment of their population, to build centers of research excellence, and to attract international students, the U.S.'s HT advantage, and more generally its historical competitive advantages, are eroding—although there remain a number of advantages, chiefly related to an entrepreneurial culture and the highest concentration of venture capital in the world.[26]

The role of science and technology in society continues to grow; many countries have assessed their weaknesses, and have strategic approaches largely focused on educational attainment, building their higher education systems, and increased R&D output; most, and in particular the E.U., are constantly assessing their relative competitiveness compared to that of the U.S. and other developed economies; U.S. policymakers are thus far less strategic, assume that the nation's high tech advantage is intact, and are generally not conscious of the breadth of change within the global economy.

---

[25] See John Aubrey Douglass, "The Higher Education Race," International Higher Education, Fall 2007.

[26] For a discussion of the convergence of national efforts to increasing higher education attainment rates, see: John Aubrey Douglass, "A Global Scenario for Higher Education Systems," GUNI-UNESCO Dec. 2007, <http://www.guni-rmies.net/news/detail.php?id=1141>.

Chapter 15

University Roles in Technological Innovation in California

C. Judson King[1]

The public universities in the United States were established with goals of providing widespread, affordable access to higher education. Starting with agriculture and the mechanical arts well over a century ago, it has been recognized more and more that another important role of research universities, public and private, is in building the economy and improving societal conditions through innovation. This role has been well appreciated in California for the electronics, software, biotechnology, and communications industries, and in other areas such as health care and agriculture.

The purpose of this chapter is to indicate some of the ways in which universities, and the University of California in particular, have contributed to the development of California industries; to explore several recent organized structural and project efforts that are various forms of university, industry and/or government partnerships; to assess some of the most important factors for success and for meeting concerns about detrimental effects of such partnerships; and finally to assess reasons for the relative success of California. The state had no grand design for promoting technological innovation, but the wisdom of putting major state

---

[1] Center for Studies in Higher Education, UC Berkeley. Helpful review comments from Irwin Feller have brought about some important points in this chapter.

resources into public higher education has been a major spur to the large success that California has had in technological innovation.

Some Measures of Impact

The broadest contributions of California universities, or indeed universities anywhere, to the state are the educational development of the populace and the flow of graduates at all degree levels to positions in business, government, universities, and self-employment. Influences that are more specific to technological innovation are the education of holders of graduate and professional degrees, the flow to industry of inventions and relevant background information stemming from university research, and transitions of faculty and senior researchers to roles as entrepreneurs themselves. Some facts and figures pertaining to the biotechnology and wine industries provide more specific examples.

Biotechnology

Yarkin and Murray[2] have studied the flow of people from the University of California to the California biotechnology industry and the contributions that they have made to the development of that industry. In 2001, stemming from the original 1980 Cohen (Stanford University) and Boyer (University of California) patent on recombinant DNA technology[3] and subsequent research, over one-third of U.S. biotechnology companies were situated in California.

- These companies accounted for over 47 percent of research expenditures of the U.S. biotechnology industry and accounted for 53 percent of revenues.
- The California biotechnology industry provided 60,000 jobs at an average salary of $71,000, i.e., $4.3 billion of personal income.
- At least 35 percent of California biotechnology firms were founded by University of California faculty.
- At least 302 persons with University of California Ph.D.s were working in California biotechnology companies.
- Licenses to technology from the University of California were held by 82 biotechnology companies.

---

[2] Cherisa Yarkin and Andrew Murray, "Assessing the Role of the University of California in the State's Biotechnology Economy: Heightened Impact Over Time," Working Paper No. 02–5, Industry-University Cooperative Research Program, University of California, March 2003, <http://ucdiscoverygrant.org/pdf/UC_Role_in_CA_Biotech_Economy_March 2003.pdf>.

[3] Maryann Feldman, "Commercializing Cohen-Boyer," <http://www.kauffman.org/pdf/tt/Feldman_Maryann.pdf>. See also <http://bancroft.berkeley.edu/Exhibits/Biotech/25.html>.

- Large clusters of biotechnology companies exist in the San Francisco Bay Area and San Diego, and 96 percent of California biotechnology companies are located within 35 miles of a University of California campus.

A less detailed companion study deals with the R&D-intensive communications industry.[4]

Wine and Viticulture

Historically, another very tangible contribution of University of California research has been to the development of the California wine industry.[5] Interestingly, the University of California programs in viticulture and enology originated through an act of the state legislature in 1880, sensing the economic potential of the industry and mandating that the state university take on the task of improving it. This research has largely been carried out at the University Farm at Davis, which became the Davis campus. During the period of prohibition of alcoholic beverages in the United States (1919–1933), research was carried out on viticulture, leading to the development of plant strains used now for over 95 percent of wine made in the United States and much of that made in other countries. Research in the 1930s focused upon the influence of climate on the growth of different varietals, leading to knowledge that underlies site locations for vineyards around the world. The Davis campus also developed malo-lactic fermentation, which allows the wine-making process to be chemically controlled to produce distinctive flavors and to exercise quality control. Maynard Amerine and associates at UC Davis developed a methodology of sensory evaluation that is in widespread use today. Nearly all wineries in the United States now have a UC Davis graduate as wine maker or manager. As well, students are sent to the UC Davis enology and viticulture programs from wine-making countries around the world. It is this long-term, sustained line of research that has made California wines excellent and highly competitive.

As of 2005,[6] the California wine industry

- contributed $51.8 billion to the California state economy and $125.3 billion to the United States economy;
- created 309,000 full-time-equivalent jobs in California, with $10.1 billion gross wages;

---

[4] Cherisa Yarkin, Andrew Murray, and Sam Chou, "The Role of University of California Scientists and Engineers in the State's R&D-Intensive Communications Industry," Working Paper No. 03–1, University-Industry Cooperative Research Program, University of California, April 2003, <http://ucdiscoverygrant.org/pdf/UC_Role_in_ CA_Commnications_Economy_April2003.pdf>.

[5] Lisa Lapin, "A Fine Blend," *UC Davis Magazine* 19, no. 2, 2002, <http://ucdavismagazine.ucdavis.edu/issues/win02/feature_1.html>.

[6] MKF Research LLC, "Economic Impact of California Wine 2006," MKF Research LLC, 2006. See also <http://www.wineinstitute.org/industry/statistics/2006/ca_wine_ economic_impact.php>.

- sold 74 percent of its output in the other 49 U.S. states, creating 875,000 jobs in the U. S. as a whole;
- paid $3.2 billion in taxes and license fees to the state of California, and $1.8 billion in federal taxes to the U.S. government; and
- contributed over 95 percent of U.S. wine exports, which totaled $658 million.[7]

The developments of the biotechnology industry and the wine industry are but two examples of the contribution of university research and industry-university-government research projects to the economy of California. The role of university research in the development of California agriculture in general is another prime example. A recent consultant report explores the economic, health-related, and cultural contributions of the University of California more widely.[8]

Structural Organization and Support Initiatives

It is important to recognize that California achieved its status and reputation as a center for technological innovation and entrepreneurship without a grand design or substantial stimulation by the state government or other organized entities. The necessary ingredients were there, and the flower blossomed on its own. As one prominent example, the origins and reasons for the success of Silicon Valley are well analyzed in a classic work by Saxenian.[9] Silicon Valley worked so well because of cultural factors and modes of interaction that were peculiar to California. That Stanford University and the Berkeley campus of the University of California were close at hand was also important, as was the fact that the early, post-World War II development of what became Silicon Valley was favored and fostered by the Stanford provost, Frederick Terman.[10] Structured organizational and supporting initiatives have come later. I will explore six of these, in rough chronological order.

Industry-University Cooperative Research and MICRO Programs

Launched in 1981, the MICRO Program is designed "to support innovative research in microelectronics technology, its applications in computer and infor-

---

[7] The Wine Institute, "California Wine Statistical Highlights," September 2006, <http://www.ineinstitute.org/industry/statistics/2004/ca_industry_highlights.php>.

[8] ICF Consulting, "California's Future: It Starts Here," report prepared for University of California, March 2003, <http://www.universityofcalifornia.edu/itstartshere/report/fullreport.pdf>.

[9] Anna-Lee Saxenian, *Regional Advantage: Culture and Competition in Silicon Valley and Route 128* (Cambridge, Mass.: Harvard University Press, new ed., 1996).

[10] C. S. Gillmor, *Fred Terman at Stanford: Building a Discipline, a University, and Silicon Valley* (Stanford, Calif.: Stanford University Press, 2004).

mation sciences, and its necessary antecedents in other physical science disciplines."[11] The program involves industrial grants for research at the University of California, supplemented with matching state funds expressly designated for the program. The state and the university waive the usual university overhead for these projects. The program is overseen by a policy board with representatives from the state, industry, and the university. Peer review plays a strong role.

While the design of the program is not all that unusual, the size and success are. More than 500 companies have participated in the program over the years. In the year 2005–2006, 97 companies supplied $6.5 million for 104 projects, with another $3.8 million coming through the program from state funds, and yet another $3+ million corresponding to waived overhead.

In 1996, MICRO was augmented by creation of the Industry-University Cooperative Research Program (I/UCRP).[12] This program gives what are now known as discovery grants in a manner similar to MICRO, except that indirect costs are not waived. Five fields are covered—biotechnology, communications and networking, digital media, electronics manufacturing and new materials, and information technology for life sciences. As of 2008, since the 1996 inception of the program, 897 projects have been funded. On an annual basis, about $22 million of state and UC funds bring in about $36 million from industry. By any measure, these programs are a large success, serving to bring university researchers together with industrial scientists and engineers and contributing substantially through their outputs to the state economy. The programs fit the needs of both state industry and university research well.

UC CONNECT

In 1985, working with the San Diego business community, the San Diego campus of the University of California formed UC CONNECT,[13] an organization designed to facilitate the development of entrepreneurial businesses in the region. The organization is free-standing and connects entrepreneurs with technology, money, markets, management, partners, and support services. Approaches used include consultation regarding support resources for start-up ventures, networking events, educational opportunities, and recognition of outstanding accomplishments. In many respects, CONNECT is an organized effort aimed at replicating what occurred naturally in Silicon Valley. It recognized the need for these diverse services and networking in order for technological innovation to occur in as unimpeded a fashion as possible. CONNECT has been an important player in the establishment of the biotech and wireless communications industries in San Diego. It

---

[11] <http://www.ucop.edu/research/micro/>.
[12] <http://www.ucdiscoverygrant.org/AnnualReport.pdf>; <http://www.ucdiscovery grant.org/>.
[13] <http://www.connect.org/>.

has since been replicated at the Davis campus of the University of California,[14] and in Scotland, Denmark, Norway, Sweden, and Taiwan.[15]

California Council for Science and Technology

Founded in 1988 as a not-for-profit corporation through enabling legislation from the state of California, the California Council on Science and Technology[16] emulates the roles that the National Research Council and the National Academies have on the federal level. The council consists of 30 members, supplemented by a much larger number of fellows, who are scientists, engineers, and technology leaders drawn from California's universities, corporations, and national laboratories. Council members are appointed for once-renewable three-year terms. Studies are undertaken at the request of branches of the state government, with the nature of the request often being developed jointly with CCST, at the initiative of either body. Project funding comes from state agencies and private foundations. An interrelated series of recent studies has dealt with the environment for science and technology in California, a critical-path analysis of the science and technology system within the state, and a critical-path analysis of the production of math and science teachers within California. Other example projects include a series of reviews of the state's $60 million per year Public Interest Energy Research Program and development of a recommended policy framework for intellectual property developed through state-funded research.

CCST studies generally get attention and action because they are requested from within the state government. Because of the lack of a state science advisor or office of science and technology function, CCST carries some of the roles that fall to the science advisor on the federal level. Examples are advising on recent landmark legislation for greenhouse-gas reduction and low-carbon fuel standards, analysis of the issues surrounding use of hydrogen as a fuel, and suggestions for components of a state science initiative.

California Technology, Trade, and Commerce Agency (TTCA)

TTCA was established in 1992 as an agency of the California state government. The missions of the agency were to promote business, employment, and trade, as well as economic competitiveness in general. The agency was also the primary state vehicle for projects associated with conversions of military bases to civilian uses. In addition, it had a $6 million program that gave matching grants of up to $200,000 for proposals to federal government agencies made by entities within the state for projects that held the potential of developing technology-based

---

[14] <http://www.connect.ucdavis.edu/home.cfm?id=OVC,6>.
[15] <http://www.connect.org/programs/index.htm>.
[16] <http://www.ccst.us/>.

business in California. Reflecting political contention over the appropriateness of this role and a seeming consensus that the value added by the agency was not large, TTCA was discontinued in 2003 during a new administration.

California Institutes for Science and Innovation

Four major research institutes were launched in the year 2000, as a gubernatorial initiative to support the role of innovation in spurring the California economy. As originally defined, the initiative provided $100 million for each of three institutes, spread over four years, with a requirement that the institutes raise even greater funds as a 2:1 match. The institutes were to be on University of California campuses and would carry out research in fields believed to be promising for the economic growth of the state. They were envisioned as catalytic partnerships between university research and private industry that could expand the state economy into new industries and "speed the movement of innovation from the laboratory into people's daily lives" (Governor Gray Davis's Budget Summary, 2001–02).[17]

The university held an internal competition, encouraging multidisciplinary approaches and the involvement of multiple campuses. Topics for the institutes were not specified; instead the topics were a part of the competition. Final proposals were subjected to extensive peer review and were judged by a multidimensional, highly distinguished panel, external to the university. The use of a competition was essential to the quality of the proposals, as well as effective multidisciplinary and multicampus design. Because of the strength of the ultimate proposals, a fourth institute was funded by the state as well. The four institutes are:

- California Institute for Telecommunications and Information Technology [Cal-(IT)^2]— San Diego and Irvine campuses,
- California Institute for Quantitative Biomedical Research [QB3]—San Francisco, Berkeley, and Santa Cruz campuses,
- California Nanosystems Institute [CNSI]—Los Angeles and Santa Barbara campuses,
- Center for Information Technology Research in the Interest of Society [CITRIS]—Berkeley, Davis, Merced, and Santa Cruz campuses.

The needed aggregate match ($800 million) was a very large sum, yet it was raised and then some, with the total initial match being over $1 billion. The acquisition of these matching funds was facilitated by having the competition, since it was clear to donors that the match would be required to bring a particular institute into existence. The fact that the subject matters of the institutes were not specified before the competition provided yet another incentive for corporations to provide

---

[17] Brenda Foust, "The California Institutes for Science and Innovation (Cal ISIs)," *The Senate Source*, University of California, January 2005, <http://www.universityof california.edu/senate/news/source/Calisi.pdf>. See also http://www.ucop.edu/california-institutes/>.

funding, since the institute in question would have to be selected in order for there to be an institute matching the particular interests of a corporation. The matching funds were raised primarily from industry for three of the institutes and primarily as federal government funds for the fourth (CNSI).

Because of the nature of the state budgetary situation at the time, the state funding was almost totally for capital expenditures. Thus the state funding has gone primarily into building the campus facilities that bring the researchers of an institute together. Core operating funds have been more of a problem, and have been provided so far from overhead[18] derived from incremental grants and other campus sources.

California Institute for Regenerative Medicine (CIRM)

CIRM is an organization that came to be in a very different way. California has a system of direct initiative ballot referenda that can be, and often are, used to enact laws directly by popular vote. In 2004, for the first time, this approach was used to establish a program of scientific research, through an initiative titled the California Stem Cell Research and Cures Act. It created the California Institute for Regenerative Medicine[19] to administer an "average of $295 million per year in bonds over a 10-year period to fund stem cell research and dedicated facilities for scientists at California's universities and other advanced medical research facilities throughout the state."[20] CIRM is overseen by an Independent Citizen's Oversight Committee (ICOC) with a specified composition appointed by designated officials and consisting of persons from specific, designated backgrounds. The initiative language is added to the state constitution, cannot be amended for three years, and requires 70 percent votes from both houses of the legislature along with approval by the governor in order to be amended (or negated) thereafter. Thus it is popularly described as "iron-clad."

This initiative did not arise from universities themselves institutionally. The prime mover was a group of advocates for medical cures and stem-cell research. The ballot proposition was promoted heavily, and indeed named, from the standpoint that stem-cell research would lead to therapy for incurable diseases such as diabetes, spinal-cord injury, and Alzheimer's disease.[21] The initiative was a very visible and tangible step placing California as a state in a forefront position within the United States in stem-cell research, as contrasted with federal policy which is currently quite restrictive.

---

[18] Overhead, also known as indirect costs, is typically supplied by government agencies and other funding bodies in the United States as a percentage of direct, identifiable cost. Overhead allows for the many noncosts associated with making research possible and effective that are not specific to the project, e.g., administration, buildings, maintenance, libraries, and computing support.

[19] <http://www.cirm.ca.gov/>.

[20] <http://www.cirm.ca.gov/prop71/pdf/prop71.pdf>.

[21] <http://www.signonsandiego.com/uniontrib/20041219/news_1n19stemcell.html>.

The ability of the state to sell the bonds was held up for about two years in a legal process initiated by those who oppose the use of embryonic stem cells for research. Meanwhile support of research commenced, drawing from a $150 million loan from state general funds authorized by the governor, supplemented by loans and gifts from private California foundations and individuals.

The initiative states that "the ICOC shall establish standards that require that all grants and loan awards be subject to intellectual property agreements that balance the opportunity of the state of California to benefit from the patents, royalties, and licenses that result from basic research, therapy development, and clinical trials with the need to assure that essential medical research is not unreasonably hindered by the intellectual property agreements." This language has muddied already unclear waters on ownership of intellectual property from state-funded research. This language and expectations of close-at-hand profitability stemming from the marketing of the initiative have led to considerable controversy surrounding ways in which the state of California can "recover" some of its investment in this and other research.

This venture, still ongoing, exhibits what can happen when the funding of research is tied so closely to the political process. Although, when all is said and done, much good may come of research sponsored through CIRM, the research itself and the research world in general will likely suffer from science becoming such an activist force in the political process and from the unrealistic expectations and constant public scrutiny thereby generated. It will also lead to other efforts to use the same process for restrictive new funding of research. A more detailed analysis of several of these issues has been given by Riordan.[22]

Indeed, there has already been another such initiative in 2006,[23] modeled in the earlier stem-cell initiative, which would have taxed producers of oil extracted in California to generate a fund of $4 billion over time, 27 percent of which would have been used for research on reduction of petroleum usage, renewable energy, energy efficiency, and alternative fuel technologies and products. It did not pass, reflecting in part after-the-fact voter dissatisfaction with the stem-cell initiative.

Project-Oriented Initiatives

In addition to the structures and mechanisms described above, there are four recent, major, California-based industry-university project initiatives that deserve consideration in connection with the theme of this chapter.[24]

---

[22] D. G. Riordan, "Research Funding via Direct Democracy: Is It Good for Science?" *Issues in Science and Technology* 24, no. 4 (2008): 23–27.

[23] <http://www.voterguide.ss.ca.gov/props/prop87/prop87.html>.

[24] I should point out that I was not involved in the creation or review of any of these project partnerships in my administrative capacities at the University of California. Research agreements are executed by individual campuses of the University of California,

Novartis Agreement with UC Berkeley

In 1998 a controversial research agreement was made between the Berkeley campus of the University of California and Novartis, a large Swiss pharmaceutical and biotechnology company. This arrangement was one of many made between large biotechnology/pharmaceutical companies and major universities over the years, reflecting the very close relationship between academic research and commercial innovation within that field. However, it was unique in its design and in that it made such a sizeable arrangement between a commercial firm and a public university. A useful and insightful analysis of the drivers for the arrangement and the benefits and concerns has been made by Todd LaPorte.[25]

The agreement[26] followed a formal, two-year process in which the College of Natural Resources of the Berkeley campus solicited proposals from six major corporations, with four responding. By the terms of the agreement, Novartis contributed $5 million per year for five years, or $25 million total, for support of research in the Department of Plant and Microbial Biology. This was about 30 percent of the total extramurally funded research budget of the department. The portion of the funds devoted to overhead was 33 percent, covering renovations, support of the general graduate program, and general campus overhead.

Another very important component was access by Berkeley researchers on a confidential basis to the Novartis agricultural genomic database, coupled with $3 million for a Novartis facility near the campus with workstations through which that database could be accessed, and for advisory Novartis employees to help with access. The value of this aspect of the arrangement lay in the fact that a substantial amount of genomic data are confidential to large companies, thereby placing the academic sector in a situation where they carry out research without full access to the available knowledge base.

In return, Novartis received first rights to license a percentage of inventions from research in the department, whether or not supported with actual Novartis funds. That percentage was the ratio of the Novartis funding to the total departmental extramural research support, cited as a method of calculation recommended by National Institutes of Health guidelines for arrangements involving both NIH and private support. Novartis also received the conventional 30-day opportunity to review potential publications for patentable items, and an addi-

---

not by the systemwide administration. The opinions expressed concerning them are solely my own as a hopefully objective observer.

[25] Todd LaPorte, "Diluting Public Patrimony or Inventive Response to Increasing Knowledge Asymmetries: Watershed for Land Grant Universities? Reflections on the University of California, Berkeley-Novartis Agreement," in *Commission on Physical Sciences, Mathematics and Applications, Research Teams and Partnerships: Trends in Chemical Sciences*, Report of a Workshop, 66–84, National Research Council, National Academy Press, Washington, D.C., 2000, <http://www.nap.edu/openbook/0309068274/html/66.html>.

[26] <http://www.berkeley.edu/news/media/releases/98legacy/11-23-98.html>.

tional 60 days if the decision was made to patent. Such a component of industry-university agreements is not unusual.

The project was overseen by a six-member advisory committee with three members from the campus (vice chancellor for research, dean, and a non-involved faculty member), and three members from Novartis. There was also a five-member research committee, three of whom were from the campus, to award actual grants.

There were a number of concerns expressed at the time and throughout the term of the agreement. These are summarized by LaPorte (*loc. cit.*). Many of the concerns dealt with academic freedom—the right of faculty to choose and pursue research as they see fit. Those concerns eventually formed the lead item for a story in the *Atlantic Monthly*.[27] As the controversy continued, there was an internal review commissioned, followed by an external review undertaken at the behest of the Academic Senate with the concurrence of the administration. That review,[28] since published as a book,[29] concluded that academic freedom and the academic conduct of the department had not been seriously compromised. The reviewers also made a number of recommendations, one of which was that the university should consider avoiding industry agreements that involve complete academic units or comparable large groups of researchers.

During the five-year period of the agreement, there was a major restructuring of Novartis that eliminated the unit that had made the agreement. Hence renewal of the agreement became moot.

In addition to the academic-freedom issue, which was probably well enough addressed with regard to the specifics of research, the essential issue surrounding this venture was the extent to which a public institution, and an entire department within that institution, can pair themselves with a private corporation. Can academic objectivity be maintained amid such a presence? And is it appropriate for a public institution that derives substantial taxpayer support, including corporation taxes, to match itself so visibly with one corporation? Conversely, it can be argued that a large amount of the total revenue of public universities (of order 77 percent for the University of California) comes from sources other than the state budget, and that corporations within the state do receive the benefit of

---

[27] Eyal Press and Jennifer Washburn, "The Kept University: UC Berkeley's Recent Agreement with a Swiss Pharmaceutical Company Has Raised Concerns over Who Ultimately Directs Research," *Atlantic Monthly* 285, no. 3 (2000): 39–54. See also <http://www.aaas.org/spp/rd/ch26.pdf>.

[28] Lawrence Busch, R. Allison, C. Harris, A. Rudy, B. T. Shaw, T. Ten Eyck, D. Coppin, J. Konefal, and C. Oliver, "External Review of the Collaborative Research Agreement between Novartis Agricultural Discovery Institute, Inc. and The Regents of the University of California", Inst. For Food and Agricultural Standards, Michigan State University, July 13, 2004, <http://evcp.chance.berkeley.edu/documents/Reports/documents/NovartisBerkeleyFinaReport071204.pdf>.

[29] A. P. Rudy, D. Coppin, J. Konefal, B. T. Shaw, T. A. Ten Eyck, C. Harris, and L. Busch, *Universities in the Age of Corporate Science: The UC-Novartis Controversy*, (Philadelphia, Pa.: Temple University Press, 2007).

their taxes, even when such arrangements are made with single corporations. A final substantive issue is how confidential data can be used in publishable research while fulfilling simultaneously the requirements of the openness of science and the ability for others to seek to reproduce results.

The Artemisinin Project: Development of a Low-Cost Malaria Drug

A large and highly innovative partnership was put together in late 2004 to work towards making artemisinin, the precursor to a potent antimalaria drug, available to the undeveloped world at a cost that will enable widespread use. Malaria strikes up to 500 million people annually, killing about 1.5 million who are mostly from very poor areas of Africa and Asia. Derivatives of artemisinin, when mixed with other substances to form artemisinin combination therapies (ACTs) and used for only three days, are nearly 100 percent effective in preventing deaths from malaria. Artemisinin is currently derived from the wormwood tree, yet even at the current price of $2.40 per treatment is too expensive for widespread use in the poor countries that are most affected.

There are four participants in the five-year project[30]—the Bill and Melinda Gates Foundation, the Institute for OneWorld Health (IOWH), Amyris Biotechnologies, Inc., and the University of California, Berkeley. The aim is to use synthetic molecular biology to create artemisinic acid, a direct precursor of artemisinin, with the goal of reducing the cost of artemisinin by an order of magnitude. The Gates Foundation, with strong interests in health in underdeveloped countries, provides $42.6 million. Of that amount, $8 million goes to Professor Jay Keasling and his group at the Berkeley campus for pertinent research on the synthetic biology route to artemisinic acid, including engineering the microbe. Twelve million dollars goes to Amyris Biotechnologies, a for-profit company, for applied research on the pertinent processing techniques. The final $22.6 million goes to IOWH, a nonprofit pharmaceutical company, which will lead development of commercialization, marketing, and distribution, including meeting regulatory requirements for different countries and analysis and improvement of ACT manufacturing, supply chain, and distribution.

In contrast to most other pharmaceutical development, this partnership is designed to address the need for extremely low product cost. The Gates Foundation funds provide seed and start-up funding of a sort that would not be available from the venture-capital community. Similarly, the not-for-profit IOWH, with the Gates Foundation funding, can address the regulatory and distribution needs in ways that would not be viable in the for-profit sector. Finally, the intellectual property arrangements[31] are also unusual and are designed to promote low cost. The University of California has given royalty-free licenses to IOWH and to Amyris for the developing-world market, i.e., the market being addressed by

---

[30] <http://www.artemisininproject.org/>.
[31] <http://www.tmgh.org/case-studies-treatment-for-malaria.php>.

IOWH. The license to Amyris is royalty-bearing for the developed world and for uses of artemisinin other that for malaria.

A key aspect of this project lies in the incentives that attract the various partners. The university benefits from having a very visible example of the utilization of university research for a great worldwide need, and as well can derive royalties from uses for malaria in the developed world and for other purposes. The nonprofit pharmaceutical company, IOWH, directly works toward its mission of making an effective malaria treatment available at a low enough cost in the underdeveloped world. The for-profit company, Amyris, can apply the processing technology that is developed in this project to other projects that rely upon the same platform technology; it develops a base of expertise and processing capability. The Gates Foundation has put together an effective team that can make a major contribution to world health, in the underdeveloped countries in particular, thereby addressing a primary mission of the foundation.

Climate and Energy Projects

The major world needs associated with greenhouse gases and sources and utilization of energy have led to two unusually large university-industry projects located in California. One is coordinated by Stanford University and the other by the University of California, Berkeley.

Stanford Global Climate and Energy Project

In 2002, Stanford University concluded an agreement with four corporations—ExxonMobil, General Electric, Toyota, and Schlumberger—for a Global Climate and Energy Project (G-CEP).[32] The sponsors pledged $225 million over 10 or more years to support a diverse program of precommercial research designed to lead to technological options for energy production and use with reduced greenhouse gas emissions. The project supports research teams at Stanford and elsewhere, and is not restricted to university research. Stanford administers the project. In an unusual step for such a consortium and a private university, the full wording of the founding agreement is available on the Internet.[33]

The project is governed by a management committee composed of single voting representatives of the four corporations, who rotate as chair, and the project director as a nonvoting member. Subject to general approval of topical areas by the management committee, the project director, who is a Stanford faculty member, and his staff oversee a peer review process whereby proposals are solicited, judged, and selected for funding. Thus, in essence, the four sponsoring corporations, acting in a consortium as a funding agency, have engaged Stanford

---

[32] <http://gcep.stanford.edu/>.
[33] <http://gcep.stanford.edu/pdfs/gcep_agreement.pdf>.

to administer a grant process to select projects, distribute funds, and monitor results.

Stanford holds legal title to inventions; however, the sponsoring corporations exercise guidance as to which inventions should be pursued for patent coverage. Sponsors also have exclusive rights to commercialize inventions for the first five years, royalty-free.

It is interesting to speculate regarding the motives for the industrial partners. First, it is important that the four corporations for the most part do not compete with one another; they are in complementary lines of business. Second, the sponsors engender a broad portfolio of underlying research, from which they may draw technologies that they may wish to develop, in most cases without competition from a direct competitor.

Funding agencies run by a university are relatively rare, but do exist in other forms. For example, the University of California administers three programs of state-funded research—breast cancer, AIDS, and tobacco-related disease—that are not restricted to University of California grantees.

BP Energy Biosciences Institute

In 2006, the multinational oil firm BP announced an intention to create an Energy Biosciences Institute, in conjunction with a major university. After preliminary explorations, BP invited five universities to form teams to submit proposals to join with BP in an Energy Biosciences Institute, which would be funded by $500 million spread over 10 years. This institute would bring BP researchers together with university researchers and would emphasize innovative means of creating and producing fuels from biological sources. In early 2007, the competition was won by a team headed by the University of California, Berkeley (UCB) and also including the Lawrence Berkeley National Laboratory (LBNL) and the University of Illinois at Urbana-Champaign (UIUC). BP spokespersons indicated that important factors in the selection of the Berkeley-led team were the large and diverse array of distinguished researchers, the tradition of technological innovation and entrepreneurship in the San Francisco Bay Area, and the history of successful, large, interdisciplinary science at LBNL. The recent attention given to the Artemisinin Project and Amyris Biotechnologies, for which the CEO was formerly president of U.S. Fuels Operations for BP, may have been helpful as well.

It is worth noting that LBNL is a laboratory of the U.S. Department of Energy, managed under contract by the University of California system. The inclusion of LBNL thereby brings the federal government into the arrangement. LBNL and the Department of Energy had earlier made major commitments to LBNL's new Helios project, which deals with renewable and solar energy.

The full proposal from the UCB-LBNL-UIUC team and other information on the Energy Biosciences Institute is available.[34] Elements of the arrangement and governance described in the proposal and mentioned elsewhere[35] include:

- construction of a 50,000 sq. ft., $120 million building on University of California land adjoining LBNL to house both the Energy Biosciences Institute and LBNL's Helios project, funded largely by state funds along with some private gifts;
- 35,000 sq. ft. of space in existing buildings on the Berkeley campus for three years before completion and occupancy of the new building;
- division of the institute into open and proprietary research portions, with 50 BP researchers who will do BP proprietary research accommodated in the building along with UC and LBNL scientists;
- up to 30 percent of the total funding being spent on the BP scientists;
- use of $100 million of the total funding at UIUC to fund research on crops for ethanol and other biofuels;
- a director who is both a UCB faculty member and a faculty senior scientist at LBNL, an associate director who is a BP employee, and a deputy director who is a UIUC faculty member;
- a governing board composed of eight senior persons from the various participating organizations (two from BP, one each from UCB, LBNL, and UIUC, and the director, associate director and deputy director of the Institute;
- 25 themed research teams, seven of which will be located at UIUC;
- payment of full institutional overhead to UCB and UIUC on all open research funded by BP, with 75 percent of these indirect costs returned by those institutions to the Energy Biosciences Institute for administrative purposes; and
- intellectual property to be owned by the participating institution that generates it, with BP having the right to license, royalty-free and nonexclusively, inventions made by researchers supported with BP money. Joint inventions will have joint ownership. BP as well has the right to take royalty-bearing exclusive licenses in a time-limited fashion.

An apparent motive for BP in setting up such an institute is close access to leading-edge research in an area that is seen as vital to the future of the corporation. By contrast to the Stanford G-CEP project, the company has placed a high premium on intimate day-to-day interactions of BP researchers with those from the other institutions.

There are a number of potential concerns to be dealt with in the relationship. One is how to handle proprietary research that is being carried out in close proximity with academic and national-laboratory researchers. The presence of proprietary corporate research on a university campus is not unprecedented, however. A second concern, familiar from the Novartis agreement described above, is the preferential position being given by a public university to a single private corpora-

---

[34] "Energy Biosciences Institute," <http://www.ebiweb.org>.
[35] Eli Kintisch, "BP Bets Big on UC Berkeley for Novel Biofuels Center," *Science* 315 (February 9, 2007): 746, 790.

tion with regard to the research of a large number of distinguished faculty members. A third concern is the need to ensure academic freedom in the choice and conduct of research. Recognizing such concerns, the Berkeley campus developed the proposal in close consultation with the leadership of the faculty Academic Senate.

Concerns about Industry-University Partnerships and How to Address Them

Several common concerns about industry-university partnerships have been mentioned already in connection with the preceding example. Concerns of this sort have been tallied, explored in a contemplative fashion and balanced against advantages by Bok,[36] Calhoun,[37] and Kirp,[38] among others. They have also been elaborated from a more uniformly negative point of view by Washburn.[39] For the most part, the concerns can be grouped into categories, as follows.

- Companies may unduly influence the research agenda; there will not be free inquiry.
- A conflict of interest occurs when a faculty member has industrial ties and related university research.
- Companies or faculty with ulterior motives may hold back damaging research results. This concern often occurs in connection with clinical trials.
- Public access to knowledge may be restricted. Knowledge that is inherently a public good may go into private hands because of exclusive licensing, publication delay, or not being published at all.
- Cross-fertilization of research may be impeded if universities accept confidentiality arrangements with corporations.
- A conflict of interest may arise if a faculty member determines whether an invention in which s/he has participated belongs to the university, a private entity, or both.
- Reliance upon private funding such as licensing revenue or corporate research support, or even upon government agency funding, may distort academic purposes and the academic agenda.
- Entrepreneurial faculty may be less engaged in classroom education.
- The humanities and social sciences will decline in attention and importance, because government and industrial funding is primarily directed towards the

---

[36] Derek Bok, *Universities in the Marketplace* (Princeton, N.J.: Princeton University Press, 2003).

[37] Craig Calhoun, "Is the University in Crisis?," *Society* 43, no. 4 (2006): 8–18.

[38] D. L. Kirp, "Shakespeare, Einstein, and the Bottom Line" (Cambridge, Mass.: Harvard University Press, 2003).

[39] Jennifer Washburn, "University Inc.: The Corporate Corruption of Higher Education" (New York, N.Y.: Basic Books, 2005).

sciences and engineering. Put another way, the emphasis of the university will go to where the money is.

In the other direction, it must be recognized that academic research would become sterile if not cross-fertilized with industry. As well, the synergy gained by close linkages between universities and industry moves society and the economy forward much more efficaciously than would be the case if interactions did not occur frequently. Also, the nature of financing of public universities by state governments in the U.S. has changed because of budgetary stringencies and other commitments. Interactions between universities, industry, and the government should and must occur. The need is to manage them effectively so as to reap as many of the gains as is consistent with minimizing the concerns.

Universities have instituted, and continue to institute, numerous policies to deal with these concerns, in some cases working within federal or state guidelines. In addition to having policies, universities must have means of monitoring and enforcing them as well. The array of such policies and mechanisms for the University of California can be found at two web sites,[40] and a more general review has been given by Sugarman.[41] *Inter alia*, they cover such subjects as conflict of commitment, conflict of interest and disclosure of financial interests, consulting and other activities outside the university, disclosure of inventions, research misconduct, technology licensing, university-industry relations, use of university research facilities, publication policy, patent and copyright policies, research integrity, and reporting of improper activities.

Assessment of What Works Well

As is shown by the measures of success described earlier, the most universal contributions of universities to innovation are the flow of university graduates to both new and established technological companies, along with the flow of research-engaged faculty members themselves to these companies as both founders of start-up ventures and ongoing consultants.

Partnership initiatives of the sorts described above are clearly also very important. The partnerships work best when there are clear incentives for each of the parties to participate. Leveraging the resources of all parties can be attractive. Partnerships should be structured so as to minimize concerns regarding conflicts or improper influences and/or benefits. Potential points of concern should be addressed openly with understandable ways of meeting them.

Serious competition and selective choice of awardees are effective avenues toward high-quality projects and partnerships. Examples already cited where competition has clearly been a benefit are the California Institutes for Science and In-

---

[40] <http://www.research.chance.berkeley.edu/main.cfm?id=9>; <http://www.ucop.edu/research/policies/welcome>.

[41] S. D. Sugarman, "Conflicts of Interest in the Roles of the University Professor," *Theoretical Inquiries in Law* 6, no. 1 (2005): 255–75.

novation, the Industry/University Cooperative Research Program, G-CEP and the BP Energy Biosciences Institute. Success breeds success, in the sense that a record of positive accomplishment is reassuring to investors.

Project design and/or active participation by government generally does not work well, because of political influences and contention. Government is best as a silent and enabling partner. This is a reason for the successes of UC CONNECT and the California Council for Science and Technology, as opposed to the short-lived California Technology, Trade and Commerce Agency.

From the viewpoint of industry, the Industry-University Cooperative research and MICRO programs afford ways to select and invest in research where industrial expenses are substantially leveraged with public funds. This is advantageous to both established and start-up companies. The California Institutes for Science and Innovation afforded another way to leverage funds, by assuring that an institute in an area of corporate interest would come into existence and by establishing liaisons with an institute. Neither of these structures advantaged single or few companies more than others.

In the case of the Artemisinin Project, the Gates Foundation has a different motive—to make a potent antimalarial drug available at very low cost worldwide. Profit or even recovery of investment are not issues, and that partnership has been constructed in ways and with licensing policies that will lead to the desired very-low-cost product.

University motives include (1) getting research results used in the marketplace and/or for public benefit (a mission of a public university), (2) enabling the conduct of well chosen research, and (3) gaining revenue from licensing, in what should be that order. The Artemisinin Partnership and UC CONNECT address the first goal. The Industry-University Cooperative Research Program, The California Institutes for Science and Innovation, and the Berkeley agreements with BP and Novartis addressed all three goals

For the state of California, the rationale is to foster the establishment of new industries and retention of existing industries, and thereby to build the economy and employment, as well as the standard of living of the state. Second, the state is interested in the overall health of its university system. The Industry-University Cooperative Research Program, the California Institutes for Science and Innovation, the California Council on Science and Technology, the California Institute for Regenerative Medicine, and the state investment in facilities for the BP Energy Biosciences Institute all address that goal, as did the California Technology, Trade and Commerce Agency. The California Institute for Regenerative Medicine has the feature of positioning the state to carry out research and attract scientists in an area currently discouraged by federal government policy. However, it has the drawbacks of lack of flexibility for the state in investing its resources (because of it being locked into the constitution) and attractiveness for political challenge because of both the way it came about and the nature of the research.

Why California?

California's success in launching new, technologically based industries and the close involvement of its universities in developing areas such as biotechnology stand in contrast to most other states in the U.S.[42] Why is it California that has flourished?

One key component is the strength of California's universities and the research output from them. Building the state's public-university systems has historically been a priority of the state government. A post-World War II economic boom provided the state with considerable resources during the 1950s and early 1960s to build its public universities and set a standard of strong budgetary support for them. The California Master Plan for higher education,[43] set in place in 1960, set a framework for the public university systems whereby the research mission and Ph.D. production were matched with the University of California, which was given a generous funding level commensurate with that mission.

Highly capable faculty were drawn to California and responded with high-quality research, as is evidenced, for example, by the considerable succession of Nobel Prizes awarded to California scientists in the postwar era. The universities produced excellent graduates, who were drawn by the salubrious climate and intellectual stimulation to want to stay in the state. Strong research universities and strong scientific talent drew science-based industries, which valued the proximity to and opportunities for interaction with such universities.

The University of California and the major private research universities in California have maintained their stature, allure, and research productivity by wise policies that base faculty advancement upon intensive peer review, continuing throughout a faculty member's career. As has been pointed out, California's strength in academic research has been built upon peer-reviewed competition and has thereby thrived. Both Stanford, through Terman, and later the University of California have made it a priority to spawn, assist, and work synergistically with California industry. California universities have also found ways to promote and reward multidisciplinary efforts, through buildings dedicated to multidisciplinary purposes, policies that promote multidisciplinarity, and close interaction with national laboratories (e.g., the Lawrence Berkeley National Laboratory and the Jet Propulsion Laboratory).

California was fertile ground for the development of Silicon Valley because of its strong scientific and technological base, an entrepreneurial spirit, and a tradition of easy, informal interactions. The various elements necessary to support entrepreneurship and start-ups were either present or readily developed. Once devel-

---

[42] R. L. Geiger and Creso Sá, "Beyond Technology Transfer: U. S. State Policies to Harness University Research for Economic Development," *Minerva*, 43, no. 1 (2005): 1–21.

[43] J. A. Douglass, *The California Idea and American Higher Education, 1850 to the 1960 Master Plan* (Stanford, Calif.: Stanford University Press, 2000).

oped, they provided fertile ground for launching additional new technologically based industries. Again, success breeds success.

Strikingly, California developed as a hotbed of "high-tech" industries without an overall design, state-government structures incubating such industries, or even state-government policies that were particularly favorable to such industries. The contrast with efforts of other states over the past several decades is that California supported its state universities strongly at the time that set the stage for innovation, but did not until recently create innovation institutes or other state supporting structures. One early exception was the 1880 decision of the state legislature to foster a California wine industry, driven by the recognition that climatic conditions within regions of the state were favorable. The state has chosen to enable and occasionally to help co-fund technological initiatives, rather than create a plan, create state laboratories, or create incubators. The state has not had a science advisor, or even science committees within the legislature. But it has created and nurtured a body (the California Council on Science and Technology) to provide science advice when needed and useful, and both groups of companies in specific areas of industry and regions have provided structures such as UC CONNECT, Joint Venture: Silicon Valley,[44] the California Biomedical Research Association[45] and the California Healthcare Institute[46] to sustain and foster what has developed.

---

[44] <http://www.jointventure.org/>.

[45] <http://www.ca-biomed.org/>.

[46] <http://www.chi.org/>.

Chapter 16

Bridging University and Industry: Taiwan's Model of a National Innovation System

Otto C. Lin[1]

Over the last 30-year period, Taiwan has developed an innovation system that links the research and development in academia with the commercialization of products in the private sector. As in many societies, national universities with research capacity tended to operate in a separate sphere from business and industry. This is only natural since the university and the industry are concerned with different missions, goals, risks, job output, skill sets, and criteria for measurement of success and reward systems. Thus it is no surprise to see the gulf existed between the interests of the university and the industry.

In the United States, and in a few other selected case examples, the academic culture has been linked to regional and national economic development over the last century—or at least more so than in Asia. In Taiwan, the key for creating a symbiotic relationship between the university and the industry, and specifically the development of commercial technology, has come through the establishment of the Industrial Technology Research Institute (ITRI) aided by a set of government policies to nurture and support commercial applications. This is a model that has increasingly gained popularity in other developing economies in Asia, such as

---

[1] Hong Kong University of Science and Technology and China Nansha Technology Enterprises, Ltd.

Singapore and China. The idea of the institute as an interlinkage to promote the interactions of the players of the innovation systems has proven highly successful.

The Idea of the Institute as a Bridge

Among the four institutional players of the national innovation system, the nature and roles of the government, business, and the university are historical and easily understood. The same cannot be said of the institute, however. A major function of the institute is to develop industrial technology based on the results of scientific research so that they can be implemented by the industry. Unlike the university, the institute is mission-oriented and profit conscious, at least to the extent of its long-term sustainability. However, unlike the industry, it does not run commercial operations on its own, so as not to be in direct competition with the clients it serves. Thus the institute is positioned between the university and the industry and plays the role of bridging the gap between them. See Figure 16.1.

Under this framework of national innovation system, the institute is an organization for the development and transfer of technology. It is expected to have the technical capability to survey and analyze the market for profitable applications of certain scientific discoveries or technological developments. When such an application is identified, the institute will, in collaboration with strategic industrial partners, strive to develop all the essential technical components for the manufacture and sale of the products or services, in full consideration of yield, quality, reliability, and service life efficiency. The institute can also provide recommendations and guidance to the university for future scientific pursuits. It is no wonder that the role of the institute was very complicated and often misunderstood.

While the university, especially those with major engineering capabilities, can have under its wing certain laboratories, centers, or institutes designed for applied research, it nevertheless maintains education and basic research as its primary objectives. Technology institutes will clearly focus on applications and interact intimately with the industry with full understanding of the latter's needs, urgency, and priorities. It is often noted that establishing a laboratory for scientific research is relatively straightforward; but establishing an institute for technology development and transfer is much more complicated. Not only the scope of the work is multifaceted, but the level of interactions needed is generally complex and, at times, subject to conflicting requirements of its partners and clients.

For developed economies, many technology companies are good at what they do and have plans to improve the established business or to expand to new areas of business. In that sense the industry can be, and usually is, the driver of technology. In dealing with entirely new technologies, or disruptive technologies that can make obsolete or replace what the industry has been practicing, the

Figure 16.1. The National Innovation System

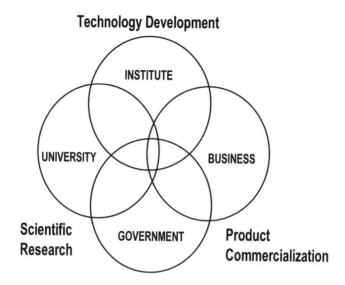

university generally plays the leadership role. The university provides the foundation, human resources, the technology breadth, the know-how and know-why, that the industry needs. Or, when new opportunities appear in the offing, the university is better positioned to organize and capture those opportunities.

Many major institutions of higher learning in the U.S., including the University of California, can take pride in their leadership in developing technology and their contribution to the growth of the U.S. economy, especially through the second half of the 20th century. In many underdeveloped or newly developed economies, however, technology capability in the university has been slower to develop. Thus, governments have to resort to institutes for technology leadership, as in the case of Taiwan in the 1970s with the Industrial Technology Research Institute (ITRI). The institute would have to source the relevant technologies, globally if needed. Subsequently, it had to further nurture and develop the technology so as to provide new, niche advantage for its products to compete in the international marketplace, often to be in the same league with the original technology provider. The institute was thus playing the role of the driver of technology progress. Similar patterns were observed in Singapore through the 1990s with its many technology institutes under the Agency of Science, Technology and Research (ASTAR). The roles of the institute in Korea and China are also remarkable.

In these cases, the linkage of the institute to the university was largely through human resources: students, faculty, and staff. With time, support and collaboration in scientific research would also proceed.

Taiwan's Transition

Taiwan was basically an agricultural economy until the 1950s. After its retreat to Taiwan, the government of Chiang Kai-shek placed an emphasis on education, land reform, and promotion of technology. Modernizing agricultural methodology was first on the economic agenda. The increased production in rice, sugar, fruits, and fisheries had rapidly become a success. Gradually, light industries targeting imports substitution have emerged. Fueled and led by a state-owned petrochemical infrastructure, industrial activities propagated rapidly through many small and medium-sized enterprises (SMEs) which are, at later decades, to become the mainstay of the economy for Taiwan. Generally speaking, SMEs were labor intensive and mostly under family-style management at around that time. Foreign direct investments were initially small and focused on assembly-type operations. FDIs were nevertheless important since they supplied employment to the society and provided opportunities to accumulate export-oriented technology and management practices for the SMEs.

By the late-1970s, under the leadership of Chiang Ching-kuo and Sun Yun-shuan, the government was able to launch 10 national strategic projects to bolster the economic infrastructure. These projects included petroleum cracking and petrochemicals, nuclear power plants, through- and cross-island highways, an international airport, seaports, steel, and ship-building. The success of these projects has given the government the resources and the stability it needed for further economic development, and, more importantly, future political reform.

With very little natural resources; Taiwan relied heavily on imports for industrial materials and energy needs. Thus the government has decided on a national initiative to accelerate the upgrade of industrial technology. By maximizing efficiency and productivity, it hoped to expedite transforming the economy from labor-intensive to technology-based. At this time, all major universities in Taiwan were publicly funded. They were all focused on undergraduate education and lacked the capability to drive the technology needed for economic growth. Therefore ITRI, the Industrial Technology Research Institute, was established in 1973 to spearhead this new strategy of economic development.

Organization and Operation Principles of ITRI

ITRI is a national institute founded through the legislature with the government commitment of an initial donation and a small recurrent budget. It was structured as a nonprofit corporation with a government-appointed board of directors and managed professionally outside the government service system. It was given the charter to assist the upgrade of industrial technology of Taiwan. Thus the positioning of ITRI as an interlinkage in the national innovation system was clear from its beginning.

ITRI has grown steadily since the mid-1980s due to its participation in the National Science and Technology Initiatives. A majority of the National Thrust Programs including information technology, energy, materials, automation, opto-electronics and environmental protection, were performed by ITRI, through competitive vetting. This funding helped the establishment of technical capacity of ITRI, both in physical infrastructure and human resources. A good portion of the high level technical and managerial staffs of ITRI were returned expatriates who had spent parts of their career in the Americas or Europe. They brought in valuable skill sets, global perspectives, and a professional network to function in a Chinese cultural and social environment. They have enhanced the ability and effectiveness of ITRI in serving industrial needs. At its peak in the 1990s, ITRI consisted of 6,000 professionals, with 650 doctorates in 11 R&D laboratories and centers. Over 30 percent of the professional staff has above 10 years of industrial experience. It became the largest technology institute in Taiwan. At the time of its establishment, ITRI was 100 percent based on government funds. In 1993, the institute had an annual budget of nearly $400 million USD from contracts and services. The initial government donation accounted for only about five percent of its total revenue.

The objectives of ITRI's technical programs can be classified into two types. One is for the development of new, high-tech industries in Taiwan. The other is for the upgrade of traditional industries to enhance their competitiveness in the world market place. Funding for the former projects was largely from the government with minor industrial participation. Funding for the latter projects was essentially from various industrial sectors with minor government matching, when appropriate.

ITRI was managed under certain sets of principles unique for the social environment of Taiwan at the time. During the period of 1985 to 1995, the principal elements of ITRI operations are (see Figure 16.2):

- Technical projects are undertaken not on the novelty or sophistication of basic science but on the potential as precompetitive technology. Project concept can be initiated internally, by external industrial panels, or by various Technical Advisory Committees participated by international experts. They are selected on the basis of scope specificity, niche advantage, market orientation, economic feasibility, and industrial participation.

- First among ITRI's criteria of the measurement of success is benefit to the industry and business. To maximize its impacts, ITRI implements technology diffusion through multi-faceted channels including technology transfer/licensing, forming industrial consortia or partnership, strategic alliances,

Figure 16.2. Role of ITRI in Taiwan's National Innovation System

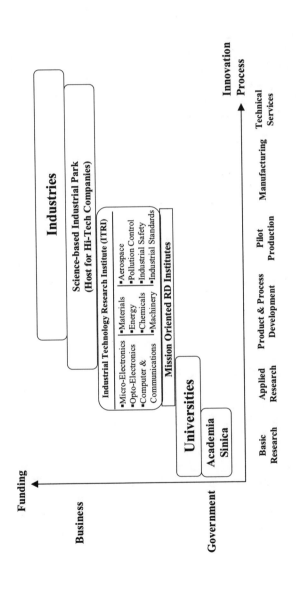

spin-off companies, dissemination by technical conferences and training of technical personnel.

- Financially ITRI aims to attain an increased portion of revenues from private sectors annually and to reach a "one to one" ratio of governmental to private sector income streams at a targeted date for each of its divisions.
- Technical transfer is conducted on the principles of nonexclusiveness, openness, and transparency. Once a technology is transferred, ITRI would strategically withdraw from operation in the same field to assure noncompetition with the client. Transfer of key professional staff was allowable on a voluntary basis and assisted by ITRI.
- ITRI pursues a close relationship with the industries. The industrial sector can be technology licensee, joint R&D developer, strategic alliance, partners in specific projects, or simply service client.
- ITRI pursues globalization, forming partnerships in technology development, market development, or strategic alliances in specific projects with international counterparts.
- ITRI adopts the principle of management by objective. All members of the technical and administrative staff undertake annual goal setting and performance appraisal and review.
- ITRI undertake quality assurance programs on customer satisfaction. External industrial review panels were established for all laboratories and centers. The board of directors conducted reviews of the corporation by an international panel of experts.
- ITRI establishes a corporate culture of "Innovation, Teamwork, Respect, Industriousness, Dedication, and Excellence" with specific implementation measures under each heading which becomes part of the individual's annual objectives.

It is noteworthy that considerations for technology transfer were first established in the planning phase of a technology project. Potential clients and the mechanisms of technology transfer were factors to consider right from the beginning of the project's formation. Therefore transfer of the technical result for commercialization was generally not an issue for ITRI, in contrast to being an agony experienced by many universities, institutes, or national academies.

The number of companies receiving technology from ITRI was generally larger than the number of technologies transferred each year. In other words, projects were transferable, on principle, to a multiplicity of clients. Nearly 50 percent of the projects were brought to market at the time of their completion, and 70 percent were on the market within three years of completion.

Since ITRI placed its focus not on scientific publications but on intellectual property, patentability of technology becomes an important consideration in project formation and project review. Patent mapping and patent strategy have gradually become keywords of conversation and the ITRI culture. The number of patent awarded to ITRI increased rapidly. Patent protection soon became an attractive feature for many ITRI technology projects. ITRI also conducted a high level of

Table 16.1. Technology Outputs of ITRI

	1983	1986	1989	1992	1995	1998	2000
Technology Transferred							
# Technologies	4	20	45	143	280	340	314
# Companies	8	22	62	217	418	510	
Patents Granted	5	15	59	274	381	560	640
Conferences/Training							
# Programs			405	643	880	957	998
# Attendees		6,500	19,706	40,150	59,492	69,000	73,959

training activities tailored to industrial needs and performed tens of thousands of technical services to companies annually. See Table 16.1.

Creation of a Technology-Based Economy

Of the success stories receiving the widest recognition was the development of semiconductors and microelectronic industries in Taiwan. In 1974, the Electronic Research and Service Organization (ERSO) of ITRI was requested, and funded, by the government to license from RCA an integrated circuit fabrication line capable of manufacturing seven micron CMOS devices on three-inch wafers. A group consisting of nearly 50 engineers spent time at the RCA site, received training, and eventually re-established the line at Hsin-Chu. Recognizing that the technical capability of the IC line acquired was rudimental and outdated, ITRI Management made conscientious efforts to improve the quality and upgrade the technology in details. In 1980, the company United Microelectronics Corporation (UMC) was spun off with an ITRI license and led by a group of technical experts. UMC built up the capability of manufacturing 3.5-micron CMOS devices and products in the adjacent Hsin-Chu Science Based Industrial Park (HSBIP). Gradually UMC grew to become a leader of the semi-conductor industry in Taiwan. See Figure 16.3.

With this spin-off, ITRI continued to pursue microelectronic technology under government support targeting at the next generation technology. In 1987, The Taiwan Semiconductor Manufacturing Corporation (TSMC) was spun off from ITRI under a similar technology transfer arrangement but at a much larger scale than the UMC. TSMC was designed to manufacture two-micron CMOS devices on a six-inch wafer. Due to the large capital investment and the potential risk, most potential investors in the private sectors have expressed skepticism. Eventually an industrial consortium was put together under government leadership and pledged supports. TSMC was finally established as a 51/49 joint venture of the local consortium with Philips Microelectronics, N.V. Philips was invited as a partner for its technological accomplishment in microelectronics, global orientation, and prolonged local presence. Soon TSMC was able to supply devices with profitable yield, building on the strength of the technical professionals. It was also very successful in pursuing a business model as a semiconductor foundry (OEM) to multinational microelectronic product manufacturers. In a relatively short time TSMC has evolved to become the flagship enterprise worldwide in the IC foundry business.

At around the same time, another semiconductor company, WINBOND Corporation, was established by ITRI scientists with local investments. The company was formed by ITRI professionals from a basic ITRI license and purchased additional technologies from a Japanese manufacturer. It was intended for the production of two-micron bipolar devices and related products. This became the first IDM (Indigenous Device Manufacturer) in Taiwan. Another joint

Figure 16.3. Formation of Taiwan's Microelectronic Industry

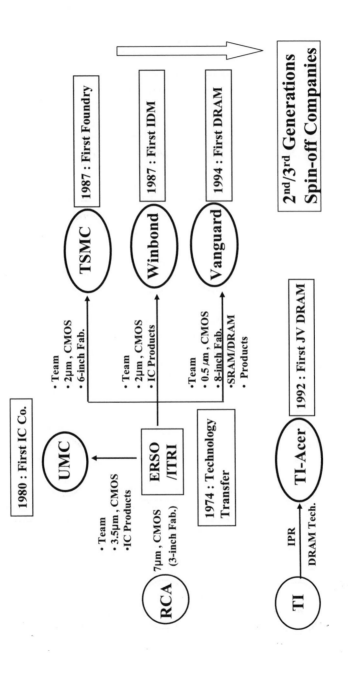

Source: Teng, 2002.

venture involved Acer Corporation and Texas Instrument was established in 1992 for the manufacturing of DRAM products. Although no ITRI technology was involved in the Acer-TI venture, transfer of technical personnel from ITRI was quite substantial.

All the while, ITRI continued its microelectronics technology development programs aiming at future generation technologies. In 1994, the Vanguard Corporation, capable of manufacturing 0.5-micron DRAM/SRAM products on an 8-inch wafer was spun off. These microelectronic companies have all set up their own R&D efforts, some overtaking ITRI laboratories in size and investments now. In the recent years, many have embarked on programs to explore nano-electronics, in conjunction with national universities and ITRI. See Table 16.2.

The continued ITRI technology transfers and the second and third generation spin-offs from the licensee companies have expanded rapidly. Together they have triggered the formation of a wave of specialty companies in IC design, packaging, and testing, resulting in the formation of very strong microelectronic clusters in Taiwan. They also led to the formation of the fab-less industry. With these technology developments and commercialization efforts, Taiwan became a world leader in semiconductor manufacturing, both in the fabrication and fab-less sectors. Today Taiwan has captured over 60 percent of the IC market worldwide. See Figure 16.4.

Similar examples can be discussed in laptop personal computers, advanced materials, communication devices, opto-electronics and industrial automation. For example, ITRI established a consortium in 1991 for the development of notebook PC with some 35 industrial partners. In one year's time, a "Made in Taiwan" notebook PC was debuted in the COMDEX show. With significant amount of entrepreneurial and industrial activities, nearly 65 percent of the world laptop PC in 2006 was manufactured by Taiwan companies.

Another interesting example to cite is the opto-electronic industries. In the late 1980s, ITRI established Taiwan's first MOCVD to demonstrate its application in LED manufacturing. Now there are over 400 units of MOCVD in the Taiwan LED industries.

The second category of technical programs in ITRI related to the upgrade of traditional industries in Taiwan. Through the application of advancement in design, material, processing and quality technologies, all are "relevant technologies," ITRI was able to help upgrade the values-in-use of many Taiwan products circulated worldwide. The list included industrial machineries, specialty chemicals, carbon fiber composite bicycles, sporting goods, etc. Therefore, ITRI's technology development has led not only to the establishment of new high-tech industries but also the renewal of traditional industries. In the early 1990s, over 15 industrial products from Taiwan had occupied number one or two market shares position worldwide.

It should be noted that enterprises receiving technology from ITRI have, indeed, dedicated a great deal of resources, or investments, to new product design, optimizing manufacturing efficiency, establishing distribution and sales channels, and pursuing a global marketing strategy. Overall this has contributed to the rapid

Table 16.2. The Top Ten in World Semi-Conductor Foundry by Revenue (2005)

2004 Rank	2005 Rank	Company	2004 Revenue	2005 Revenue	Change (%)	Market Share 2005 (%)
1	1	TSMC	7,668	8,228	7.3	44.7
2	2	UMC	3,497	2,822	-19.3	15.3
4	3	SMIC	975	1,171	20.1	6.4
3	4	Chartered Semiconductor	1,103	1,132	2.6	6.1
5	5	IBM Microelectronics	850	810	-4.7	4.4
7	6	Magnachip (Hynix)	360	396	10.0	2.1
6	7	Vanguard International	393	353	-10.2	1.9
9	8	Dongbu Electronics	333	347	4.2	1.9
10	9	HHNEC	324	305	-5.7	1.7
13	10	X-Fab	178	204	14.6	1.1
		Top 10 Foundries	15,681	15,768	0.6	85.6
		Others	3,150	2,653	-15.8	14.4
		Total Market	18,831	18,421	-2.2	100

Source: Hsu, 2006.

Figure 16.4. Taiwan's Role in the World's Notebook PC Production

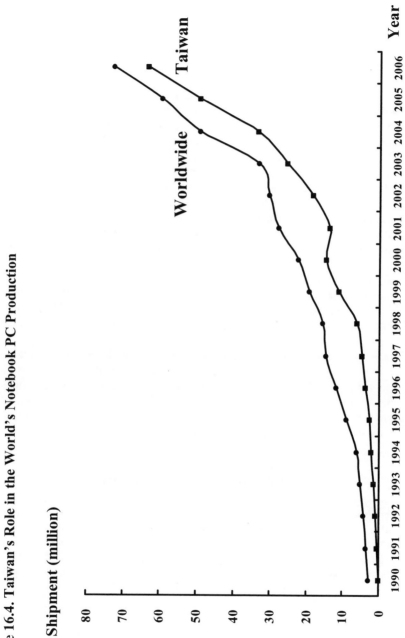

Shipment (million)

economic development of Taiwan during the period of 1985 to the end of the 20th century. This development has resulted in the transformation to a technology-based economy in Taiwan. It is this synergistic cooperation of the institute and the industry, with ample supply of well-trained human resources from the university, under the orchestration of the government that has consummated the phenomenal growth of the economy in Taiwan through the last two decades of the 20th century.

Two additional points need to be made. One relates to globalization. ITRI has actively pursued technology sourcing globally, shown in the case of semiconductor fabrication, and global marketing in many other areas. There were abundant examples in ITRI that point up the importance of globalization to the overall technical capacity and economic growth of Taiwan. Notable examples can be reviewed with Sun Microsystems, General Electrics, AT&T Bell Labs, TNO, Fraunhoffer Institute, Boeing, Lotus Engineering, and many others.

The second point relates to the migration of technology business to the Chinese Mainland and the impacts on the modernization movement of the People Republic of China. Back from the late 1980s, ITRI has organized or participated in many scientific and technology conferences and exchanges for professionals between the two sides of the Taiwan Strait. This was before any political talks or rhetoric between the two sides. These exchanges have enhanced foreign direct investments to the mainland. A significant part of the FDI was in the manufacturing sectors, especially electronics. Increasingly after the mid 1990s, a substantial portion of Taiwan's electronic products have been manufactured on the Chinese Mainland. This has served as a catalyst for the growth of indigenous high tech industries in China. Close collaboration among the R&D, product design, manufacturing, and marketing expertise of both sides of the Taiwan Strait have contributed to the global presence of Chinese technology products, a business model that can be characterized as "Global Chinese Inc." This facet of the modernization and globalization of China was arguably the most surprising effect of the national innovation system of Taiwan.

Reshaping the University Culture

It was evident that both the university and the institute could and have performed as driver of technology under different social and economic environments. Indeed, the division of responsibility between the university and the institute is an area that is creating confusions as well as opportunities.

The university traditionally attracts elite professionals to run its education and research programs. A university is judged by the quality of the graduates and the impacts of the research. Students are the most precious output, and good basic research tends to provide students with excellent training, nurturing curiosity and creativity. Basic research deals with the depth of knowledge and opens doors to future opportunities. It readily draws attention and fame for the university if any discovery, large and small, comes along the way.

For the institute, its products are relevant technology and technical service to the industry. The institute places focus on industrial and social needs, short- and long-term, and is interested in a wide range of knowledge or know-how that may address those needs. As a solution provider, the complete and quantitatively measurable services that it provides will have value. The criterion of success for an institute is generally the benefits to and, thus, support from, its clients, be it industry, society, or the government. The institute placed the creation of patents, know-how, and other forms of intellectual property as the priority over publication of scientific papers. When there is a discovery of value, the institute will first seek validation for its commercial value and patent coverage before making it public. Just as in the private sector, the question was often asked of a scientist trying to rush through a publication proposal: If it is so good, why would you want other people to know about it, and, now?

The scales of process, equipment, material, and staff requirements are generally much larger in the institute than in the university. Thus the institute was viewed, at times, by the university as a competitor for resources.

The university and the institute can indeed engage in competition as drivers of technology progress in the innovation system. There is an advantage for the university, leveraging on its historical fame and network, to recruit star scientists or engineers to establish a mission-oriented institute that can, in turn, draw large-scale funding from the government or industry. Likewise, there is a tendency for the institute to extend its technology scope to new disciplines of knowledge and offer educational programs that capitalize on its own staff and technical infrastructure. Thus the university and the institute can be drawn into a collision course on many fronts. The probability becomes even larger with the advent of nanotechnology and biotechnology, which, by nature, are multidisciplinary and have no clear lines of demarcation between science and technology.

The juxtaposition of the university and the institute can and should be restructured to become complimentary and to generate synergy. This can be facilitated by establishing in the national innovation system the mechanism to reach consensus in defining national goals, shaping strategies, and setting responsibility and accountability of the players. Equitable management of resources compatible with defined responsibilities can then follow. It is therefore desirable to conduct periodic reviews of the wealth creation process in a certain technology field of the region. A renewed definition of scientific research, technology development, and product commercialization compatible with the regional environment is a useful undertaking.

Indeed, with the increasingly rapid pace of change brought forth by information technology and the Internet, competitions in science, technology, and industry can be fiercer by the day on the world scale. In this era of globalization, competition and collaboration between organizations will take on an added dimension. With globalization, the scope of competition and collaboration goes beyond any political or geographical boundary. The "pure" national corporation may soon be extinct from the face of the earth. Players in the national innovation system should recognize this new reality.

V.   Organization and Governance:
Taking Stock of National and Supranational
Efforts at Higher Education Reform

Chapter 17

European Responses to Global Competitiveness in Higher Education

Marijk van der Wende[1]

Responses to globalization and more precisely, the growing global competition in which knowledge is a prime factor for economic growth, are increasingly shaping policies and setting the agenda for the future of European higher education. With its aim to become the world's leading knowledge economy, the European Union is concerned about its performance in the knowledge sector, in particular in research, (higher) education and innovation (the so-called "knowledge triangle"), and aims to solve the "European paradox": whereby Europe has the necessary knowledge and research, but fails to transfer this into innovation and enhanced productivity and economic growth.

Indicators to "tell the story" refer to investments in higher education and research that lag behind those in the U.S. and Japan, as is the case with the level of higher education qualifications among the E.U. working-age population, and the number of researchers in the labor force. The share of European Nobel Prize winners has declined throughout the 20th century, brain drain continues, too few European universities appear at the top of global rankings, the universities hold few registered patents, the U.S. attracts more R&D expenditure from E.U. companies than U.S. companies allocate to the E.U., and China may soon be spending the

---

[1] Amsterdam University, College and Vrije Universiteit Amsterdam.

same percentage of GDP on R&D as the E.U.—all of these facts are fueling further concern.

OECD's secretary general commented recently: "Universities in Europe are not living up to their potential. Funding is too low, and the rewards for excellence are not there yet. Links to the business world are also weak. Europe has no shortage of brilliant minds, but they are locked away in low-performing institutions" (Gurria 2007).

Awareness of these concerns is not limited to governmental levels, but is also present in the higher education sector:

> It is evident that the European university system needs to broaden access on a more equitable basis, that it has to reach out to increased excellence and that it must allow for more diversification within the system. The American university system is, as the former President of the American Council of Education, David Ward, put it, "elitist at the top, and democratic at the base"; the European university system seems to be neither [. . .]. Alarming for Europe is not only that China regards the U.S. and Japan, and not Europe, as its potential peers to be matched in research and higher education. As announced officially, China aims at matching the U.S. and Japan with respect to innovations by 2020. Given Europe's stagnation and the dynamics in East Asia, one can easily predict the day when East Asia —and not Europe—will possess "the world's leading knowledge-based economy" (Winckler 2006).

Policy responses to the pressures of growing global competitiveness cannot easily be captured as one single trend or strategy, as they are formulated and implemented at different levels: European, national, and institutional, with the regional level additionally sometimes cutting across the European/national distinction. Moreover, they are underpinned by sometimes quite different perceptions of globalization and the meaning of global competition for the sector and by major differences in their actual abilities (i.e., financial and human resources) to support action.

Consequently, European responses may seem to be somewhat preoccupied or confused. Clearly, it takes more political conviction than demonstrated so far to hold to the intended three percent GDP target for R&D expenditure and to accept the two percent GDP target for higher education expenditure, mainly through stimulating more private investments in these areas. Conceptual and practical issues are related to the need for convergence (system coherence and transparency) and more diversity (in order to allow for more access and excellence) at the same time. Other major questions in designing further policies focus on how global competitiveness can best be stimulated and achieved; what role do competition and cooperation-based strategies at the national and European level play in this respect, and what is the best mix?

E.U. Higher Education Policies

For the European Union as a whole, with the European Commission (E.C.) being a major policy actor, we can distinguish different phases and approaches (Huisman and Van der Wende 2004; 2005). Yet the way in which individual countries respond to these policy initiatives can be quite diverse.

Brief Historical Overview: the ERASMUS Era

After the E.C. of the then-countries of the European Economic Community became active in higher education in the mid-1970s, its initiatives were for a long period restricted to stimulating cooperation and mobility between "closed" national systems in which the controlling power entirely lay with the member states (based on the "subsidiarity principle"). Such initiatives were successfully extended across levels and countries until the end of the 1990s. Beginning with an initiative to stimulate action at the level of individual academics and students, the first ERASMUS program (1987) gradually developed through the SOCRATES program (1996) into an effort in which the curriculum and the institutional (policy) level were included. With the enlargement of the E.U., especially after 1992 with preparations for the joining of 10 new central and eastern European member states, the activities underwent a substantial geographic expansion. The rationales for these activities were seen as mainly academic and cultural, for example scholarly exchange, mutual learning processes, and the role of foreign languages. The agenda was strongly focused on the European integration process, and consequently on intra-European cooperation. Yet it is also undeniable that the process of European integration, cemented by the completion of the European internal market in 1992, was driven by an important economic agenda. Mindful of this, in 1991 the E.C. launched a memorandum on higher education underlining the role of higher education in the economic and social cohesion of the E.U. The response of the higher education community was particularly negative and critical of this use of an economic rationale for higher education.[2] It was 10 years before the E.C. was able to come back with another message on the role of higher education in economic growth and competitiveness.

Two Major Vehicles: the Bologna Process and the Lisbon Strategy
In the late 1990s in European higher education, awareness of global competition was raised. It was realized that despite all the success that had been

---

[2] On a larger international scale (including notably developing countries) and later in time, the same type of response emerged from the 1998 UNESCO World Conference on Higher Education, which also strongly rejected the competitive, market-driven model and stressed that appropriate [national] planning must be based on cooperation and coordination between institutions of higher education and responsible state authorities.

achieved in enhancing intra-European mobility,[3] the picture in relation to extra-European mobility was a less successful one. Europe had lost its position as the number one destination for foreign students to the United States, was losing too many of its own graduates and researchers to R&D positions in the United States, and had substantially less efficient degree structures than the United States because its graduates entered the labor market at an older age than did American graduates. Awareness of these factors led to initiatives at various levels. First, in 1998 the ministers of four countries (the United Kingdom, Germany, France, and Italy), called for the harmonization of degree structures. This was the initiative that triggered the "Bologna Process," launched in the signing of the Bologna Declaration by 29 countries one year later. This was an important bottom-up initiative—the E.C. joined the process only later—toward system convergence with a view to enhancing employability in Europe and the international competitiveness and attractiveness of European higher education as a whole.

The E.C. itself was able to become more active after 2000, which was the year that the heads of state and government declared in Lisbon that the E.U. should become by 2010 the most competitive and dynamic knowledge economy in the world. Shortly after that, education was defined as one of the key areas in achieving this goal. This provided the E.C. with an important political mandate in the area of education policy (though this mandate was not supported by any extended legal power). The E.C. quickly developed a wide range of initiatives under what became the "Lisbon Strategy."

The Bologna Process and the Lisbon Strategy are the main vehicles or frameworks guiding the European response to globalization in higher education. Although they emerged in very different ways (bottom-up versus top-down), and thus have some different patterns and origins of ownership, and could be characterized as intergovernmental (Bologna) versus supranational (Lisbon), they seem to converge slowly into one overarching approach.

After the first phase of the Bologna process, which focused strongly on the intra-European convergence and transparency agenda (i.e., reform of curriculum and degree structures for easier recognition with a view to employability in the European labor market), in the second phase, the process has become more oriented to the "external dimension," with the aim of enhancing international competitiveness and attractiveness, and to its connections to other regions. This coincided and was paralleled by the creation of the ERASMUS MUNDUS program (in 2004) and the development of the European Higher Education Area (EHEA) and the European Research Area (ERA), as part of the wider of the Lisbon Strategy which aimed to make "Europe the most competitive and dynamic knowledge economy in the world by 2010."

---

[3] In 2007, the ERASMUS Program will celebrate its 20 years, with over 1.5 million students exchanged (now 150.00 per year) and in the hope that in 2012 3M will be reached.

Lisbon clearly represents the wider agenda: "The Education and Training 2010 work programme, recognising the extreme importance of modernisation of higher education, over and above the reforms called for in the Bologna process which, *a fortiori*, are also important for achieving the Lisbon objectives" (European Commission 2005, 11). Also in a more technical sense the key instruments from the Bologna process have been integrated into the Lisbon Strategy.

Although convergence between the two agendas and processes can be observed, this is seen by many as a paradigm shift. The Bologna process is associated with mutual cooperation and in principle the equal position of all institutions and systems, whereas the Lisbon agenda is seen as more explicitly competition-driven and intended to produce more hierarchical and stratified impressions of the European higher education landscape.

Both processes and their outcomes so far will be discussed in more detail below.

The Bologna Process: Patterns of Convergence.

The Bologna Process represents the totality of commitments freely taken by each signatory country (45 nations since 2005)[4] to reform its own higher education system in order to create overall convergence at the European level, as a way to enhance international/global competitiveness. Its nonbinding character was a crucial facilitator, given the need to overcome reluctance in Europe toward standardization and harmonization. Its bottom-up character should be understood in terms of the limited competencies of the E.C. in the field of higher education policy.

The achievements of the Bologna Process have been substantial and influential. The range of policy issues included in the Bologna Process was extended throughout the medium of ministerial meetings that took place every two years to follow up on the implementation of the process. The initial focus on a change of degree structures into a two-cycle (undergraduate-graduate) system, and the wider implementation of ECTS (European Credit Transfer System) with the aim of enhancing the readability and recognition of degrees, extended into the development of a European Qualifications Framework, the description and "tuning" of competences and learning outcomes at the curriculum level, and substantial initiatives in the areas of quality assurance and accreditation (see also Reinalda and Kulesza, 2005).

Since the 2005 ministerial meeting in Bergen the work program has been extended to the "third cycle," i.e., the reform of studies at the doctoral/Ph.D. level. Reforms would focus on the length and structure of these programs, interdisciplinarity, supervision, the training of generic skills, systematic assessments, etc.

A series of biennial studies has demonstrated that the implementation of the two-cycle degree structure was established in almost all countries by 2005, al-

---

[4] Membership of the E.U. is not required for joining the process, which explains the fact that the number of Bologna signatory countries exceeds the number of E.U. member countries (25).

though in various modes and at a varying speed of introduction (Reichert and Tauch 2005). In-depth studies and comparisons between countries show that the actual implementation of the new structures can vary significantly. Lub et al. (2003) found substantial differences between the Netherlands, where the new two-cycle system replaced the existing long first-cycle degree system; and Germany, where the new system was implemented parallel to the existing system, and despite quick growth in the number of new degree programs, only a small fraction of the total student population actually participates in these programs.[5] Alesi et al. (2005) found in a comparison among six countries that there is no unified logic within the system of new degree programs. This point applies both to the breadth of the introduction—in each country different groups of subjects are excluded from the new structure, and different time frames set for the introduction—and to the duration of the new programs.

The 3+2 year model, a bachelor's degree followed by a master's degree, is the basic model; but there are many variations from this model. For example, the United Kingdom is a notable exception: In that nation master's degrees mostly take one year. Likewise Witte (2006), in a comparison of England, France, the Netherlands, and Germany, found that there is variation in the degree of change following from the Bologna process, especially if one looks at implementation. She concludes that the four countries under study weakly converged between 1998 and 2004, in the direction of the English system.

Witte also concluded that although the changes leading to that convergence all occurred within the framework of the Bologna Process, this does not necessarily mean that they have been caused by it. Rather, the Bologna Process has often served to enable, sustain, and amplify developments that have been driven by deeper underlying forces or particular interests at the national level; for example the pressures to reduce study length, the time within which a student must complete a degree or drop out. Sometimes the Bologna Process has simply provided a mental frame for developments that were unrelated to degree structures as such. This illustrates that actors align themselves with the international context and international perceptions only when those perceptions are consistent with nationally grounded preferences. At the same time, international perceptions have a very high legitimating power when they support national preferences, even though those international perceptions may be selective and biased, sometimes even wrong, and are rarely questioned (Witte 2006, 492).

Diversification Trends and Policies

Apart from the fact that the Bologna Process is implemented quite differently *across* countries, weakening its harmonizing or convergence effects, paral-

---

[5] In 2001, 10 percent of the total number of study programs was structured in bachelor-master, with one percent of the student population enrolled in them. In 2003, this had increased to 23 percent of programs, catering to 3.5 percent of the student population.

lel to it, divergent trends can be observed. This is especially the case *within* countries. Examples are Germany and France, where there is increased diversity in each case. This is partly due to the parallel existence of different degree structures in the transition phase, but also derives from the increased curricular autonomy of HEIs (Witte 2006). In a number of countries, among the trends in governmental policies are increased autonomy and a push for more diversity in the system. This is especially the case in those national systems which aim to enhance participation in higher education; for example the United Kingdom, Sweden, Finland, and the Netherlands, where participation targets of 50 percent have been formulated. More diversity is seen as a necessary condition to achieving these aims. The E.C. also advocates increased diversity, as a condition for excellence and greater access (European Commission 2005).

At the same time, another process of convergence can be observed. As both academic and professionally oriented higher education institutions offer bachelor's and master's programs, there are frequent and increasing instances of functional overlap. This convergence of the two main types of higher education may lead to a change in those nations with such binary systems. But again, in response to this situation, nations exhibit diversity, and an overall trend toward a unitary system cannot be confirmed. In Hungary it has been decided to abolish the binary system and to replace it with a more varied range of programs, especially at the master's level. The Netherlands intends to maintain the binary system and wants more institutional types to emerge. In Finland and Austria, binary systems were established only over the last decade. The United Kingdom, which abolished its binary system in the early 1990s, is now looking to re-establish more diversity with the abovementioned aim of thereby enhancing participation. These trends raise questions about the level at which diversity is defined and pursued, and whether it is systemic, institutional, or programmatic diversity (Birnbaum 1983). A more contemporary point is that "there has been a gradual shift in the meaning of 'diversity'—from diversity among national systems of higher education to a European-wide diversification in institutions and programmes with different profiles" (Hackl in Olson 2005).

An important distinction needs to be made between changes at the undergraduate and the graduate levels. Increasing participation rates require diversity to be enhanced especially at the undergraduate level, thereby enabling nontraditional students to enroll. In terms of programmatic diversity, the introduction of the associate or foundation degree, awarded after two years higher education, is important here, but often this is seen to contradict the spirit of the Bologna Declaration.[6] At the graduate level, where the patterns of activity are closely related to research strengths, there is a trend toward greater concentration and specialization.

---

[6] Because the Bologna Declaration required a minimum of three years for the first degree. This has been solved by considering this type of "short cycle higher education" as integrated into or linked to the first degree (MSTI 2005).

Both kinds of trends indicate that the current dynamics in European higher education are at one and the same time characterized by trends of convergence, aiming for harmonization and transparency; and divergence, searching for more diversity. Both kinds of trend are considered important in order to enhance competitiveness in the global context. Increased participation rates among a larger number of domestic students, fostered by diversity of provision, are seen to enhance the potential of each country as a knowledge economy. Enhanced cross-border mobility within Europe, and attracting more students from other regions, objectives fostered by harmonization and convergence, are seen to enhance the performance of the European knowledge economy as a whole.

At the same time, this implies patterns that to an extent are confusing, and it raises questions about the further direction of the process of Europeanization in higher education. Given that multilevel actions and interactions are involved, these questions are not easy to answer, and future directions are not easy to predict. But clearly, differentiation is thought to be at least as important as convergence: "European universities have for long modeled themselves along the lines of some major models, particularly the ideal model of the university envisaged nearly two centuries ago by Alexander von Humboldt, in his reform of the German university, which sets research at the heart of the university and indeed makes it the basis of teaching. Today the trend is away from these models and towards greater differentiation" (European Commission 2003a, 5–6).

The Lisbon Strategy: Coordinating Policies for a European Knowledge Economy

As noted, whereas the Bologna Process emerged bottom-up and the role of the E.C. in the process was initially limited but over time gradually developed into a leading one, the initiative for the Lisbon strategy was taken by the E.C. at the supranational level, and in its implementation it exhibits a more top-down character. Yet this strategy cannot be characterized completely as top-down, since the formal competences of the E.C. in the area of education policy have not been enlarged. Instruments used are thus not (legally binding) E.U. directives, but take the form of recommendations, communications, consultations, or other working documents. This "open method of coordination," based on common objectives, is translated into national action plans and implemented through sets of indicators, consultative follow-up, and "soft" mechanisms such peer review, peer learning, and peer pressure (see also Gornitzka 2005).

In 2001, the E.C. published a first report setting out the steps to be taken in response to the challenges of global competition in higher education (European Commission 2001). The report explicitly referred to market-oriented approaches to internationalization in the United Kingdom, Germany, France, and the Netherlands and stressed the need to attract more students from other regions to the European Union. This laid the foundation for the establishment of the ERASMUS MUNDUS program in 2004. This program includes a global scholarship scheme for third-country nationals, linked to the creation of "European Union Masters Courses," based on interuniversity cooperation networks. The program has enrolled more than 800 students and 130 scholars, about 40 percent from Asia, in 60 master's programs in the academic year 2005–2006,[7] and is expected to grow further. These figures can be compared to the 1,300 foreigners who enter the U.S. every year as fellows of the Fulbright program, on which ERASMUS MUNDUS was largely modeled.

Following up the Lisbon summit of 2000, in 2002 the E.C. published a detailed work program on the future objectives of education and training systems in the E.U. (European Commission 2002), emphasizing the central role of those systems in achieving the aim of Europe becoming the world's most competitive and dynamic knowledge society by 2010. The general goals of improving quality, enhancing access, and opening up the education and training systems to the wider world were worked through in a set of more specific objectives for the various education sectors. Those most relevant to higher education were the objective of increasing graduates in mathematics, science, and technology by 15 percent while improving gender balance, to ensure that more than 85 percent of all 22-year-olds had achieved at least an upper-secondary education level, and to ensure that 12.5 percent of the 25-to-64-year-old adult working population participated in lifelong learning.

In 2003, the E.C. launched a large-scale consultation on the role of higher education institutions in the European knowledge economy (European Commission 2003a). It showed a particular concern for the funding of higher education. The increasing underfunding of European higher education institutions was seen to be jeopardizing their capacity to attract and keep the best talent and to strengthen the excellence of their research and teaching activities. The consultation round took two years and was paralleled by a series of critical messages on growth and innovation. Two important reports published in 2003 (European Commission 2003b, 2003c) revealed that the objective of boosting E.U. spending on R&D from 1.9 percent to three percent of GDP—the principal target for research expressed in the Lisbon strategy—was far from being met; that the R&D investment gap between the European Union and the United States increasingly favored the United States;[8] and that brain drain out of Europe and notably to the U.S. was still on the rise. It was clear that the E.U. was hindered in catching up with its main global competitors by a lack of investment in human resources[9] by not producing enough higher education graduates,[10] and by

---

[7] See <http://europa.eu.int/comm/education/programmes/mundus/index_en.html>.

[8] Eighty percent of this comes from the difference in domestic business R&D expenditure between the E.U. and the U.S. Further analysis showed that the U.S. attracts one-third more R&D expenditure from E.U. companies than U.S. companies allocate to the E.U. (a net outflow of EUR 5 billion in 2000) (European Commission 2003b).

[9] Especially private investments in education in the E.U. (0.6 percent of GDP) lag behind the U. .(2.2 percent) and Japan (1.2 percent). The biggest difference is in higher education: the U.S. spends between two and five times more per student than E.U. countries (European Commission 2004).

attracting less talent than its competitors.[11] Furthermore, the E.U. had too few
women in scientific and technological fields; rates of early school leaving were
still too high and rates of completion of upper secondary education still too low,
with nearly 20 percent of young people failing to acquire key competences;
there were too few adults participating in lifelong learning; and there was a
looming shortage of qualified teachers and trainers (European Commission
2004).

Early in 2005 a new stage of the Lisbon Strategy was announced. Major
E.U. conferences on higher education and research were organized, and in a
follow-up communication on the contribution of universities to the Lisbon strategy (2005), further and wider measures were announced. These initiatives were
focused on achieving world-class quality,[12] improving governance, and increasing and diversifying funding. The European Commission stated that "while most
of Europe sees higher education as a 'public good,' tertiary enrollments have
been stronger and faster in other parts of the world, mainly thanks to much
higher private funding" (European Commission 2005, 3). This contrasted with
the strong emphasis that many in the higher education community have placed
on "higher education as a public good" and on the role of universities with respect to social and cultural objectives rather than economic purposes, especially
in the context of the Bologna Process (Van Vught et al. 2002).

The E.C. identified the main bottlenecks retarding access and excellence as
uniformity in provision, due to a tendency toward egalitarianism and a lack of
differentiation; and insularity, in that systems remained fragmented between and
even within countries, and higher education as a whole remained insulated from
industry; over-regulation, in that a strong dependence on the state inhibited reform, modernization, and efficiency; and underfunding.[13] The pathways to more

---

[10] On average in the E.U., 21 percent of the E.U. working-age population holds a
higher education qualification, compared to 38 percent in the U.S., 43 percent in Canada,
36 percent in Japan, and 26 percent in South Korea (European Commission 2005).

[11] The E.U. produces more higher education graduates and doctors in science and
technology (25.7 percent) than the U.S. (17.2 percent) and Japan (21.9 percent) but the
percentage of them at work as researchers is much lower in the E.U. (5.4 per 1000 population in 1999), than in the U.S. (8.7) and Japan (9.7). This is due to career changes, a
limited European labor market for researchers, and better opportunities and working conditions in the U.S. (European Commission 2004).

[12] It was explicitly stated as a problem that apart from some British universities there
were no European universities in the top 20 of the world and relatively few in the top 50
as ranked by Shanghai Jiao Tong University.

[13] E.U. spending on research (1.9 percent of GDP) compared badly with the U.S.,
Japan, and South Korea (all close to three percent thanks to much higher investments
from industry). Higher education spending in the EU (1.1 percent of GDP) also compared
badly with U.S. and South Korea (both 2.7 percent, again related to differences in private
investments). It was calculated that in order to match the U.S. figure, the E.U. would
need to spend an additional EUR 150 billion a year on higher education. It was suggested
to set a two percent of GDP aim for funding of higher education (European Commission
2005).

access and excellence were seen to be more diversity and enhanced flexibility. At this point the Lisbon Strategy absorbed the Bologna objectives of coherent structures, compatibility, and transparency, designed to improve the readability and attractiveness of European higher education internationally. Likewise the Bologna instruments such as the ECTS, IDS, and EQF were taken into the Lisbon agenda. The E.C. also spoke out for the first time on issues such as the governance and funding of higher education, arguing for greater institutional autonomy, deregulation, and professionalized management, combined with competition-based funding in research and more output-related funding in education, supported by more contributions from industry and from students via tuition fees.

These statements reflected a preference for new public management (NPM) techniques and related to what was seen as "good practice" in certain member states, notably the United Kingdom, where a risky political initiative to raise higher ("top-up") tuition fees in order to provide the university sector with sufficient capital to counteract global competition had succeeded by a narrow political margin; and also systems such as the Netherlands where deregulation and institutional autonomy had been advanced. At the same time there had been a more open debate in the Nordic countries about tuition fees for domestic students and differential fees for foreign (non-E.U.) students.[14] These issues remained highly controversial in other parts of Europe, however.

As well as pushing for the more widespread adoption of these practices, the E.U. made a notable effort to enhance investments in research, innovation, and excellence. In the context of the E.U. budget for 2007–2013, introducing major budget growth was planned in order to enable investment in the new Framework Programme for R&D (FP7) and an integrated program for education (the Lifelong Learning Programme).

Midterm Concerns and Challenges

During 2005 these ambitions were seriously constrained by severe obstacles in achieving a political agreement on the new E.U. Treaty (the so-called "European Constitution"), a process that was temporarily halted after French and Dutch referenda failed to gain a majority in favor of the new treaty, and on the new E.U. budget. Under the U.K. presidency of the European Union, the Hampton Court Summit failed to make the intended budget shift from an "agricultural" to a "knowledge" Union. Instead of the originally planned E.U.R 132 billion, a total of E.U.R 72 billion was attributed to all activities under the heading of competitiveness, growth, and employment.

---

[14] Denmark has, as the first country in Scandinavia, introduced tuition fees for non-EU/EEA students from September 2006 forward in an effort to become more competitive in the global arena.

This included a total (seven-year) budget of 7.5 billion Euro for the newly (2007) established European Research Council (ERC), set up to fund innovative, groundbreaking basic research, with competitive funding awarded based on peer review (as with the National Science Foundation allocations in the U.S.). And a seven-year budget of 50.5 billion Euro was established for the E.U.'s 7th Framework Programme for R&D, which is twice the financial volume of its predecessor (FP6). In comparison: This is a slightly larger budget than the U.S. NSF budget on a yearly basis (6.2 billion U.S.D for 2007), although it represents not even four percent of the total of national R&D (private plus public) budgets of the member states together. Important, therefore, are the bottom-up dynamics that are emerging at the same time through the network of national research councils (ERA-NET), which strives on a voluntary basis for more cooperation between them through transparent peer review, aiming to avoid overlap between national research agendas and pushing for joint calls for proposals (yet still very infrequent). It is expected that the E.C. may top up such common budgets as to provide a greater incentive to move toward "single pot" funding. Initiatives for such cooperation also emerge on a regional basis, as for instance between the Nordic countries (the NORIA initiative, see below), which may further encourage this type of bottom-up dynamics.

The most recent review of progress in the Lisbon Strategy displays a more optimistic view with respect to the overall objectives of economic growth, employment, and productivity. The February 2007 report of the Lisbon Council stated that: "Now in the 7th year of the Lisbon Agenda some of the objectives finally seem within reach," and that "The famous Lisbon targets have come within closer reach throughout the E.U. than many had thought possible" (5–6). It should be noted that this review only looked at the largest nine E.U. economies, comparing them to the E.U. 15 average (see Table 17.1).[15]

On this basis the report concluded that Europe was doing better economically at the time than it has done in any year since 2000, when economic growth briefly brushed four percent. In particular, growth in the E.U.-15 was a surprisingly high 2.8 percent in 2006—the first time since 2000 that E.U. countries have come close to meeting the Lisbon target in this vital policy area. And growth has become much more stable; there is no "new economy" hype as there was in 2000. But also that despite the progress that has been made recently, Europe still has low productivity in the services sector—an area which covers 70 percent of modern economic activity—a fact that many experts blame on the low application of information and communications technology (ICT) in the service sector.

Looking at higher education, it can be noted that the overall proportion of employees with tertiary education is steadily rising. In 2006, 29 percent of the

---

[15] An overview of the EU25 (and now even 27) member states would display a different average performance. The extension of the E.U. with 10+ countries coinciding with the ambition to become the world's leading knowledge economy is seen by many as the main challenge toward achieving these aims.

Table 17.1. Overall Performance on the Lisbon Objectives of the Nine Largest E.U. Economies, Compared to the E.U.15 Average

Rank	Country	Overall Score 2006 Q3	Change in Ranking since then	Rank one year ago	Score one year ago
1	Sweden	1.37	◄	1	1.26
2	Belgium	1.09	▲ ▲	8	0.72
3	Netherlands	1.02	▼	2	0.95
4	U.K.	0.98	▲	4	0.85
5	Spain	0.98	▼	3	0.87
6	Germany	0.91	▲ ▲	9	0.65
7	E.U.15	0.90	◄	7	0.73
8	Austria	0.83	▼ ▼	5	0.83
9	France	0.80	▼ ▼	6	0.78
10	Italy	0.43	◄	10	0.33

Source: Lisbon Council, 2007.

workforce in the E.U.-15 countries had tertiary or higher education, up from 25 percent in 2000 (see Figure 17.1).

For research, however, progress is still unsatisfactory; throughout the E.U.-15 the share of GDP spent on R&D remains stuck obstinately at 1.9 percent (see Figure 17.2), far below the prominent Lisbon target of 3 percent of GDP by 2010. Considerable differences between countries can be observed: Italy and Spain demonstrate very low scores, while in contrast Sweden is way out front. The report notes that education and research alone are not enough for a knowledge-based economy; equally important are the use of human capital and the diffusion of new technologies. Also, for the share of private investment in R&D, the Lisbon objectives have not yet been met. Currently the private contribution is 55 percent on average; the Lisbon target is 66 percent.

Another recent review of achievements under the Lisbon Strategy (London School of Economics 2006), which is less optimistic on the wider economic progress, criticizing the failure of E.U. members to liberalize their product and labor markets, agrees on the weak progress on the R&D side. It underlines that R&D and in particular innovation as a route to growth is sensible, but notes that the cost of patenting in Europe is still about five times the cost of patenting in the United States. And the "brain drain" from the E.U. to the United States—because of better research opportunities and higher wages—is still a significant phenomenon and the Lisbon aim of reversing this trend has not materialised (London School of Economics 2006).

Despite these disappointments, positive points can also be reported. First, the role of the E.C., especially in the higher education policy area, has expanded

Figure 17.1. Share of Tertiary Education Level Attained

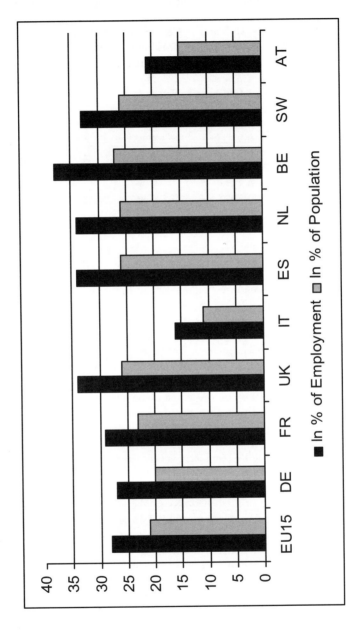

Source: Lisbon Council, 2007

Figure 17.2. R&D Expenditure in the E.U.

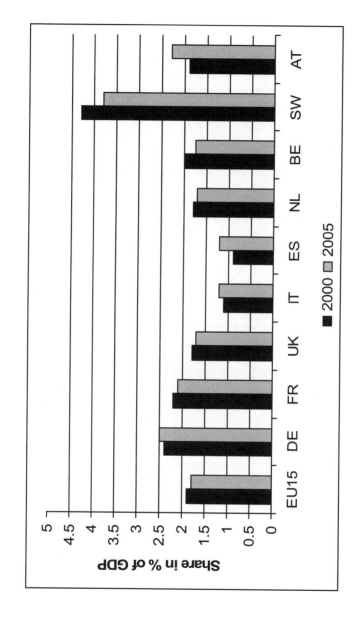

Source: Lisbon Council, 2007

and become less controversial. This is a gain in terms of both legitimacy and coordinating capacity. Second, individual countries have started to respond to the wider E.U. agenda on global competitiveness. Third, although the overall targets for investments in R&D and higher education have not been reached and many countries do not as yet reach their individual targets; and in some cases investments have even decreased, with the expected additional contributions from private sources proving especially problematic; as noted, several nations have developed initiatives to strive for more excellence and to widen access to higher education, notably the Nordic countries, the United Kingdom, Germany, and the Netherlands.

Responses to Global Competition: Some Examples

While the world envies the Nordic countries for appearing at the top of almost every global and certainly European-league table, the Nordics themselves worry about being able to keep their leading position in the field of R&D. A recent report for the Nordic Council of Ministers (intergovernmental forum for co-operation between the Nordic countries)[16] departed from the assumption that the relevance and success of research and its application in the form of innovation is limited by the size of a country. Since all the Nordic countries are small (population-wise), it looks into ways of reaching a critical mass by working more closely together. In admiration of the E.U.'s successful coordination of its member states' research policies, the Nordic countries would likewise develop a joined-up research and innovation policy, and through it, the Nordic Research and Innovation Area (NORIA) (Norden 2006).

Also, within various individual countries, efforts are underway to respond to global competition. Aimed at strengthening the country's position in the international higher education and research market(s), Denmark engaged in a merger process in order to create fewer but stronger (and larger) universities. Motivations for this merger operation are related to the challenges of increased global competition, of creating world-class universities, of achieving the three percent of GDP target for R&D by 2010 (0.7 percent public + 1.7 percent private in 2005), and of allowing 50 percent of young people to attend higher education (45 percent in 2006). The mergers are taking effect from January 1, 2007, bringing the number of universities back from twelve to nine and probably later on to six or seven (Larsen 2006).

In Germany, the government decided in 2004 to create top universities and research institutes that can compete with the global premier league.[17] The idea

---

[16] Nordic cooperation, one of the oldest and most wide-ranging regional partnerships in the world, involves Denmark, Finland, Iceland, Norway, Sweden, the Faroe Islands, Greenland, and Åland.

[17] In this year the first editions of the THES and Jiaotong global university rankings were published.

was to achieve this through nationwide competition among universities to identify the best research universities and provide them with extra funding to become "elite institutions" or "lighthouses" able to compete on a global level. A budget of 1.9 billion Euro was earmarked for 2006–2011 (Kehm 2006). In 2003, the Dutch government established an innovation platform, chaired by the prime minister, following the example of Finland. Although already initiated in a bottom-up way, the innovation platform and the Ministry of Economic Affairs encouraged with a 50 million Euro grant the formation of a federation by Delft University of Technology, Eindhoven University of Technology, and Twente University. Today the initiative is well underway and has established a joint graduate school, joint accreditation, a common framework for the quality assurance of research, and a common scheme for research chairs. On this basis it recently engaged in the joint recruitment of 30 new professors to lead the five new joint centers of excellence that have been established (3TU 2005).

Responses from the institutional level can be illustrated by the establishment of the League of European Research Universities (LERU[18]). LERU was founded in 2002 by a group of 12 European research-intensive universities concerned with the question of how to ensure that more of our European universities join Oxford and Cambridge at the top of the world university rankings. In their view, the European universities need greater autonomy to respond rapidly to challenges and opportunities, combined with much greater investment to ensure that the best compete at the highest international levels of excellence. Another example concerns the 2004 merger of UMIST and the Victoria University of Manchester to create the U.K.'s largest single-site university: the University of Manchester, in order to match the leading universities in the world, i.e., to become one of the top 25 strongest research universities in the world by 2015.

The examples presented above illustrate responses to global competition and clearly indicate the important role that international rankings of universities play in this respect. All of these responses have both cemented the role of the rankings themselves and further intensified competitive pressures. Yet as rankings seem to be here to stay, they are far from problem-free (Marginson and Van der Wende 2007). In Europe the CHE ranking developed in Germany presents a strong example of how spurious holistic ranking can be avoided and is well-positioned to develop into a Europeanwide system. In order to encourage institutions to design different missions and profiles, allowing them to excel in a variety of domains, and to ensure transparency for stakeholders at the same time, a typology (classification) of higher education institutions in Europe is being developed (Van Vught et al. 2005; forthcoming).

---

[18] LERU includes the Universities of Amsterdam, Cambridge, Edinburgh, Freiburg, Genève, Heidelberg, Helsinki, Leiden, Leuven, University College London, Lund, Milan, Munich, Oxford, Paris 6, Paris-Sud 11, Karolinska Institute, Strasbourg, Utrecht, and Zürich.

Conclusions and Reflections

Governments have to consider what is the best way to make the national higher education system more globally competitive: national or European-level cooperation or competition, or (more likely) a mix of these four options. National policies often demonstrate combinations of the various strategic options. For example measures to make national research funding more competitive through the national research council may be combined with policies that urge institutions to cooperate more closely within the national context, for example through mergers.

At the same time institutions are stimulated to cooperate at the European level by participating in E.U. R&D projects, and the government supports the establishment of the ERC as it believes that competitive funding measures are even more effective at the supranational level. Similar examples could be given for the teaching function. This illustrates how complex the environment is for institutions in terms of partners, competitors, and strategic options. Consequently the outcome of the process at a meta-level is ever more difficult to predict. Clearly, successful strategies depend on the right mix of competitive and cooperative options (Van der Wende 2007).

Overly simplistic or one-sided competitive models will enhance vertical differentiation by building strength in certain institutions or areas by weakening others and may in fact lead to a lack of diversity (Marginson and Van der Wende 2007). Therefore these choices need to be guided by a vision of an effective division of labor and a good balance between global competitiveness, European excellence, and national priorities and interests (including issues of cultural and linguistic diversity). The development of such a vision is not bound to national-level actors. Also the E.U. as a whole has been urged to better define its priorities and opportunities for cooperation and competition in a wider international context (EURAB 2006). Scenario studies indicate that specialization and concentration in the research function of the university will increase (OECD 2006) and, as mentioned before, this may lead in Europe to a concentration of this function and relate type of HEIs in the northwest of Europe (Enders et al. 2005).

On the one hand the E.U. is considered as an '"area" for higher education and research, as indicated in the European Research Area (ERA) and the European Higher Education Area (EHEA), in which cooperation is traditionally seen as the pathway towards stronger global competitiveness of the E.U. as a whole. On the other hand the E.U. is seen as an internal market subject to internal competition strategies, which were likewise introduced to achieve stronger global competitiveness. This latter principle is starting to affect the higher education sector more than before, i.e., in the ERC and notably, under the Services Directive.[19] This mixed

---

[19] The proposed E.U. directive on services in the internal market seeks to remove barriers to the freedom of establishment for service providers in member states and barriers to the freedom to provide services as between member states. Higher education (as a

reality implies a certain degree of conceptual and political confusion as to how the higher education and research sector is to be interpreted in terms of supranational steering and how its dynamics should be understood in the light of global competition.

Olson (2005) underlines the existence of competing visions in Europe, among the university as a service enterprise in competitive markets, the university as an instrument for national political agendas, and the university as a public service model based on the argument that higher education cannot be solely market-driven because the logic of the market does not apply easily to education. He regards the situation as unsettled, given the multitude of partly inconsistent criteria of success and competing understandings of what forms of organization and governance will contribute to good performance. Jacobs and Van der Ploeg (2006) also argue that higher education cannot be left to the market alone and that government interference may be necessary to correct for market failures. In their view, the challenge for reform of the European system is to achieve the diversity and quality for which the U.S. system is praised: choice, differentiation, and competition.

But Europe should not throw away the baby with the bathwater, i.e., it should not only invest in top academic universities but should also maintain and cherish the high average quality of its institutions. Van Vught (2006) is also concerned about the potential for simplistic market-type strategies in relation to the social dimension of higher education.

The introduction through public policy of increased competition does not necessarily lead to more responsiveness of higher education institutions to the needs of the knowledge society. Rather than being driven by a competition for consumer needs, higher education institutions are driven by a competition for institutional reputation. In addition, the creation of more institutional autonomy in such a "reputation race" leads to cost explosions, related to hiring the best faculty and attracting the most talented students; institutional hierarchies; and social stratification of the student body. Instead, the coordinative capacity of the market should be used, consisting of a new set of "social contracts," which lay down the mutual obligations between universities and their stakeholders, including business and industry. For the E.U., however, this implies that an inverse tendency needs to be addressed. The European business community has an increasing propensity for technological alliances with U.S. firms, while the European academic community has an increasing propensity for intra-European partnership. There is still a considerable lag in cooperation between enterprises and universities within the E.U., compared to the U.S. and Japan (Archibugi and Coco 2004).

---

sector providing services) is not excluded, although it is not clear yet what exactly the impact of the new directive will be on cross-border activities in higher education. This directive was developed by the E.C.'s directorate for the internal market and can be seen as an example of wider E.U. policy interfering with higher education policies and as an E.U. equivalent to GATS, a trade framework that also intervened with higher education, but which was dealt with by yet another E.C. directorate (for trade).

Finally, Europe demonstrates striking internal differences in performance between countries and systems, differences that are large, deep-rooted, and difficult to overcome. The E.U. includes some of the top higher education systems in the world, performing on a par with and on some measures performing higher than the U.S. and Japan, as well as a range of new member states that are at a very different overall technological level to that of the E.U.15 group. Effective solutions for accommodating this diversity and lack of cohesion in terms of supra-national decision making require major institutional reforms at E.U. level, which have yet to be established.

References

3TU. 2005. *Bestuurlijke Agenda 2005/2006. Gemeenschappelijke regeling Technische Universiteiten.* Federatie van Technische Universiteiten in Nederland i.o.

Alesi, B., S. Burger, B. Kehm and U. Teichler. 2005. *Bachelor and Master Courses in Selected Countries Compared with Germany.* Bonn/Berlin: Federal Ministry of Education and Research.

Archibugi, D., and A. Coco. 2004. "Is Europe Becoming the Most Dynamic Knowledge Economy in the World?" *Journal of Common Market Studies,* 43 (3): 433–59, <http://papers.ssrn.com/sol3/papers.cfm?abstract_id= 786101>. See also <http://www.ces.fas.harvard.edu/publications/ArchibugiTech.pdf>.

Birnbaum, R. 1983. *Maintaining Diversity in Higher Education.* Washington: Jossey-Bass Publishers.

Enders, J., J. File, J. Huisman, and D. Westerheijden, eds. 2005. *The European Higher Education and Research Landscape 2020. Scenarios and Strategic Debates.* CHEPS/UT.

E.U.A. 2006. *The Contribution of Universities to Europe's Competitiveness.* Speech of E.U.A President Prof. Georg Winckler to the Conference of the European Ministers of Education, Vienna, 16–17 March 2006, <http://www. eua.be/eua/jsp/en/upload/E.U.A_Winckler_Speech_160306.1142503291615. pdf>.

European Commission. 2001. *Communication of the European Commission to the European Parliament and the Council on Strengthening Co-operation with Third Countries in the Field of Higher Education.* Brussels: E.C..

———. 2002. *The Concrete Future Objectives of Education Systems.* Report from the Commission. Brussels: E.C..

———. 2003a. *Communication from the Commission. The Role of Universities in the Europe of Knowledge.* COM(2003) 58 final. Brussels: E.C..

———. 2003b. *Key Figures 2003–2004. Towards a European Research Area. Science, Technology and Innovation.* Brussels: E.C..

———. 2003c. *Brain Drain Study—Emigration Flows of Qualified Scientist.* Study carried out by Merit, <http://ec.europa.eu/research/era/pdf/indicators/ merit_exsum.pdf>.

———. 2004. *Education & Training 2010. The Success of the Lisbon Strategy Hinges on Urgent Reforms.* COM(2004) 685 final.

———. 2005. *Communication from the Commission. Mobilising the Brainpower of Europe: Enabling Universities to Make Their Full Contribution to the Lisbon Strategy.* COM(2005) 152 final.

———. 2006. Communication of the European Commission to the European Council. *The European Institute of Technology: Further Steps Towards Its Creation.* COM(2006) 276 final.

European Research Advisory Board (EURAB). 2006. *International Research Co-operation.* Final Report EURAB.

Gornitzka, A. 2005. "Coordinating Policies for a 'Europe of Knowledge.' Emerging "Practices of the 'Open Method of Coordination' in Education and Research." Arena Working Paper No. 16, Oslo. <http://www.arena.uio.no>.

Gurria, A. 2007. *Human Capital: Europe's Next Frontier.* Schuman Lecture 2007, for the Lisbon Council. Brussels, February 27.

Huisman, J., and M. C. van der Wende, eds. 2004. *On Cooperation and Competition. National and European Policies for Internationalisation of Higher Education.* ACA Papers on International Cooperation. Lemmens, Bonn.

———, eds. 2005. *On Cooperation and Competition II. Institutional Responses to Internationalisation, Europeanisation and Globalisation.* ACA Papers on International Cooperation. Lemmens, Bonn.

Jacobs, B., and R. van der Ploeg. 2006. "Guide to Reform of Higher Education: A European Perspective." *Economic Policy*, vol. 21, no. 47: 535–92.

Kehm, B. 2006. *The German Initiative for Excellence: Restructuring the German University Landscape.* Paper presented at the EIB/EJE Joint Workshop European Universities in Search of Excellence. November 17, Luxembourg.

Larsen, S. 2006. Mergers among Danish Universities—Research *Policy* Considerations. Danish Council for Research Policy. Meeting of the Heads of Secretariats of the National Advisory Councils for Science and Technology Policy of the E.U. member countries. Dublin, 2006.

LERU. 2006. Putting European Research and Higher Education First. Annual report 2005.

Lisbon Council. 2007. European Growth and Jobs Monitor. Indicators for Success in the Knowledge Economy. Frankfurt/Main: Allianz Dresdner Economic Research.

London School of Economics and Political Science. 2006. "Boosting Innovation and Productivity Growth in Europe: The Hope and the Realities of the E.U.'s 'Lisbon Agenda.'" London: LSE, Centre for Economic Performance.

Lub, A., M. van der Wende, and J. Witte. 2003. The Implementation of the Bachelor-Master System in Germany and the Netherlands, *TEAM*, 9, 249–66.

Marginson, S., and M. C. van der Wende. 2007. *Globalization and Higher Education.* Paris: O.E.C.D, <http://www.oecd.org/dataoecd/33/12/38918635.pdf>.

Ministry of Science, Technology and Innovation (MSTI). 2005. "A Framework for Qualifications of the European Higher Education Area." Copenhagen: Bologna Working Group on Qualifications Frameworks.

Norden. 2006. *Building Nordic Strength through More Open R&D Funding—Study 3 . The Next Step in NORIA.* Copenhagen, Nordic Council of Ministers.

Olson, J. P. 2005. *The Institutional Dynamics of the (European) University.* Arena Working Paper, <www.arena.uio.no>.

Organization for Economic Cooperation and Development, O.E.C.D. 2006. *Four Futures Scenarios for Higher Education,* <http://www.oecd.org/dataoecd/30/5/36960598.pdf>.

Reichert, S., and C. Tauch. 2005. "Trends IV: European universities implementing Bologna." E.U.A, Brussels.

Reinalda, B., and E. Kulesza. 2005. *The Bologna Process: Harmonizing Europe's Higher Education*. Barbara Budrich Publishers.

Vught, F. A. van. 2006. Higher Education System Dynamics and Useful Knowledge Creation, in *Universities and Business: Partnering for the Knowledge Society*, ed. J. Duderstadt and L. Weber. New York: Economica, 63–79.

Vught, F. A van, M. C. van der Wende, and D. F. Westerheijden. 2002. "Globalisation and Internationalisation. Policy Agendas Compared," in *Higher Education in a Globalizing World. International Trends and Mutual Observations*, ed. J. Enders and O. Fulton. Kluwer, Dordrecht, 103–21.

Vught, F. A. van, J. Bartelse, D. Bohmert, N. Burquel, J. Divis, J. Huisman, and M. C. van der Wende. 2005. *Institutional Profiles. Towards a Typology of Higher Education Institutions in Europe*. Report to the European Commission, <http://www.utwente.nl/cheps/documenten/engreport05institutional profiles. pdf>.

Van Vught, F. A., J. Bartelse, D. Bohmert, J. File, C. Gaethgens, S. Hansen, F. Kaiser, R. Peter, S. Reichert, P. West, M. C. van der Wende (forthcoming). "Mapping Diversity: Developing a Classification of European Higher Education Institutions." Report to the European Commission.

Wende, M. C. van der. 2007. "Internationalisation of Higher Education in the O.E.C.D Countries: Challenges and Opportunities for the Coming Decade." *Journal on Studies in International Education,* vol. 11, no. 3–4: 274–90.

Winckler, Georg. 2006. "The Contribution of Universities to Europe's Competitiveness." Vienna: Conference of the European Ministers of Education.

Witte, J. 2006. Change of Degrees and Degrees of Change. *Comparing Adaptations of European Higher Education Systems in the Context of the Bologna Process.* CHEPS/UT: Dissertation.

Chapter 18

Recreating the Elite Research Universities in Germany: Policy Transfer Then and Now

Daniel Fallon[1]

From Germany to America

A book is a vector of knowledge transmission that often provokes unforeseeable consequences. At the beginning of the 19th century, such a surprise forged an unlikely link from a liberated European intellectual, Madame de Staël, to a strait-laced American prodigy, George Ticknor. This connection, it seems, blazed the trail toward the creation of the American research university. Madame de Staël was already a cultural icon when she left France for Germany in October 1803, her heart heavy with anxiety and sorrow. Her essays on the revolution, published in pamphlet form, and her stunning novel, *Delphine*, which praised the ideal of the free and independent woman, had won her an enthusiastic audience. Not among her admirers was the emperor Napoleon, who ordered her exile to diminish the threat he felt from her ideas and her persona.

The several years Madame de Staël spent in the German states gave her extended access to artists and intellectuals and consequently through the lens of their fervor, insight into the German enlightenment. Convinced that the world beyond Germany needed to know more about German ideas, she undertook to

---

[1] Carnegie Corporation of New York.

write about them. *D'Allemagne* was first published in 1810, but Napoleon ensured that all 10,000 copies were destroyed before they left the publishing house, so the functional publication date was postponed until after the restoration, in 1813.

Although *D'Allemagne* is justly famous in its own right, I support a further argument for its historic impact on our contemporary world of higher education. George Ticknor, a gifted young student in the distant, rough, and newly formed American Republic read Madame de Staël's new book with unabated excitement. Having graduated from Dartmouth at the age of 15, Ticknor had continued his studies independently in Boston, decided to read for the bar, was admitted at the age of 21, but quickly tired of practicing law. His active intellect thirsted for a greater challenge. In the early years of the United States, there was little prospect of advanced study of any kind. If a talented scholar was interested in science, the study of literatures in the modern languages of Europe, or advanced philosophy, study in Europe was the only option. But where?

The seemingly natural target, England, was inhospitable because of mutual animosity. For example, as Ticknor was trying to decide where to continue his study, the British were in the act of burning down the public buildings of the city of Washington, District of Columbia, in the frustrating final years of the War of 1812. France was similarly out of bounds since the aftershocks of the revolution were still trembling, education from grammar school through university was in various stages of confusing rearrangement, and many prominent intellectuals were either in exile or had lost their lives. Therefore, Madame de Staël's inspiring book, *D'Allemagne*, with its unstinting praise of German intellectual progress, became a beacon for the precocious American.

Ticknor wrote to de Staël for advice and made arrangements to embark for Germany via England and France. In the meantime, he befriended another gifted young intellectual in Boston, Edward Everett, who was also eager for German scholarship. Everett had graduated as valedictorian of Harvard College at the age of 17, continued the study of theology, and was ordained pastor of the Brattle Street Unitarian Church less than three years later. Thus in April of 1815, George Ticknor, then 23 years old, and Edward Everett, about to turn 21, set sail from Boston for Liverpool. After fruitful travel through England, with visits to centers of thought and culture, and France, where Ticknor was invited to dinner with the then dying Madame de Staël, the two studious Americans settled in for serious academic work at the University of Göttingen.

Ticknor did not take a degree, but his study of classical literature started him on a journey of discovery that led him through multiple nations in Europe during which he received notice that Harvard was offering him a chair in French and Spanish languages and *belle lettres*. Everett stayed in Göttingen and received a Ph.D. degree there in 1817, the first such degree awarded to an American, and returned to Harvard to assume a professorship in Greek literature, joining Ticknor on the faculty. Both men experienced long lives and careers, achieving fame later in the century: Ticknor with publication of a monumentally important contribution to scholarship, the three-volume *History of Spanish Litera-*

ture (1849), and Edward Everett as a great orator, perhaps best known for his two-hour address at the dedication of the Soldiers' National Cemetery at Gettysburg, Pennsylvania, on September 23, 1863, where he was outshone by President Abraham Lincoln's two-minute remarks.

Although Ticknor and Everett were far ahead of their time and thus unable in their years at Harvard to transform it, both sought to institutionalize the enlightenment reforms that characterized the newly modern German university. That stunning achievement had been realized by the founding of the Friedrich Wilhelm University of Berlin in 1810 by Wilhelm von Humboldt. The revolutionary principles that infused the University of Berlin quickly spread throughout German-speaking Europe, beginning in the universities of the North, where Göttingen was an outstanding example. Northern Germany possessed another advantage for the pious young Americans. Unlike the largely Catholic South, universities in the North did not require an oath of allegiance to the Church as a prerequisite for matriculation.

Following Ticknor and Everett in the nineteenth century, a trickle and then a flood of American scholars studied at northern German universities, primarily at Berlin, Göttingen, and Leipzig. They brought back to the United States the reformist ideals of the German enlightenment that Humboldt sought to promote. For the Americans, these clustered around three essential ideas:

- Academic freedom, the freedom to teach (professors should design their own courses), and the freedom to learn (students should freely elect the courses they would take);

- The unity of teaching and research (professors should create new knowledge at the frontier of the discipline and should both be led to the frontier and make it comprehensible through their teaching);

- The centrality of the Faculties of Arts and Sciences to the modern university (the ancient study of philosophy being the root of all learning, now branching out to create new areas of specialized study).

The ideas at the center of a highly idealized generic concept described by American intellectuals as simply "the German university" ultimately became the driving force in the latter nineteenth century for the creation of what we know today as the American research university.

William S. Eliot, who assumed the presidency of Harvard in 1869 after a brief sojourn in Germany, was determined to remake Harvard in the image of the German enlightenment ideals and succeeded in astonishing measure, primarily by championing free electives and the seminar method of instruction in disciplinary departments, before his retirement from the presidency 40 years later in 1909. The Johns Hopkins University intended on its founding in 1876 to be the first truly German university on American soil. Of the 53 members of the faculty appointed during its first seven years, virtually all had studied in Germany, and 13 had received Ph.D. degrees from German universities. The first president of Clark University, G. Stanley Hall, spoke for an era when he wrote in 1891:

The German University is today the freest spot on earth. . . . Never was such burning and curiosity. . . . Shallow, bad ideas have died and truth has always attained power. . . . Nowhere has the passion to push on to the frontier of human knowledge been so general. Never have so many men stood so close to nature and history or striven with such reverence to think God's thoughts after Him exactly.

By the early twentieth century, the American research university was firmly established. American scholars no longer needed to study abroad, even though the prominence of German scholarly accomplishment continued to confer benefits on those American academics who studied in Germany. Relative comparisons between the two nations became meaningless during the rise of the Nazi dictatorship and the ensuing Second World War.

The Trouble with Equity over Quality

After the war, the western occupying powers were determined as part of the program of denazification to "democratize" universities in Germany. A commission was convened, headed by American officers, and composed in part of German professors who had been in exile during the war or were known to be part of the resistance movement against the Nazis. Among the ideas proposed were boards of trustees, endowments, admissions offices, and similar features that were utterly foreign to the German tradition. When the Russians blockaded Berlin in 1948, however, the attention of the western Allies was diverted to the new "Cold War," especially the necessity of establishing a common currency and banking system in the western zones of occupation, and cobbling together a federal form of government. University reform fell off the table. What little attention was left was devoted primarily to ensuring that, in a federal system, principal responsibility for universities would be vested in the German states rather than in the central government.

Left to do business on their own, the academics within universities, and the civil servants responsible for them, rebuilt the universities along traditional lines, resembling the German universities of the late nineteenth century. The noble function of the university in German life functioned reasonably well throughout the rebuilding years of the 1950s, as scholars in many disciplines began producing work of high quality, university students were well prepared for their civil service examinations, and advanced students proceeded toward a doctorate. The elegantly reconstructed university, however, had in an earlier day been designed for an aristocracy consisting of about four percent of the cohort of 19 year olds, who were overwhelmingly male, upper class, and politically conservative. In the mid-1960s, twentieth century reality upended this nineteenth-century universe. A new generation of German baby boomers, politically diverse, including women and working-class students, began to arrive in large numbers.

Changing conditions everywhere in the western world led to rising expectations for change and were accompanied in Germany by the first significant peaceful transfer of power under a democratic constitution in the nation's history, to a socialist government headed by Willy Brandt. Untenured junior academics demanded a share of academic authority; students demanded curricular modernization. A conservative reaction by some threatened senior professors was inevitable, and was supported by alarmed politicians and by a civil service bureaucracy comfortable with the status quo. Although reform ideas were widespread, the German university, embedded within a diffuse state government that distributed responsibility for making decisions throughout its many parts, was unable to adapt with the agility that the times demanded.

Increasing dissatisfaction among government policymakers with the lack of clarity about boundary conditions for reform led in January 1976 to a nationwide federal "framework law" for universities. Although the law was conceived as a means of facilitating reform, in the end it served primarily to inhibit innovation and add an additional layer of constraint. The instruments of state regulation found themselves choked with too many students, too few teaching faculty, and a curriculum and examination structure poorly matched to the requirements of a modernizing economy. Finally, postsecondary education in Germany was dominated, as it had been in the past, by basically one institution to serve all purposes: a comprehensive doctoral-granting university charged with full teaching and research functions. There was only modest differentiation of mission among institutions of higher learning.

And thus the tables turned. By the late 1980s it was clear that enrollment by foreign students in German universities had decreased dramatically in both quantity and quality. Worse still, the most able and promising of German youth were increasingly looking toward other nations for high quality postsecondary education, and the United States was considered the prime destination. Although many factors contributed to the sluggishness of the German university, the most obvious was the tenacity of adherence to the idea that a German university must be the same wherever it was located, offering essentially the same full range of study, by faculty who were treated essentially the same everywhere. Throughout the nation, salaries were regulated within narrow ranges for a full professor no matter where that person taught, and the same was true for all of the academic positions. Although some universities were small and could offer limited curricular opportunity, they were treated the same as if they were large and could offer the full spectrum. Furthermore, if some universities managed to assemble academic talent to produce excellence in a given field, they were offered no advantages over others that appeared mediocre. German academics and policymakers increasingly looked to United States higher education as an exemplary model, and aspired to produce similar conditions in Germany.

Investing in the Research University

As advanced economies worldwide began to shift from an industrial mode of wealth production to a knowledge- and information-based economy, a consensus developed within Germany that the university structure needed dramatic change. Professors proposed reform ideas, but could not bring themselves to champion a differentiation of mission and purpose among universities. The European Union adopted rules for higher education among the participating nation states of the E.U., which led to the introduction of bachelor's degrees and master's degrees, and the prospect of awarding academic credit for coursework to facilitate the orderly and meaningful transfer of students among institutions. These innovations, which would have been regarded as dangerously radical as recently as the 1970s, were adopted with alacrity throughout Germany in the 1990s. Still, more than 100 institutions responsible for educating more than 80 percent of the nation's postsecondary students, regarded themselves as universities fully equal in privilege and status to any other. Differentiation among these universities was a reform idea that could not be introduced without threatening the status of both universities and professors and was, therefore, off the table.

Finally, on January 27, 2004, the federal minister for higher education and research in the socialist government of Gerhard Schroeder electrified the academic community with a speech in which she declared that the university system as it existed was intolerable. For the sake of the nation's future, Minister Edelgard Bulmahn declared, the government needed to invest heavily in higher education, and specifically in finding a way to elevate a small number of universities to elite status, capable of competing with the best universities in the world. She proposed that the government select six universities to be Germany's top institutions of higher learning, and provide just those with exceptional supplemental funds. The Christian Democratic Party was delighted, since differentiation of mission among universities was an idea they found compatible with their political values. The two leading political parties, in an unusual alliance, began building strong momentum for radical change. The state ministers of education (*Kultusministerkonferenz*) pointed out, however, that the constitution made university education a state rather than a federal responsibility. They did not want to stop the reform. Rather, they wanted some control over the shape of it. The voices of the professoriate insisted upon being heard and were expressed through their representatives in the German Research Society (*die deutsche Forschungsgemeinschaft*) and the Science Council (*der Wissenschaftsrat*). Hard and earnest negotiations then ensued among all of these parties.

By June 2005, a consensus had been reached that permitted passage of a bill by the federal parliament (*der Bundestag*) and each of the individual state governments (*die Landtage*) that appropriated 1.9 billion Euros (about $2.6 billion) for a process called the "Excellence Initiative" (*Exzellenzinitiative*). Under the terms of the agreement, the funding was divided between federal and state budgets, and all universities were given an opportunity to participate in activities that hold the promise of improvement, even though only a small number could be formally designated as "elite," with substantial supplemental budget allocations. Three concurrent competitions were designed to strengthen research and doctoral education broadly, while also permitting the selection of an elite group for special attention.

- Universities were to compete for extra funding by proposing a winning idea for a "graduate school," conceived as a new and better way of preparing doctoral students. The government would provide about one million Euros per year for five years in extra funds, and about 40 awards were expected in this category.

- Similarly, a competitive process was to govern selection of proposals for "excellence clusters," in which universities arrange to combine a small number of their very best academic departments in innovative ways to promote high-quality interdisciplinary research and teaching. The government would provide about 6.5 million Euros per year for five years in extra funds, and about 30 awards were expected in this category.

- Finally, universities could participate in a special competition with proposals for a "futures concept" that described an institutional strategy for achieving world-class status within 5–10 years. To qualify for funding under the futures concept, an institution would have to enter the other competitions and win at least one graduate school and one excellence cluster. The government would provide about 13 million Euros per year for five years in extra funds, and no more than 10 awards were expected in this category. Since these universities would also have funding for graduate schools and excellence clusters, their total extra funding would be at least 20 million Euros per year for five years. These universities, expected to number no more than 10, would be considered the elite universities on which the German nation would be making its big bet.

The competition guidelines explicitly encouraged all proposals to include partners in business and industry, to stress interdisciplinary research and teaching, to focus on creating a positive impact on academic fields in the future, and to include plans for turning research results into practical applications. They were required to demonstrate participation by established excellent scholars and scientists, provide career development opportunities for junior faculty, create new ways of preparing junior faculty to do research, and encourage the participation of women. Finally, unconventional ideas were given priority, and assurances were sought for effective leadership and efficient management.

The German Research Society was given responsibility for managing the competition for graduate schools and excellence clusters. The Science Council managed the competition for futures concepts. Because each competition was measured against international academic standards, and top scholars from nations around the world were invited to serve as external evaluators, all proposals in all categories had to be written in English. In some cases, a German version was also submitted for informational purposes, but the evaluated proposal was in English. To manage cash flow, the appropriated funds were distributed in two successive rounds separated by two years, so that about half of the awards were made in the first year of the competition and the remainder in the second.

An intricate process coordinated the complex matrix of decisions. A Discipline Committee (*Fachkommission*) of fourteen renowned scholars, some from Germany but many from other countries, recommended awards in the competition for graduate schools and for excellence clusters. The committee commissioned external reviewers from institutions around the world to assist in the process. A Strategy Committee (*Strategiekommission*) of 12 equally renowned scholars recommended awards in the competition for futures concepts. Strategy committee members were responsible for leading site visit teams to each of the universities selected as finalists for awards, and the members of the visiting teams came from distinguished universities worldwide. These two committees then combined to form a Common Committee (*die gemeinsame Kommission*) of 26 people that negotiated differences in marginal cases, ensured that prerequisites were met, and arrived at a final recommendation for all categories.

After the Common Committee completed its deliberations, the politicians were invited to become participants in a process designed to yield 16 votes for the federal education officials and 16 votes for the state education officials (one vote for each of the 16 states of the federal republic). The Common Committee joined with the political representatives to form the Awards Committee (*Bewilligungsausschuss*) and in this setting the Discipline Committee was allocated 21 votes and the Strategy Committee 18. The Awards Committee was designed to ensure explicitly that the academic participants, with a total of 39 votes, would have a majority over the political participants, with a total of 32 votes.

The process to carry out the German excellence initiative began in fall 2005, the first round winners were announced in fall 2006, and the final round concluded in fall 2007. I was privileged to sit as a member of the Strategy Committee. An overview of the scope of the initiative is shown in Tables 18.1, 18.2 and 18.3. In the first round, only three universities survived all phases of the evaluation for elite status: the University of Munich, the Technical University of Munich, and Karlsruhe University. Karlsruhe is a special case, in that its success depended upon the merger of the university with an independent federal government research laboratory, the Gustav Helmholtz Institute that is located in Karlsruhe. Such an arrangement is highly promising but without precedent. It required difficult negotiations and a number of specific approvals. If the union of these two entities had not in the end been achieved, then funding for elite status for Karlsruhe would have been withdrawn.

Deliberations within the Strategy Committee were meticulous, serious, and driven entirely by judgments of academic excellence. The completed first round serves as an example. Two committee members were assigned to prepare independent evaluative summaries of each of the 27 preliminary proposals, using a standard format requiring answers to questions framed to encompass the published criteria for selection. At the first of two day-long meetings of the full committee, each proposal was discussed in depth and the committee arrived at a preliminary assessment.

Table 18.1. Germany's Excellence Initiative Outcome, Round 1 (Fall 2006)

Competition	Graduate Schools	Excellence Clusters	Futures Concepts
Number to be selected	~ 20	~ 15	~ 5
Preliminary proposals received	135	157	27
Finalists (Full proposal requested)	39	39	10
Winners	17	18	3

Table 18.2. Germany's Excellence Initiative: Outcome of Round 2 (Winners announced Fall 2007)

Competition	Graduate Schools	Excellence Clusters	Futures Concepts
Estimated number of winners	~ 20	~ 15	~ 5
New preliminary proposals	118	123	20
Round I proposals carried forward	+ 21	+ 22	+ 7
Total Round 2 Proposals Evaluated	139	145	27
Finalists Selected (Full proposal requested)	44	40	8
Winners	21	20	6

Table18.3. Germany's Excellence Initiative: Final Outcome, Both Rounds (October 2007)

Competition	Graduate Schools	Excellence Clusters	Futures Concepts
Estimated number of winners	~ 40	~ 30	~ 10
Preliminary proposals	253	280	47
Finalists Selected (Full proposal requested)	83	81	18
Winners	39	37	9

Proposals were determined either likely to be successful, not likely to be competitive, or needing further discussion. At the second meeting, the committee considered additional analyses of the strength of the proposals and arrived without difficulty at a preliminary selection of 8–12 likely finalists. A third meeting took place in conjunction with the Discipline Committee, which allowed the Strategy Committee to learn which universities were likely to succeed in qualifying for selection by virtue of having at least one proposal for a graduate school and one proposal for an excellence cluster accepted for finalist status. The selection of 10 finalists for the futures concept competition was then straightforward, reflecting strong consensus.

When the committee arrived at its selection of 10 finalists for the first round, we realized that the list was politically sensitive and would be uncomfortable for many. Most of the finalists, 6 of 10, were from two states in southern Germany known to be bastions of conservative academic policy. There were no universities selected from the heavily populated industrial regions of the North, which had a history of socialist political control. One university, Bremen, was a small institution of limited breadth that had a highly publicized reputation during the 1970s as a hotbed of radical politics; its transformation since that time by a generation of serious new academics had gone largely unnoticed by the public. No universities from the former German Democratic Republic survived the evaluation. The committee reviewed its work carefully and discussed the outcome earnestly. We concluded comfortably and without dissent that our charge was to select the best proposals on criteria of academic excellence alone. If the outcome caused political difficulties, then it would have to be the responsibility of a subsequent public political process to seek a solution.

The finalists selected in January 2006 were given three months to prepare full final proposals. Guidelines and expectations were explicit. In the case of proposals for futures concepts, each proposal, in English, was to be no longer than 25 type-written pages, not including budget requests, for which additional clear instructions were provided. Unprecedented for a German academic proposal, 20 percent of the budget was reserved for indirect costs, a concept borrowed directly from U.S. experience. Certain clarifying appendices were allowed.

Beginning about six weeks after submission of the full proposals, site visits were conducted at each of the 10 universities. The chair and vice chair of each visiting team were members of the Strategy Commission. I served as vice chair of the team visiting Freiburg University, and as chair of the team visiting the Free University of Berlin. Each team was made up of an impressive group of scholars. For example, the team that I chaired included an Arabist from Yale, an American historian from Yale, a mathematician from Oxford, a dean from Indiana University, a prize-winning young scientist from Göttingen, a former university chancellor from Switzerland, and two directors of independent research laboratories in Germany.

The site visit encompassed two full days and was conducted largely in English. Occasionally, there were times when some of the local participants were unable to express themselves clearly in English, and in those instances German was permitted. A simultaneous translator was provided for visiting team members who did not understand German. The host institution made presentations and selected local participants. Each of the 10 visits followed an identical format as closely as possible. Although the institution might try to provide additional printed material, it could not be considered in the formal evaluation.

At the conclusion of the visit, the visiting team gathered alone for a session of three to five hours to agree upon a common evaluative judgment and framework. Each of the 10 visiting teams was required to complete together a single common questionnaire conforming to the criteria for selection, with identical questions for all sites. A team of analysts from the Science Council accompanied each visit and took copious notes. A representative of the German Research Council attended each site visit as an observer, including the confidential sessions of the visiting team.

Following the site visits, the analytical staff from the Science Council, in consultation with the chair and vice chair of the visiting team, prepared a comprehensive descriptive and evaluative summary of the proposal, informed by the site visit. This summary was then shared with each member of the visiting team in a collective editing process that ended with a document upon which all could agree. The Strategy Committee then had three artifacts to assist its deliberations for final selection: (1) the institution's written proposal; (2) the common evaluative questionnaire completed by the visiting team while on site; and (3) the comprehensive descriptive and evaluative summary approved by the chair, vice chair, and visiting team. The Strategy Committee met at the end of the summer for one full day for a preliminary review of all 10 proposals, and then again for another full day in conjunction with the Discipline Committee. Some proposals for futures concepts that might have been approved had to be set aside at that point because the institutions did not succeed in winning support for either a graduate school or an excellence cluster.

The final meeting of the Common Committee to agree on recommendations in all categories was scheduled for a full day, and lasted well into the evening. A festive dinner, originally scheduled for 6:00 pm, was postponed because of ongoing deliberations and did not begin until 10:00 pm. The meeting of the Awards Committee on the following day occasioned moments of high drama. The political participants had anticipated some leeway for their input, at least with respect to marginal or boundary cases. The Common Committee had been so thorough, however, that the representatives from the political sector felt closed out, presented with a *fait accompli*. After delivering several high-minded speeches, the political delegation walked out of the meeting to caucus separately. A tense 90 minutes later, the group returned, led by the Minister for Higher Education and Research of the Grand Coalition federal government, the Christian Democrat Annette Schavan, who announced that the government representatives had agreed unanimously to support the recommendations of the Common Committee, without comment. On the afternoon of October 13, 2006, the results of round one of the Excellence Initiative were announced to an eager audience at a well-attended press conference.

The second round of the competition proceeded in the same way as the first round, with minor modifications. For example, promising proposals from finalists in the first round were permitted to continue as finalists in the second round, with modifications based upon comments received during the first round. To avoid discomfort among the political participants, a process was established that permitted the politicians to receive a preliminary report of the Common Committee's recommendations the evening before the scheduled meeting of the Awards Committee.

Because the 17 universities that were not selected as finalists in the first round of the Futures Concepts competition were allowed to submit wholly new proposals in the second round, the total number of applications overstates the actual number of universities that participated. In fact, in the end, 32 universities competed in the "Futures Concepts" competition, and a total of nine were selected. Joining the three selected in the first round were the Technical University of Aachen, Free University of Berlin, University of Freiburg, University of Göttingen, University of Heidelberg, and the University of Konstanz. Similarly, a university was not restricted in the number of proposals it could submit for graduate schools or excellence clusters. Thus, the number of proposals submitted in these competitions overstates the number of individual universities that participated. At the end of the competition, from among 110 institutions recognized as universities in Germany, 70 participated in at least one of the competitions, and 37 universities were among the winners of at least one award.

Germany's Excellence Initiative has dominated national news for more than a year now. There has been, of course, considerable criticism of the methods and the selection process, but on the whole the initiative has been very well received. There is strong political consensus to continue the effort in some form at the conclusion of this first five year investment. The 16 states of the Federal Republic of Germany understand the importance of the initiative for their local constituents. The Federal Government, including both major political parties, appears strongly committed to a reorientation of the nation's higher education sector to make it more competitive in a new global economy in which the production of intellectual capital must have priority.

I strongly support the Excellence Initiative in Germany, even though the priorities for change I would have championed would have gone much further. The fundamental difficulties for German university academic policy are exceptionally difficult to address because they are embedded in reliance on state civil service agencies. For example, universities at present have virtually no authority to set standards for admission or to select their own students. The federal constitution, honoring two centuries of tradition, states that every graduate of a German academic high school (*das Gymnasium*) who passes the school-leaving examination (*das Abitur*) has a constitutional right to study at a German university.

To manage overcrowding at some universities, and in certain oversubscribed disciplines, the government higher education framework law created a central office for student placement, known by its initials, ZVS (*die Zentralstelle für die Vergabe von Studienplätzen*), which is now responsible for finding study opportunities for about one-third of all German students. The state governments also regulate conditions within their boundaries governing which students can go where. The constitutional right to student matriculation extends to all degree levels, including graduate study. In my view, it is essential, if Germany is to develop strong world class universities, that the authority to develop admission standards and admit students devolve in significant measure to the universities themselves.

Strong governmental regulation, although the prerogative of the German states rather than the central government, has nonetheless moved all universities toward common standards of financing and operation. For example, there is a near universal expectation throughout all 16 of the German states that each professor will be responsible for the equivalent of four courses to be taught each semester. Although some relief from such high teaching responsibilities may be negotiated in special cases, no German university today can come close to the lower median annual teaching assignments at leading U.S. research universities. It is difficult to compare student/faculty ratios between the U.S. and Germany because, unlike the Full-Time-Equivalent faculty calculation in the U.S., it is unclear in Germany exactly who is to be counted on the faculty side of the equation or how they are to be counted. Nonetheless, it seems clear that student/faculty ratios are unreasonably high in Germany, especially in comparison with leading U.S. research universities. Salaries for university faculty are also tightly regulated within a fairly narrow band throughout the Federal Republic of Germany, permitting little discrepancy between faculty salaries at any one university compared to another, in stark contrast to the U.S., where market prices determine sharply higher salaries for faculty at leading research universities.

The university system in Germany is structurally underfinanced. According to the most recent analysis of the Office for Economic Cooperation and Development

(OECD), obtained from budgets for 2005, Germany spent 1.1 percent of its Gross Domestic Product on higher education, compared to 2.9 percent spent in the United States, and to an average figure for all European Union nations of 1.3 percent. It is difficult to see how German universities, no matter how radically reformed, can build toward competition with the best in the world without greater investment, and a strong commitment to focusing resources on just a few universities. The United Kingdom attempts to keep no more than three universities in the elite class (Cambridge, London, and Oxford) and Switzerland only one (The University of Zürich). It would seem in the end that Germany could actually afford, at the most, no more than five. Yet for many political and cultural reasons, the pressure in Germany will be to widen the circle of participants proclaiming "elite" status rather than narrow it. Both of these issues, the matter of general finance and the need for focus, are being earnestly discussed in considerations for how to structure another round of the Excellence Initiative.

Looking at Germany through American eyes, it seems to me that the effort to create "elite" institutions capable of competing on the world stage with excellent research universities anywhere will require considerably more than the current Excellence Initiative offers. The initiative may well founder on the rocks of financial challenge, a civil service bureaucracy intent on managing essential university functions, and a general inability to allocate authority and resources to the institutions themselves to manage their affairs in accord with what society expects of them. This culturally bound perception, however, may well be flawed and thus excessively pessimistic.

One impressive lesson I have learned by participation in this bold national experiment is a heartening surprise—one shared, I believe, by the many foreign participants invited to assist the enterprise. It is not that the "German university," as a collective concept, lags behind universities elsewhere, but rather that, despite what appear to be formidable handicaps, it is so extraordinarily good. A seriousness of purpose pervades the commitment that academic scholars have made to their profession. Although the barriers to producing high quality scholarship are high, there are many important scholars intent on overcoming them. They are working to create the conditions, as one said to me, of supporting "genuine research in place of intelligent conversation." Virtually all of the German scholars I have encountered are industrious, efficient, focused on their academic goals, and well aware of the proud traditions and accomplishments that comprise the legacy of the storied history of their academic institutions. They are prepared to work themselves through difficult conflicts of values and obstacles of clumsy state policy. They fully intend to measure themselves against the contributions of the best moments of the great European universities of which they are but the present manifestation.

I strongly support the Excellence Initiative because it is an act of national courage at a time when a progressive orientation toward the future is necessary in the national policies of advanced economies. The initiative has challenged stultifying myths about higher education in Germany and through this act of will put all of the old assumptions on the agenda for examination. From this moment forward, the university will not be the same; everything is in motion. No one can claim any longer that all universities are fundamentally the same comprehensive institution. Differentiation of mission has arrived in the university sector of Germany, and it is surely only the vanguard of a modernized university.

Razor-sharp analytical thinking about the needs of the present and the future shaped the Excellence Initiative. The parties who designed this adventure reasoned that the future of productive research in a knowledge-based economy was going to be interdisciplinary; that it would productively engage partners in the local and national economy; that it must encourage the youth of the nation to pursue academic work and provide smooth trajectories for them to advance within the academy; that it must explicitly support and develop women scholars in all areas; that it must pursue bold creative ideas; and that it must find new and efficient means to manage this work. These goals were at the heart of all three competitions and the evaluating committees aggressively pursued them at all stages. The future speaks through this process.

We saw the tables turned in the latter twentieth century, as the American research university became the ideal pursued by German reformers, just as the German research university had once been the ideal pursued by American reformers. The Excellence Initiative does not intend to turn the tables once again, but rather to permit German academic scholarship to be measured against the best in the world, and to encourage German scholars to participate actively on the world stage in the production of new knowledge. What motivated Minister Bulmahn and her fellow citizens in the Federal Republic of Germany was recognition of fundamental changes in the underlying political economy of those advanced nations that have crossed the threshold toward a new economy based on knowledge and information in a globalized world. We can see similar activity in the United Kingdom, in Australia and New Zealand, in Japan and Singapore, and elsewhere in developed countries.

In the U.S., the changing economic realities are reflected at the elementary and secondary level by such initiatives as the "No Child Left Behind" legislation, and at the postsecondary level by U.S. Secretary of Education Margaret Spellings' Commission on the Future of Higher Education. The danger in the U.S. is that American postsecondary institutions, well aware of their vaunted leadership, face the future with complacent tinkering rather than with the need for imaginative energy that the times demand. The U.S. is already losing market share among foreign students, and not only because of new visa requirements occasioned by the terrorist attack of September 11, 2001. Perhaps the first nation to reach a point where more than 50 percent of all adults had participated in some form of higher education, the U.S. has now been overtaken by many other nations in the proportion of educated adults. The production of baccalaureate degrees in the U.S. is for the first time now falling behind other advanced nations. Statistics compiled by the OECD show the U.S. still ranks highest, at 35 percent, among advanced nations in the proportion of the population holding baccalaureate degrees among adults between the ages of 55 to 64, but the U.S. has sunk to eighth in the world among adults between the ages of 25 and 34. The U.S. stands at 37 percent on this measure, compared to more than 50 percent by both Canada and Japan.

Somewhere today in a developing country, perhaps in Africa or the Middle East, there is a precocious 21st century scholar, the equivalent of George Ticknor or Edward Everett. Seeking to quench a thirst for knowledge, the aspiring student is trying to determine where best to seek the future. Perhaps those youthful eyes will fall upon a book, essay, or Internet article describing Germany's Excellence Initiative and thus sense how universities everywhere in the advanced economies of the world are forging ahead to try to meet a challenging future. If the current bold experiment in Germany succeeds, that student may well choose a university in Germany.

Chapter 19

Governing European Higher Education

Jeroen Huisman[1]

The institutional governance arrangements within higher education institutions in Europe have changed considerably in the past decade and many authors have documented these changes (see e.g., Amaral, Jones, and Karseth 2002b; Begg 2001; Braun and Merrien 1999 for comparative studies on governance). At the minor risk of oversimplifying these developments, the main changes can be captured under three headings.

- Governments have stepped back and granted more institutional autonomy— be it legal or more informal—to higher education institutions. Whereas signs of increasing autonomy are ubiquitous, various studies have made it clear that "stepping" back is not necessarily a zero-sum game, and that increased autonomy often comes with strings attached (see e.g., Maassen and Van Vught 1988 for a critical analysis of steering in the Netherlands). Steering from a distance has often been accompanied, for better or worse, by government measures that "compensate" their loss of control over higher education institutions (see also Neave 1988; Neave 1998 on the shift from *ex ante* to *ex post* state control).
- Related to the first development, higher education institutions are obviously in a more competitive, global environment, which has prompted both gov-

---

[1] International Center for Higher Education Management, University of Bath.

ernments and higher education institutions themselves to reconsider governance arrangements, particularly in terms of strengthening the "steering core" (Clark 1998) of the institution.

- New Public Management ideas (Hood 1991; Pollitt and Bouckaert 2000) have infused the debate on governance arrangements, raising issues regarding the performance of public institutions, and regarding the accountability and transparency of governance arrangements in higher education institutions.

Again with the risk of painting with broad strokes, the general answer prompted by national governments in Europe was to (a) strengthen institutional leadership at the top level of higher education institutions, sometimes at the cost of the role and power of senates; (b) stress or reiterate the requirements regarding institutional accountability; and (c) increase the role of outsiders in strategy and policymaking (see also Amaral and Magelhaes 2002). What we are particularly interested in is the emergence of new bodies (*Raad van Toezicht*—the Netherlands, *Kuratoorium*—Estonia, *Universitätsrat*—Austria, *Bestyrelsen*—Denmark) and their roles and changes in the roles of existing bodies (such as councils in the U.K.).

This chapter describes a number of actual changes in governance arrangements across Europe, focusing on the role of governing bodies, why these changes came about, and comparing developments in the U.S. and Europe in order to address lessons to be learned.

European Models: Hungary, Estonia, Austria, U.K. and the Netherlands

To start with a possibly less obvious example, in Hungary, advisory lay boards at the institutional level have been introduced in the second half of the 1990s to play a kind of buffer function between governments and universities, and to link Hungarian universities to their (regional) communities, particularly in business and industry (Morgan and Bergerson 2000). The *1996 Higher Education Law* stipulated that supervisory boards, with representatives from outside the university and one member being a representative of the state, were to "supervise, judge, and evaluate the economic management of the institution and make proposals to improve it" (Morgan and Bergerson 2000, 439). An amendment to the regulations in 1999 changed some of the functions and workings of the board: they were renamed advisory councils, they were made optional, and the regulations indicate that some of the representatives should have recognized expertise in economic, financial, or scientific public life. The latter change was introduced to meet the criticism that lay board members would not be able to understand university matters sufficiently.

In Estonia, advisory boards of governors (kuratoorium) have been introduced to support institutional decision-making in the beginning of the 1990s.

Their main role is to provide a better link between the (public) university and society. Apart from a counseling role for the university, the kuratoorium may make proposals to the Minister of Education and Research, and the kuratoorium must present its assessment of the university to the public once a year. A recent evaluation of tertiary education in Estonia addressed the functioning of the kuratoorium and concluded that these boards do not live up to expectation (Huisman, Santiago, Högselius, Lemaitre, and Thorn 2007).

In Austria, a new law for higher education was introduced in 2002 (Universitäts-gesetz). It entailed a rigorous break with the previous regulations regarding university governance, rooted in Humboldtian traditions. Universities were granted full autonomy, its employees no longer were civil servants, and the university could decide upon its own organizational structures (Lanzendorf 2004; Meister-Scheytt and Laske 2005). The new regulations also implied more power for the executive (Rektor or Rektorat), who could now nominate the deans and heads of departments, allocate budgets, and propose the university's strategy. Finally, a board of governors (Universitätsrat) was introduced. Its main task is to contribute to the attainment of the objectives and the fulfillment of the duties of the university. Its responsibilities include selecting the Rektor from a shortlist drafted by the Senat, concluding the working contract with the Rektor, approving the university development plan and the three-year contract between Rektor and Ministry, approving the obligatory (mostly financial) reports of the Rektor to the responsible minister, and reporting to the minister in the event of serious breaches of the law by the universities or the danger of serious financial loss. Depending on the size of the university, boards consist of five, seven, or nine members. Two, three, or four of the members, respectively, are nominated by the Senat; two, three, or four members, respectively, are nominated by the federal minister. The remaining member is appointed by the other governors. The regulations require that members of the board should be past or present holders of responsible positions in academe (but not from the same university), culture, or business, and should have exceptional knowledge and experience.

Having shortly described three less obvious cases, we cannot escape addressing the usual suspects. In the U.K., governing bodies are part and parcel of governance arrangements and these arrangements have been rather stable throughout the last decade. Some changes in governance structures took place in the aftermath of the Dearing Report (National Committee of Inquiry into Higher Education 1997), but it has to be acknowledged that given the diversity in arrangements across the system, (Ackroyd and Ackroyd 1999; Shattock 1999) there is not a general pattern of change.

The Dearing Report argued that governance structures needed to be updated. A major issue was the need for greater control of governing bodies and stronger roles for external stakeholders in governance, although critical analyses doubt whether there really was such a need (see e.g., Shattock 1998). Furthermore, the report argued for a move to smaller councils, to frequent reviews of the body itself and its (and the institution's) effectiveness (actually enforcing compliance and threatening the withdrawal of funds), more openness in terms of the outcomes of these reviews (annual reports), and the development of a governance code of practice. The recommendations of the Dearing Report itself have been received critically, but the Committee of University Chairmen (CUC) took up the invitation, not wholeheartedly, but to some extent stimulated by a number of governance scandals at universities and colleges, and produced Guides on Governance in the late 1990s. The codes particularly addressed general principles of governance. The Lambert Review (2003), addressing university-business cooperation, reinforced the debate and argued for more corporate-type structures, including a more profound role for governing boards (instead of senates), and more lay involvement in these boards. The latest version of the Governance Code of the CUC (2004) was adopted in light of these recommendations.

The Dutch case is another usual suspect, the Netherlands being a frontrunner in Europe when it comes to changing steering and governance practices in higher education. Part of the roots for change in the Netherlands can be found almost two decades ago (De Boer 2003). In the 1997 University Governance Reform, three major changes took place in the governance structure. First, university and faculty senates no longer had decision-making power (e.g., the approval of the institutional or faculty budget); their role changed into a representative advisory body. Second, executive boards were granted more power (e.g., appointing the deans of faculties). Deans before that time were elected by councils at the faculty level and they often were chosen for two years. And third, supervisory boards (Raad van Toezicht) were introduced. The five members of these new bodies were to be appointed by and accountable to the minister. The supervisory board has to approve the most important plans of the university, including the strategic and budget plans. Furthermore, the supervisory board appoints the members of the executive board (see below for more details). Shortly after the introduction of the new structure, an implementation study took place (Commissie Datema 1998). In 2004–2005, the university governance structure was more formally evaluated (De Boer, Goedegebuure, and Huisman 2005).

Change for the Better?

Various questions come to mind when reflecting on the changes in institutional governance arrangements. An important question, if not the crucial question, is whether the new governance structures live up to expectation, and whether they are better than the old regimes.

Surprisingly, the policy documents addressing governance change in higher education are quite equivocal when it comes to the arguments for introducing particular new governance regimes, in the sense that almost all of the reports are silent, or at most, rather vague, about the "why" question. Most government documents more or less adequately address the changing environment in which higher education institutions exist, but most of the time it is unclear why a particular governance solution is suggested. Sometimes, the presumed conservative nature of academia and the slowness of decision-making (if not indecisiveness) if academics are involved, are referred to. Such characteristics are deemed inappropriate when higher education institutions live life in the fast lane. This argument echoes the New Public Management discourse that stresses the need for priority setting in institutional strategies. In a similar vein, the lack of expertise and knowledge of students is mentioned as a risk to adequate strategy setting. But empirical evidence beyond the anecdote cannot be found to support the assumption of inertia or indecisiveness, and consequently cannot support the necessity to change the existing arrangements, let alone the direction of change.

To be honest, neither can evidence be found that the "collegial" decision-making model has ever existed and fully worked in academia, nor that this model should be qualified as superior to any other decision-making or governance model. But overall, it is important to note that governments felt an urge to change the governance arrangements with some (theoretical) arguments for change, but without a thought-out analysis of the shortcomings of existing arrangements, and lacking compelling arguments why the alternatives proposed would do better. The following quotes, commenting on reports that formulated recommendations on governance, may further illustrate this point. Tilley (1998, 6) comments on the changes in governance in Australian higher education: "All three recent Government reviews of higher education have sought, in essence, to apply modern management processes to the governance of universities. There has been little empirical justification for criticism of university management." And Shattock (1998, 35) comments on the Dearing recommendations for U.K. higher education: "But the merits of this [institutional governance] model against others is not discussed, merely asserted, nor is there evidence of any research into effective university governance that might have underpinned the recommendations" (see also Ackroyd and Ackroyd 1999; Knight 2002).

Here we can make an interesting link to the area of corporate governance research. As has been set out above, government initiatives have implicitly or explicitly been inspired or, if you wish, polluted by new public management ideas or, more generally, concepts from the corporate sector. We would argue that this is not necessarily wrong (see Birnbaum 2001), but rather that the point is we should carefully consider whether corporate practices can be transplanted to the public sphere. Moreover, as researchers studying private and public sector governance contend (Exworthy and Halford 1999; Ferlie, Ashburner, Fitzgerald, and Pettigrew 1996), there is only limited knowledge of how corporate governance works, and what can be seen as best practice (see also Bennett 2002, 296). So the question actually is why we should implement corporate practices if there is not sufficient support that these would cure the problem (if there is a need for a remedy at all).

The suspicion that the new arrangements are not necessarily more effective or efficient than the old ones is further fuelled by the fact that strikingly similar solutions across higher education systems have been suggested, which is difficult to reconcile with the variety of problems these systems confront and the

various political, historical, and sociocultural contexts the institutions are situated in. It strikes us as odd that a "universal" governance arrangement—one size
fits all—would work for systems that were or are in transition (e.g., Hungary
and Estonia), that have to deal with declining government resources and mass
higher education (U.K.), and those that try to balance the power of academics in
institutional decision-making (e.g., Austria).

The volume of studies focusing on the impact of changing governance arrangements in European higher education is low. At present, there are papers
describing the changes proposed and implemented, and various papers critically
discussing the sense and nonsense of such changes. In addition, surveys are used
to "measure" the extent to which certain objectives are met, but the number of
actual evaluations or impact studies is low. Although there is some more empirically oriented research (Bennett 2002; De Boer et al. 2005; Huisman, de Boer,
and Goedegebuure 2006; Laske, Lederbauer, Loacker, and Meister-Scheytt
2006), we have hardly scratched the surface. This leaves us with the contention
that we cannot tell whether new structures function better. There are methodo-
logical tools at hand that would easily lead to relevant insights, such as analyzing existing governance practices through case studies. Or, we can gather views
and perceptions through surveys among those involved in institutional governance and use the outcomes as proxies for effectiveness (see e.g., De Boer 2003;
De Boer et al. 2005 on evaluating governance arrangements in the Dutch university sector). Combinations of both would allow us to triangulate findings from
different methods and sources. Most importantly, to fully reap the benefits of
such research, a proper conceptual and theoretical approach is invaluable.

Governing Bodies in the Netherlands

Fortunately, a number of authors in the general area of governance studies have
addressed conceptual and theoretical issues of governance. We take Hung's
1998 paper, distinguishing six roles and theories to analyze roles of governing
boards, as a point of departure (see also Cornforth 2003 for building on Hung's
work; and Meister-Scheytt and Laske 2005 for using Cornforth's work) to illustrate how we could gain more insight into the functioning of governing bodies,
using the example of the *Raad van Toezicht* in Dutch universities. We will confront the conceptual analysis with findings from our own research (De Boer et
al. 2005) to reveal shortcomings in the Dutch government's view on institutional
governance.

One of the theoretical approaches that Hung addresses is resource dependency. This theory (Pfeffer and Salancik 1978) posits that stakeholders and organizations have different interests and that their interrelationships, both within
and outside the focal organization, are affected by the nature and amount of the
resources that are exchanged within and between organizations. Its main assumption is that organizations and individuals will try to reduce their dependencies. Whereas most work on institutional governance from a resource depend-

ency perspective focused on interlocking directorates (Pennings 1980), there is a broader application. From this theoretical perspective, governing boards fulfill a boundary-spanning role between organization and environment, focusing on a decrease of dependency and uncertainty. An important role would be to develop good relations with key external stakeholders and possibly to secure funds for the organization (Cornforth 2003, 8–9). As such, it would be interesting to try to disentangle the various dependencies of and with governing boards. Figure 19.1 attempts to illustrate the dependency relationships in Dutch university governance, focusing on the top-level of the organization, meaning that we do not address relationships at the faculty and department level. Since we are focusing on governance relationships, financial resources play a less dominant role, and information as a resource is considered to be of crucial importance.

Let us first of all mention that this figure is not complete. Specifically, the executive board has the power to decide (after being advised by various internal bodies) on the internal regulations (*bestuurs- en beheersreglement*). These internal regulations may further specify certain dependency relations not visible in this figure. Furthermore, the picture is drawn on the basis of the existing regulations, while the actual practice of information flow and decision-making is considerably dependent on factors such as individual discretion and organizational culture. In other words, if we were to draw dependency relations for a specific institution, the figure may differ from the one above. Finally, like in many other higher education systems, there are attempts to fill "gaps" in the structure by developing guides or codes of good practice. Such codes do not replace regulation but could be seen as norms complementing the regulations (see e.g., VSNU 2007) and existing dependencies.

Most important in the figure is the organization of the triangular dependency relationships between the minister, the supervisory board, and the executive board.

- The executive board is accountable to the supervisory board regarding institutional governance and management (with further specifications including strategic planning, budget, annual report, etc.) and the supervisory board controls and checks whether the executive board adheres to the existing regulations and procedures. When asked, the executive board should give the necessary information to the supervisory board.
- The supervisory board is accountable to the minister and has the duty to inform him/her.
- The executive board has the duty to inform the minister on university matters.

It is striking, from a resource dependency perspective, that there are a number of unnecessary "double loops" in the system. To start with a minor issue, we address accountability, approval, and giving advice. Accountability implies that the "accountee" explains what he did, and how and why he performed a given action, and the notion (Bovens 2007) would imply that the "accountor" responds to this. This suggests the exchange of information, and ultimately, advice. Also, the supervisory board's duty is to approve several documents. We cannot imagine that the approval of substantial documents is possible without an exchange

Figure 19.1. Resource Dependencies in Dutch University Governance

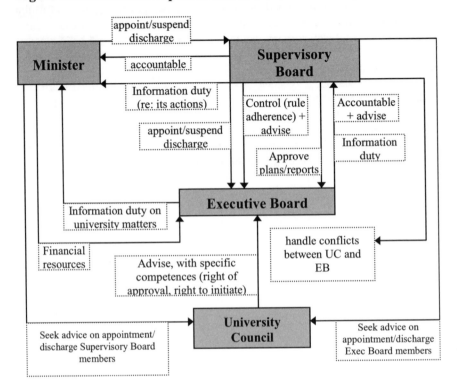

between supervisory board and executive board, which entails *de facto* that advice will be given by the supervisory board. The same goes *vice versa* for the executive board, which obviously will defend and explain the choices made in strategic and budget plans: *de facto* it is advising the supervisory board to accept its proposal. In sum, the prescription of advice—from supervisory board to executive board and the other way around—is superfluous.

Of more concern, however, is the fact that the minister requires the supervisory board to be accountable and to give information to the minister, whereas the minister can simultaneously ask the executive board to supply information regarding university matters. Here it seems that the government has insufficient trust in the supervisory board, and as a kind of safety net would like to be able to be directly in touch with the executive board. Whatever the motivation, it seems superfluous to maintain this relation, for this is adequately covered by the dependencies between the minister and the supervisory board, and the executive board and the supervisory board.

A third concern is that the regulations are not sufficiently clear on what it actually expects from the supervisory board: it is unclear what the supervisory board is accountable for. It seems logical that the supervisory board can only be held accountable for actions specified in the regulations, which would imply that the supervisory board should account for how and why it supervises and controls the executive board. These definitions should be specified to prevent role confusion. Moreover, whereas it is clear in the relationship between the supervisory board and the executive board that feedback on actions or proposals (see above) is an important element of the dependency relations, this is obviously missing in the relationship between the minister and the supervisory board. Indeed, the Education Inspectorate (2004, 313) found that supervisory boards hardly receive substantial feedback from the ministry on their accountable activities.

A fourth concern relates to the combination of various dependency relations. It might be unavoidable to charge certain bodies with certain tasks and conse- quently, dependency relations, but it will be difficult for such a body, in this case the supervisory board, to set priorities. It might be worthwhile to rank the tasks presented to each body (e.g., supervision before advice, see also Adviesraad voor het Wetenschaps-en Technologiebeleid 2003).

These four concerns coincide with the findings of our survey (De Boer et al. 2005) that indicate that the role of the supervisory board is not understood by most of the internal stakeholders. Even for almost half (46 percent) of the members of the University Council and for 17 percent of the deans, it is unclear what the su- pervisory board's role is within the university. The further a respondent is located from the top-levels of governance, the less he or she understands the supervisory board's role. More than half of those active in governance bodies at the level of the faculties and departments think the supervisory council's role is unclear. The members of the supervisory board themselves indicate that they consider their role to be sufficiently clear and unproblematic.

A fifth and final concern relates to the broader objective of the government to increase institutional autonomy. Certainly, our evaluation has indicated that insti- tutional autonomy by and large has increased, but the role of the supervisory board in this matter is marginal. If the idea was to allow the institutions—through their supervisory boards—to be better embedded in regional and national networks, this element is still largely undeveloped. Our survey pointed out that supervisory board members have remarkably few external contacts with other stakeholders in higher education. And if the idea was to make the institution more effective in being in- dependent from the minister, it would be worthwhile to set certain requirements regarding the skills and expertise of supervisory board members, allowing these bodies to make a distinctive contribution to strategy-making (Adviesraad voor het Wetenschaps-en Technologiebeleid 2003).

There are shortcomings to this analysis of governance in the Netherlands. One of these is that it is a macro-level analysis, which does not inform us (yet) about actual governance practices—hence the need to carry out case studies that reveal these practices. Another concern, closely linked to the previous point, is that how- ever important structures and dependency relationships are, personal contributions to the exchange relationships (either in the form of relatively tangible assets such as skills and knowledge, or in less tangible form such as "chemistry" within and between persons and bodies) are of crucial importance. A structural approach, like

resource dependency, tends to downplay these elements in dependency relationships and gives priority to structure above agency. Although it seems that in continental Europe, structure also seems to dominate agency in governance issues, one
should not forget the role of people in governance issues. Furthermore, given that
governance is riddled with paradox (Cornforth 2003, 11–14), one may posit that
rational-structural approaches, that neglect the human factor to some extent, are
not necessarily the best analytical tools (see also Kezar and Eckel 2004).

Lessons for or from the U.S.

Institutional governance has been on the political agenda in the United States for
decades. One could argue, however, that the issue is currently less prominent
than in Europe. An indication of the relatively lower levels of attention in the
U.S. is that board accountability figured at the 6th position among the top-10
public policy issues for higher education (Association of Governing Boards
2007). Attention to board accountability is superseded by attention to student
matters, such as price of tuition, student aid policy, access and success, accountability for student learning, and consumer information. In the previous ranking
(Association of Governing Boards 2005), two governance issues were ranked 8th
and 10th in the top 10: accountability to the public and the after effects of Sar-
banes-Oxley, respectively. This is in rather sharp contrast to the European developments, characterized by firm government decisions to change institutional
governance arrangements, set out in the first part of this chapter.

Despite the low profile character of governance issues, periodically there is
attention to specific topics in the U.S.

- First, governing boards' intrusion upon academic freedom and tenure has
  been dominant in the U.S. in the 1990s. Currently, the topic only occasionally keeps academia occupied, but possibly, the media are more interested.
  We would argue that the situation regarding this issue is not different from
  that in Europe. In individual cases, governing bodies sometimes misuse
  their power and unjustifiably limit the academic freedom of a particular
  staff member. And at the same time, some scholars misinterpret their right
  to academic freedom by forgetting that freedom comes with obligations.
  The issue of academic freedom and governance, however, needs attention in
  light of the increasing marketization of higher education (since pipers other
  than traditional governments institutions now also determine the financial
  tune, with a potential impact on academic freedom. For this, see the special
  issue of *Higher Education Policy*, vol. 20, no 3, 2007). Furthermore, antiter-
  rorism policies may have repercussions on academic freedom (Palfreyman
  2007).
- Second, the possible waning of shared governance (see e.g., Rhoades 2003),
  or more generally the tension between boards and senates (Tierney 2005), is
  a topic that appears now and then on the agenda. Shared governance in this
  context should be understood as the division of authority and decision-

making responsibility between faculty and administration, based on distinctive expertise (American Association of University Professors 1966). Again, the parallels with Europe are apparent, although the pressures under which academics have become less powerful are different. In Europe, governments rather vigorously tipped the power balance in the advantage of the executives (Amaral, Jones, and Karseth 2002a), partly under the influence of the new public management.

In the U.S., the debate seems to be largely on finding a balance between serving the public interest and preserving professional autonomy, but it should be mentioned that there are multiple challenges that impact on this balance (see Tierney and Minor 2003). Remarkably, the seeming demise of academic power and authority in decision-making in U.S. higher education is not fully supported by empirical evidence. Kaplan reports (2002) on the basis of a large-scale governance survey that respondents thought almost all groups that play a role in governance have more authority than 20 years ago.

- Third, accountability and transparency issues around board decision-making and selection procedures for presidents are prevailing issues on the governance agenda (McLendon and Hearn 2006; Tierney and Minor 2003). More recently, board performance and effectiveness (Kezar and Tierney 2004; Tierney and Kezar 2006) are emerging topics that clearly link to the general accountability and transparency debate. And again, this resonates with the debate in Europe, where governing bodies (but not only governing boards) are under pressure to explain to governments and other stakeholders what they do and why they perform a certain set of actions. The issue of transparency looms large in European codes of governance (see Committee of University Chairmen 2004; De Boer and Goedegebuure 2007) .

What clearly distinguishes the U.S. from Europe, or actually better, the U.S. and U.K. on the one hand, and the European continent on the other, relates to the time dimension. The U.S. and U.K. have a much longer tradition of and experience with relatively strong governing bodies. Scholars from these countries studying their governing bodies in higher education may come to the conclusion that these bodies are relatively weak and possibly ineffective (Bennett 2002). But compared to their continental counterparts, they are much more advanced in various respects: induction and training of board members *in spe*, more clarity about roles and functions of persons and bodies in governance matters, more attention to the functioning of boards and board members through effectiveness reviews, and more transparency regarding codes of conduct and conflicts of interest. Without assuming that governing boards in the U.S. and U.K. are necessarily performing better than in continental Europe—since we simply lack the evidence for such a statement—those involved in higher education governance (such as national policymakers in Europe) in the latter countries should certainly try to reap the benefits of lessons learned, both positive and negative, in the U.S. and U.K., however fragile the findings may be. Comparative analyses of developments in the U.S. and Europe would certainly be appropriate to contextualize and support such learning experiences.

References

Ackroyd, P., and S. Ackroyd, S. 1999. "Problems of University Governance in Britain. Is More Accountability the Solution?" *International Journal of Public Sector Management* 12, no. 2: 171–85.

Adviesraad voor het Wetenschaps- en Technologiebeleid. 2003. *Wijsheid achteraf: De verantwoording van universitair onderzoek.* The Hague: AWT.

Amaral, A., G. A. Jones, and B. Karseth. 2002a. "Governing Higher Education: Comparing National Perspectives." In *Governing Higher Education: National Perspectives on Institutional Governance*, ed. A. Amaral, G. A. Jones and B. Karseth. Dordrecht: Kluwer, 279–98.

———. 2002b. Governing Higher Education: National Perspectives on Institutional Governance. Dordrecht: Kluwer.

Amaral, A., and A. M. Magelhaes. 2002. "The Emergent Role of External Stakeholders." In *Governing Higher Education: National Perspectives on Institutional Governance*, ed. A. Amaral, G. Jones, and B. Karseth. Dordrecht: Kluwer, 1–21.

American Association of University Professors. 1966. *Statement on Government of Colleges and Universities.* Washington: AAUP.

Association of Governing Boards. 2005. Ten Public Policy Issues for Higher Education in 2005 and 2006. Washington: AGB.

———. 2007. Ten Public Policy Issues for Higher Education in 2007 and 2008. Washington: AGB.

Association of Universities in the Netherlands (VSNU). 2007. Code goed bestuur universiteiten. The Hague: VSNU.

Begg, R. 2001. Special issue on governance. *Tertiary Education and Management,* 7(2).

Bennett, B. 2002. "The New Style Boards of Governors—Are They Working?" *Higher Education Quarterly* 56, no. 3: 287–302.

Birnbaum, R. 2001. *Management Fads in Higher Education. Where They Come From, What They Do, and Why They Fail.* San Francisco: Jossey-Bass.

Bovens, M. 2007. "Public Accountability." In *The Oxford Handbook of Public Management*, ed. E. Ferlie, Laurence E. Lynn, and C. Pollitt. Oxford: Oxford University Press, 182–208.

Bovens, M. 2003. "Public Accountability." Paper presented at the EGPA Annual Conference, Oeiras, Portugal, September 3–6.

Braun, D., and J. X. Merrien, eds. 1999. Towards a New Model of Governance for Universities? A Comparative View. London: Jessica Kingsley.

Clark, B. R. 1998. Creating Entrepreneurial Universities: Organizational Pathways of Transformation. Oxford: Pergamon.

Commissie Datema. 1998. *De kanteling van het universitaire bestuur.* Zoetermeer: Klankbordgroep invoering MUB.

Committee of University Chairmen. 2004. Guide for Members of Higher Education Governing Bodies in the U.K. Governance Code of Practice and General Principles: CUC.

Cornforth, C. 2003. The Governance of Public and Non-Profit Organizations. What Do Boards Do? London: Routledge.

De Boer, H. 2003. *Institutionele verandering en professionele autonomie*. Enschede: Center for Higher Education Policy Studies.

De Boer, H., and L. Goedegebuure. 2007. "'Modern' Ggovernance and Codes of Conduct in Dutch Higher Education." *Higher Education Research and Development* 26, no. 1: 45–55.

De Boer, H., L. Goedegebuure, and J. Huisman. 2005. *Gezonde spanning. Beleidsevaluatie van de MUB*. Enschede: Center for Higher Education Policy Studies.

Education Inspectorate. 2004. *Onderwijsverslag 2003/2004*. Utrecht: Education Inspectorate.

Exworthy, M., and S. Halford, eds. 1999. *Professionals and the New Managerialism in the Public Sector*. Buckingham: Open University Press.

Ferlie, E., L. Ashburner, L. Fitzgerald, and A. Pettigrew. 1996. *The New Public Management in Action*. Oxford: Oxford University Press.

Hood, C. 1991. "A Public Management for All Seasons?" *Public Adminstration* 69: 3–19.

Huisman, J., H. de Boer, and L. Goedegebuure. 2006. "The Perception of Participation in Executive Governance Structures in Dutch Universities." *Tertiary Education and Management* 12, no. 3: 227–39.

Huisman, J., P. Santiago, P. Högselius, M.-J. Lemaitre, and W. Thorn. 2007. *Thematic Reveiw of Tertiary Education Estonia. Country note*. Paris: OECD.

Hung, H. 1998. "A Typology of the Theories of the Roles of Governing Boards." *Corporate Governance* 6, no. 2: 101–11.

Kaplan, G. E. 2002. Preliminary Results from the 2001 Survey on Higher Education Governance. Washington: AAUP.

Kezar, A., and P. Eckel. 2004. "Meeting Today's Governance Challenges. A Synthesis of the Literature and Examination of a Future Agenda for Scholarship." *Journal of Higher Education* 75, no. 4: 371–99.

Kezar, A. and Tierney, W. 2004. *Assessing Board Performance*. Los Angeles: Center for Higher Education Policy Analysis, University of Southern California.

Knight, M. 2002. "Governance in Higher Education Corporations: A Consideration of the Constitution Created by the 1992 Act." *Higher Education Quarterly* 56, no. 3: 276–86.

Lambert Committee. 2003. Lambert Review of Business-University Collaboration. London: HM Treasury.

Lanzendorf, U. 2004. *Humboldt Well Advised? University Councils in Austria and Germany*. Paper presented at the 17th Annual CHER Conference, Enschede, the Netherlands, September 17–19.

Laske, S., D. Lederbauer, B. Loacker, and C. Meister-Scheytt. 2006. *Struktur und Selbstverständnis österreichischer Universitätsräte*. Innsbruck.

Maassen, P., and F. A. Van Vught. 1988. "An Intriguing Janus-Head: The Two Faces of the New Governmental Strategy for Higher Education in the Netherlands." *European Journal of Education* 23: 65–77.

McLendon, M. K., amd J. C. Hearn. 2006. "Mandated Openness in Public Higher Education: A Field Study of State Sunshine Laws and Institutional Governance." *Journal of Higher Education* 77, no. 4: 645–83.

Meister-Scheytt, C., and S. Laske. 2005. *Reinventing Governance—Fact(ion) and Fiction about Board of Governors in Austrian Universities.* Paper presented at the 27th Annual EAIR Forum, Riga, Latvia, August 28-31.

Morgan, A. W., and A. A. Bergerson. 2000. "Importing Organizational Reform: The Case of Lay Boards in Hungary." *Higher Education* 40: 423–48.

National Committee of Inquiry into Higher Education. 1997. *Higher Education in the Learning Society.* London: Stationary Office.

Neave, G. 1988. On the Cultivation of Quality, Efficiency and Enterprise: An Overview of Recent Trends in Higher Education in Western Europe, 1986–1988. *European Journal of Education* 23, no. 1/2: 7–23.

Neave, G. 1998. "The Evaluative State Reconsidered." *European Journal of Education* 33, no. 3: 265–84.

Palfreyman, D. 2007. "Is Academic Freedom under Threat in U.K. and U.S. Higher Education?" Oxford: OxCHEPS Occasional paper 23.

Pennings, J. M. 1980. *Interlocking Directorates.* San Francisco: Jossey-Bass.

Pfeffer, J., and G. R. Salancik. 1978. The External Control of Organizations. A Resource Dependence Perspective. New York: Harper & Row.

Pollitt, C., and G. Bouckaert, eds. 2000. *Public Management Reform. A Comparative Analysis.* Oxford: Oxford University Press.

Rhoades, G. 2003. "Democracy and Capitalism, Academic Style: Governance in Contemporary Higher Education." Paper presented at the Governance Roundtable, Santa Fe, U.S., June 12-14.

Shattock, M. 1998. "Dearing on Governance—The Wrong Prescription." *Higher Education Quarterly* 52, no. 1: 35–47.

Shattock, M. 1999. "Governance and Management in Universities: The Way We Live Now." *Journal of Education Policy* 14, no. 3: 271–82.

Tierney, W. G. 2005. "When Divorce Is Not an Option: The Board and the Faculty." *Academe* 91, no. 3: 43–46.

Tierney, W. and A. Kezar. 2006. *The Role of Boards in College Access Programs: Creating and Maintaining Quality.* Los Angeles: Center for Higher Education Policy Analysis, University of Southern California.

Tierney, W. G., and J. T. Minor. 2003. *Challenges for Governance: A National Report.* Los Angeles: Center for Higher Education Policy Analysis.

Tilley, A. G. 1998. "University Governance and Policy-Making." *Journal of Higher Education Policy and Management* 20, no. 1: 5–11.

Chapter 20

New Management Responsibilities: The Organizational Transformation of European Universities

Christine Musselin[1]

The transformation of European public universities does not consist in the mutation of the public higher education institutions into private entities, but in the "construction of these universities into organizations" as argued by N. Brunsson and K. Sahlin-Andersonn (2000). According to these authors, this process does not only affect higher education but the public sector at large. But it can be clearly shown (Musselin 2006) that European public universities have experienced the three main processes which are characteristics of such an evolution for Brunsson and Shalin-Andersonn: the construction of an identity (i.e., strengthened autonomy, clearer boundaries and "being special," the construction of a hierarchy (thanks to a reinforced executive leadership), and the construction of rationality (setting objectives, measuring results, and allocating responsibility).

This happened with the complicity of, and incentives from, public authorities that reinforced the executive leadership within higher education institutions and simultaneously delegated some of its previous prerogatives to the latter. This process sometimes happened through new laws, as in the case of the Netherlands with

---

[1] Centre de Sociologie des Organisations (Sciences Po et CNRS).

the 1998 MOB (de Boer., Denters, and Goedegebuure 1998; de Boer and Goedegebuure 2001), or in Germany with the 2001 *Fünftes Gesetz zur Änderung des
Hochschulrahmengesetzes*, but also through the introduction of new tools, as in
France, with the development of four-year contracts between the French ministry
for higher education and research and each university. Being transformed into
organizations, many European universities now have to make decisions on issues
on which they had very little prior influence. This is the case for the management
of academic staff, specifically regarding the assignment of academic positions.
While most European public authorities were previously in charge of controlling
the overall number of positions, their allocation among disciplines, the construction of salary-scales, and the definition of academic duties, such issues have increasingly devolved to higher education institutions.

Building mainly on a comparison between Germany and France, this chapter
addresses the potential consequences this will have on the governance of universities on the one hand and on the management of the academic profession on the
other.

The French and German Contexts

In this perspective, Germany and France are interesting cases for two reasons.
First, the role of public authorities in the management of academic staff and
positions was, and is still in some respect, very strong but the nature of their role
has changed. In France, academics are state civil servants[2] and until 2007 their
salaries were centralized in a national budget managed by the state. Central public authorities, such as the ministry for higher education and research and central
deliberative bodies such as the CNU[3] still are the key players in this issue, and
they have long maintained a corporatist style of management where diverse representatives of the academic profession strongly control, and negotiate with, the
central administration (Musselin 2001/2004), thus leaving the individual universities at the outskirts of staff management. On paper, the authority of the ministry is still rather strong insofar as it must validate the reopening of all vacant
positions, and also decide the number of positions to be created each year in
each university, while the CNU is responsible for deciding who is qualified
enough to be allowed to apply to an academic position. But in recent decades,
French universities have gained more and more leeway in the management of
their staff. Within the forthcoming five years they should become in charge of
the management of their academic and nonacademic staff.

---

[2] With the new act of August 2007, French universities now have the possibility, under certain conditions to recruit faculty members on private contracts and no more on
public servants agreements.

[3] Conseil National des Universités. It is organized into 57 discipline-based sections
which are composed of professors and maîtres de conférences (tenured assistant professors).

In Germany, by contrast, even if university professors are federal civil servants, the regional authorities (the *Länder*) are mostly in charge of staff expenses and directly negotiate with the universities for the creation, suppression, or reallocation of positions. They are also entitled to control the short list of candidates chosen by peers at the end of a recruitment process, and to modify the established ranking. They are also involved in the negotiation of the funds to be allocated to a newly recruited professor, if university resources are not sufficient to fulfil the candidate's requirements. Nevertheless, the academic profession is not engaged in a form of comanagement with the ministries of the *Land*, as is the case in France, since German universities traditionally have enjoyed greater margins of manoeuvre in the management of their positions and in the recruitment of their academic personnel.

Second, the two countries are experiencing some changes, which may be not as radical as in some other countries,[4] but provide an interesting occasion to look at their consequences. In Germany, the 1998 *Vierten Gesetzes zur Änderung des Hochschulrahmengesetzes,* which allowed the *Länder* to develop their higher education systems more independently from one another, thus permitting each region to differentiate itself, and the 2001 reform mentioned above have had heavy repercussions on the management of academic staff. The introduction of merit-based salaries for newly recruited professors, in particular, creates the possibility for each university to sanction or reward its staff according to its performance. Previously, higher education institutions had no leeway at all once the recruitment negotiation was finished.

In France, the introduction of four-year contracts by the end of the 1980s favored the emergence of stronger university presidents and promoted their increasing involvement in the management of academic positions, and sometimes also of academic staff. While university leaders could hardly decide the redistribution of vacant positions in the past, it is more and more frequent now: building on the priorities set in the four-year contracts and on the evolutions of students' numbers,[5] they reallocate positions among schools. Some university presidential teams modified the rules that prevailed in the decision for the creation of new positions: the university strategic priorities become the main reference while previously alternately choices prevailed. Even if it is still very rare, it has also become some-

---

[4] One of the more radical cases in Europe being Austria: newly recruited professors are no more civil servants and are directly managed by their university.

[5] In France, there is no selection for undergraduates entering the universities. Each students having his/her Baccalaureate can become a student in the discipline he/she chooses at one of the 85 French universities (by contrast, the access to the alternative higher education sector called "grandes écoles" is highly selective). Since the overall increase in student numbers from the mid 1990s has slowed, some disciplines (in sciences, economics, etc.) lose students each year while others (in management or in psychology, for instance) are very attractive. University presidential teams use this evolution in the distribution of students to support the reallocation of positions within their institution.

what more frequent for university management to refuse the candidates to recruitment selected by local hiring committees.[6]

In France, this trend will probably develop for three reasons. First, the introduction of the "LOLF" Act (*Loi organique relative aux lois de finances*) will
transform the preparation, allocation, and implementation of the French national
public budget, and as a consequence, the higher education and research budget.
Second, the Research Act of April 2006 should also lead to some changes. It
creates a national agency for the evaluation of research and higher education
(AERES) which, among others, will provide more information and indicators to
the individual institutions (and to the public in general) on their performance in
training, research, and governance.[7] Third, with the forthcoming devolution of
the budget for staff at the institutional level, French universities will get more
responsibility in the management of positions, staff budget, and academic careers and many predict that there will be more evaluation of the performance of
academic staff by the universities themselves. This will be a major change as
today many French faculty members escape any kind of regular assessment: if
French universities develop their own self-evaluation processes, it will provide
the possibility for university managers to develop a more individual style of
managing their staff.

Few, if any, empirical studies exist on the effects of all these measures on the
management of staff in the two countries. It is, of course, still too early in France
as some of the new measures have not yet been implemented. In Germany, it only
very recently became realistic to draw some first conclusions, since the concrete
implementation of the 2001 act took some time and is still not finished. Moreover,
some of its consequences cannot be assessed until a greater period of time has
elapsed.[8] But in a rather provisional way, one can already identify some of the

---

[6] It is still very rare, but the percentage of positions (on the total number of assistant
professor positions opened in France) that have not been filled because the university
level refused to agree on the rankings produced by the hiring committee raised from 0.5
percent in 2002 to 0.7 percent in 2005.

[7] Evaluation existed before the creation of the AERES but was widespread among
different places and bodies. The ministry for higher education and research was in charge
of the four-year accreditation of training programs and also led the evaluation of the university research units not affiliated to national research centers such as the CNRS, while
the affiliated units were evaluated by their respective national research centers. The CNE
(Comité National d'Evaluation) was in charge of the institutional evaluation of higher
education institutions. All these evaluations activities are now concentrated in one single
agency, the AERES, which is publicly funded but independent from the ministry. The
achieved evaluations are all published on the website of this agency.

[8] It is for instance the case with the introduction of the Junior professor positions.
These are time-limited posts for three years renewable once, for young academics who
are recognized a complete autonomy to lead their research projects (while in Germany
junior staff depends on a full professor) and will be allowed at the end of the six years to
apply for a professor position, without having an Habilitation. Some first reports have
already been published about the less than 800 Junior professoren positions already created (Federkeil and Buch 2007), but at least a 10-year period of time is needed to assess

challenges French and German universities will confront in the near future, and the impact this could have on the academic profession in both countries.

Impacts on the Governance of Universities

The devolution of the management of positions and staff to universities is not only a technical administrative measure. Internalizing such issues in higher education institutions can affect the internal balance in power, the nature of the relationships among the members of the university and the role of university and administrative leaders.

A Challenge for University Leaders

When public authorities are in charge of the management of staff and positions, they can ground the legitimacy of their decisions in two rather opposite ways. The first one consists in justifying the decisions made by the needs and objectives of the nation. In research led in the late '90s (Fresse 1998, 1999) on recruitment in German universities, this clearly was the principal rationale used by the ministries of the *Länder*. The cuts in mathematics and history were rationalized by the need to develop disciplines important for future development, such as science and technology. This interventionist role can be performed by public authorities as depositaries of the general interest, thus defined in a Weberian perspective, to be coercive and to make difficult decisions for the benefit of the whole society.

The second form of legitimation follows a more Mertonian perspective, and relies on the recognition of the strong autonomy of the academic sphere. The role of the state is then to protect science by implementing the demands and preferences of this sphere. The French comanagement system between the ministry and representatives of the profession was quite close to this second model. In this case, the legitimacy of decisions made by the state relies on the fact that they respect the interests and preferences of the academic profession and this is legitimate because it is believed that, what is good for science is good for the society.

With the delegation of the management of staff and positions to the university, academic leaders now have to choose between these two possibilities on their own terms. They can either listen to the demands emerging from their institution, or identify society's needs and adapt their institution to them. But in both cases, they face a problem of legitimacy. .In the first case, they will be confronted with the obligation to discriminate among the demands emerging from the various disciplines. They can either behave as a traditional *primus inter pares* and mobilize

---

whether this, as expected, will make the German academic career more attractive, transformed the path of access to professorship and stimulate innovative and internationally recognized research production.

nonpainful and well-established methods (reproduction of the existing equilibrium, or "tour de role"[9]), or they can develop methods to evaluate the most relevant demands from an academic point of view and set priorities among them accordingly. But notwithstanding the feasibility of such methods, this first option is rarely observed. In the French case, most presidential teams want to depart from the *primus inter pares* conception and intend to develop institutional projects or strategies, and do not conceive of their role as pure mediators of academic demands. In the German case, this first option is also unlikely: years of restrictive policies have further obliged university leaders to depart from this traditional vision.

If the second option is therefore more probable, it is not easier to adopt. What was already contested by public authorities is even less legitimate with university leaders. How can they legitimate their actions as general interest builders? Deciding to give more staff to a certain department rather than to another because the former is more "relevant" to the university's future plans, the society at large, or the economic growth of the country, is particularly difficult to justify. In her Ph.D. dissertation, Stephanie Mignot-Gérard (2006) clearly shows how French presidents are balancing between managerial demands and academic rationales, and how it is crucial for them to reconcile managerial goals with academic rationales if they want their projects to succeed.

Despite this ambiguity, university leaders have become increasingly intrusive in making delicate decisions in French and in German universities, leading departments to lose positions and forcing them to follow reduction plans (in Germany) or redistribute posts (in France). Here it is interesting to observe the strong parallel between the rationales observed in some American private universities (Musselin 2005b) and those used in these European universities. Two arguments are usually mobilized to justify such decisions.

- On one hand, the scientific reputation of each department, as assessed by peers through external evaluation processes, can be used by the president to justify the pressure put on certain departments. This argument was used in two mathematics departments, one in Germany and one in the U.S., to introduce budget cuts in the first case, and to refuse the reoccupation of vacant positions in the second.

- On the other hand, invoking the "demands of the students"[10] is a common tactic on both sides of the Atlantic. For instance, the diminution in student en-

---

[9] These are two methods we frequently observe in French universities. In order not to provoke conflicts, some university leaders preferred to re-allocate the vacant positions to the department where they were (reproduction of the existing equilibrium) and to ask for new positions for each department one after another (*tour de role*).

[10] The students can be invoked in many ways. In France where the access to universities is not selective, some discipline (management for instance) are overwhelmed by numbers, while others (economics, physics . . .) suffer from penury. The ratio number of students/teachers is then used as criteria for redistribution (even if never in an automatic way, in order to preserve the research potential of the declining disciplines). In the U.S. the sociology of the students can become a criteria: in history for instance, the increase in

rollment in some disciplines has been used by some French university presidents to impose that all or a certain percentage of newly vacant positions would be reallocated to a common pool that is open to redistribution to other disciplines.

Such decisions by university leaders provide good evidence of the ongoing transformation in university governance in Europe, even in countries where less radical changes have been introduced in higher education, and also where new public management rhetoric has been less successful and influential (Pollitt and Bouckaert 2004). In these countries too, university leaders are facing decisions that they previously could avoid (or which they could attribute or leave to public authorities). For such difficult decisions to be accepted by their staff, university leaders have to develop compatible rationales.

The Transformation of the University/Academic Relationships

The devolution of the management of academic staff and positions does not only increase the scope of decision-making for European university leaders. It also transforms the relationship between academics and their universities.

As already described and analyzed (Friedberg and Musselin 1989; Musselin 2005a), these relationships were very different in France and in Germany. In France, the management of positions at the national level (and the reluctance—or incapacity—of university leaders to be involved this domain until recently), and the bureaucratic management of academic staff left no possibility at the university level to determine salaries (which were set by a national income scale), to negotiate recruitment funds, or to reward/sanction its staff. As a consequence, the intensity and the content of the university-academic relationship were weak. Universities could be described as shelters in which academics were allocated, which do not offer much to their staff, and to which most parties do not feel strongly affiliated.

In Germany, universities have had for a long time the possibility to negotiate recruitment funds with the professors (but only the professors) they recruit. This created the conditions for the existence of an implicit contract between each academic and his/her institution: while the institution provides resources allowing academics to develop their own research project and recognizes (through the resources allocated) their scientific value, the academics feel obliged to meet the expectations made on them and to be loyal to their institution. I qualify this situation as an "investment relationship": when recruiting, the university bets resources

---

Asian students was an argument to replace vacant position in European history, by position in Asian history. The supposed attractiveness of some thematic for the labor market can also be an argument: in Germany, some departments in history were transforming positions in medieval history into a position in contemporary history of Europe, in order to train more employable historians (or at least use this argument to avoid a cut).

on a person and expects a return on its investment in the long run, but has no means to control, reward, or sanction its staff once the recruitment is made.

These typical situations have changed. In Germany, the introduction of merit-based salaries, but also the recourse to time-limited recruitment funds, provide universities with incentives to manage their academic staff after hiring. According to interviews led with German university leaders (university president, director for human resources, registrars) in June 2008, they set objectives to the newly re-cruited professors. It is common to ask for the successful development of a new training program and to fix a certain amount of grants to be obtained during a three- to four-year period. The allocation of the variable part of the salary will depend on the attainment achieved by the professor.

France has not progressed so far yet, even if some incentives were introduced in the form of bonuses[11] at the beginning of the '90s. But three reports at the be-ginning of the 21st century, the Rapport Espéret (2001), the Rapport Belloc (2003) and the Rapport Schwartz (2008), suggested giving more power to the president. All three proposed the introduction of individual agreements between each aca-demic and his/her university, defining for a four- or five-year period, the percent-age of time he/she will should spend on research, teaching, and administrative activities.[12] To date, these reports did not lead to any concrete decisions or change. But, with the creation of the AERES (see above), the devolution of human re-sources management to the universities and the implementation of regular individ-ual assessments for each academic, one can expect stronger involvement of uni-versity leaders in the management of academic careers. This would inevitably strongly affect the relationships between the university leadership and their aca-demics.

In sum, two main transformations are happening in France and in Germany.

First, the emergence of internal labor markets (Doeringer and Piore 1971, Musselin 2005a and 2005b) can be observed in the devolution of management of staff and in the tools universities are creating for internal assessment and reward. As a result, universities will not be shelters or pure investors anymore: they be-come closer to employers, having the power to lead assessment procedures, and to reward and sanction their staff.

---

[11] They have had a modest influence as one of them is allocated by national proce-dures and the attribution of the two others are rather regulated.

[12] According to the latest report (Rapport Schwartz 2008), the assessment of the re-search performance should be led by external peers, most probably at the national level, while the teaching performance will be led by the institution. Relying on these results, the university president should then regularly negotiate with each individual academic but also consults the concerned deans, department chairs, and directors of research unit.

A Challenge for the University Administration

A final implication at the university level concerns the university's administrative staff. When French and German universities respectively worked as shelters or investors, the competence of their administrative staff could be reduced. The attributions of university administrations were traditional and bureaucratic. If universities have to manage their staff at a more local level, this style of management will no longer be efficient, and new tools and practices will be needed. This is probably one of the main problems that would have faced the suggestions developed in the French reports mentioned above and the introduction of individual agreements between each academic and his/her university. Such measures suppose strong administrative support and a professionalized staff able to manage these kinds of instruments.

The devolution of the management of academic staff at the university level is therefore deeply affecting the governance of universities, the relationships between academics and their institutions, and the competence of the university administrative staff.

Consequences on the Management of the Academic Profession

If this evolution has important consequences at the university level, it also more broadly affects the management of the academic profession. On one hand, it changes (at least partly) the internal dynamics of development in the academic profession. On the other, it questions the strength of the professional power. Let us develop these two points.

The Regulation of the Academic Profession

Different interpretations conflict in the understanding of the internal dynamics of development within the academic profession. Some studies focus on endogenous processes, such as the development of the profession resulting from the diversification of science itself (Clark 1997). As science progresses, new specialties, new domains, and new disciplines appear. The relative power and influence of each specialty and its capacity to expand can therefore be analyzed as the result of the conflicts and debates within the field of science (Bourdieu 1984), or as a question of the controversies affecting the scientific sphere (Latour 1987; Callon 1989). Others (mostly economists) point to exogenous processes such as the role of social demand and the allocation of public funding in the development of different areas of science.

These two opposing views can help qualify the situations in France and in Germany. The strong comanagement that prevailed between the central administration and the academic profession in France left more room for the first interpretation. Even if one should not underestimate the role of the French government in steering the developments of nuclear science or electronics, and in leading Colbertist industrial plans[13] (Cohen 1992), the main explanations for the increase in the relative strength of the certain disciplines in the French universities during the '90s include the rise in student numbers in some sectors,[14] and most of all the pressure for stability led by the various representatives of the disciplines within the ministry. As a result, the balance between the humanities, the sciences, and law has not been strongly affected. In contrast, in Germany, over the same period of time, certain exogenous factors played a stronger role. The *Länder* developed more interventionist strategies and strongly pressured the traditional disciplines in order to find resources and positions for what they consider to be the promising domains for the future and for economic growth.

Two conclusions can be drawn from this rapid overview. First, public authorities are not a guarantee against the disappearance of some disciplines or their decreased importance. Second, the central management of positions does not prevent corporatist style management decisions (or alternatively, it does not guarantee decisions based on the general interest of the discipline). Thus, the traditional fears raised by those opposed to the decentralization of the management of academic staff and positions to institutions do not seem to be avoided when one leaves the decision to public authorities or to the academic profession. Neither the former, nor the latter warrant the preservation of academic interests. Reciprocally, individual institutions (and their leaders) can be very respectful of academic "culture" and norms. In the study I led in three American private research universities (Musselin 2005b), it was remarkable to observe that they all remained "complete" institutions and were protecting the integrity of each discipline, by including undergraduate courses in those disciplines (thus maintaining a certain demand for faculty members), but also by securing some graduate studies and research in these domains in order to attract the best academic talent. The rationale was that a research university must display a large spectrum of disciplines and cannot only (or primarily) reflect the needs of the market.[15]

At this point, for American research universities, there seem to be no sharp differences between public and private not-for-profit entities. They share the same definition of what a "university" is and private nonprofit universities feel con-

---

[13] Linking public sectors of research with big national public firms.

[14] The suppression (after a legal recourse) of the selective access that prevailed in sport, led for instance in the '90s to an explosion in student numbers in this discipline, provoked an impressive increase in faculty members in this sector (+3,019 percent between 1986 and 2001!)

[15] Such considerations are certainly less present in less academic institutions (two-year colleges for instance). This shows the importance of differentiating among the subsectors and the needs for looking at the "crisis of the publics," subsectors by subsectors, rather than in general terms.

cerned with public missions. By contrast, this seems rather different in the U.K. where, the idea of university seems no more not associated with the presence of a complete range of disciplines: many departments have been suppressed in British institutions, and even in prestigious ones, in the recent years.

These different examples remind us that there is no evidence that the devolution of the management of academic staff and positions to universities will worsen or improve the development of science. Nor will this devolution threaten or protect the less market-oriented disciplines than when this responsibility is left to public authorities or to the profession itself.

Nevertheless, this devolution raises a series of questions about the forms of regulation to be created and maintained at regional, national, or even supranational (i.e., European) levels. Should everything rely on market mechanisms among institutions or should some issues (such as the equilibrium among regions) rest in the hands of public authorities? More broadly, it raises questions about the transformation of the role of the state after it delegates its management functions.

Auto-Regulation or Institutional Control

The second issue raised by the involvement of the university in the management of academic staff and positions deals with the potential decrease in the power of the academic profession. In France and in Germany, academic power was almost the only mechanism regulating the profession. As described above, even if in Germany the university was a player in the recruitment process when negotiating with highly ranked candidates, this institutional intervention was rather limited.[16] Thus, in the decisions pertaining to recruitment or promotion, in the assessment of the quality of publications or teaching, peer-level review was dominant in the two countries. But at the same time, the exercise of this academic power was rather concentrated. It occurred on specific (nonregular) occasions, was mostly based on voluntarism (i.e., nobody was obliged to apply for new positions, or to submit papers for publication), and the possibility of exercising pressure on deviance[17] was very low.

This rather weak capacity of the academic profession to strongly regulate itself (which is a recurrent issue in many professions, see for instance Karpik 1995) leaves room for other forms of control and power to develop and occupy the vacuum. This can happen without directly infringing on academic power, but rather by adding other mechanisms on top of the professional ones. From my point of view, this much better describes what is happening in the French and German pub-

---

[16] It could nevertheless have a certain impact on the career or this candidate if he/she obtains a rather consequent amount of resources in terms of assistants, equipment, specific budgets, etc.

[17] Here, I do not mean deviance such as frauds or illegal practices, but behaviors such as not renewing one's courses, disinvesting in research activities, refusing any kind of administrative task or responsibility, etc.

lic universities than the traditional complaint on the regressing power of the guild. Other forms, and among them institutional tools and processes, have been added to the traditional professional ones. The overall amount of control on academics therefore increased, and changed in nature (as it now mixes professional and institutional dimensions), but the absolute amount of academic power did not diminish. One could even argue it increased (Enders and Musselin 2008): as mentioned above, university leaders must build their legitimacy when making decisions on academic staff and positions. One common way to succeed in this construction is to mobilize external peer reviews. The label received from being funded by research councils such as the DFG (Deutsche Forschungsgemeinschaft) in Germany or the ANR (Agence Nationale pour la Recherche) in France, or from the individual evaluation that will be led by the future AERES, or the department evaluation led by German assessment agencies, are welcome by university leaders as a means to identify the specific sectors, or individuals, to support.

The expansion of these new evaluation and funding bodies based on peer review provides an opportunity for academic power to increase, while being at the same time at the service of institutional control. This is one of the paradoxes of the recent and future development in academic management.

More Convergence?

How will the recent empowerment of French and German universities in the management of their academic staff and positions influence their long-term development? On one level, it appears that it will lead, in some form, to a convergence of the management choices and approaches of the universities of these two countries. It will also lead to less decentralized decision-making with the following effects.

- It will strengthen university leaders, the scope of intervention of university governance, and the constitution of universities in organizations.
- It will modify the nature of the relationships between academics and their institutions. Even if the state remains the employer, as is the case of France, the possibility of intervention university leaders have in managing positions or to negotiate individual contracts regarding the expected activities of each faculty member, will strengthen the role and the perception of these leaders as "principals" (exercising a sort of hierarchical authority and some employers' privileges).
- It can at the same time increase control over academics, favor the development of alternative forms of evaluation and steering, while simultaneously emphasizing the need for more academic assessment, thus indirectly reinforcing the academic guild.

References

Bourdieu, P. 1984. *Distinctions: A Social Critique of the Judgement of Taste.* Cambridge, U.K.: Cambridge University Press.

Brunsson, Nils, and Kerstin Sahlin-Andersonn. 2000. "Constructing Organisations: The Example of Public Reform Sector." *Organisation Studies* 4.

Callon, Michel. 1989. *La Science et Ses Réseaux : Genèse et Circulation des Faits Scientifiques.* Paris: La Découverte.

Clark, Burton R. 1997. "Diversification of Higher Education: Viability and Change." In *The Mockers and the Mocked: Comparative Perspectives on Differentiation, Convergence and Diversity in Higher Education*, ed. Lynn V. Meek, Leo Goedegebuure, Osmo Kivinen, and R. Risto Rinne. IAU Issues on Higher Education. Oxford, New York, Tokyo: Pergamon Press, 16–25.

Cohen, Elie. 1992. Le Colbertisme "High Tech": Economie des Télécom et du Grand Projet. Paris: Hachette.

De Boer, H., B. Denters, and L. Goedegebuure. 1998. "Dutch Disease or Dutch Model? An Evaluation of the Pre-1998 System of Democratic University Government in the Netherlands." *Policy Studies Review* 15(4): 37–50.

———. 2001. "On Boards and Councils; Shaky Balances Considered. The Governance of Dutch Universities." *Higher Education Policy* 11.2/3: 153–64.

De Boer, H., and L. Goedegebuure. 2001. "On Limitations and Consequences of Change: Dutch University Governance in Transition." *Tertiary Education and Management* 7, no. 2: 163–80.

Doeringer, Peter B., Michael J. Piore. 1971. *Internal Labor Markets and Manpower Analysis.* Lexington: Heath Lexington Books.

Enders, Jürgen, and Christine Musselin. 2008. "Back to the Future: The Academic Professions in the 21st Century." In OECD. *Higher Education 2030*, vol. 1: Demography, Paris: OECD Editions (*L'enseignement supérieur en 2030*, vol. 1: Démographie. Paris: Editions OCDE).

Federkeil, Gero, Florian Buch, Fünf Jahre Juniorprofessur. 2007. "Zweite CHE-Befragung zum Stand der Einführung." Working Paper No. 90, CHE.

Fresse, Alexandra. 1998. Commissions de Recrutement: Commissions de Spécialistes. Etude du Recrutement des Professeurs d'Histoire dans Quatre Universités Allemandes, Mémoire de DEA de l'Institut d'Etudes Politiques de Paris.

———. 1999. L'Expertise Importée: Monographie sur le Recrutement des Professeurs de Mathématiques dans Quatre Universités Allemandes, Rapport d'Enquête CSO, Paris.

Friedberg, Erhard, Christine Musselin. 1989. *En Quête d'Universités.* Paris: L'Harmattan.

Karpik, Lucien. 1995. *Les Avocats. Entre l'Etat, le Public et le Marché—XIIIème-XXème Siècles,* Paris: Gallimard.

Latour, Bruno. 1987. Science in Action: How to Follow Scientists and Engineers through Society. Cambridge: Harvard University Press.

Mignot-Gerard, Stéphanie. 2006. "Echanger et Argumenter Les Dimensions Politiques du Gouvernement des Universités Françaises." Ph.D. in Sociology, Sciences Po, Paris.

Musselin, Christine. 2004. *La Longue Marche des Universités*. Paris: PUF. 2001, published as *The Long March of French Universities*. New York: Routledge.

———. 2005a. *Le Marché des Universitaires*. France Allemagne, Etats-Unis, Paris : Presses de Sciences Po.

———. 2005b. "European Academic Labor Markets in Transition." *Higher Education*, 49: 135–54.

———.2006. "Are Universities Specific Organizations?" In *Towards a Multiversity? Universities between Global Trends and National Traditions*, ed. G. Krücken, A. Kosmützky, and M. Torka. Bielefeld: Transcript Verlag, 63–84.

Pollitt, Christopher, and Geert Bourckeart. 2004. *Public Management Reform: A Comparative Analysis*. Oxford: Oxford University Press.

Rapport Belloc. 2003. *Propositions pour une Modification du Décret 84–431 portant Statut des Enseignants*. Paris: Ministère de la Jeunesse, de l'Education Nationale et de la Recherche.

Rapport Esperet. 2001. *Nouvelle Définition des Tâches des Enseignants et des Enseignants Chercheurs dans l'Enseignement Supérieur Français*. Paris: Ministère de l'Education Nationale.

Rapport Schwartz. 2008. *Commission de Réflexion sur l'Aavenir des Personnels de l'Enseignement Supérieur*. Paris: Ministère de l'Enseignement Supérieur et de la Recherche.

Chapter 21

Rethinking the Mandates of Sub-Saharan African University Systems

Ahmed Bawa[1]

Higher education in Sub-Saharan African has been in a state of crisis now for several decades, and this has been documented by the Secretary-General of the Association of African Universities (AAU), Aki Sawyerr (2004). In addition, several national and regional analyses have been performed to understand the nature of the challenges and how the sector may be regeared to play the kind of role that is expected of it.[2] One observes too that significant formal literature has emerged in the recent past, an example of which is a new *Journal for African Higher Education* published by CODESRIA (the Council for the Development of Social Research in Africa) based in Dakar, Senegal. For the first time, there is a journal that serves as a venue for debate and discussion relating specifically to African higher education.[3] In addition, and we shall look at this in more detail later, there is renewed local and international interest in rebuilding the sector. It is against this background that a discussion of the future of higher education on

---

[1] Deputy Vice-Chancellor, University of KwaZulu-Natal, South Africa.

[2] For example, the Partnership for Higher Education in Africa commissioned a series of country studies of the higher education systems.

[3] There are other national journals such as the *South African Journal of Higher Education*.

the African continent should be discussed, and an interrogation of what the impact of such interest might be.

Contexts and Challenges

The dismal failure of most African governments to make headway in achieving the U.N.'s Millennium Development Goals (2004) has been a major impetus in the reemergence of a serious discussion on higher education transformation. This has also brought into sharp relief the debates that surround the impact of the World Bank-inspired structural adjustment programs on higher education of a few decades ago. This discussion about transformation is made interesting by folding into it the impact of globalization on higher education on the one hand, and on the impact of higher education on the economy, society, and polity under conditions of globalization on the other. There has been much written about this, and one example is a very interesting set of articles in two volumes also published by CODESRIA titled *African Universities in the 21st Century* (Zeleza 2004).

The editors of these volumes indicate that the impact of globalization on African higher education will have the effect of forcing "a reconstitution of the basic principles that underpin the entire higher education system." This has to be seen in light of the fact that globalization brings into play on the sector a very substantial set of new features, conditions, and forces.

Let's examine a few of these. First, in terms of the WTO's General Agreement on Trade in Services, education (including higher education) is seen as a service, and therefore has forced upon it a fundamentally neo-liberal approach to global trade in higher education (c.f. Knight 2005). This has enormous implications for the way that governments have to construct policy frameworks within which to organize higher education. We will address at a later stage why it is important to consider this. Second, globalization has opened up the "trade" in skills, and there continues to be acceleration in the number of highly skilled Africans who are mobile and move to better conditions of work and living. It is estimated, for instance, that the percentage of newly qualified medical doctors that emigrated from Ghana in 2002 (as a fraction of those that remained) was 94 percent. This migration was mainly to the U.K. and other developed English-speaking nations around the globe (Anarfi et al. 2003). The brain drain continues to be an extremely big issue for higher education, and raises the specter of leaving behind unsustainable systems in many African nations. Third, globalization is underpinned by the vast successes in improving the power of information technology and the increasing social ubiquity of the technology coupled with declining costs. This has enormous potential for the delivery of higher education and thus for access to it, for research, for improving the quality of learning and teaching, and for improving the quality of the management processes. Fourth, globalization and the unfolding of the knowledge economy with its thirst for the production of new knowledge, the continuous flow of information, and the infusion of these outputs into production processes, has been a rather important impetus in galvanizing both national and international forces to understand how African higher education could be revitalized—how to gear the universities so that they are more able to take Africa into the globalized economy (Castells 1991). One recent instance of this is the study done by the World Bank, the ideas of which are captured in a book titled *Constructing Knowledge Societies: New Challenges for Tertiary Education* (Salmi 2002).

In terms of the theme of this chapter, the question that has to be asked is whether there exists a suitable philosophical and policy framework within which to hold a discussion about the role of African higher education in a globalizing world. Where discussions have been held, it appears that the framework has been borrowed from the global north. It must be asked if this is likely to be a suitable framework. One has to take into account the vastly different contexts in which these discussions are taking place, even though there is a strong historical connection between these universities in Africa and the colonial systems from which they derived their early mandates and forms. The postindependence experience of these universities, and the systems in which they are embedded, has been one of systematic crisis and this has generated various levels of dysfunctionality on the one hand, and complexity on the other.

The most important factor contributing to the crisis is chronic underfunding over a decades-long period. This has resulted in systems across the continent (including South Africa's much more substantial system) being fundamentally unsustainable. Enormous strains on infrastructure, the erosion of the capacity of these systems to produce new academics, extraordinarily low student participation rates, poor learning/teaching, the failure of these institutions to develop decent research cultures, and archaic management systems, are a few outcomes of these crises. What this results in is a crisis of social and political legitimacy, producing a circular condition of crisis. In the following sections we explore some of these crises.

Rethinking the African University

At the heart of the challenge facing African higher education is its ability to reproduce itself. The first generation of postindependence scholars that gave Makerere, Dar-es-Salaam, and Ibadan their sheen were almost all trained in the global north. They helped to shape a period of high-quality research and teaching that made these institutions the beacons of hope in the postindependence period. It was a period that was soon to fade away as the political and economic crises began to set in and its conclusion arrived with the onset of the World Bank-inspired structural adjustment programs as they began to impact the nature of the academic enterprise at these universities.

The question, then, is how are African nations, in the context of the political and economic crises they face, to produce higher education systems that are sustainable? A prerequisite condition for this is that these systems must generate research activities at a sufficiently large scale because it is only through the performance of research that new cohorts of researchers and academics may be produced. This is obviously a requirement for the systems to be intellectually sustainable.

Although there have been some very well-publicized recent relapses, the general trend on the continent has been towards the emergence of processes of national democratization. This is important for the transformation of higher education, since there is an increasing opportunity for internal discussion about higher education policy and especially about the way that the sector should interface with the social, political, and economic spheres. It is important for these discussions to be led by local intellectuals rather than by consultants from the World Bank or other international agencies. This is to reduce the tendency for these discussions on higher education to slide towards the more dominant forms that have emerged elsewhere in the world. While it is very important to take into account global trends and developments, it is crucially important that policy development processes be reflective of the particular contexts in which they are located.

This opening of policy space has also permitted the emergence of a new generation of higher education leadership, which more readily permits the flourishing of creativity and innovation within the universities. This is very important if the brightest people are to remain at these institutions. And in some universities, finally, vice chancellors (or presidents or rectors) are now appointed by the universities rather than by the government. This serves to increase the level of connection and accountability between these appointees and the various constituencies at the institutions.

This is progress. There is however, still an important question. Much of the debate is about the current crises rather than about *the nature of higher education;*[4] that is, there is not yet a serious discussion about rethinking the mandates of higher education in society. The geneses of these universities and of the systems in which they occur are colonial. But the concern being expressed here is that the discussion continues to be somewhat colonial in nature. This means that the emergence of higher education during the colonial period was shaped by the colonial project, and the universities were seen to be the producers of human resources for the local populations; the teachers, health professionals, and civil servants for the colonial governments. They were not conceived as institutions that would engage in research, in the production of new knowledge, in the development of cohorts of exceptional local intellectuals, or to act as bridges between African societies and the rest of the world. Further, the dominant imagination of the African university that emerged in the postindependence period is

---

[4] Look for example, at the country case studies commissioned by the Partnership for Higher Education in Africa. Its website is <http://www.foundations-partnership.org>.

that of the "development university," which has as its primary impetus an instrumentalist notion of the university (Ajayi 1996). These notions of the African university emerged mainly by default rather than through a positive attempt to conceive of a new university form. The "development university" therefore lacks a coherent philosophical basis on which to pin its academic enterprise.

This way of describing the African higher education system may not apply fully to those systems that developed in regimes that we might consider to be settler states such as South Africa, Namibia, and Zimbabwe. In these nations, there are parts of the higher education system that were originally designed for the European settler communities, and were therefore strongly tied (both in spirit and practice) to the university systems in the global north. But there are also institutions (such as the historically black universities in South Africa) that were seen to be of the kind described above. And it has been argued elsewhere that even the historically white universities have as their fundamental underpinning, a "colonial imagination" (Bawa 2007).

And in terms of the new thinking on the impact of globalization on the African university, one sees the impetus of the influence of the World Bank and other kinds of development agencies, and it may be argued that the situation repeats much of the same. There has been very little, if any, attempt to reimagine the nature of African higher education. And one sees similar interpretations being proposed by governments and by other local political forces, such as the trade union movements. Thus, the notion of "the development university" (used to describe instrumentalist mandates) is a very pervasive notion of the university in Africa, but I argue that it is a colonial variant.

It would appear, then, that the key challenge to reestablishing a sustainable model for African higher education systems would depend first and foremost on the ability of the nations to reimagine the role of universities in society as essentially producers and transmitters of new knowledge. Without this, the default imagination continues to be colonial.

Access to Higher Education

The World Bank study on the role of higher education in development placed much of its focus on the broadening of access to higher education, while at the same time placing emphasis on the importance of driving up student participation in science, engineering, and technology programs. Universities in sub-Saharan Africa face a tremendous challenge. Higher education participation rates globally have grown rapidly in the last 40 years. In 1960, there were just 13 million participants (about 0.4 percent of the total population then), and in 2004 this figure was 132 million (about two percent of the total population)—a five-fold growth in the participation rate (Haddad 2006). In sub-Saharan Africa, the participation rate as a fraction of the population of 18 to 24 year olds is no more than about 3.3 percent. To this we must fold in the fact that the participation rates of the two larger systems, South Africa and Nigeria, are 16 percent and 10 percent respectively. In fact, the participation in several countries is less than one percent. There are only 300 universities on the continent to serve 700 million people. The density is simply too low (Morley et al. 2007).

However, having said this, there is also a clear indication that the demand for higher education is growing. This is reflected partly in the fact that the participation rate across the sub-Saharan continent increased by some 7.2 percent over the last year, and is indeed a good sign. Then, there is the growing proliferation of private higher education providers—from small single qualification colleges to foreign international institutions operating locally. We shall return to this trend later in the chapter. Further, several national public institutions such as Makerere University in Kampala, are experimenting with new ways of broadening access through controversial income generating mechanisms. And along these lines, there are several experiments under way with new funding mechanisms, which include the charging of tuition, which is quite foreign in many systems across the continent (Johnstone 2006).

But what does this increase in demand for higher education mean? The new demand builds on an extraordinarily low base in most cases, and so the challenge for these systems (and for the societies in which they are embedded), is to understand how they might sustain growth over an extended period. This depends on a range of factors, only some of which are resolvable within the higher education sector.

Increasing access to higher education is expensive when the university systems in question have neither the infrastructure nor the academic capacity to extend their student intake to scale. Thus the broadening of access can only be achieved with a sustained injection of core funding that will address these needs. One way of achieving this would be to diversify and strengthen the income streams of the national higher education sectors and that of specific institutions. This would depend on the development of multiple strategies, such as the introduction of tuition in public institutions, and the optimization of new capacities being introduced through private sector providers.

Increased levels of funding also require the creation of a platform upon which a new kind of social contract might emerge between higher education and the state—one that is built on trust. This implicit contract is important to the extent that there has to be buy-in. There has to be an understanding by the state that higher education produces social goods that are of value to the society, and that this requires large-scale and sustained social investment. There has also to be a partnership between higher education and the broader population, establishing an understanding among participants of higher education that there will have to be a commitment to pay for the right to achieve this private good. This has to be seen in light of both anecdotal and inferred evidence that the gradual broadening of access to higher education in sub-Saharan Africa has generally strengthened the status and financial well-being of those that are in the upper social strata rather than the poor (Morley et al. 2007). The emergence of such a social contract will contribute to the legitimacy of the sector, and hence its capacity to engage fruitfully with government and society more generally. In an interesting twist on this line of thought, a Rand Corporation analysis of U.S. higher education was titled *Breaking the Social Contract* (Rand 1997).

Investment in infrastructure is crucial. Makerere University in Kampala was built for 5,000 students. It now has an enrollment of about 20,000. The existing infrastructure is simply under extreme pressure. So, essentially, consideration has to be given to building new colleges and universities. Only a few of these have to be research universities. The majority may well be technical-type colleges or community colleges that offer prebaccalaureate qualification. We would have to see the emergence of *systems* of higher education, which include different types of postsecondary institutions in systems that are differentiated and articulated. This would help to construct cost-efficient systems.

And then there is the question of how access is to be broadened. Which academic areas should be seen to be growth areas? What are the pertinent demand-side pressures? How should demand-side forces be brought to bear on the choices that are made? Many analyses on the issue of access in African higher education treat the matter as simply something that should be achieved. The articulation of access with the needs of the economy and the capacity of the societies to absorb qualified graduates has not been fully explored. In South Africa, there have been serious attempts to address this issue, and yet there are indications that the rate of unemployment among graduates is increasing. And there are anecdotal indications that there is a growing disjunction between the nature of the higher education output and the human resource needs of the economy. This is not meant to undermine the argument for the broadening of access, but only to say that there has yet to be a serious analysis of the labor market and its impact on higher education planning. Thus one sees that in Lesotho, for instance, only six percent of the total enrollment is involved in science courses. This must be compared with 16 percent in South Africa, 12 percent in the USA, and about 30 percent in Finland and France. What is the best way to interpret these figures? And how should such targets be set for each of the individual economies?

At the national systemic level, there are other issues that would impact access and throughput rates. For instance, questions have to be asked as to whether the throughput rate and the quality of secondary schools are at a sufficient level to allow meaningful increases in access to higher education. This is the major impediment to extending access in South Africa beyond the 20 percent level. But there are other serious issues, and these are often system specific. In Nigeria, for instance, one reads about the role of "cults" in university dorms and their negative impact on the culture of learning and teaching.

At the institutional level, there are the issues of curriculum and quality. There are deep concerns about the nature and quality of teaching and the student experience at higher education institutions, and whether there is sufficient human capacity to take access to higher levels. These have to be seen in the context that several national systems are developing quality systems that will hopefully address issues of capacity and innovation.

There are new and interesting ways to affordably broaden access through the use of technology and the establishment of satellite campuses. Experiments have been rolled out, and there are now some interesting case studies.

The challenge for African higher education is for it to reinsert itself into national development strategies and national imaginations. What opportunities exist for this? This remains the most important question, since strong, coherent arguments must be put forward for higher education to be considered as a required social institution in the holistic development of nations. This is the only way that the sector (on a nation-by-nation basis) may compete successfully against a host of other demands on the strained budgets of these developing nations. In this section, we look at what might influence such a reimagination process.

Universities in Nation Building

Universities in Africa have a critical role to play in nation building, with issues of identity and citizenship continuing to be critical determinants in the way that societies organize themselves in terms of viable socio-political systems. It also has to be noted that issues of identity and citizenship are regarded as important factors in the cases of genocide and ethnic strife that have engulfed parts of the continent from time to time. Universities and higher education systems have a crucial role to play in citizenship development and nation building, especially in the context of complex multi-ethnic societies. And as the processes of globalization engulf the continent, this challenge increases since local identities are put under strain. The powerful arguments made by Readings (1996) and others about higher education's diminishing role in nation building may apply to the particular contexts in which they were located. These arguments are not applicable in these young nations. As the processes of democratization take hold in these nations, there are growing expectations placed on higher education systems. These challenges take on many forms, and are shaped by the contexts in which the universities are located.

Universities and Information Technology

There has been a strong thrust among governments, universities, and donor organizations to understand how best the power of the information technologies might help these institutions to overcome some of their impediments. There are many large projects aimed at addressing this issue, and in most cases, these are aimed at addressing the serious infrastructure deficits in both the institutions themselves, and in the national telecommunication systems. Among these impediments are the extraordinarily high costs of bandwidth, the nonavailability of standard basic equipment and technology, the lack of high-level technical skills to manage the networks, the lack of technical support to clients, and the very low skill levels among users. While there has been much experimentation with small-scale projects, it is understood that for the utilization of technology to be effective, it has to be rolled out on a significant scale. And it is understood that technology must provide the basis for the improvement of learning/teaching and access, provide resources for research, provide for high-density communication, and help to improve the quality of higher education management. Much still needs to be done, and it is hoped that once roll out occurs, the technology and its effective deployment will be rapidly scaled-up.

There are many concomitant challenges. The first is that the regulatory frameworks within countries need to be set up to begin to address in a systematic way the issue of affordable bandwidth provision. Otherwise, all attempts are based on *ad hoc* and temporary solutions.[5] This is a large issue, and it has taken South Africa, for instance, many decades to begin to address the establishment of a regulatory framework that is finally allowing sufficient bandwidth to become affordable to middle- and high-income groups.

The second challenge relates to the fact that if high bandwidth does become available in these countries, it also opens the way for external private providers of higher education to operate via mixed-mode learning, where the start-up investments are high. The danger with this is that they will enter these markets with tremendous legacy advantages. In the context of the WTO's *General Agreement on Trade in Services*, this could place local higher education systems at severe risk, even though there may be huge benefits to accrue, for instance, through the broadening of access (see Altbach 1996), and the creation of new competitive pressures on the local sector. And unless (as in South Africa), these nations have developed a rigorous quality system that impacts the registration of these providers locally, there is a grave danger that, for instance, the nation-building role of higher education might be eroded.

Notwithstanding such issues, the opportunities that flow from the effective deployment of these technologies in higher education are an important development. In addition to the possible areas mentioned above, these technologies may provide the basis for new kinds of relationships between institutions in the global south and those in the north. And technology may provide for the emergence of new forms of developmental engagement, which allow for symmetrical intellectual engagement, but at asymmetrical scales. There are new and interesting examples on the table, such as the "OpenLearn" initiative set up by the U.K.'s Open University.[6]

Perhaps the most important outcome of the deployment of IT in higher education is the opportunity that it provides to young people on the continent to begin to engage with a technology that allows them to interact with large global

---

[5] The bandwidth project funded by the Partnership for Higher Education in Africa and which is described on its website: <http://www.foundation-partnership.org>, indicates how such projects can default to ad hoc solutions unless there is some intervention at a more systemic intergovernmental level.

[6] For more information look at <http://www.openlearn.open.ac.uk>.

networks—not just through courseware, but also through the opportunity of simply exploring the outcomes of ubiquitous connectivity.

Regional Integration

"Regional integration" is a generic term for attempts to build better, more effective, and higher levels of collaboration and cohesion across the continent. This is particularly important in the African context, given that resources of all kinds are very limited, but also substantially scattered across the continent. Formal structures for regional integration have now been created in the form of NEPAD (the New Partnership for Africa's Development), and more recently the African Union —with several heads of state making important visionary statements about the place of universities in society (See for example Mbeki 2005). On the higher education terrain, there are a few continental institutions, only some of which function well. The two most prominent ones are the AAU and CODESRIA. There are also large consortia that bring together researchers and scholars around disciplinary themes and graduate programs. One example is the African Economic Research Consortium, which offers graduate programs by drawing on the best academics in economics from across a number of institutions.

In this regard, the commitment of international agencies to provide large amounts of developmental funding to higher education is real. This is in the form of grants and loans—both of a short- and long-term nature. These funds, which amount to hundreds of millions of U.S. dollars each year, are extremely important to these reform exercises since they permit institutions to reach beyond their limited core funding for interesting innovations. An example of this is the 6 (or 7) foundation Partnership for Higher Education in Africa, which has *regional networks* as one of its strategic themes. The question is whether there is sufficient reimagination to make these investments move the discourse of transformation beyond the state of constant crisis that so many institutions face. More recently, there has been the creation of a large number of smaller, but highly effective intranational and international consortia on this question. Examples are the African Institute of Mathematics and the National Astrophysics and Space Science Program, both of which are based in South Africa, but which serve students from across the continent.

These consortia may be most effective in the experimental sciences where large-scale laboratories may be set up, expertly staffed, and maintained as a means to set up facilities for research groups that are drawn from a range of institutions from around the continent. Such facilities exist already, but without the policy and financial infrastructure to make them operate at a continental level. If this is done well, such facilities may be set up to be globally competitive, and thereby attract scientists from around the world. The new 11 meter Southern African Large Telescope (SALT) is one such facility that has institutional collaboration from Europe, North America, India, and elsewhere. The same would apply to the establishment of high performance computing facilities that would permit various kinds of research from remote sites. These are possible to achieve now.

In the same light, there is no reason, except for political lethargy, to prevent the establishment of a continental facility that provides the African research community with access to the necessary literature and other information databases. While the bandwidth at most sites is still very limited, there is no reason why one or two research sites should not be identified in each country to be provided with sufficient satellite-borne bandwidth. There are a number of projects that already perform an important basis for such a facility.

International Interest

There is a very substantial renewal of interest in African higher education. The reasons for this are largely those presented above, but there is also a renewed understanding that societies (especially those that are developing) need universities. One would be able to identify at least four such streams of interest.

The first is the very substantial interest being shown by the development agencies of the developed nations, such as the United Kingdom's DfID, Sweden's SIDA/SAREC, the Dutch Department of International Development, and Norway's NORAD. These bodies make large grants either through government agencies or directly to the institutions.

The second category is that of the large multilateral agencies. The World Bank is an example. After advising these very same societies to cut back on investment in higher education through the structural adjustment programs in the 1980s, it has in recent years begun to do some interesting work in trying to move the debate about the linkage between higher education and the economy in developing contexts. The World Bank has recently made large loans for higher education development to Nigeria and Mozambique. Other examples include UNESCO and the World Health Organization.

The third set of actors is the large U.S. philanthropic foundations, such as the Ford Foundation, the Carnegie Corporation, and so on. These have a longstanding relationship with African higher education through grantmaking—though at a much smaller scale than the previously mentioned categories. The better grantmakers among them see their role as strategic, as providing resources to facilitate experimentation with interesting ideas, and to allow the grantees (and the grantmakers) to make sound arguments to their respective governments, and to the larger development agencies described above. This is, therefore, an important area of grantsmanship.

The fourth set of actors are the newer, spend-down philanthropic organizations such as the Gates Foundation and the Open Society Foundation. These are more direct and focused on grantmaking themes such as HIV/AIDS intervention. This group of donor agencies is now investing considerable sums of money in the African higher education system, to the tune of hundreds of millions of U.S. dollars annually.

More importantly, there are a growing number of intracontinental and inter-continental collaborations that have emerged in the recent past that augur well for the growing interconnectedness between systems of higher education. However, the problem remains that these are often still largely in an archaic, debilitating south-north framework that undermines the scope of the African institution to shape these engagements.

Reimagining African Higher Education

It is in the light of such a rich mixture of intersecting themes that we must begin to look at the revitalization of African higher education. If these opportunities are not developed as levers for change and transformation, then there is the real danger that resources of various kinds that are directed at higher education de-velopment, and for which there is much competition, will be utilized in ways that are not sufficiently farsighted and progressive. Another way of saying this is that there is a real danger that these resources might be directed at attempting to resolve existing crises that have their origins in the very fabric of those systems.

The key issue that should be focused on as consideration is given to a proc-ess of reimagination is the construction of *a knowledge intensive role for African higher education.* At the present time, the research profile of most institutions is limited, and the research environment is very precarious. As was pointed out earlier, this has many debilitating consequences for these systems. Consider the following four. These points have been made above, but are important enough to be repeated here.

- The sustainability of these higher education systems depend fundamentally on their being able to generate new cohorts of university-based scholars and aca-demics. The only way that they can do this is if they have large, vibrant re-search enterprises where graduate students are educated and trained. Thus a poor research infrastructure, and a poor research ethos leave these systems unsustainable since there isn't any hope of reproducing the academy—even if there is strong collaboration with other university systems.
- The impact of the brain drain is real. The best young scholars leave for other, more developed research systems to study, and then the most talented remain at the various metropoles—whether they be metropoles in the global north (such as New York, Paris, or London), or those in the global south (such as Johannesburg or São Paulo). But it also ought to be said that if the higher education systems do not have vibrant knowledge-producing systems in place, the brightest young people also leave (after their first degrees) for ca-reers in commerce or in the private sector—a second kind of brain drain. And perhaps more insidiously, if the expectation of academics to perform research is outstripped by the expectation of generating income by extra teaching (as occurs at Makerere University and elsewhere), or by moonlighting through

consulting, then this undermines the traditional roles of a university. This is in fact a third kind of brain drain.

- The failure of these systems to foreground research and knowledge production as key enterprises undermines completely their capacity to act as bridges between the societies that they serve and other societies. They have to see themselves, and be seen by their societies, as complementary partners with other higher education institutions around the world, rather than supplementary ones—to be as competent and interesting as generators of knowledge as those other institutions. And this shift in perspective must happen especially in relation to their own social, cultural, and physical contexts, so that these societies may enter the global community of knowledge on their own terms.

- And perhaps, when higher education systems lack depth and breadth in research, it is difficult for them to generate sufficient social and political legitimacy, and thus to make the arguments that would allow them to be funded seriously. If the perceptions are that all they do is good (or poor) undergraduate teaching, and if they are not seen as generators of knowledge and ideas that facilitate the creation of solutions for problems that face the societies in which they are located, that argument is very difficult to make.

It is therefore fundamental for these institutions to develop sound and vibrant research systems that can draw on the deepest levels of talent, creativity, and innovation in their local contexts, and be able to attract the best minds from other parts of the world.

Seeking Lessons

The state of continuous crisis that African higher education finds itself in is not likely to emerge in parts of the world where the systems are considerably more substantial and developed, such as in the U.S. The *Crisis of the Publics* has very different connotations in Africa. However, it is important to understand what lessons may be learned, since we have seen that this state of crisis has many roots, and some of them spread quietly and over a period of time. In what follows, we look at three or four issues that may be lessons for the higher education sector in the U.S., in terms of how it may prevent a *Crisis of the Publics*.

- First, it is important to understand that the roots of the crisis are embedded in the political fabric of the societies in which they exist. Thus, we see that in the postindependence period, there was a rapid erosion of institutional autonomy and academic freedom. This gave rise to the emergence (or rather imposition) of new institutional "mandates" that were usually deeply utilitarian in nature, which saw research as an unnecessary activity unless it was directed at some specific development project, and the emergence of various kinds of censure (including imprisonment) against academics who were critical and challenging of the dominant regimes. It is important for universities and academics to understand that they are tightly related to the conditions of the societies in which they are located. Thus it is always important to defend the space for intellectual engagement and unfettered search for truth through academic research. It is therefore important for universities to constantly work at defending academic freedom and institutional autonomy, and to constantly renew the arguments for this. This latter point is important to ensure that new generations of academics understand the importance of these actions.

- Second, on a more general note, in terms of their research agendas, African institutions are largely unlinked from their local contexts. For instance, there is little research related to the African languages at a time when these languages are under severe threat. English, Arabic, French, and Portuguese have established themselves as lingua franca, and this is exacerbated by the impact of globalized media and popular culture. The emphasis in the utilitarian imagination (including the international advice offered to the governments by the World Bank and others) is to shift the emphasis to science and technology, and one witnesses the continuing erosion of the humanities and social sciences. This is an extraordinarily dangerous trend, as it is through vibrant research in the humanities and social sciences that universities become locally legitimized, as communities see themselves represented in these elitist institutions. The development of the society's capacity to engage in high level policy development also depends on a vibrant social science enterprise. It is therefore important for universities to constantly survey the way that they relate to their local contexts, and to ensure that they are seen to be (at least in part) representative of those contexts.

- Third, chronic underfunding of universities and higher education systems has devastating effects. It is always the case that the areas that are most impacted are the conditions of service of faculty and staff (leading to various kinds of brain drain), and then research, first impacting experimental research, and gradually spreading to all aspects of the higher education enterprise. This kind of erosion undermines the core of the university. It is therefore imperative that academics, universities, and higher education systems constantly argue for the value of higher education to society, and the extent to which higher education contributes to the public good. These arguments must regularly be renewed since socio-economic conditions change with time. One example of this is the impact of globalization on the conditions under which higher education operates.

- Fourth, the importance of being globally connected cannot be underestimated. This is one way of ensuring that systems of higher education are benchmarked against best practices, and are able to respond to the challenges of economic and political globalization. In particular, this kind of articulation provides universities with natural mechanisms to connect with communities globally, and ensure that societies have the opportunity to think globally.

- Fifth, higher education systems have to find effective ways to communicate with, and respond to, the needs of the economy—in terms of its research needs, its human resource needs, and in terms of developing innovation cycles. If this is not done, then there is the very real danger that the research enterprise will move out of the university systems into industrial laboratories.

- Sixth, it is critically important that higher education plays a role in shaping good citizens, and ensuring that the learning and personal and social development experiences of students are optimized.

Amidst a host of others, these are real challenges for African higher education, and it is clear that it is not simply a case of fixing things by massive investment. There has also to be a major process of rethinking higher education on the continent, and revisiting and reshaping the mandates of those institutions and systems, so that they are seen to be, and act as if they are, critical to the well-being of the societies in which they rest. Most importantly, they have to present these arguments of the public good in a convincing way. These imperatives apply to universities all over the world.

References

Ade Ajayi, J. F., L.K.H. Goma, and G. A. Johnson. 1996. *The African Experience with Higher Education*. London: James Currey Ltd, Islington.

Altbach, P. G. 1996. *The Challenge of the Market: Privatization and Publishing in Africa*. Chestnut Hill, Mass.: Bellagio Pub.

Altbach, P., and D. Levy, eds. 2005. *Private Higher Education: A Global Revolution*. Southampton: Sense Publications.

Anarfi, J., S. Kwankye with O-M. Ababio and R. Tiemoko. 2003. *Migration from and to Ghana: A Background Paper*. Development Research Centre on Migration, Globalisation and Poverty, Sussex.

Bawa, A. C. and D. Herwitz. 2007. *Re-Thinking the Mandates of African Universities*. In preparation.

Castells, M. 1991. "The University as Engine of Development in the New World Economy." Report prepared for the World Bank, Washington, D.C.

Haddad, G. 2006. *The Importance of Internationalization of Higher Education*. IAU 2006 International Conference: Internationalization of Higher Education: New Directions, New Challenges, Beijing, October 13.

Johnstone, D. B. 2006. *Financing Higher Education: Cost-Sharing in International Perspective*. Boston: Boston College Center for International Higher Education; and Rotterdam: Sense Publishers.

Knight, J. 2005. "GATS and Crossborder Education: Developments and Implications in Asia- Pacific." Background Report for UNESCO Seminar on "The Implications of WTO/GATS for Higher Education in Asia and the Pacific." Seoul, Korea. See also: Knight, J. 2004. "Crossborder Education in a Trade Environment: Complexities and Policy Implications. The Implications of WTO/GATS for Higher Education in Africa." Proceedings of the Accra workshop on GATS. Accra, Ghana: Association of African Universities.

Mbeki, T. 2005. Address of the president of South Africa at the conference of the Association of African Universities. Cape Town, February 22.

Morley, L., F. Leach, and R. Lugg. 2007. *Democratising Higher Education in Ghana and Tanzania: Opportunity Structures and Capacity Challenges*. Higher education and economic growth theme, UKFIET Conference, Oxford, September.

Rand Corporation. 1997. Breaking the Social Contract. The Fiscal Crisis in Higher Education. Santa Monica, California.

Readings, Bill. 1996. *The University in Ruins*. Harvard: Harvard University Press.

Salmi, J. 2002. Constructing Knowledge Societies: New Challenges for Tertiary Education. The World Bank, Washington, D.C.

Sawyerr, A. 2004. "Challenges Facing African Universities: Selected Issues." *African Studies Review*, April.

Singh, M. 2001. *Re-Inserting the Public Good into Higher Education Transformation*. In *Kagisano*, Council on Higher Education Discussion Series, No 1, Summer.

United Nations Department of Public Information. 2004. *Millennium Development Goals: Status 2004.* UN DPI2363/A.

Zeleza, P. T., and A. Olukoshi. 2004. African Universities in the 21st Century. Volume 1: Liberalization and Internationalization. Dakar, Senegal: CODESRIA Publications.

———. 2004. African Universities in the 21st Century. Volume 2 Knowledge and Society. Dakar, Senegal: CODESRIA Publication.

Contributors

Philip G. Altbach is J. Donald Monan University Professor and director of the Center for International Higher Education at Boston College. He is author of *Tradition and Transition: The International Imperative in Higher Education*, co-editor of *Worldclass World Wide: Research Universities in Asia and Latin America*, and other books.

Ahmed Bawa is a distinguished lecturer in the Department of Physics at Hunter College, City University of New York. He was until recently Deputy Vice Chancellor at the University of KwaZulu-Natal, and he also served as Program Officer for Higher Education with the Ford Foundation. He holds a Ph.D. in physics from the University of Durham. In the post-1994 period he served on a number of South African policy development teams and was an inaugural member of the National Advisory Council on Innovation and fellow of the Academy of Science of South Africa. He is also a fellow of the Royal Society of South Africa.

Juliet Chester is a senior researcher at the Higher Education Policy Institute (HEPI), based in the United Kingdom. She has undertaken research for HEPI on fees and funding for Home and E.U. undergraduate students at English universities, including the implications of raising the current tuition fee cap for these students and the case in support of a national bursary scheme. She also has an interest in research policy across the U.K.

John Aubrey Douglass is Senior Research Fellow—Public Policy and Higher Education at the Center for Studies in Higher Education (CSHE) at the University of California, Berkeley. He is the author of *The Conditions for Admissions* (Stanford Press 2007*)* and *The California Idea and American Higher Education* (Stanford University Press, 2000; published in Chinese in 2008). Among the research projects he founded is the Student Experience in the Research University (SERU) Consortium. He is also the editor of the CSHE Research and Occasional Paper Series (ROPS) and sits on the editorial board of a number of international higher education journals.

Kerstin Eliasson is a former deputy minister for Sweden's Ministry of Education, Science, and Culture. Prior to her time as deputy minister, Eliasson served in a variety of positions including director for research policy for the Ministry of Education, Science, and Culture; advisor to the prime minister's office; and chair of the OECD Committee for Scientific and Technological Policy. She currently serves as chief negotiator for Sweden's participation in two international research organizations, serves on the Board of the Joint Research Centre (E.U.), is a member of the Strategic Forum for International S&T Cooperation (E.U.), chair of the Biobank Committee within the Swedish Research Council, and serves as a consultant for Uppsala University on international cooperation.

Henry Etzkowitz is chair in Management of Innovation, Creativity, and Enterprise at the Business School, Newcastle University. He is also visiting professor in the Department of Technology and Society, School of Engineering and Applied Sciences, Stony Brook University. Etzkowitz is author of *Triple Helix: A New Model of Innovation*; *MIT and the Rise of Entrepreneurial Science,* and coauthor of *Public Venture Capital* and of *Athena Unbound: The Advancement of Women in Science and Technology*. He is cofounder of the Triple Helix international conference series on university-industry-government relations.

Daniel Fallon is professor of psychology, emeritus, and professor of public policy, emeritus, at the University of Maryland at College Park, where he also served as provost and vice president for academic affairs. He recently retired from Carnegie Corporation of New York, where he served as program director for higher education. He is a continuing member of the Strategy Commission of the German Excellence Initiative, and author of *The German University* (1980), Colorado Associated University Press, which won the Eugene M. Kayden Prize for excellence in the humanities.

Irwin Feller is a senior visiting scientist at the American Association for the Advancement of Science (AAAS) and professor emeritus of economics at the Pennsylvania State University, where he was on the faculty between 1963 and 2002. His research interests include science and technology policy, economics of higher education, and program evaluation. He has been a consultant to the President's Office of Science and Technology Policy, Carnegie Commission on Science, Technology, and Government, The Ford Foundation, National Science Foundation, National Institute of Standards and Technology, COSMOS Corporation, SRI International, U.S. General Accounting Office, and the U.S. Departments of Education and Energy, among others.

Grant Harman is professor of educational management and director of the Centre for Higher Education Management and Policy at the University of New England, Armidale, New South Wales, Australia. His main research interests are in university-industry research links, quality assurance in higher education systems, internationalization of higher education, and studies of aspects of the academic profession. He is editor in chief of the journal *Higher Education*, published in the Netherlands by Springer.

Jeroen Huisman is professor of higher education management and director of the International Centre for Higher Education Management, University of Bath. He is editor of *Higher Education Policy* and co-editor of *Tertiary Education and Management*. His current research interests include higher education governance; leadership and management; institutional diversity; internationalization and globalization; and Europeanization and the Bologna process.

C. Judson King directs the Center for Studies in Higher Education on the University of California, Berkeley campus. He was from 1995 until 2004 provost and senior vice president of academic affairs of the University of California system. Before that, he was provost of professional schools and colleges on the Berkeley campus. He has been at Berkeley since 1963 as a faculty member in chemical engineering, chaired that department, and was dean of the College of Chemistry. He is a member of the National Academy of Engineering and has received a number of national awards from the American Institute of Chemical Engineers, the American Chemical Society, the American Society for Engineering Education, and the Council for Chemical Research.

Wilhelm Krull is the secretary general of the Volkswagen Foundation, which is located in Hanover, Germany. From 2006 to 2008 he was the chairman of the European Foundation Centre. He is currently the chairman of the German Bundesverband Deutscher Stiftungen. From 2003 to 2005 he was chairman of the Hague Club of major European foundations. He has been and still is a member of numerous advisory committees and governing boards of universities, Max Planck Institutes, academies, and research organizations. At the European level he chaired expert panels on benchmarking of scientific and technological productivity as well as on monitoring and evaluation of the Sixth Framework Programme. He was also strongly involved in developing the concept for establishing the European Research Council.

Otto Lin has served as president of the Industrial Technology Research Institute (Taiwan) and vice president of the Hong Kong University of Science and Technology. He now lives in Hong Kong, engaging in writing on social issues and lecturing on the management of innovation and technology. In the recent years, he has also devoted himself to the study of global innovation through the Salzburg Seminar (Austria) and regional technology development of the Greater Pearl River Delta area.

Katharine Lyall is president emeritus of the University of Wisconsin system, professor of economics at UW-Madison, and visiting senior scholar at the Carnegie Foundation for the Advancement of Teaching. She served as deputy assistant secretary at the U.S. Department of Housing and Urban Development in the Carter administration, and has held faculty positions at Syracuse University and the Johns Hopkins University. Her most recent book is *The True Genius of America at Risk: Are We Losing Our Public Universities to De Facto Privatization?* (Praeger/Greenwood, 2006).

Wanhua Ma is a professor at the Graduate School of Education, Peking University, and holds a master's degree and Ph.D. from Cornell University. She came to work at Peking University in 1997, specializing in educational psychology and higher education administration. Since then she has carried out many research projects funded by UNDP, UNESCO, the Ford Foundation, and the National Science Foundation in China, concerning the issues of higher education reform, girls' education, research university development and building, internationalization, and globalization of higher education.

Christine Musselin is the director of the Centre de Sociologie des Organisations, a research unit of Sciences Po and the CNRS. She leads comparative studies on university governance, public policies in higher education and research, state-universities relationships, and academic labor markets. One of her books, *La longue marche des universités françaises,* published by the P.U.F. in 2001, has recently been edited in English (*The Long March of French Universities*) by Routledge (2004). A new book, *Le marché des universitaires*, dealing with hiring committees and academic labor markets in French, German, and American universities was published in November 2005 by the Presses de Sciences Po.

Ruth K. Sobótka is a research associate at the University of Cambridge, where she also coordinates the European Education Policy Network, a research network affiliated with the Centre of International Studies. Sobótka is currently involved in several higher education policy studies at the European level, such as the European University Association's "Bologna Masters" study and the "Trends 2010" review of the Bologna Process reforms in European universities. Since March 2008, she has also been working on an in-depth study of European research career structures and employment policies for the League of European Research Universities.

Stéphan Vincent-Lancrin is a senior analyst at the OECD Centre for Educational Research and Innovation (Directorate for Education). His recent work is about higher education (globalization, trade, technology, demography) and innovation in education. He has co-authored and edited several OECD/CERI publications on higher education, including on cross-border higher education and a new book series on the future of higher education, titled *Higher Education to 2030*. Before joining the OECD, Vincent-Lancrin worked as a lecturer and researcher in economics at the University of Paris-Nanterre and the London School of Economics. He holds a Ph.D. in economics and master's degrees in philosophy and in business administration.

Marijk van der Wende is the founding dean of Amsterdam University College and holds a chair in higher education at the Vrije Universiteit Amsterdam, and is a visiting professor at the Center for Higher Education Policy Studies (CHEPS) at the University of Twente. She also chairs the VU Honours Programme and the universities Internationalisation Board. She was a visiting scholar at CSHE at UC Berkeley in 2001. Her research focuses on the impact of globalization on higher education and related processes of internationalization and Europeanization; in particular on how these processes affect higher education systems, their structure and governance, institutional strategies, curriculum design, innovation, quality assurance methods, and the use of technology.

Chunyan Zhou is a professor and the manager of the International Institute of Triple Helix (IITH). With a B.S. in physics, a master's degree in science education, and a Ph.D. in science and technology innovation, she does interdisciplinary research in innovation, including the university-industry-government triple helix for regional innovation as well as science and technology innovation. With Professor Henry Etzkowitz, she also contributed to an Entrepreneurial University Special Issue for Science and Public Policy as a co-editor in January of 2009.